# Reshaping Financial Systems and Fostering Sustainability Through Embedded Finance

Chin Yee Lee
*Taylor's University, Malaysia*

Thilageswary Arumugam
*University Malaya Wales, Malaysia*

IGI Global
Scientific Publishing
Publishing Tomorrow's Research Today

Vice President of Editorial Melissa Wagner
Director of Acquisitions Mikaela Felty
Director of Book Development Jocelynn Hessler
Production Manager Mike Brehm
Cover Design Jose Rosado

Published in the United States of America by
IGI Global Scientific Publishing
701 East Chocolate Avenue
Hershey, PA, 17033, USA
Tel: 717-533-8845 | Fax: 717-533-7115
Website: https://www.igi-global.com E-mail: cust@igi-global.com



Library of Congress Cataloging-in-Publication Data

Names: Lee, Chin Yee, 1988- editor http://id.loc.gov/authorities/names/n2025013913 http://id.loc.gov/rwo/agents/n2025013913 | Arumugam, Thilageswary, 1975- editor http://id.loc.gov/authorities/names/n2025013920 http://id.loc.gov/rwo/agents/n2025013920
Title: Reshaping financial systems and fostering sustainability through embedded finance / [edited by] Chin Yee Lee, Thilageswary Arumugam.
Description: Hershey, PA : IGI Global Scientific Publishing, [2026] | Includes bibliographical references and index. | Summary: "The book aims to accomplish the following goals by emphasizing the incorporation of financial services into non-financial platforms and coordinating these innovations with sustainability "-- Provided by publisher.
Identifiers: LCCN 2025013531 (print) | LCCN 2025013532 (ebook) | ISBN 9798337324647 hardcover | ISBN 9798337324654 paperback | ISBN 9798337324661 ebook
Subjects: LCSH: Financial services industry--Environmental aspects
Classification: LCC HG173 .R444 2026 (print) | LCC HG173 (ebook) | DDC 332--dc23/eng/20250616
LC record available at https://lccn.loc.gov/2025013531
LC ebook record available at https://lccn.loc.gov/2025013532

British Cataloguing in Publication Data
A Cataloguing in Publication record for this book is available from the British Library.

# Table of Contents

**Preface** .......... x

**Chapter 1**
The Rise of Neobanks in India: Digitizing the Future of Banking and Financial Inclusion .......... 1
*Priti Dadasaheb Mane, Saibalaji International Institute of Management Sciences, India*
*Indrajeet Kole, Ramachandran International Institute of Management, India*
*Sarika Rajabhau Khandekar, Dr. D.Y. Patil Vidyapeeth, Pune, India*
*Hrishikesh Kokate, Dr. D.Y. Patil Vidyapeeth, Pune, India*

**Chapter 2**
Embedded Finance and Financial Inclusion in Emerging Markets: Opportunities and Challenges .......... 21
*Silvio Andrae, Independent Researcher, Germany*

**Chapter 3**
Embedded Finance and Sustainable Financial Inclusion: A Conceptual Framework for Integrating Financial Services Into Non-Financial Platforms .......... 61
*Shuchi Gupta, University of Hail, Saudi Arabia*
*Manika Garg, Maharaja Agrasen Institute of Management Studies, India*
*Gargee Banerjee, Raja Madhusudan Dev Degree College, India*

**Chapter 4**
The Role of Embedded Finance in Business Innovation: Technology Enablers and Industry Applications .......... 91
*Gouri Sathvika Garapati, Christ University, India*
*Abhijeet Birari, Christ University, India*

**Chapter 5**
Artificial Intelligence-Integrated Embedded Finance for a Sustainable Future: Can AI-Embedded Finance Enable Sustainability? .......... 129
*Wasswa Shafik, Dig Connectivity Research Laboratory (DCRLab), Uganda*

**Chapter 6**
Sustainable Finance in the Digital Age: The Function of Embedded Finance in Eco-Friendly Investments ........ 163
*Rismawati Rismawati, Universitas Muhammadiyah Palopo, Indonesia*
*Monika Handayani, Politeknik Negeri Banjarmasin, Indonesia*
*Ela Elliyana, Universitas Indonesia Timur, Indonesia*
*Indra Pahala, Universitas Negeri Jakarta, Indonesia*

**Chapter 7**
Embedded Finance in Action: A Pathway to Sustainable Growth........ 197
*Arindam Nag, Christ University, India*

**Chapter 8**
The Intersection of Integrated Finance, Sustainability, and ESG: An Overview........ 227
*Rosimah Ahmad, Taylor's University, Malaysia*
*Premagowrie Sivanandan, Sunway University, Malaysia*

**Chapter 9**
The Role of Social Workers in Fostering a Green Economy Within the Sustainable Development Goals: Promoting Social Justice, Environmental Responsibility, and Inclusive Growth ........ 257
*Thi Thi Win, Lincoln University College, Malaysia*
*Jahid Siraz Chowdhury, Lincoln University College, Malaysia*
*Mujawir Hussain, Lincoln University College, Malaysia*
*Blikis Blikis, Lincoln University College, Malaysia*
*Md. Taraqual Islam, Lincoln University College, Malaysia*

**Compilation of References** ........ 281

**About the Contributors** ........ 319

**Index** ........ 325

# Detailed Table of Contents

**Preface** ........................................................................................................ x

**Chapter 1**
The Rise of Neobanks in India: Digitizing the Future of Banking and Financial Inclusion ........................................................................................ 1
*Priti Dadasaheb Mane, Saibalaji International Institute of Management Sciences, India*
*Indrajeet Kole, Ramachandran International Institute of Management, India*
*Sarika Rajabhau Khandekar, Dr. D.Y. Patil Vidyapeeth, Pune, India*
*Hrishikesh Kokate, Dr. D.Y. Patil Vidyapeeth, Pune, India*

Rise of neobanks in India is a key moment in digital banking and financial inclusion. The journey of digital banking in India from 1990s through core banking systems (CBS), its growth in internet & mobile banking in 2000s & 2010s and the catalytic support of the government including Digital India campaign and Aadhaar based systems for financial inclusion are explored in this paper. Neobanks emerged with the advent of the Unified Payments Interface (UPI) taking digital transactions to next level. Neobanks are unlike the traditional banks, they are — in fact — fully digital, inexpensive, easy to use, and provide personalized services. In this paper, I examine how neobanks are disrupting the Indian financial landscape and facilitating financial inclusion, thereby challenging traditional banking systems of the world.

**Chapter 2**
Embedded Finance and Financial Inclusion in Emerging Markets: Opportunities and Challenges ........................................................................ 21
*Silvio Andrae, Independent Researcher, Germany*

This study examines the potential of embedded finance (EmFi) to improve financial inclusion in emerging economies by seamlessly integrating financial services into everyday applications. The aim is to systematically analyze the effects, prerequisites, and risks of this development. Methodologically, the study combines panel data analysis, case studies (China, India, Kenya, Brazil), and network visualizations of digital financial ecosystems. The results show that EmFi significantly increases account penetration, digital payments, and credit usage, especially where public real-time payment systems, digital identities, and proportional regulation interact. At the same time, risks arise from data misuse, algorithmic distortions, and platform concentration. The study, therefore, underscores the importance of open infrastructures, transparent governance, and technical standards in shaping EmFi as an inclusive financial system, not as a mere disruptor, but as a socially embedded innovation.

**Chapter 3**
Embedded Finance and Sustainable Financial Inclusion: A Conceptual Framework for Integrating Financial Services Into Non-Financial Platforms..... 61
*Shuchi Gupta, University of Hail, Saudi Arabia*
*Manika Garg, Maharaja Agrasen Institute of Management Studies, India*
*Gargee Banerjee, Raja Madhusudan Dev Degree College, India*

The paper aims to develop a conceptual framework that explains how embedded finance can drive financial inclusion while aligning with sustainability goals. It explores the role of digital financial services integrated into non-financial platforms, such as e-commerce, mobility, and social media, in promoting accessibility and responsible financial practices. This study adopts a conceptual research approach by reviewing existing literature on embedded finance, financial inclusion, and sustainable finance. It synthesizes theoretical perspectives such as Access to Finance Theory to propose a structured model for policymakers and business leaders. The research identifies embedded finance as a transformative force that lowers financial barriers, improves accessibility for underserved populations, and facilitates sustainable financial solutions. It highlights key mechanisms, including digital wallets, API-based banking, and ESG-linked financial products, that contribute to inclusive economic growth while promoting responsible investment.

**Chapter 4**
The Role of Embedded Finance in Business Innovation: Technology Enablers and Industry Applications........................................................................ 91
*Gouri Sathvika Garapati, Christ University, India*
*Abhijeet Birari, Christ University, India*

This study explores the role of embedded finance (EF) in driving business model innovation and consumer engagement in India's digital economy, focusing on e-commerce and transportation/food delivery. EF, which integrates services like payments, lending, and insurance into non-financial platforms, is analyzed for its impact on revenue, satisfaction, and inclusion. Using case studies of Flipkart, Amazon, Ola, and Swiggy, and a survey of 250 respondents, the research shows how EF boosts convenience, conversion, and access for underserved users. However, data reveals EF alone doesn't ensure satisfaction without seamless UX and personalization. The study highlights the role of APIs and AI in delivering EF benefits while noting regulatory and privacy concerns. Findings show EF's potential to reshape business and consumer behavior in India

**Chapter 5**
Artificial Intelligence-Integrated Embedded Finance for a Sustainable Future: Can AI-Embedded Finance Enable Sustainability? ........................................ 129
*Wasswa Shafik, Dig Connectivity Research Laboratory (DCRLab), Uganda*

Artificial Intelligence (AI)-integrated embedded finance is transforming financial services by enabling seamless, data-driven solutions that promote sustainability. This study details how embedding AI-driven financial tools into non-financial platforms, businesses and consumers gain real-time access to personalized, transparent, and efficient financial services. AI enhances risk assessment, fraud detection, and credit scoring while optimizing resource allocation for sustainable investments. Its predictive analytics support green financing, ethical lending, and financial inclusion, fostering long-term economic and environmental benefits. Therefore, as AI continues to evolve, its integration in embedded finance holds the potential to drive a more resilient, inclusive, and sustainable financial ecosystem.

**Chapter 6**
Sustainable Finance in the Digital Age: The Function of Embedded Finance in Eco-Friendly Investments ................................................................ 163
*Rismawati Rismawati, Universitas Muhammadiyah Palopo, Indonesia*
*Monika Handayani, Politeknik Negeri Banjarmasin, Indonesia*
*Ela Elliyana, Universitas Indonesia Timur, Indonesia*
*Indra Pahala, Universitas Negeri Jakarta, Indonesia*

Sustainable embedded finance is transforming the financial sector by incorporating green investing strategies into digital platforms. This study examines how embedded finance, fintech innovations, and decentralized financial models enhance access to sustainability-linked financial products. Essential elements encompass the function of AI-driven ESG analytics, blockchain-enabled transparency, and digital payment systems in promoting financial access for environmentally sustainable initiatives. The study analyzes policy frameworks and regulatory obstacles, highlighting the necessity of integrating financial plans with the UN Sustainable Development Goals (SDGs). As embedded finance progresses, it presents novel options for scalable, transparent, and technology-driven sustainable investments. The results underscore the essential interaction among finance, technology, and sustainability, offering guidance for investors, politicians, and enterprises in steering the future of sustainable finance.

**Chapter 7**
Embedded Finance in Action: A Pathway to Sustainable Growth..................... 197
*Arindam Nag, Christ University, India*

This chapter examines how embedded finance reshapes sustainable investment through AI, machine learning, and DeFi integration with ESG practices. These technologies can address behavioral biases such as loss aversion, yet major challenges remain. ESG data is fragmented, with rating providers often showing correlations below 0.6, weakening automated screening. Greenwashing risks rise as automation favors convenience over impact checks, while regulation lags behind and leaves fiduciary duties unclear. The discussion links these issues to finance theory, applying CAPM to test whether ESG factors improve risk-adjusted returns and using behavioral insights to assess how embedded systems may correct cognitive limits. Case studies show that while embedded finance reduces transaction friction, turning convenience into measurable sustainability outcomes is still uncertain. The chapter contributes by connecting finance theory with emerging technologies to evaluate real versus promised effects on sustainable investment.

**Chapter 8**
The Intersection of Integrated Finance, Sustainability, and ESG: An Overview............................................................................................. 227
*Rosimah Ahmad, Taylor's University, Malaysia*
*Premagowrie Sivanandan, Sunway University, Malaysia*

Integrated finance is a progressive financial approach that integrates ESG principles into financial systems to promote long-term sustainability. It bridges global sustainability goals with measurable ESG frameworks, enabling capital to be directed toward inclusive, ethical and resilient growth. Instruments such as green bonds, ESG-aligned portfolios and sustainability-linked loans exemplify this alignment. Integrated finance supports the UN Sustainable Development Goals (SDGs) by promoting inclusive digital financial services and financial products. It enhances financial system resilience by embedding ESG risks into strategic decisions like pricing and cash flow management. Despite benefits such as transparency and stakeholder trust, challenges include regulatory complexity and socio-economic issues. Ultimately, integrated finance seeks to redefine finance as a driver of sustainable transformation, supporting a quadruple-bottom-line approach, i.e., people, planet, profit, and purpose.

**Chapter 9**
The Role of Social Workers in Fostering a Green Economy Within the Sustainable Development Goals: Promoting Social Justice, Environmental Responsibility, and Inclusive Growth ........ 257
*Thi Thi Win, Lincoln University College, Malaysia*
*Jahid Siraz Chowdhury, Lincoln University College, Malaysia*
*Mujawir Hussain, Lincoln University College, Malaysia*
*Blikis Blikis, Lincoln University College, Malaysia*
*Md. Taraqual Islam, Lincoln University College, Malaysia*

Sustainable development has become a global-criterion as environmental challenges like floods, biodiversity loss, and pollution increasingly threaten human well-being. This paper explores the role of social workers in promoting the Sustainable Development Goals (SDGs) by fostering a green economy, particularly in ecologically fragile regions. It explains how social workers can collaborate with policymakers, investors, and corporate leaders to implement sustainable practices that reduce environmental risks, create jobs, and support local economic growth. Through qualitative analysis of existing articles, journals, and books, the role of social workers is highlighted as an advocate for community-based green projects, policies, and capacity building initiatives. This paper describes practical strategies for social workers in the contribution of sustainable development goals through social justice and environmental sustainability. In this way, social workers ensure the economy is growing in an environmentally friendly way and is socially inclusive.

**Compilation of References** ........ 281

**About the Contributors** ........ 319

**Index** ........ 325

# Preface

## INTRODUCTION

In an era defined by rapid technological change and global interconnectedness, the boundaries between finance, business operations, and sustainability are being redrawn. The chapters compiled in *Reshaping Financial Systems and Fostering Sustainability Through Embedded Finance* reflect the collective efforts of scholars, practitioners, and innovators to understand and shape this transformation.

Businesses today no longer rely solely on traditional financial intermediaries to power their growth. The integration of financial services directly into non-financial platforms—known as embedded finance—is revolutionizing how value is created, customers are engaged, and innovation is driven. This phenomenon is not merely a technological shift; it represents a fundamental reconfiguration of economic relationships, business models, and the financial landscape itself. By embedding payments, lending, insurance, and investment mechanisms into everyday transactions, businesses are unlocking new efficiencies and creating seamless experiences that enhance both accessibility and inclusion.

Simultaneously, the urgency of sustainability compels organizations to reassess their priorities. In a world facing climate, social, and governance challenges, companies must align their growth strategies with global sustainability goals. This convergence of sustainable business practices and embedded finance offers an extraordinary opportunity—to design resilient ecosystems that balance profitability with social responsibility and long-term environmental stewardship.

This volume explores the crucial role of embedded finance in reshaping corporate operations and advancing sustainability agendas. Through interdisciplinary insights, empirical research, and case-based discussions, the contributors examine how the fusion of technology, finance, and purpose-driven innovation can foster equitable and sustainable growth.

The book seeks to achieve five key objectives:

1. Examine the role of embedded finance in business innovation;
2. Promote financial inclusion and accessibility;
3. Align financial systems with sustainability goals;
4. Provide a framework for business leaders and policymakers; and
5. Bridge the gap between technology and financial systems.

Our intended readership includes academicians, marketers, managers, professionals, entrepreneurs, researchers, and students across the fields of finance, business, digital transformation, and sustainability. We hope that this collection not only informs but also inspires new thinking about how financial systems can be reimagined to serve both economic progress and societal well-being.

As editors, we extend our sincere gratitude to the authors whose contributions bring depth and diversity to this work, and to the reviewers and partners who helped shape its direction. We invite readers to engage with these ideas critically and creatively—to envision and build a future where financial innovation and sustainability are not competing goals, but mutually reinforcing pillars of global prosperity.

## ORGANIZATION OF THE BOOK

### Chapter 1: The Rise of Neobanks in India: Digitizing the Future of Banking and Financial Inclusion

The opening chapter charts the dynamic evolution of digital banking in India, tracing its path from the introduction of core banking systems (CBS) in the 1990s to the expansive reach of mobile and internet banking in subsequent decades. Against this backdrop, the rise of neobanks—fully digital, customer-centric platforms—marks a transformative moment in financial inclusion and innovation. Supported by initiatives like *Digital India* and *Aadhaar*-based verification, India's financial ecosystem has become fertile ground for technology-driven banking solutions. This chapter explores how the Unified Payments Interface (UPI) acted as a catalyst for the emergence of neobanks, offering low-cost, personalized, and frictionless financial experiences. By contrasting neobanks with traditional banking institutions, the author demonstrates how these digital-first entities are democratizing access to finance, empowering underserved populations, and setting a global precedent for inclusive banking innovation.

## Chapter 2: Embedded Finance and Financial Inclusion in Emerging Markets: Opportunities and Challenges

The second chapter delves into the global impact of embedded finance (EmFi) in expanding financial inclusion across emerging markets. Drawing from empirical data and case studies in China, India, Kenya, and Brazil, the research investigates how the integration of financial services into everyday applications enhances access to accounts, digital payments, and credit. The analysis reveals that countries with strong digital infrastructure, real-time payment systems, and clear regulatory frameworks have experienced the most substantial gains. However, the chapter also cautions against potential risks—such as data misuse, algorithmic bias, and platform monopolization—that could undermine inclusivity. Through quantitative modeling and network visualizations, the author highlights the delicate balance between innovation and regulation, concluding that open infrastructure and transparent governance are essential for ensuring EmFi functions as a socially embedded, inclusive force rather than a purely disruptive one.

## Chapter 3: Embedded Finance and Sustainable Financial Inclusion: A Conceptual Framework for Integrating Financial Services into Non-Financial Platforms

In this conceptual study, the author constructs a framework linking embedded finance with sustainability and inclusion. By synthesizing theories such as the *Access to Finance Theory*, the chapter explains how embedding financial services into non-financial platforms—like e-commerce, mobility, and social media—can foster equitable access and responsible financial behavior. The research identifies digital wallets, API-based banking, and ESG-linked financial products as key enablers of sustainable inclusion, offering pathways to financial empowerment while supporting global sustainability goals. The conceptual model proposed here serves as both a theoretical contribution and a practical guide for policymakers and business leaders aiming to align innovation with ethical growth. This chapter stands as a cornerstone in articulating how embedded finance can evolve into a **transformative, sustainability-oriented financial paradigm**.

## Chapter 4: The Role of Embedded Finance in Business Innovation: Technology Enablers and Industry Applications

Chapter 4 explores the pivotal role of embedded finance in business model innovation and consumer engagement, particularly within India's rapidly digitizing economy. Through case studies of Flipkart, Amazon, Ola, and Swiggy, the research illustrates how embedded financial tools—ranging from payments to micro-lending and insurance—are seamlessly integrated into digital ecosystems, driving customer convenience and operational efficiency. Empirical findings from surveys and case analyses reveal that while embedded finance increases access and conversion rates, user satisfaction hinges heavily on intuitive design, trust, and personalization. The study also identifies APIs, artificial intelligence, and data analytics as core enablers of embedded financial ecosystems, while addressing emerging concerns related to privacy, regulation, and digital literacy. Ultimately, this chapter highlights embedded finance as a strategic lever for innovation, bridging technological advancement with inclusive business practices.

## Chapter 5: Artificial Intelligence-Integrated Embedded Finance for a Sustainable Future: Can AI-Embedded Finance Enable Sustainability?

This chapter investigates the intersection of artificial intelligence (AI) and embedded finance, presenting a vision for how AI-driven tools can revolutionize sustainability in the financial sector. By embedding AI within financial services, platforms can deliver personalized, transparent, and efficient solutions that enhance risk assessment, fraud detection, and sustainable investment allocation. The chapter demonstrates how predictive analytics facilitate green financing, ethical lending, and inclusive credit access, creating both economic and environmental value. As AI technologies continue to evolve, the author emphasizes their potential to drive sustainable, data-informed financial ecosystems. Yet, the chapter also urges careful attention to ethical design, algorithmic accountability, and equitable access to ensure that AI-enabled embedded finance truly fosters long-term resilience and inclusion.

## Chapter 6: Sustainable Finance in the Digital Age: The Function of Embedded Finance in Eco-Friendly Investments

Focusing on the convergence of sustainability and digital finance, this chapter examines how embedded finance can accelerate green investment and eco-conscious economic growth. The analysis highlights the synergy between fintech innovations, AI-driven ESG analytics, blockchain-enabled transparency, and decentralized finance models in promoting access to sustainability-linked products. Policy frameworks and regulatory challenges are discussed in relation to the UN Sustainable Development Goals (SDGs), underscoring the need for harmonized strategies that align digital innovation with sustainability imperatives. The chapter concludes that embedded finance can serve as a scalable, transparent engine for eco-friendly investments, enabling businesses, policymakers, and investors to participate in building greener, more equitable financial systems.

## Chapter 7: Embedded Finance in Action: A Pathway to Sustainable Growth

Chapter 7 offers a critical evaluation of embedded finance as a practical instrument for sustainable investment, integrating insights from finance theory, behavioral economics, and ESG analytics. The author examines how technologies such as AI, machine learning, and decentralized finance (DeFi) can mitigate behavioral biases and increase participation in sustainable markets. However, challenges such as inconsistent ESG data, greenwashing, and regulatory lag complicate the pathway to meaningful impact. The discussion bridges theoretical frameworks—like the Capital Asset Pricing Model (CAPM)—with real-world examples to test whether ESG factors genuinely improve risk-adjusted returns. Ultimately, this chapter demonstrates that while embedded finance reduces transactional barriers and enhances convenience, translating these efficiencies into verified sustainability outcomes remains an evolving challenge that demands further interdisciplinary inquiry.

## Chapter 8: The Intersection of Integrated Finance, Sustainability, and ESG: An Overview

This chapter presents a comprehensive overview of integrated finance—a model that embeds Environmental, Social, and Governance (ESG) principles into the core of financial decision-making. It explores how instruments like green bonds, ESG-aligned portfolios, and sustainability-linked loans align capital allocation with long-term societal and environmental goals. The discussion highlights integrated finance as a mechanism that strengthens resilience, transparency, and stakeholder trust while supporting the UN SDGs. Despite the benefits, the author identifies regulatory complexity and socio-economic disparities as persistent challenges. The chapter concludes that integrated finance redefines the purpose of financial systems, positioning them as engines for inclusive, ethical, and purpose-driven growth, encapsulated in the "quadruple bottom line" of people, planet, profit, and purpose.

### Chapter 9: The Role of Social Workers in Fostering a Green Economy Within the Sustainable Development Goals: Promoting Social Justice, Environmental Responsibility, and Inclusive Growth

The final chapter broadens the lens of sustainability by introducing the human and social dimensions of financial transformation. It explores how social workers play a pivotal role in promoting green economies and advancing the Sustainable Development Goals (SDGs) through advocacy, education, and community-driven initiatives. Drawing on qualitative analyses of global research, the chapter underscores the importance of collaboration among policymakers, investors, and community organizations to ensure environmental responsibility and social equity. Social workers are portrayed as catalysts for inclusive and environmentally conscious growth, championing policies that balance economic advancement with ecological preservation. This concluding chapter ties the volume together by emphasizing that sustainable finance and embedded systems must ultimately serve people and communities, reinforcing social justice as the cornerstone of a truly sustainable financial future.

## CONCLUSION

As editors of *Reshaping Financial Systems and Fostering Sustainability Through Embedded Finance*, we close this volume with a deep sense of optimism and responsibility. The chapters presented throughout this book collectively underscore a profound transformation underway at the intersection of technology, finance, and sustainability. Together, they demonstrate that embedded finance is not merely a technological trend—it is a structural reimagining of how value is created, shared, and sustained in a rapidly digitizing world.

From the rise of neobanks and the integration of AI-driven financial tools to the alignment of embedded finance with sustainability goals and ESG principles, each contribution reveals both the promise and the complexity of this evolving ecosystem. Embedded finance has emerged as a catalyst for inclusion, democratizing access to financial services and enabling underserved communities to participate in the formal economy. At the same time, it has become a platform for sustainability, channeling resources toward environmentally responsible investments, ethical consumption, and long-term resilience.

Yet, as the insights in these chapters make clear, this transformation is not without its challenges. The growth of digital and embedded financial systems raises pressing questions about data ethics, regulatory governance, algorithmic accountability, and social equity. The success of these systems depends on transparent frameworks, responsible innovation, and collaboration among governments, businesses, and civil society. To ensure that technological progress translates into inclusive prosperity, stakeholders must cultivate financial ecosystems that are not only efficient and innovative but also equitable and sustainable.

Ultimately, the convergence of embedded finance and sustainability offers an unprecedented opportunity to reshape the global financial architecture in service of people and the planet. The ideas shared in this book invite researchers, practitioners, and policymakers to think beyond traditional silos—to envision financial systems that are seamlessly integrated, ethically grounded, and purpose-driven.

We hope this collection will serve as both a scholarly resource and a call to action—encouraging continued inquiry, experimentation, and dialogue on how embedded finance can power a more inclusive and sustainable future.

Chapter 1

# The Rise of Neobanks in India: Digitizing the Future of Banking and Financial Inclusion

**Priti Dadasaheb Mane**
https://orcid.org/0009-0005-6293-9579
*Saibalaji International Institute of Management Sciences, India*

**Indrajeet Kole**
*Ramachandran International Institute of Management, India*

**Sarika Rajabhau Khandekar**
*Dr. D.Y. Patil Vidyapeeth, Pune, India*

**Hrishikesh Kokate**
https://orcid.org/0000-0001-7931-9003
*Dr. D.Y. Patil Vidyapeeth, Pune, India*

## ABSTRACT

*Rise of neobanks in India is a key moment in digital banking and financial inclusion. The journey of digital banking in India from 1990s through core banking systems (CBS), its growth in internet & mobile banking in 2000s & 2010s and the catalytic support of the government including Digital India campaign and Aadhaar based systems for financial inclusion are explored in this paper. Neobanks emerged with the advent of the Unified Payments Interface (UPI) taking digital transactions to next level. Neobanks are unlike the traditional banks, they are — in fact — fully*

DOI: 10.4018/979-8-3373-2464-7.ch001

*digital, inexpensive, easy to use, and provide personalized services. In this paper, I examine how neobanks are disrupting the Indian financial landscape and facilitating financial inclusion, thereby challenging traditional banking systems of the world.*

## INTRODUCTION TO NEOBANKS

Neobanks are becoming an important part of India's banking system by offering fully digital services that are easy to use and more convenient than traditional branches. Their rise is supported by the widespread use of smartphones, low-cost internet, and the strong growth of digital payment systems. By cutting paperwork, speeding up transactions, and offering customized financial tools, these platforms are helping more people take part in formal banking. They are also improving financial inclusion by reaching people who have limited access to physical banks through simple mobile apps and quick onboarding. However, issues like unclear regulations, data security risks, and the need to build customer trust remain. Continued cooperation between fintech firms, established banks, and regulators will be important for long-term success. With thoughtful guidance, neobanks can support better financial habits, increase financial awareness, and play a meaningful role in India's digital banking future.

### Overview of Digital Banking Evolution in India

In the 1990s the first wave of digital banking arrived in the form of core banking systems (CBS), which allowed traditional banks to centralize their operations for delivery of services across multiple branches. This was the first of the large steps towards digitization: banks streamlined their operations and started offering basic online services in the 2000s, when banks started providing internet banking, involving their customers in doing important banking functions, such as balance checks, fund transfers or bill payments using web-based platforms, (Iona cu et al., 2023). Secondly, the mobile banking surge in the 2010s enabled those with smartphones to access banking services on the affordable and accessible mobile devices being used by more and more people across the country.

Other important initiatives of the government, such as Digital India campaign and Aadhaar based identification systems helped the government promote digital banking by making financial inclusion easier and streamlining account opening, (Buteau, Rao, & Valenti, 2021). The introduction of the Unified Payments Interface (UPI) by the National Payments Corporation of India (NPCI) in 2016 revolutionized digital payments by merging peer to peer and merchant payments giving way for further digitalization of the financial services space while traditional banks continued to provide such digital service as an extension of their branch-based services. Neobanks came with a new point of view, they were 100% digital from the beginning, creating user friendly interfaces, decreased costs and personalized financial services without physical branches, (Monis & Pai, 2023).

## Defining Neobanks

A neobank is a digital only financial technology (fintech) company providing a range of banking and financial services to consumers through an app or online platform but generally without a physical branch network, (Sharma, 2024). Unlike traditional bank, neobank works exclusively in the digital space and not in the offline environment. As a rule, they often partner with licensed banks to offer their services, particularly in regulatory environments like India when they may not have own banking licenses, (Caussat, Prime, & Wilken, 2019). Pawn banks, also known as neobanks, were created to balance out a few shortcomings of standard banks that supply a friendlier and more utilitarian banking experience, commonly focused on tech-fluent clients as well as price levels inspired by freelancers, little businesses or youthful grownups. They typically focus on:

1. ***Low fees and transparency:*** In most cases, neobanks eliminate or at least considerably cut down on fees that apply to standard services like maintaining of accounts, fund transfers, or ATM usage. It is an appealing thing to customers fed up with surprise charges.
2. ***Seamless, fast onboarding:*** Unlike traditional banks, neobanks do their onboarding digitally — without the need for users to physically visit branches to gain access to an account. Frequently, the fulfilment of KYC is completed through mobile apps.
3. ***Data-driven insights and financial management:*** Data analytics is being used by neobanks to integrate this data and provide the user with insights on what they spent, what savings goals they prioritize, and how they can invest.
4. Jupiter, for example, is aimed primarily at young professionals with personalized rewards and insights to manage how much you spend, whereas Niyo targets salaried individuals and international travelers to provide forex services and salary, bank accounts in digital form.

Thanks to working online, neobanks have reduced the overhead costs as compared to traditional banks, allowing them to set competitive rates, engage in innovative services, and provide tailored solutions that speak to their customer markets. But because they lack physical branches, they rely heavily on technology and experience to develop trust and satisfy regulatory standards.

## GLOBAL NEOBANK TRENDS

While the concept of neobanks sprouted in Europe and the States, it grows fast across other regions such as Asia and Latin America, (Ziouache, & Bouteraa, 2023). Notable neobanks rose up in Europe during the early 2010s including Revoluta in the UK and N26 in Germany. However, these platforms provided banking services at ease from their mobile apps, mobile foreign exchange services, spent analysis tools, would check the range of transferred money very easily. As these neobanks all focus on a specific segment of the market – e.g. underbanked individuals – thats where they were are quickly able to expand userbase, their low fees and user friendly Interfaces attracted millions of users, especially younger generations, looking for alternatives to traditional Banks. The catch was that despite the shiny new features these neobanks brought to the table, they tended to take their cue from the major US banks, designing free checking accounts with savings tools, and providing access to early direct deposits for paychecks.

Neobanking has also taken off in Asia with WeBank in China and Tonik in the Philippines. For example, We Bank, one of the first digital only banks in China, used Tencent's ecosystem to create a range of financial products, (Sirakova-Yordanova, 2024). In the Philippines, with low banking penetration, Tonik brought neobanking to market, enabling customers to open digital savings accounts and loan products. The gap between India and these global trends is closing, but the regulation is in a more cautious place(Kandpal, 2024). Neobanks in India like Jupiter, Open and Fi Money are creating new digital banking services targeted at fine customers like small businesses, salaried professionals and gig workers. The RBI (Reserve Bank of India) hasn't given full banking licenses to these neobanks yet, but they can operate in tandem with licensed banks. With this hybrid approach, they can comply with the restrictions and provide a variety of service.

Given India's rapid digital adoption and high smartphone penetration coupled with the rise of UPI, neobanks were enabled in India's conducive environment. The growth in India's neo banking sector can be attributed to increasing customer demand for convenience, transparency and personalization, but it is also facilitating the inclusion of people, and changing the conventional banking frame of mind.

## THE INDIAN NEOBANK LANDSCAPE

### Current Players

There are many players in India's neobank ecosystem and each focus on a particular segment and service tailored to their needs. Here is a closer look at some of the prominent neobanks in India and their focus areas:

#### Jupiter

Developing specifically for younger professionals or digital banking aficionados, Jupiter is aimed at meeting both of these needs. Features such as personalized rewards, budgeting tools, spending habits insights, are provided by it, (Dwivedi et al., 2021). Jupiter wants to make financial management easy for clients by focusing on making great customer experience, total transparency, and low fees. What its app lacks is the appealing simpler experience that the card's competitors offer to younger users, who generally value financial insight and simplicity.

#### Niyo

Niyo has made a bet on itself as a neobank targeting international travelers, the salaried set and blue-collar workers. A digital layout account and often with a multi-currency forex card makes this ideal for anybody traveling overseas. Salaried employees will be able to use a salary account available on Niyo that does not demand minimum balance and allow easy access to salary deposits and other banking services. Niyo is ideal for travelers and professionals abroad that want to make international currency transactions with low fees.

#### Fi Money

Fi Money is geared toward tech savvy, salaried millennials and Gen Z customers. Designed with intuitive tools for financial planning, savings goals and investment advice, its app. Save Smart helps users automatically save money with the Fi Money and personalizes spending insights. Additionally, the app has UPI integration and users, through the app, can set budgets, open smart savings accounts, measure the progress in the areas of financial growth. My goal with Fi Money, was for a young user to get a comprehensive financial tool.

## Open

India's first neobank targeted at SMEs is Open. These services are business accounts, invoicing, expense management, and integration with the accounting software. Open makes financial operations of SMEs easier by providing a digital first experience tailored to a business requirement; automatic reconciliation of invoices and payments, expense categorization, and help in tax filing, among others. Open is a great option for SMEs as it makes banking, such as corporate cards, automated bookkeeping, and even credit facilities, easy.

## RazorpayX

RazorpayX is the neobanking unit of India's largest payments solutions provider, Razorpay. Basically, RazorpayX is in the business of bringing business banking solutions for startups, freelancers and SMEs. What it does is it provides automated payroll, payments to vendors, current accounts — which is helping businesses manage money better. The integration with Razorpay's payment gateway makes it very useful for startups and online businesses as it aggregates the businesses finance and payment collection.

## Zolve

The neobank Zolve works with international travellers and Indian migrants in the U.S. It provides cross border banking solutions whereby users can open bank accounts and use Credit cards in the U.S. before getting to the U.S. For that, Zolve, as they call themselves, helps students, employees and other migrants moving to the U.S, simplify the financial transition, making it seamless from India and ensuring that they have instant access to credit and banking services upon arrival.

Speaking of, each of these neobanks is addressing a particular topic in India's financial landscape: from personal finance tools for individuals, to freelancers and small businesses looking for finance solutions tailored to their needs. For neobanks, this segmentation enables them to carve out distinct competitive positions in targeting the distinct needs of their target audience and promote customer loyalty and increased engagement.

# TARGET AUDIENCE

The target audiences for neobanks in India vary widely, allowing each neobank to address specific pain points and cater to the financial needs of distinct user groups:

- ***Salaried Individuals:*** Neobanks such as Jupiter and Fi Money are aimed specifically at what is called salaried persons, mainly young professionals who are given budgeting tools, understanding the spending insights and seamless integration with UPI. So that they can better manage money, track expenses and set savings goals, these features make banking more interactive and informative.
- ***Freelancers and Gig Workers:*** Freelancers and gig workers often find it difficult to bank with traditional banking, and platforms like Open and RazorpayX offer services that help them. Neobanks provide easily usable current accounts, automatic invoice, expense management tools for freelancers to keep track of income, manage business expenses and ensure timely payment.
- ***Small and Medium Enterprises (SMEs):*** Specifically, Open and RazorpayX serve SMEs with business focused banking solutions. Neobanks offer businesses such as corporate cards, payroll management as well as banking integration with accounting software to help them manage cash flow, streamline expenses; and even access credit facilities, (Onunka et al., 2023). Banking tools for this segment are based on business needs rather than personal finance.
- ***Teenagers and Students:*** But while there aren't as many neobanks, some are beginning to experiment with services targeting younger audiences. Most neobanks targeting this demographic offer pre-paid cards, or restricted accounts that teach teenagers early financial management. The idea is to design these services so that they could attract parents who wish to have their children know about money management in a safe environment.
- ***International Travelers and Migrants:*** People who travel internationally or migrate often are the focus of Niyo and Zolve. As a foreign exchange service, Niyo offers competitive rates and low transaction fees for frequent travelers through multi-currency cards. However, Zolve is meant for the Indian migrants, especially students and professionals who are shifting to the U.S. to open bank accounts and take credit in the new country, to create a financial footprint abroad.

These neobanks focus on specific user segments, and accordingly, offer a unique experience that meets unique financial needs. With this approach, they have found a way to carve out a place in India's much larger financial ecosystem.

*Table 1. Overview of leading neobanks in India and their target audiences*

| Sr No | Neobank | Target Audience | Key Features/Focus |
|---|---|---|---|
| 1 | Jupiter | Young professionals, individuals seeking digital banking | Customized rewards, spending insights, budgeting tools, saving pots for dedicated goals, transparency, low fees and customer focus. |
| 2 | Niyo | International travelers, salaried individuals, blue-collar workers | Multi-currency forex card, digital savings account, salary account with zero minimum balance, low fee international banking services. |
| 3 | Fi Money | Tech-savvy, salaried millennials and Gen Z customers | Savings goals, Financial planning tools, Investment advice, Smart savings automation, UPI integration, Spending behavior insights, and more. |
| 4 | Open | Small and medium enterprises (SMEs), freelancers | Invoicing, expense management, accounting software integration, automated reconciliation, corporate cards, taxes filing, credits facilities. |
| 5 | RazorpayX | Startups, SMEs, freelancers | Vendor payments, automated payroll, current accounts, financial management tools for business, seamless payments and collections, payment gateway integration. |
| 6 | Zolve | International travelers, Indian migrants to the U.S. | U.S. bank accounts and credit cards; cross border banking; managing financial services prior to arrival in the U.S.; simplifying financial transitions for migrants. |

(Author's work)

## PARTNERSHIP WITH TRADITIONAL BANKS

Another reason is that in India, neobanks often have to partner with traditional licensed banks to provide their services, as they don't have full banking licenses themselves. The partnership model this allows the neobanks operate within the regulatory framework of the Reserve Bank of India (RBI) and depositing of customers' deposits and banking services can be adhered to the set standards of safety and compliance. Here's how this partnership model works and why it's essential:

- ***Leveraging Banking Infrastructure:*** Like the traditional banks, the neobanks are digital platforms that have their own unique user interface and customer experience, but are only able to support their core operations, maintaining accounts, processing transactions and managing funds, through the traditional banks, (Barroso & Laborda, 2022). Jupiter, for instance, is a partnership with Federal Bank for savings accounts, and Niyo is with ICICI and SBM for salary and travel accounts. This arrangement frees neobanks from thinking about the bank infrastructure while focusing on the customer experience.
- ***Regulatory Compliance:*** Financial institutions have stringent regulation by RBI in respect of capital adequacy, risk management and consumer protec-

tion, (Jayadev, 2013). Neobanks are technology based financial service providers that are not fully licensed banks and hence cannot keep deposits in their own. Neobanks do this by partnering with licensed banks that follow RBI rules and make sure their funds are safe. Through this partnership approach, neobanks don't need a banking license to operate within the legal and regulatory framework.

- ***Product Innovation and Rapid Market Entry:*** Traditional banks are stuck in bureaucratic structures and legacy systems that don't allow for fast innovation, (Alshwayat et al., 2023). With agile technology platforms, one of the strengths of neobanks is the ability to develop and deploy new products and features much faster. Through partnerships between these products and traditional banks, they can access the backend support needed to launch these products, including current accounts, forex services and loans without the full regulatory burden of a full banking license, (Chuhan-Pole & Angwafo, 2011). This allows them to be able to get into the market quickly and have the ability to scale their service.
- ***Access to Trust and Credibility:*** Neobanks get credibility through partnering up with established banks, which can also be useful to gain customers trust considering that many of them have no physical branches, (Nagy, Molnár, & Papp, 2024). A bank licensed to handle customers' funds may make customers feel more secure. For instance, the partnership of Zolve with banking institutions in the United States enables the lender to offer credit products to Indian migrants knowing that they are being backed by well-established financial institutions.

Neobanks and traditional banks have teamed up to create a synergistic relationship that sees neobanks bring innovation, digital expertise and customer experience, while traditional banks bring regulatory support, infrastructure and credibility. This model helps Indian neobanks innovate and grow as it keeps in mind the regulatory standards to fill the void between technology driven banking and traditional financial services.

## REGULATORY ENVIRONMENT AND RBI'S ROLE

### RBI's Stance on Neobanks

The Reserve Bank of India (RBI) has been somewhat cautious in approving the opening of fully digital, branchless banks – i.e. neobanks. Unlike some countries that have allowed neobanks to operate with license as a full banking system, the

RBI has not granted any such licenses to a neobank operating in India. Multiple reasons drive these precautions:

## Risk Management

The RBI has priority of the financial system's stability and security. While any digital-only entity doesn't have a physical presence, most are built on agile, cloud based systems that might be more susceptible to cybersecurity risks, (Murinde, Rizopoulos, & Zachariadis, 2022). By not approving the full banking licenses to neobanks, the RBI can also eliminate operational and technological failures which can disrupt the banking system.

## Consumer Protection

Consumer protection, grievance handling, and dispute resolution processes are extensive in the traditional banks, and they are usually physical verification or support based, (Ejuma Martha Adaga et al., 2024). RBI might worry that digital banks, in the absence of a physical branch network, might find it difficult to make effective customer service and protection available to less tech savvy customers.

## Financial Inclusion

RBI is also looking at increasing financial inclusion in rural and underserved areas where physical branches also play a big part. RBI may not be in sync with broader financial inclusion goals, and may not be the place for neobanks, which cater to digitally savvy, urban customers.

## Compliance and Oversight

Supervision, auditing and oversight of fully digital entities is new for the RBI, and it is challenging to regulate them as new frameworks are needed. The RBI has limited regulatory infrastructure to monitor digital only banks properly. For this reason, it is cautious and chooses to regulate neobanks indirectly by way of partnerships with licensed banks.

Due to these concerns, neobanks in India operate as fintech companies rather than full-fledged banks. The partnership of these neobanks with traditional banks that hold the needed license allows the neobanks to function as banks without any regulation from the RBI. It allows neobanks to innovate while the RBI keeps the stability of the financial ecosystem under control.

## IN-PRINCIPLE APPROVAL VS. FINAL AUTHORIZATION

In India, the RBI has a long and often multiple stage process for approvals of new banking entities, from in principle approval to final authorization. Here's how this process works and why it's important:

1. ***In-Principle Approval:*** When the RBI gives in principle approval to a new financial entity it is tantamount to granting permission to the entity to begin its business operations and start making arrangements to start. The entity can build the infrastructure, make partnerships, and put technology systems in place as well as comply with RBI's regulatory requirements in this stage(Thommandru & Chakka, 2023). But this approval is not a rubber stamp: the entity still has to fulfill additional requirements before it can do so fully.

For example, the popular neobank Jupiter received in principle approval from the RBI to operate in liaison with a licensed bank. This first approval made way for Jupiter to begin scaling out their digital infrastructure, security systems and regulatory development work in order to become first fully licensed.

2. ***Compliance and Evaluation:*** They also have to abide by RBI's own regulatory guidelines and once they get in principle approval they have to set up data protection systems, customer verification protocols (such as KYC) and anti-money laundering norms. In this phase, RBI is observing and keeping a watch on their progress on meeting stringent requirement of secure and responsible financial services.
3. ***Final Authorization:*** Before the entity can offer services to the public, the RBI authorizes the entity only when it is sure that the entity is operational and complies with all regulatory requirements. With that out of the way, the neobank can begin full operations but must remain under regulatory oversight and regular check of compliance. It's a critical milestone, in that it final authorizes the neobank in that it confirms that the neobank has met all the regulatory standards to protect consumers and ensure stability.

## KEY FEATURES AND BENEFITS OF INDIAN NEOBANKS

### User-Centric Design and Experience

Neobanks are built on mobile first and web-based platforms and place a high emphasis on delivering a seamless and intuitive user experience. Unlike traditional banks, neobanks have a clean, user-friendly design that appeals to tech savvy population. With user journey in place, these platforms support easy navigation, immediate access to banking services, as well as personalized dashboards. It enables simpler, available anytime, any location banking for customers. It focuses on a modern, user centered experience that makes banking less intimidating to millennials and Gen Z users.

## Lower Fees and Transparent Pricing

Disrupting traditional banking, Neobanks are banks that provide low cost or no fee banking. Account maintenance, fund transfers, ATM withdrawals and a host of other services are often charged by traditional banks, and they can add up quite quickly. But, neobanks can deliver those services for a fraction of the cost or for free. That's because they run with a lighter infrastructure that avoids the overhead costs of physical branches. For example, most neobanks offer free online transfers, free or discounted ATM withdrawals and no annual account fees. This pricing structure is especially appealing to younger users—digital natives—and small businesses seeking cheap banking solutions. The cost conscious customers are attracted to neobanks because they are able to trust everything from simple account pricing to lack of hidden fees and surprising charges.

## Financial Tools and Smart Insights

The tricky part of it all is neobanks are giving you sophisticated financial tools that you don't get even from banking. Budgeting tools, real time spending insights and automatic categorization of spending are key features aimed at helping users manage and track their finances properly. To give an example: It lets users see what they're spending their money on the most, set saving goals, and get wise insights or reminders not to spend too much. Neobanks have access to Machine learning algorithms to better understand user's behavior and recommend personal financial advice based on user's behavior. But traditional banks, with their paper based or old system records cannot offer such insights. That provides the ability to another layer of support on the customer to help them make better financial decisions and make better use of their finances.

## Quick Onboarding and KYC

One of the most important benefits of neobanks is being able to offer a fast and paperless onboarding process. Traditionally, opening accounts with a bank needs customers to walk into a branch and present physical documents and undergo a long verification process. When it comes to neobanks, however, the process is as simple as that; you can do a little KYC verification via video call or just upload your digital copies of identity proofs and you're good to go. One thing that it means is no in person visits, and this is especially important for people that live in remote areas or people that don't have easy access to bank branches. This means that the digital onboarding process generally takes only a matter of minutes and users are able to begin banking almost immediately, which makes not only a huge difference in terms of convenience and access.

### Focus on Financial Inclusion

Unlike conventional banks, neobanks aim for reaching underserved, or financially excluded parts of the population that small traditional banks have often neglected to serve. It includes rural populations, blue collar workers, and even teenagers. Neobanks offer banking services to individuals without traditional brick-and-mortar banks through their easy-to-use mobile platforms. Not only do they generally have lower terms, for example offering lower minimum balance requirements, the flexibility of how you make a payment, and specialized products like microloans or savings accounts created to serve these underserved groups. Financial inclusion is made possible by extending basic financial services to those who don't have credit histories. The democratization of banking is bridging the unbanked populations, by bringing them into the formal financial system.

## CHALLENGES FACED BY NEOBANKS IN INDIA

But India is also the hotbed of neobanks — digital first, mobile based financial services that promise convenience and personalization. Although, as they grow, neobanks come across a few hurdles that make it hard for them to scale and become popular. Issues come into play with everything from regulatory to customer trust issues, to being in competition with traditional banks and data security risks. Let's explore each of these challenges in detail:

### Regulatory Constraints

In India's case, the regulatory environment itself is one of the major hurdles. Digital banking is growing, but the Reserve Bank of India (RBI) is still cautious about taking to full digital only banking platforms for fear of money laundering, fraud and consumer protection issues.

Neobanks are internet only, and do not have physical branches by definition. This puts them under more scrutiny by the RBI and to work a little more than with traditional banks on some things. Consider the case of most neobanks in India – they must partner with established banks to fulfil savings, lending, and payment services. That restricts the freedom neobanks have in operating and forces them to pass on their customer data and revenues to traditional banking partners. Neobanks also don't have banking licenses themselves, so they're dependent on banks for core banking services such as deposits and withdrawals.

## Customer Trust and Awareness

The same can be said about the surge in digital adoption, as the majority of Indian consumers continue to bank with traditional banks, keeping faith for decades in the trust they have amassed over time. The banks, such as State Bank of India (SBI), HDFC, and ICICI already have a long history and they speak volumes about the reliability of financial matters.

Being new in the market, neobanks have a hard time to build up the same level of trust. Security, fraud, and the general legitimacy of these new players are keeping many customers, especially those in nonmetro areas or older age group, from embracing digital only banking platforms. To prove that they can deliver the same reliability, security, and customer service as traditional banks, neobanks have to move forward.

## Traditional Banks Competition

Traditional banks have their infrastructure and conservatism, but they are not blind to the digital wave sweeping through the financial market. Leading banks in India such as HDFC Bank, Axis Bank and ICICI Bank are spending big on digital services and have launched their own versions of digital accounts, apps and payments.

Therefore, this becomes a very competitive world for neobanks. Neobanks are great because they're a digital first and offer services like AI driven financial advice, spending analysis and automated saving, but traditional banks are able to leverage their existing customer base and huge branch network to offer a broader set of financial services.

## Data Security and Privacy

Data security and privacy is one of the biggest concerns over neobanks. The very nature of neobanks relies on digital platforms and mobile apps, which means they keep your transaction history, account details and personal ID information, (Citterio, Marques, & Tanda, 2024). In the financial services industry, customers are wary about sharing their personal data with digital-only platforms, which are increasingly getting attacked by cyber-attacks and data breaches.

To gain trust and scale for neobanks, they need to put serious money into advanced security protocols. That includes end-to-end encryption, two factor authentication, as well as continuous monitoring of transaction activities to detect and prevent fraud. They also have to ensure that their performance works as per the laws like the Personal Data Protection Bill (PDPB) which provides protection of customer data and is used for its intended usage.

While security is needed, so is transparency in privacy policies. As neobanks are increasingly partnering with other fintech firms and institutions, customers are questioning how their data is being used, stored and shared with third party companies; and old timers, like myself, are asking; 'What's a neobank?' Having compromised security system of a neobank can be critical and result in very serious consequence: reputational consequences, loss of customer trust and even legal consequences.

# NEOBANKS AND FINANCIAL INCLUSION, DIGITAL TRANSFORMATION

Neobanks are transforming the Indian banking landscape in a huge way, in terms of financial inclusion and digital transformation of the banking sector. They can introduce, in the form of services, technology and an innovative business model to populations that were ignored or underserved by traditional banks.

## Neobanks: Future in India and Contribution

### Bridging Urban-Rural Divide

In rural India, neobanks overcome the barrier of the limited physical branches as well as high costs through digital banking services that can only be accessed via smartphones. Low cost models, educational content and partnerships with local agents make them good vehicles for financial inclusion and literacy.

## Supporting the Gig Economy

Gig and freelance workers find it easy to get serviced like instant payments, flexible loans through financial planning tools that caters to their needs. In addition, they also use alternative data to determine creditworthiness and offer loans that banks would normally have refused to grant.

## Making Young and Underbanked Users Empowered

Neobanks are focused on millennials and have easy account setup, financial literacy tools, and free services. A feature of features allows them to promote early financial independence with features like savings tools and parent-controlled accounts.

## Future Outlook

Potential regulatory reforms that could grant full digital banking licenses could see India's neobanks grow. These banks are likely to further strengthen their tie ups with traditional banks, adopt advanced technologies, like AI and Blockchain and innovate to stay relevant in a growing market with new entrants.

In India, Neobanks are transforming financial services, enabling inclusion, and fostering digital transformation for underserved, and emerging customer segments.

# CONCLUSION

The introduction of neobanks in India signifies a significant transformation in the nation's financial services sector. Utilizing advanced technology, these exclusively digital platforms have revolutionized banking into a more convenient, affordable, and user-friendly experience. Neobanks have shown their ability to fill the voids left by conventional banking systems, especially by enhancing financial inclusion, catering to neglected groups, and providing innovative financial solutions.

The regulatory framework in India, influenced by the Reserve Bank of India (RBI), has taken a careful but supportive approach to encouraging this growth. Although neobanks currently collaborate with licensed banks, possible regulatory changes might create opportunities for independent functioning, thereby enhancing their acceptance.

Major players like Jupiter, Niyo, Fi Money, and RazorpayX have effectively served niche markets, targeting salaried workers, small enterprises, freelancers, and global travelers. Their emphasis on tailored services, smooth digital onboarding, and clear pricing has appealed to tech-savvy customers and younger demographics.

Even with their potential, obstacles persist. Regulatory challenges, lack of trust, rivalry from conventional banks, and worries about data protection must be tackled for neobanks to grow sustainably. Ongoing investment in cybersecurity, compliance structures, and customer awareness will be essential to addressing these challenges.

Neobanks are not just disruptors but also drivers of financial change in India. As they keep evolving, adopting cutting-edge technologies, and broadening collaborations, they hold the potential to transform banking standards and speed up financial inclusion. By adopting a balanced strategy of regulation and innovation, India can establish itself as a worldwide frontrunner in digital banking.

## REFERENCES

Adaga, E. M., Egieya, Z. E., Ewuga, S. K., Abdul, A. A., & Abrahams, T. O. (2024). A COMPREHENSIVE REVIEW OF ETHICAL PRACTICES IN BANKING AND FINANCE. *Finance & Accounting Research Journal*, *6*(1), 1–20. DOI: 10.51594/farj.v6i1.705

Alshwayat, D., Elrehail, H., Shehadeh, E., Alsalhi, N., Shamout, M. D., & Rehman, S. U. (2023). An exploratory examination of the barriers to innovation and change as perceived by senior management. *International Journal of Innovation Studies*, *7*(2), 159–170. DOI: 10.1016/j.ijis.2022.12.005

Barroso, M., & Laborda, J. (2022). Digital transformation and the emergence of the Fintech sector: Systematic literature review. *Digital Business*, *2*(2), 100028. DOI: 10.1016/j.digbus.2022.100028

Buteau, S., Rao, P., & Valenti, F. (2021). Emerging insights from digital solutions in financial inclusion. *CSI Transactions on ICT*, *9*(2), 105–114. DOI: 10.1007/s40012-021-00330-x

Caussat, P., Prime, N., & Wilken, R. (2019). How Multinational Banks in India Gain Legitimacy: Organisational Practices and Resources Required for Implementation. *MIR. Management International Review*, *59*(4), 561–591. DOI: 10.1007/s11575-019-00387-6

Chuhan-Pole, P., & Angwafo, M. (Eds.). (2011). *Yes, Africa Can: Success Stories from a Dynamic Continent*. The World Bank., DOI: 10.1596/978-0-8213-8745-0

Citterio, A., Marques, B. P., & Tanda, A. (2024). The Early Days of Neobanks in Europe: Identification, Performance, and Riskiness. *Journal of Financial Services Research*. Advance online publication. DOI: 10.1007/s10693-024-00433-x

Dwivedi, Y. K., Ismagilova, E., Hughes, D. L., Carlson, J., Filieri, R., Jacobson, J., Jain, V., Karjaluoto, H., Kefi, H., Krishen, A. S., Kumar, V., Rahman, M. M., Raman, R., Rauschnabel, P. A., Rowley, J., Salo, J., Tran, G. A., & Wang, Y. (2021). Setting the future of digital and social media marketing research: Perspectives and research propositions. *International Journal of Information Management*, *59*, 102168. DOI: 10.1016/j.ijinfomgt.2020.102168

Iona cu, A. E., Gheorghiu, G., Spătariu, E. C., Munteanu, I., Grigorescu, A., & Dănilă, A. (2023). Unraveling Digital Transformation in Banking: Evidence from Romania. *Systems*, *11*(11), 534. DOI: 10.3390/systems11110534

Jayadev, M. (2013). Basel III implementation: Issues and challenges for Indian banks. *IIMB Management Review*, *25*(2), 115–130. DOI: 10.1016/j.iimb.2013.03.010

Kandpal, P. C. (2024). India's policy response to the COVID-19 pandemic: Lessons for a post-COVID society. *Discover Global Society*, *2*(1), 16. DOI: 10.1007/s44282-024-00043-x

Monis, E., & Pai, R. (2023). Neo Banks: A Paradigm Shift in Banking. *International Journal of Case Studies in Business, IT, and Education*, 318–332. DOI: 10.47992/IJCSBE.2581.6942.0275

Murinde, V., Rizopoulos, E., & Zachariadis, M. (2022). The impact of the FinTech revolution on the future of banking: Opportunities and risks. *International Review of Financial Analysis, 81*, 102103. DOI: 10.1016/j.irfa.2022.102103

Nagy, S., Molnár, L., & Papp, A. (2024). Customer adoption of neobank services from a technology acceptance perspective–evidence from Hungary. *Decision Making: Applications in Management and Engineering*, *7*(1), 187–208.

Onunka, T., Raji, A., Nkemchor Osafiele, A., Daraojimba, C., Afeyokalo Egbokhaebho, B., & Chinazo Okoye, C. (2023). BANKING: A COMPREHENSIVE REVIEW OF THE EVOLUTION AND IMPACT OF INNOVATIVE BANKING SERVICES ON ENTREPRENEURIAL GROWTH. *Economic Growth and Environment Sustainability*, *2*(2), 66–78. DOI: 10.26480/egnes.02.2023.66.78

Sharma, S. (2024). Digital Disruption in Banking: A Comparative Analysis of Neo Banks and Traditional Institutions. *International Journal of Management and Development Studies, 13*(3), 01–12. DOI: 10.53983/ijmds.v13n3.001

Sirakova-Yordanova, G. (2024). Banks Go Beyond Banking: The Expansion Towards Non-Banking Services. *Proceedings of the International Conference on Business Excellence, 18*(1), 391–404. DOI: 10.2478/picbe-2024-0034

Thommandru, A., & Chakka, D. B. (2023). Recalibrating the Banking Sector with Blockchain Technology for Effective Anti-Money Laundering Compliances by Banks. *Sustainable Futures : An Applied Journal of Technology, Environment and Society*, *5*, 100107. DOI: 10.1016/j.sftr.2023.100107

Ziouache, A., & Bouteraa, M. (2023). Descriptive approach of neo-banking system: Conception, challenges and global practices. *International Journal of Business and Technology Management*, *5*(2), 194–204.

# Chapter 2
# Embedded Finance and Financial Inclusion in Emerging Markets:
## Opportunities and Challenges

**Silvio Andrae**
https://orcid.org/0000-0002-8586-7812
*Independent Researcher, Germany*

## ABSTRACT

*This study examines the potential of embedded finance (EmFi) to improve financial inclusion in emerging economies by seamlessly integrating financial services into everyday applications. The aim is to systematically analyze the effects, prerequisites, and risks of this development. Methodologically, the study combines panel data analysis, case studies (China, India, Kenya, Brazil), and network visualizations of digital financial ecosystems. The results show that EmFi significantly increases account penetration, digital payments, and credit usage, especially where public real-time payment systems, digital identities, and proportional regulation interact. At the same time, risks arise from data misuse, algorithmic distortions, and platform concentration. The study, therefore, underscores the importance of open infrastructures, transparent governance, and technical standards in shaping EmFi as an inclusive financial system, not as a mere disruptor, but as a socially embedded innovation.*

DOI: 10.4018/979-8-3373-2464-7.ch002

# INTRODUCTION

## Background and Relevance

Over the past decade, embedded finance (EmFi)—understood as the seamless integration of financial services into non-financial digital environments—has evolved from a marginal field of innovation to a structural element of the global platform economy. In developed markets, EmFi primarily appears as a convenience layer: Ride-hailing apps bundle instant insurance, e-commerce checkouts offer one-click credit capabilities, and social media wallets increasingly blur the lines between content consumption and payment functionality, (Ozili, 2023).

According to forecasts, the global EmFi market is expected to reach a volume of over USD 228 billion by 2028, with an average annual growth rate of 23.8%. The market volume already amounted to USD 185 billion in 2024, an increase of 25% in just two years, driven by favorable refinancing costs and rising earnings in platform banking, (Ifrim, 2024; Paypers, 2024). This growth trajectory suggests that EmFi has the potential to significantly enhance financial inclusion, with only around 20% of the market potential currently tapped. This makes EmFi a promising field for platforms that are prepared to integrate financial solutions into digital journeys in a functional and data-driven manner.

However, the transformative potential of EmFi is particularly profound in emerging markets. There, access to formal banking services remains highly unevenly distributed. At the same time, mobile network coverage is increasingly available across traditional physical infrastructure, and digital data streams are being tapped in real-time. According to the Global Findex 2021, approximately 1.2 billion adults worldwide still lack a transaction account, with a particularly high concentration in sub-Saharan Africa, South Asia, and certain parts of Latin America. At the same time, smartphone penetration among adults under the age of 35 is already over 70% in many of these regions. The coincidence of a largely underserved population and widespread use of mobile devices creates a transformative environment for the emergence of platform-based financial services. Big techs, mobile network providers, and FinTechs are increasingly using this constellation to integrate payments, microloans, and microinsurance directly into everyday digital interactions—be it when ordering agricultural inputs, topping up mobile phone credit, or booking carpooling services.

Financial inclusion is not only a tool for individual protection against income shocks and a vehicle for wealth creation, but also a macroeconomic driver for overall economic development. Empirical studies document robust correlations between the possession of payment accounts and improved consumption smoothing, higher female labor force participation, and rising GDP per capita. Nevertheless, the traditional banking system is facing structural limitations in many emerging countries: branch banks are scarce in sparsely populated regions, micro-transactions are challenging to present in business terms, and informal incomes make standardized credit checks difficult.

Embedded finance offers an alternative access route by utilizing existing digital contact points, such as super apps or digital marketplaces, to distribute financial services. This approach reduces customer acquisition costs, enables the establishment of transaction-based credit rating models, and allows for the integration of so-called 'invisible' financial services into everyday contexts. It is precisely where the potential for inclusive system innovation lies.

At the same time, the rise of EmFi raises complex political, economic, and regulatory issues. Data flows are highly fragmented, run via proprietary APIs, and, in many cases, are beyond the control of national governments. Global platform providers, such as Apple, Ant Group, or Meta, increasingly define EmFi as app logic, rather than a regulated process architecture. This not only makes uniform supervisory practice more difficult, but also harbors substantial risks: without appropriate guardrails, embedded credit offerings could lead to new cycles of over-indebtedness, algorithmic credit models could reproduce systematic distortions, and the market structure could be destabilized by increasing platform concentration. The existing academic literature on EmFi has so far remained highly descriptive, Western-dominated, and lacking in context. This paper fills an analytical gap by employing a comparative and methodologically plural design to examine how EmFi is transforming the financial landscape in four representative emerging markets—Kenya, India, China, and Brazil—and what urgent regulatory responses are necessary to strike a new balance between innovation promotion and consumer protection.

## Objectives and Research Questions

Against the background of this problem, this study aims to systematically investigate whether and under what institutional, technological, and socio-economic conditions embedded finance (EmFi) contributes to a substantial and sustainable improvement in financial inclusion in emerging economies. In this context, meaningful inclusion' is not merely understood as the numerical expansion of account openings or digital payment transactions, but rather a qualitative gain: what is meant is long-term access to affordable, responsibly designed financial products that expand real economic capabilities and contribute to the economic resilience of households and micro-enterprises.

This leads to three interlinked, empirically based research questions:

RQ1 - Diffusion and impact dimensions: To what extent have the introduction and use of embedded payment systems, buy-now-pay-later (BNPL) models, and microcredit solutions led to measurable changes in key inclusion indicators, such as account usage, savings behavior, borrowing, and transaction intensity, in the selected countries?

RQ2 - Ecosystem configuration: How do API-driven system architectures and platform governance structures change value creation and risk distribution in local financial ecosystems? Who creates economic value, what new forms of intermediation are emerging, and how are dependency relationships shifting between established banks, telecommunications providers, FinTech start-ups, and global platform players?

RQ3 - Regulatory adequacy: To what extent are existing regulatory regimes - including e-money regulations, data protection regulations, and guidelines for digital lending - suitable for meeting the challenges of EmFi in terms of consumer protection, competitive dynamics, and systemic stability? What normative and institutional design principles can be derived for innovation-promoting but risk-sensitive supervision?

By combining quantitative macro indicators and qualitative case analyses, the aim is to generate generalizable insights while also revealing context-specific mechanisms that explain the success or failure of embedded finance initiatives in emerging markets.

## Structure of the Study

The structure of the paper follows a step-by-step unfolding of theoretical foundations, methodological approaches, empirical findings, and normative implications:

Section 2 develops the conceptual foundation. Here, central terms and definitions related to embedded finance are explained. The analysis distinguishes EmFi from related approaches, such as open banking or banking-as-a-service, and describes the technical and institutional functioning of BNPL, embedded payments, and microcredit. It situates EmFi within the framework of current theoretical discourses on the platform economy, API governance, and digital inclusion.

Section 3 examines the structural and contextual drivers of EmFi in emerging markets. The focus is on technological foundations, such as mobile network coverage, digital identity infrastructures, and real-time payment systems, as well as socio-economic influencing factors, including the role of informal economies, gender-specific access differences, and capital bottlenecks in micro-enterprises. Particular attention is paid to the orchestrating function of Big tech corporations and telecommunications providers in the design of hybrid platform ecosystems.

Section 4 presents methodological design. The study combines a panel-based quantitative impact analysis with in-depth case studies in four countries: Kenya, India, China, and Brazil. These case studies draw on qualitative interviews, document analysis, and API-based network visualizations to reveal both the institutional frameworks and the topology of EmFi value chains.

Section 5 presents comparative case analysis along a standardized analytical grid. For each country, EmFi-specific developments, inclusion effects, governance structures, and regulatory responses are analyzed. Section 6 systematizes the opportunities and risks arising from the case studies. In addition to positive effects such as easier access to credit, increased transaction security, and everyday integration, structural risks, including algorithmic distortions, data protection violations, platform dominance, and over-indebtedness, are also critically examined.

Section 7 is dedicated to the regulatory and tax policy implications. Sandbox models, RegTech instruments, licensing regimes, and the need for interoperable and privacy-sensitive infrastructure are discussed as prerequisites for fair market conditions. Section 8 concludes with an overarching assessment. The section summarizes key findings, formulates recommendations for action for political and institutional actors, and outlines research desiderata, for example, regarding the interface between EmFi and digital central bank currencies or the cross-border regulation of API-based financial intermediation.

Together, these eight sections provide a comprehensive analysis that combines theoretical depth, empirical evidence, and regulatory perspectives to inform action, to understand embedded finance as a potentially inclusive yet highly configuration-dependent mechanism within the future financial system.

## CONCEPTUAL FOUNDATIONS: EMBEDDED FINANCE AND FINANCIAL INCLUSION

### Definition and Delineation of Embedded Finance

Embedded finance refers to the seamless integration of financial products, such as payments, loans, insurance, or investments, into non-financial digital processes and interaction surfaces. The user does not come into direct contact with a bank but carries out financial transactions as part of another activity, such as online shopping, ride-hailing, social networking, or business software. Third-party providers process the transaction via standardized API interfaces in the background. EmFi is therefore characterized by contextuality - financial services do not appear as a stand-alone service, but as an embedded, often invisible functional element.

Three demarcations sharpen the profile of EmFi:

- Open Banking vs. EmFi - Open Banking focuses on data portability and customer-controlled access to bank accounts, for example, via third-party apps. EmFi, on the other hand, shifts the focus to the distribution of financial products in non-bank-centric digital ecosystems. Open banking is an infrastructural enabler, and EmFi is a strategic distribution paradigm.

- Banking-as-a-Service (BaaS) - BaaS providers provide regulated financial functions via APIs. EmFi uses this infrastructure as a use case and wraps it into digital end-user experiences orchestrated by platforms outside the banking sector.
- Traditional co-branding vs. EmFi - While traditional alliances are based on bilateral contracts and file transfers, EmFi is API-native, modular, and operates in real-time. It allows dynamic pricing, instant KYC checks, and granular risk management at the platform level.

This represents a paradigm shift: from traditional channel orientation (branch, website, banking app) to 'surface thinking' - financial services are integrated where digital attention is already available. Banks are becoming middleware providers, and platforms are transforming everyday interactions into monetizable touchpoints.

## Forms and Mechanics of Embedded Finance

Embedded payments are the most widespread form. Wallet tokens in ride-hailing or grocery apps enable one-click payments, with the payment process virtually disappearing from the interface. In the background, payment service providers (PSPs) orchestrate transactions via APIs—for example, via UPI (India) or PIX (Brazil). It reduces shopping cart abandonment, increases data collection, and opens up sources of revenue such as interchange or float effects.

Buy-Now-Pay-Later (BNPL) integrates real-time lending at the point of sale. Decision engines access device and behavioral data and approve installment purchases within milliseconds. BNPL often replaces traditional credit cards in emerging markets, creating formalized credit histories for the first time (e.g., Lazada BNPL in Southeast Asia).

Integrated microloans and working capital financing enable platforms to use sales data from gig workers or microenterprises as alternative collateral. For example, M-Shwari (Kenya) uses mobile phone usage and remittance behavior to set individual credit limits. In China, Huabei and Jiebei grant loans directly from the Alipay wallet.

Embedded insurance and asset management are being developed but are growing. Parametric micro-insurance can be integrated into product purchases, with cashback or cashback functions automatically flowing into micro-investments, such as MercadoFondo in Latin America.

Technically, all these models are based on four layers: (1) digital identification (KYC), usually via national ID systems; (2) data collection via SDKs; (3) regulatory licensed balance sheet providers or underwriters; (4) user interaction via orchestrated platform interfaces. Low-code dashboards significantly accelerate the configuration of new products - market launches often take just a few days.

## Financial Inclusion in Emerging Economies: Challenges and Opportunities

Despite technological advances, structural barriers persist, including high transaction costs for small sums, the limited reach of physical bank branches, restricted access to creditworthiness data, and KYC processes that often require formal identification documents —documents that are not readily available in precarious living situations. Additionally, informal incomes and cultural mistrust of banks hinder the widespread adoption of formal financial services.

In contrast, three developments open up opportunities for sustainable inclusion:

- Mobile penetration: In many emerging markets, smartphone penetration among young adults exceeds 70%, making mobile devices de facto bank branches.
- Regulatory innovation: Sandbox approaches and graduated KYC requirements enable the operation of low-threshold wallets with simplified legitimization requirements.
- Real-time payment infrastructure: Interoperable systems, such as UPI and Pix, reduce transfer costs to almost zero, making proprietary networks superfluous.

However, the depth of use remains central: an account alone is not an indicator of inclusion. Only recurring micropayments, credit cycles, and savings instruments create sustainable financial relationships. Studies from Kenya and Bangladesh show that multi-functionality significantly increases the intensity of use and length of stay.

At the same time, EmFi harbors new risks: Excessive BNPL usage can lead to over-indebtedness, algorithmic scoring models may reproduce social distortions, and the cross-border reach of large platforms poses significant challenges for national regulatory regimes, from oversight of capital flows to avoiding data exclusion.

## Theoretical Lenses: Platform Economics, API Ecosystems, Digital Inclusion

Platform economics provides the first theoretical frame of reference. Platforms act as multi-sided markets, in which reduced transaction costs generate network effects: more users attract more providers, which in turn favor extended functionalities, such as embedded financial services. In this logic, EmFi is not viewed as a separate business area, but rather as a means to increase user engagement, monetization, and penetration. Competition increasingly takes place not at the product level, but at the ecosystem level.

API governance theories complement this picture. APIs act as 'boundary resources' (Ghazawneh & Henfridsson, 2013) that enable third-party actors to integrate without giving up central control rights. Modularity reduces innovation costs, but also allows strategic control through access restrictions, versioning, and rate limiting. Network analyses show that if individual BaaS providers supply several dominant platforms, concentration risks arise that can overlay classic system risks.

The literature on digital inclusion (Heeks, 2010; Donner, 2015) highlights that technical access alone is insufficient; affordability, digital literacy, context-specific relevance, and institutional security are also crucial. EmFi can be effective in all of these dimensions: subsidized fee models increase access opportunities, embedded UI functions lower usage barriers, context-sensitive financial products (such as loans for seeds or storage costs) increase proximity to everyday life, and regulation creates a framework of trust.

A particularly dynamic development path in the context of digital inclusion results from the combination of embedded finance (EmFi) with mobile artificial intelligence (mobile AI). It refers to AI-supported functions that are executed directly on mobile devices, for example, through voice processing, scoring algorithms, or behavior-based recommendation systems (Goggin, 2025). Mobile AI can act as a contextualization engine for embedded finance: Financial services such as micro-loans, savings accounts, or BNPL offers are typically embedded in mobile apps. The AI models running locally on the end device enable the adaptation of these functions to individual usage situations, such as personalized fraud detection, alternative scoring procedures, or voice-based navigation. Especially in contexts with unreliable connectivity or infrastructural gaps, on-device AI solutions offer the opportunity to make financial interactions secure and efficient even under semi-offline conditions.

This form of edge intelligence is not only functionally relevant, but also advantageous from a regulatory perspective: local data processing enables better compliance with data protection requirements, which is becoming increasingly important in many emerging countries - for example in the context of new data protection laws such as India's DPDP 2023 or Brazil's LGPD. At the same time, mobile AI components enable a more situational user approach that can better address illiterate or linguistically disadvantaged population groups, for example, through voice interfaces, adaptive interfaces, or locally trained models.

In synthesis, this results in an expanded understanding of embedded finance: not just as the technical or economic embedding of financial functions in digital platforms, but as 'embedded intelligence' that reacts adaptively to usage contexts, language areas, and infrastructure levels. Mobile AI thus adds an inclusive, decentralized, and context-sensitive dimension to the EmFi paradigm, with particular relevance for regions where traditional banking infrastructure is insufficiently available. This perspective complements theory-based approaches to the platform economy and digital inclusion, which understand EmFi as a socio-technical stack whose impact is primarily determined by the quality of the interfaces and the context-sensitivity of the interaction. Recent studies on disruption by FinTechs and BigTechs confirm these findings. Anagnostopoulos, Sails, and Alexandrou (2025) show, based on stakeholder interviews, that these technology companies generate extreme concentration tendencies through data monetization and platform effects. However, it's the FinTechs that truly stand out, innovating more strongly in niches. Banks, in their role, contribute crucial regulatory stability, providing a reassuring anchor in the midst of disruption. For EmFi, this means that inclusion successes are inextricably linked to the regulation of platform power and data economies. The socio-technical stack approach developed in this article can thus be understood as a bridge between disruption theory and inclusion research.

In a conceptual evaluation framework, the inclusion contribution of embedded finance depends mainly on: (i) the structural power constellations in the platform market, (ii) the technical and institutional governance of API ecosystems, and (iii) the actual ability of EmFi offerings to expand user-side spaces for action.

## DRIVERS AND ENABLING CONDITIONS FOR EMBEDDED FINANCE IN EMERGING MARKETS

Embedded finance does not proliferate in a vacuum; its development in low- and middle-income economies reflects the interplay of technological infrastructures, market actors, and socio-economic realities. This section identifies four interrelated factors that determine both the speed and inclusivity of EmFi adoption.

### Digital Ecosystems and Mobile-First Markets

The most significant factor driving the spread of embedded finance in the Global South is the mobile nature of everyday life. By 2024, the Global System for Mobile Communications Association (GSMA) estimates smartphone penetration in sub-Saharan Africa at 51%, in South Asia at 71%, and in Latin America at 79%. Among young people in cities, the figures are 10 to 15 percentage points higher. A decade of falling device prices and bandwidth costs has created a mobile-first, sometimes mobile-only user base whose primary access to commerce, communication, and entertainment is a handheld screen.

Digital platforms, from ride-hailing and food delivery apps to marketplaces for agricultural inputs, act as multi-service hubs. In Kenya, Safaricom's M-Pesa Super App bundles P2P transfers, merchant payments, credit ratings, and utility bill payment modules into a single interface; in Indonesia, Gojek's GoTo ecosystem combines logistics, streaming, and micro-investment products with transportation services. These 'super apps' shorten the distance between a non-financial need (ordering fertilizer, booking a motorcycle cab) and the embedded financial solution (payment on delivery, working capital advance).

A second, less conspicuous driver is the persistence of feature phone users who rely on USSD menus and STK applications. Many EmFi vendors are therefore investing in a dual design: smartphone front-ends for affluent urban customers and USSD fallbacks for rural or lower-income segments. The technical discipline of keeping products 'USSD-compatible by default' lowers marginal inclusion costs and protects against a bifurcated digital financial system.

Finally, the data generated by continuous in-app activity—geolocation traces, clickstreams, and post-purchase reviews—feeds alternative credit scoring models. The richer the digital ecosystem, the larger the data surface from which machine learning algorithms can derive repayment probabilities, enabling nano-loans at service costs that are unimaginable for branch-based banks.

## The Pivotal Role of Big Techs and Fintechs in Shaping Embedded Finance

Regardless of regional differences, big tech companies in emerging markets have several strategic advantages: they have direct access to a broad user and merchant base, are often initially subject to less stringent regulation, operate with low capital and scalable structures, and have advanced, silo-free data architectures. This combination makes them ideal orchestrators of embedded financial solutions. Their entry strategy into the financial sector almost always begins with payment services—the simplest financial function in terms of technology, yet the one with the broadest reach, (Andrae, 2022; Doerr et al., 2025).

Fintech apps have a high penetration in advanced economies, while big tech apps are more prevalent in developing and emerging economies (Figure 1).

*Figure 1. Distribution of fintech and big tech apps*

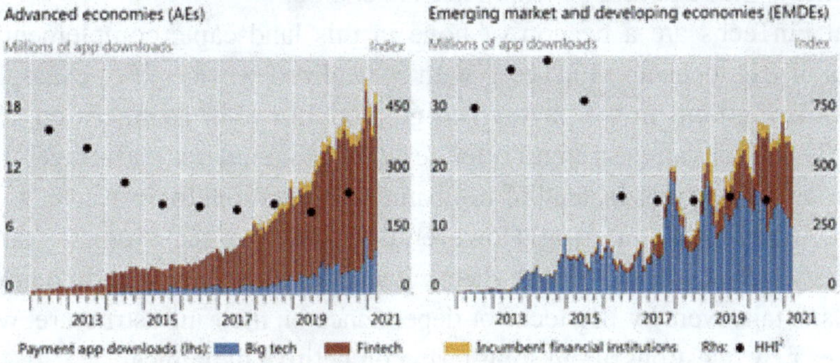


HHI = Herfindahl-Hirschman Index of market concentration.

[1] Downloads of all payment apps among the top 50 finance apps as classified by Sensor Tower. "Fintech" refers to apps by new entrants specialised in financial technology; "big tech" refers to apps by large technology companies whose primary activity is digital services, rather than financial services, and "incumbent financial institutions" refers to apps from commercial banks, insurers, card networks and other financial institutions. [2] Yearly average; calculated on the top 50 finance apps as classified by Sensor Tower.

Source: Croxson et al (2023).

The Chinese EmFi ecosystem serves as a beacon of advancement, boasting over 850 million internet users and a mobile payment volume equivalent to around 16% of its GDP, making China a global pioneer. The Ant Group is a prime example of a vertically integrated Big tech ecosystem, with more than one billion users accessing embedded financial services, including BNPL (Huabei), working capital financing (Jiebei), money market funds (Yu'e Bao), and microinsurance, all via the Alipay app. Lending is driven by Zhima Credit, a proprietary behavioral and scoring engine that considers over 3,000 data points per user. This example illustrates how network effects, brand trust, and closed platform structures can integrate embedded finance into a comprehensive, everyday infrastructure, largely independent of traditional banking institutions.

In India and Brazil, Meta is pursuing a different but equally influential strategy. Through WhatsApp Pay, the company is using the massive reach of its messaging platform to introduce peer-to-merchant (P2M) payments, first in Brazil and later in India. In both countries, Meta collaborates with local acquirers and banks and integrates with government-provided real-time payment systems, such as UPI and Pix. The case demonstrates that interoperability, enforced by regulation, enables foreign platforms to utilize local payment systems and overcome market entry barriers.

A hybrid model is evident in Africa, as seen with JumiaPay, which emerged from the regional e-commerce platform Jumia. In order to minimize cash-on-delivery risks, Jumia developed its wallet, which was later expanded to include BNPL functions and airtime credit. Without its banking license, JumiaPay relies on banking-as-a-service partners—an example of EmFi's modular partner architecture, where lending, risk management, and regulatory compliance are shared.

Local FinTechs are a beacon of hope in this landscape, complementing the offerings of Big techs and FinTechs with specialized services. For example, they finance solar systems in the pay-as-you-go model or offer advances on gig work income. Their innovative strength often results from regulatory arbitrage - they are subject to e-money rules instead of full banking regulation, for example, as well as from a focused product offering. However, their ability to scale remains limited as long as they lack access to balance sheet capacity or growth capital. In many cases, this leads to takeovers by Big techs or dependence on their infrastructure, which in turn raises new questions about long-term competitive dynamics.

## Infrastructure Prerequisites: Network Coverage, Digital identity, Payment Interoperability

The success of embedded finance depends mainly on the digital infrastructure, i.e., the stability of networks, the availability of electronic identities, and the openness of payment systems. Three levels stand out here:

Firstly, network connectivity: while 4G and increasingly 5G networks achieve coverage of over 90% in the urban centers of many emerging countries, there are still significant gaps in peri-urban and rural regions. Additionally, unstable power grids, load shedding, and infrastructural bottlenecks make maintaining continuous online availability challenging. EmFi providers are responding with technical workarounds, such as offline-capable SDKs that buffer authentication tokens locally, or USSD bridges that do not require a mobile data connection. In this way, electricity access becomes an indirect but essential factor of financial inclusion.

Secondly, digital identity and e-KYC procedures: Scalable ID systems significantly reduce onboarding costs. In India, the biometric-based Aadhaar system enables video KYC to be carried out within a few minutes. In Brazil, gov.br combines various administrative data into a digital proof of identity. Open-source models, such as MOSIP, allow even low-income countries to set up national ID systems cost-effectively. Where such infrastructures are lacking, for example, in the Democratic Republic of the Congo, providers fall back on SIM registration data or social references. However, this increases the susceptibility to errors and reinforces existing exclusions, for example, among women, who are less likely to have formally registered mobile phone contracts.

Thirdly, real-time payment systems with API access: platform-independent systems, such as UPI (India), Pix (Brazil), or PAPSS (Pan-Africa), enable low-cost micropayments with high transaction security. Their openness enables FinTechs to offer payments without proprietary networks—a key success factor for BNPL models or pay-per-use insurance. At the same time, interoperability reduces the risk of lock-in effects: users can transfer funds between wallets, and providers must compete on the quality of their services instead of relying on access restrictions.

The convergence of these three layers—connectivity, digital identity, and interoperable payments—explains the explosive growth of EmFi in countries like India. Public infrastructure, such as fast payment systems (FPS), can promote competition (Figure 2) where these prerequisites are lacking, fragmented solutions with limited reach dominate.

*Figure 2. Public infrastructures like fast payment systems can foster competition*

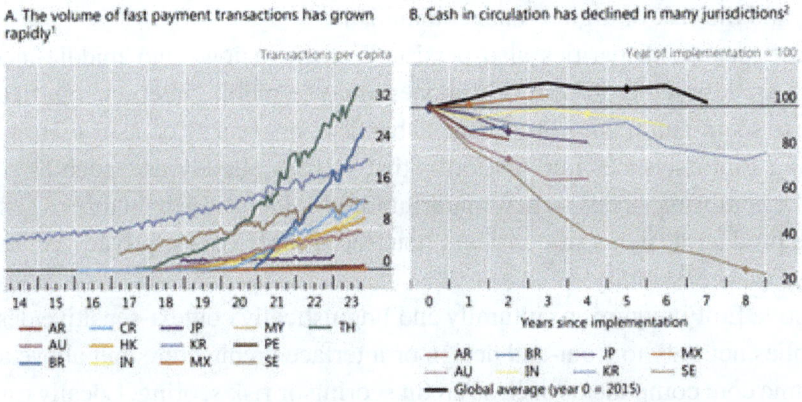


¹ Monthly data. See technical annex for details. ² Banknotes and coins in circulation are shown as a percentage of narrow money, except for KR for which currency in circulation/narrow money is shown. The markers indicate the year of the Covid-19 pandemic, 2020, except for KR, which shows only eight years after 2009.

Source: CPMI Red Book Statistics (2025); Frost et al (2024).

## Societal and Economic Contexts: Informality, Gender Gaps, Access to Capital

Digital infrastructure and technological solutions do not develop their impact independently of social realities. Instead, social structures act as a filter to determine who benefits from embedded finance and who remains excluded from it. An inclusive finance approach is one way of understanding how people's context facilitates or hinders their movement towards wellbeing. Embedding EmFi in the inclusive finance approach takes into account the country's context, including community assets, governance, and institutional norms; the local context through social norms surrounding decision-making, mobility, and responsibility; norms regarding the roles of different types of people within social networks; and customer characteristics (Andrae, 2025a).

A key feature of many emerging countries is the high proportion of informal employment, which ranges from 50% to 70%, depending on the region. These forms of employment are often characterized by irregular income streams, a lack of documentation, and limited evidence of creditworthiness. EmFi can help to make informal activities 'visible' - for example, by analyzing sales data or travel turnover on platforms - and thus create access to credit where conventional banks fail. At the same time, data-based credit models pose new risks of exclusion: algorithms could negatively assess unstable income patterns and thereby reinforce existing structural disadvantages. It raises fundamental questions about data sovereignty, algorithmic fairness, and the risk of digital 'data colonialism'.

Gender-specific disparities also persist. Women in low- and middle-income countries are less likely to own cell phones and use mobile internet significantly less, due to socio-cultural norms, financial barriers, or security concerns. However, integrating EmFi services into platforms that women already use, such as social commerce platforms, opens up new opportunities for inclusion. It requires a gender-sensitive product design that considers household preferences, privacy concerns, and language accessibility.

Effective EmFi requires a culturally and linguistically context-sensitive design. This applies not only to front-end design or interface architecture, but above all to algorithmic core components such as credit scoring or risk scoring. Locally trained models, language-sensitive interfaces, and differentiated UX designs tailored to the specific everyday routines of users are considered integral components of an adaptive EmFi system. This orientation not only strengthens the usability but also the legitimacy of the services.

The participatory character emphasizes that users are not just passive recipients, but active data producers and generators of feedback. This understanding supports governance instruments such as data trusts or data cooperatives (Andrae, 2025b), which enable collective control over data flows, as well as bias audits, in which algorithmic models are regularly checked for fairness and representativeness. Participation thus becomes a mechanism of algorithmic accountability—a crucial element in reducing power asymmetries in data-based EmFi ecosystems.

Finally, the concept emphasizes institutional embedding, ensuring that technological innovation cannot generate trust or inclusion in the long term without robust governance frameworks that evolve alongside it. Last but not least, user trust remains a key prerequisite. In countries with experience of payment fraud, Ponzi schemes, or platform collapses, widespread mistrust prevails. Building trust, therefore, depends not only on technical security but also on institutional signals, such as the involvement of local agents or clear proof of state licensing in apps. Individual scandals, whether through data misuse or aggressive collection practices, can discredit the entire EmFi sector. This perspective corresponds with key findings from EmFi regulatory research: only where embedded supervision, multi-level licensing regimes, or regulatory sandboxes accompany technical evolution is it possible to stabilize inclusion gains and control systemic risks institutionally.

Embedded finance should not be thought of solely as a technological or economic innovation, but as a multidimensional intervention at the interface of technology, society, and regulation. This view opens up new perspectives for designing inclusive financial systems that go beyond traditional microfinance or FinTech paradigms in terms of their architectural openness, social responsiveness, and regulatory embedding. EmFi thus becomes not just a tool, but a touchstone for the institutional learning and adaptability of digital economies.

Another structural problem is the financing gap for micro and small enterprises. The estimated global financing shortfall for this group is approximately USD 5 trillion (Andrae, 2025a). EmFi offerings that rely on cash flow-based repayment concepts, such as revenue shares instead of fixed installments, offer a promising alternative. At the same time, there is a risk that non-transparent interest rates and short-term maturities could lead to a debt trap if regulatory standards for product transparency and risk disclosure are lacking.

## METHODOLOGY

This section explains how the study integrates quantitative metrics, qualitative evidence, and network analysis to develop a multi-layered understanding of EmFi in emerging markets. The approach is explicitly explanatory-sequential: statistical patterns are first identified and then interpreted through country-level case studies and ecosystem mapping.

### Mixed-Methods Design

A convergent parallel mixed-methods design is employed, in which quantitative and qualitative strands are conducted simultaneously and integrated in the interpretation phase. There are three reasons for this:

- Complementarity: Macro-statistics capture breadth, while case studies reveal causal mechanisms and context dependencies.
- Triangulation: Independent streams of evidence reduce methodological bias and increase internal validity.

- Development: network analysis informs the qualitative interview guide (e.g., by identifying gatekeeper APIs), and qualitative findings refine variable specifications in regression models.

### Quantitative Module

A balanced panel (2013-2024) of 25 emerging countries is created. The key explanatory variable is an index of EmFi adoption intensity based on: (i) BNPL transaction volume per capita, (ii) share of e-commerce GMV transacted via embedded wallets, and (iii) number of publicly documented EmFi APIs per million population. A fixed-effects model is used to test the relationship with four key inclusion indicators: Account ownership, digital payments, credit utilization, and savings rate. Control variables include GDP per capita, urbanization, and mobile data costs. Robust results are tested using a staggered difference-in-differences estimator (Callaway & Sant'Anna, 2021).

### Qualitative Module

Four country cases are analyzed using 38 semi-structured expert interviews, a document analysis, and ethnographic user observations. The transcripts are coded in NVivo using an iterative-abductive procedure: deductive codes from platform economy theory are supplemented by inductive ones (e.g., data colonialism, trust in agent networks).

## Integration Strategy

According to Creswell & Plano Clark (2010), results are merged in joint display matrices in which statistical coefficients are contrasted with citations and network centrality values. Convergences confirm causal statements, while divergences lead to deeper analysis (e.g., why India has higher credit growth than Brazil, despite similar EmFI intensity).

Case-Selection Rationale: China, Kenya, India, Brazil

The four country cases (China, Kenya, India, Brazil) were selected on theoretical grounds to capture maximum variance in three key dimensions (Table 1):

- Maturity level of digital platform markets
- Regulatory level of development
- Socio-economic heterogeneity

*Table 1. Country selection*

| Dimension | China | Kenya | India | Brazil |
|---|---|---|---|---|
| **Platform architecture** | Closed, Big tech-centric (Ant Group, Tencent) | Telco-led super-app (Safaricom/M-Pesa) | Open-rail UPI + competitive FinTech layer | Central-bank-orchestrated Pix + private super-apps |
| **Regulatory stance** | Ex-post crackdown on Big tech finance | Pro-innovation sandbox regime | Proactive open-rail policy | Strong pro-competition mandates |
| **Socio-economic profile** | Upper-middle income, high urbanization | Lower-middle income, rural majority | Lower-middle income, high digital ID coverage | Upper-middle income, high inequality |

This configurative diversity enables the identification and generalization of robust patterns across diverse institutional contexts. The selection of the four country cases—Kenya, India, China, and Brazil—demonstrates the breadth of our research, as it follows the principle of maximum functional diversity. Each country represents a unique aspect of financial innovation: a telco-driven model in Kenya, a state-orchestrated API infrastructure in India, a BigTech-centered super app integration in China, and neobank and real-time payment innovation in Brazil. These cases cover key EmFi typologies and provide a comprehensive view of the digital financial ecosystem. However, it's important to note that important regions such as West Africa, MENA, and the rest of Latin America are not included. To address these gaps, selective references to initiatives in Nigeria (e.g., Kuda, Flutterwave), Ghana (e.g., E-Zwich, Sandbox program), and Mexico (CoDi, Banxico fintech regime) are included in the synthesis sections. Generalizability is explicitly reflected upon in the concluding discussion (Section 8.1).

## Data Sources and Financial-Inclusion Metrics

Primary quantitative data sets:

- Global Findex (World Bank, 2021): Account ownership, savings behavior, credit usage.
- IMF Financial Access Survey (annual): Number of ATMs and bank branches, outstanding mobile money accounts, transaction volumes.
- GSMA Mobile Money Metrics (monthly): Wallet activity rates, merchant payment volumes.

Crunchbase and CB Insights API databases: annual counts of EmFi API endpoints and funding flows.

Derived indicators:

- Account activity rate - proportion of registered mobile money accounts that have processed transactions within a period of ≥90 days
- Digital credit penetration rate - number of individual borrowers using mobile or BNPL loans per 1,000 adults.
- Savings rate - Median balance in mobile wallets divided by GDP per capita.
- Inclusion composite index - principal component score of the above metrics normalized to 0-1.

Missing values are replaced with multiple imputations (chained equations) under the assumption of missing-at-random; robustness analyses ensure the stability of the results.

Interview corpus. Regulators, platform managers, telecommunications companies, NGOs, and retailers were interviewed and recruited through snowball sampling and public conferences. All interviews comply with GDPR-compliant standards.

## Network and API Analysis for Ecosystem Mapping

The aim is to map EmFi ecosystems in a structural manner. Two network layers are constructed:

1. API graph: All publicly documented EmFi APIs in the case study countries are extracted. Each API is a directed edge between a provider (e.g., BaaS) and a consumer application (e.g., e-commerce platform), classified by function and authentication.
2. Multiplex network: The platform nodes are additionally linked via participation and partnerships. It allows technical dependencies to be overlaid with economic power structures.

The following analytical measures are used:

- The degree of centrality and intermediate centrality identify 'gatekeeper' APIs whose failure could lead to the fragmentation of user flows.
- The Herfindahl-Hirschman Index (HHI) for API calls measures the concentration of technical power.
- The K-Core decomposition isolates a resilient subnetwork of deeply anchored partnerships.

Visualizations are carried out with Gephi. Centrality values serve as moderators in quantitative models (e.g., influence on switching costs and inclusion dynamics).

Network maps are triangulated using regulatory reports, press sources, and feedback from interviews. Deviations lead to targeted follow-up research.

Limitations exist in the selection of experts and the visibility of proprietary APIs. Nevertheless, the integrative design approach enables reliable statements to be made about the paths, conditions, and risks associated with EmFi-based inclusion.

By integrating panel econometrics, detailed case descriptions, and granular network mapping, this methodological framework clarifies not only whether embedded finance promotes financial inclusion, but also through which pathways—technical, organizational, and institutional—it occurs and under what conditions these pathways remain equitable and resilient.

## CASE STUDY ANALYSIS

The four case studies illustrate different development pathways through which EmFi drives, or limits, financial inclusion in emerging markets. Each analysis follows the same framework: (i) market and product architecture, (ii) measurable inclusion effects, (iii) risks and governance responses, and (iv) transferable lessons learned.

### Kenya: M-Pesa and the Integration of Mobile Payment Services

#### Architecture and Products

Since its launch in 2007, Safaricom's M-Pesa has revolutionized Kenya's payments system, operating on a mobile-first platform. By 2024, the platform had processed an impressive 30 billion transactions worth KES 38.29 trillion (≈ USD 296 billion) and served over 34 million users. The introduction of new functional modules, such as Ratiba (standing orders) and Fuliza Biashara (an overdraft facility for merchants), has further expanded the ecosystem, enabling recurring payments and providing working capital.

#### Inclusive Effect

Mobile money subscriptions reached 45.4 million accounts in early 2025 - a penetration rate of 86.6% of the adult population. Over 400,000 micro-merchants now accept QR payments; nano-loans via M-Shwari have created a formal credit history for 6 million customers for the first time, according to the central bank (Kim & Duvendack, 2024).

## Risks & Governance

Safaricom retains a market share of over 80% in transaction volume, despite Airtel's efforts to catch up. The Central Bank of Kenya is therefore planning for agent interoperability, where each agent will be able to process services from all wallets in the future, thereby reducing lock-in effects. At the same time, the data protection authority is targeting scoring-based credit products to prevent algorithmic discrimination.

## Lessons Learned

EmFi scales fastest where (a) telcos maintain a dense agent network, (b) simplified tier KYC takes effect, and (c) regulators open sandbox spaces early. However, concentration risks require proactive interoperability rules and real-time oversight (Andrae, 2022). Micro-level experiences illustrate that digital credit products not only open up financial opportunities but also have psychosocial dimensions. A qualitative study conducted by CGAP (2018) among Kenyan users shows that Fuliza loans are often used for school expenses, demonstrating a direct inclusion effect. At the same time, many respondents express concerns about a lack of transparency regarding fees, which undermines trust. The development of M-Pesa illustrates the logic of the platform economy: the more users and merchants are connected to the system, the stronger the network effects, which in turn make new functions such as microloans or insurance attractive. At the same time, it becomes apparent that a lack of interoperability increases the risk of a winner-takes-most market – a core problem from the perspective of platform theory.

# India: UPI, Embedded Microfinance, and Digital Identities

## Architecture

Launched in 2016, the Unified Payments Interface (UPI) combines real-time clearing, virtual payment addresses (VPA), and Open API access. In May 2025, UPI processed 18.68 billion payments worth the equivalent of 25.14 lakh crore (approximately USD 302 billion); 673 banks were connected live. Despite short-term defaults, the average daily volume in June was 613 million transactions.

## Embedded Microfinance

The account aggregator framework and Aadhaar-based video KYC drastically reduce onboarding costs. FinTechs such as Jupiter or PayNearby link $\leq$ 10,000 microloans directly to UPI handles; repayments are made flexibly with each incoming payment. A survey of 14,000 MSMEs shows that 73% attribute their sales growth to smartphone tools and UPI.

### Inclusive Impact

UPI has narrowed the gender gap in account ownership from 9% (2017) to <2% (2024); rural transaction shares increased from 14% to 29% in 2021-25. At the same time, over 50 million first-time loans were granted to households with thin credit files.

### Risks & Debates

The zero-fee policy (0% MDR) secures access costs but limits the scope of payment players' business models. The government and the RBI are discussing an MDR of 0.2-0.3% for wholesalers in 2025 to refinance operational investments.

### Lessons

A state-driven, interoperable rail can catalyze private sector innovation when (i) open APIs, (ii) digital identities, and (iii) proportional licensing regimes come together. However, the sustainability of monetization remains unclear (Andrae, 2022). UPI clearly illustrates the role of open API ecosystems: banks, fintechs, and big tech companies are connected via uniform interfaces, allowing a wide range of innovative products to be integrated on a plug-and-play basis. The Indian case thus shows that the governance of API standards is crucial for promoting both competition and inclusion.

## China: Ant Group, MyBank, and the BNPL Ecosystem

### Architecture

In China, a Big tech-centric version of EmFi dominates. Alipay's Huabei (revolving credit) and Jiebei (short-term loans) together reached around 500 million users by 2024. The total market for buy-now-pay-later is estimated to be USD 122 billion by 2025. At the same time, MyBank - a purely digital institution within the Ant Group - provides over 53 million SMEs with data-supported microloans (≤ CNY 1 million).

### Inclusive Impact

Ant's credit algorithms use more than 3,000 behavioral variables and deliver real-time limits within 60 seconds. Internal analysis shows that 80% of MyBank customers had not previously obtained a bank loan. Social micro-add-on products, such as Xianghubao (peer-to-peer mutual aid), extend the protective umbrella but were discontinued in 2024 due to regulatory uncertainties.

### Risks & Regulation

Following the IPO freeze in 2020, Ant was compelled to adopt a financial holding structure; Huabei data has been flowing into the national credit register since 2022. New regulations require a 30% equity share in consumer loans to ensure a stake in the game. At the same time, the PBoC caps BNPL interest rates at 15% per annum, thereby shrinking margins.

### Lessons

Big tech-powered EmFi can close inclusion gaps en masse as long as (a) huge data lakes are collected, (b) cloud core banking delivers economies of scale. However, without clear capital and data oversight, systemic risks and power asymmetries arise (Andrae, 2022). The Chinese example confirms the theoretical perspective of the platform economy in its extreme form: Ant Group bundles financial services in a closed ecosystem whose network effects generate massive gains in inclusion, but at the same time also reinforce market power and cluster risks. This dynamic is consistent with the winner-takes-most logic of digital platform markets.

## Brazil: Nubank, Open Finance, and Pix-driven Inclusion

### Architecture

With Pix (2020), Brazil's central bank has created a real-time payment rail as a public utility. By 2025, Pix will already be processing > 2 trillion. R$ per month and is expected to overtake credit cards as the leading online payment method by 2025, according to the Ebanx study. A new installment function (Pix Parcelado) will be launched in September 2025, bringing interest-free partial payments to the core protocol. In parallel, Nubank has gained ~90 million customers in Brazil (across its 119 million group-wide customer base) through a streamlined app onboarding process and fee-free accounts (Figure 3); 83% of these customers remain active every month. Open Finance APIs enables third-party providers to securely integrate account information (with consent) into credit scoring models.

*Figure 3. Pix has introduced fast payments for over 90% of adults*

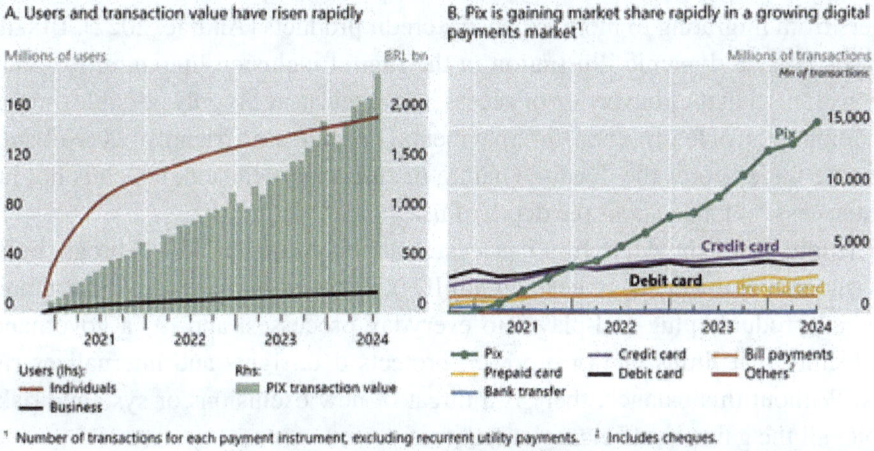


Source: Duarte et al (2022); Frost et al (2025); updated as of November 2024.

## Inclusive Effect

According to the central bank, 12 million previously unbanked Brazilians had a Pix-enabled account for the first time by the end of 2024. Nubank reports that 58% of its new female credit card customers did not previously have a card. Micro-savings features such as Caixinhas auto-round up everyday purchases and park small amounts in Tesouro-Direto funds.

## Risks & Supervision

The unrestricted use of Pix lowers merchant costs but threatens bank interchange revenues. In regulatory terms, the Autoridade Nacional de Proteção de Dados (ANPD) requires detailed consent flows for open finance data. At the same time, the central bank conducts stress tests on default scenarios for Pix.

## Lessons

A government-developed, openly licensable payment rail can spur private neo-banks on a large scale, provided that (i) data protection is strictly enforced and (ii) functional enhancements such as installment payments prevent low-income consumers from migrating to more expensive credit products (Andrae, 2022). Brazil's case serves as a dynamic illustration in the digital inclusion literature. It vividly demonstrates that the conversion of access into actual usage is only possible through the combination of fee-free real-time payments (Pix) and user-friendly UX (Nubank). This case underscores the dynamic nature of financial inclusion, which is not just about access, but also about the depth of usage.

The four cases show that EmFi successes are based on a triad: (1) broad digital rails (mobile, real-time payments, digital IDs), (2) modular API stacks that embed financial products plug-and-play into everyday processes, and (3) a governance architecture that limits platform power, protects data rights and internalizes risk costs. Without this balance, there is a threat of new exclusions or systemic risks, despite all the gains in efficiency and access.

# OPPORTUNITIES AND RISKS OF EMBEDDED FINANCE FOR FINANCIAL INCLUSION

## Potential: Access to Credit, Transaction Security, Suitability for Everyday Use

Embedded finance (EmFi) is a transformative force that is reshaping market dynamics. It achieves this by lowering barriers to entry in three key ways. Firstly, it opens up credit markets for previously data-poor customers by using transaction traces from everyday apps as 'alternative' scoring. MyBank in China is a prime example, with 80% of its 53 million SME customers who had not received a bank loan before digital onboarding now making decisions in less than 60 seconds. In Kenya, M-Shwari and Fuliza collectively achieved over 6 million first-time loans, while also establishing a formal credit history in the national database. Secondly, real-time rails such as India's UPI or Brazil's Pix increase transaction security, making authorized payments irrevocable and linked to two-factor approvals via APIs, thereby reducing fraud rates below those of traditional card networks. Thirdly, everyday usability - including checkout, QR cash-in/out, and micro-savings accounts in super apps - increases the frequency of use. Global Findex data indicate that adults who receive digital payments are, on average, twice as likely to save or borrow as those who do not.

Ghana also illustrates early experiments with EmFi-like architectures. E-Zwich, Africa's first biometric e-money system, was launched in 2008 to provide account access to previously unbanked groups based on fingerprint authentication (Breckenridge, 2010). At the same time, sandbox programs and MTN Mobile Money are driving the spread of digital payment services. According to the Bank of Ghana, the transaction volume of Mobile Money increased by more than 500% between 2017 and 2022, facilitated by simplified KYC rules that included rural populations (Bank of Ghana, 2019). Ghana thus illustrates that even smaller markets can provide impetus for inclusive EmFi through biometric innovations and regulatory experiments.

The adoption dynamics of EmFi are heavily influenced by digital literacy and trust. Studies by GSMA (2023) show that in LMICs, up to 30% of registered mobile wallets remain inactive due to users' lack of understanding of the system's functions or fear of financial loss. Trust is often built through social networks and, notably, local merchant agencies that act as gatekeepers (Donner & Tellez, 2008). These local partnerships play a crucial role in promoting digital financial inclusion. However, a lack of transparency regarding fees and data usage can quickly undermine this fragile trust.

The panel data show that EmFi is expanding access and usage. From a platform economy perspective, this reinforces positive network effects: more users make the products more attractive to providers, which in turn broadens access to credit and digital payments.

## Risks: Data Misuse, Algorithmic Discrimination, Risk of Debt

The same data exhaust that makes scoring possible harbors privacy risks. In Africa, studies have raised concerns about unclear consent and third-party data access, with data protection identified as the 'biggest obstacle' to sustainable growth for EmFi. Historical incidents, such as the 2019 leak of 11.5 million gambling transactions at M-Pesa, illustrate the potential for escalation.

Algorithmic biases exacerbate existing inequalities when there are gender or region-specific gaps in training data: Frontiers analyses show systematic misclassifications in loans that undervalue women and rural users. Nevertheless, CFI comparative studies show that well-calibrated algorithms can reduce human discrimination by up to 40%—an indication of governance rather than technological abandonment.

Leverage risks are particularly prevalent in 'Buy Now, Pay Later' (BNPL) models. These models, although currently anticipated to have low default rates by institutions like Morgan Stanley and the Richmond Fed, carry the risk of 'stacked loans' for young users as soon as BNPL payments accumulate across multiple apps. In Kenya, the consumer protection authority reported 63 complaints against digital lenders in 2024, almost four times as many as in 2023, mainly due to non-transparent fees and aggressive collection methods.

Mexico is particularly relevant for Latin America beyond Brazil. In 2019, the central bank (Banxico) introduced CoDi, a QR-based real-time payment system that is directly linked to bank accounts. The aim was to reduce the proportion of cash in the economy and promote financial inclusion. Despite regulatory support and technical infrastructure, adoption has so far fallen short of expectations: at the end of 2023, less than 15% of the potential target group was actively using CoDi (Alliance for Financial Inclusion (AFI), 2024). Studies point to a lack of user-friendliness and the requirement to have an existing bank account as key barriers. Mexico thus demonstrates the limitations of purely top-down EmFi implementations without a stronger user focus.

The risks associated with embedded finance can be precisely located along three theoretical strands. From the perspective of the platform economy, the central danger lies in increasing market concentration: network effects and economies of scale favor 'winner-takes-most' dynamics, where a few dominant providers determine market activity, thereby restricting competition and innovation diversity. The perspective of API ecosystems points to a second risk. If interfaces remain proprietary and standards are fragmented, lock-in effects arise that tie users to specific platforms and make it difficult to switch to alternative providers. Finally, the digital inclusion literature highlights a third risk: 'exclusion by design.' For instance, if a digital payment system only supports a specific language or requires a certain level of digital literacy, it can exclude those who do not meet these criteria. If embedded financial solutions do not take cultural differences, gender inequalities, or deficits in digital literacy into account, there is a risk of reinforcing existing inequalities instead of overcoming them. Overall, it is clear that EmFi not only opens up new opportunities for access but also carries the risk of structural distortions, fueled equally by economic, technical, and social logic.

## Market Structure: Platform Dominance, Lock-in Effects, Interoperability

Embedded finance tends to concentrate technical and economic power. This is evident in cases like Ant Group, which controls around 1.3 billion users and 80 million merchants through Alipay, enabling it to bundle lending, insurance, and wealth products within a proprietary data loop. In Kenya, despite recent erosion,

M-Pesa still holds 90.8% of mobile money subscriptions—a quasi-monopoly that de facto sets fees and product design.

Exclusive wallet tokens, loyalty programs, and API throttling create lock-in mechanisms that prevent users from switching to alternative services. Sponsor bank studies show that more than 50% of their deposits and revenues already come from EmFi partnerships; this dependency shifts systemic risks from bank balance sheets to less-regulated FinTech nodes. However, where real-time payment rails remain open, lock-ins can be mitigated. UPI alias addresses enable provider changes with a single click, and Pix enforces interoperability down to the agent level. IMF analyses quantify that country-wide interoperability increases adoption by an additional 8-12 percentage points (Copestake, Kirti, & Martinez Peria, 2025).

However, interoperability deficits remain: In Nigeria, the K-Switch fee causes fragmentation, while in the US, heterogeneous RTP coverage shifts fraud risks and slows down the spread of open use cases. The lack of technical standards increases integration costs for newcomers and reinforces the first-mover advantages of established platforms.

A key example in West Africa is Nigeria, where providers such as Kuda and Flutterwave are energizing the EmFi sector. Flutterwave has become a regional gateway for merchants and consumers with its API-based payment services. At the same time, Kuda, as a 'neobank for Africans,' operates entirely on mobile and has opened over 6 million accounts since 2019. However, both players have a tense relationship with the Nigerian Central Bank, which has repeatedly tightened licensing requirements and temporarily blocked international payments (Okekenwa, 2025; Global Legal Insights, 2025). Nigeria thus demonstrates the opportunities offered by data-driven wallet and API models, but also the regulatory risks of fragmented supervision.

Empirical observations – such as the high betweenness centrality of a few API nodes in China and Kenya – illustrate the power asymmetries described in the API ecosystem literature. The greater the dependence on a few technical gatekeepers, the more vulnerable the system becomes to systemic risks.

## Replacement of Traditional Financial Intermediation?

Embedded finance is altering the balance of roles between banks, FinTechs, and non-financial platforms, without completely replacing traditional institutions to date. Four trend lines are emerging:

1. Banks as 'balance-sheet-as-a-service': community and sponsor banks in the US, or tier 2 institutions in Brazil, are shifting to a background function, providing license, capital, and compliance, while front-end UX lies with Big- or

FinTechs. It threatens to erode margins for transaction-related products, with banks compensating them with wholesale loans or API fees.

2. Disintermediate payment transactions: Pix and UPI volumes are replacing cards and ATM fees - an internal central bank rail is displacing private intermediary revenues. Pix is set to overtake online cards in Brazil for checkouts as early as 2025.
3. Re-intermediation via data and risk: Banks are trying to reoccupy customer touchpoints with their open finance stacks (e.g., Itaú Open Banking). The probability of success depends on the quality of the API and FinTech partnerships.
4. Regulatory burdens remain with the licensed entity: In many BNPL models, banks bear minimum capital and stress test obligations, while platforms skim margins. If margins fall (e.g., China: 30% self-funding ratio), banks could reprice EmFi partnerships.

Embedded finance is inevitably forcing banks to adopt new strategies because two developments cannot be stopped: standard financial products are moving away from the banks' sphere of sovereignty to customer interfaces that are increasingly dominated by embedded finance providers, whether tech giants or e-commerce merchants that enrich their offerings with financial services. Conversely, this means that banks pursuing a business model with less differentiating standard financial products for end customers will find it more challenging to survive. The combination of threats to banks' standard business model from EmFi and market opportunities from BaaS approaches turns BaaS from a niche strategy into an option that every bank should consider. To do this, banks need to understand digital technologies such as APIs, blockchain, or cloud computing, as well as the business models based on them, including platform, streaming, or marketplace approaches. With the right mindset, they should develop their own BaaS offerings in a targeted and creative manner to capitalize on the opportunities. This highlights the relevance of the platform economy: banks are losing their customer interface because platforms are monopolizing them as economic interfaces. From the perspective of digital inclusion research, however, it is crucial that this new division of labor not only creates access but also builds trust and competence.

The net result is not a complete displacement, but rather a division of functions: banks become suppliers of regulation and liquidity, while platforms orchestrate user journeys. Whether this division of labor is stable depends on two factors:

- Capital regulatory regime: if regulators force platforms to hold capital (as with Ant Group), they move closer to bank return logics.
- Data rights: If open data mandates enforce portability, the customer relationship can diffuse back.

Overall, this results in the following synthesis: embedded finance offers measurable opportunities for inclusion, including more loans, secure real-time payments, and seamless everyday integration; however, it is based on a fragile web of data governance, market power, and consumer protection. Privacy leaks, bias, and over-indebtedness are real dangers, exacerbated by high levels of concentration and proprietary API lock-ins. Regulation is therefore facing a balancing act:

- Open, interoperable payment and identity infrastructure minimizes lock-in, lowers entry costs, and increases competition.
- Proportional licensing regimes and embedded supervision, facilitated by API access, strike a balance between the pace of innovation and risk control.
- Algorithm audit, data minimization, and purpose limitation protect consumers and reduce systemic bias.
- Debt sustainability checks and transparency obligations limit BNPL over-indebtedness.

If this policy mix succeeds, EmFi can mature from a 'disruptor' to an inclusive public-private utility that complements, but does not replace, traditional financial intermediationn, closing the last mile of financial inclusion without creating new inequalities.

## REGULATORY CHALLENGES AND GOVERNANCE ISSUES

Embedded finance, a term referring to the integration of financial services into non-financial platforms, poses new challenges for regulatory authorities worldwide. The rapid diffusion of data-driven financial offerings via these non-bank platforms necessitates institutional responses that facilitate innovation without compromising consumer protection, system stability, and competitive fairness. The regulatory responses can be summarized in four key areas: existing approaches, consumer protection, global-local tensions, and future proposals for stable governance structures.

### Existing Regulatory Approaches: RegTech, Sandboxes, Open Banking/Finance

In many emerging markets, regulatory sandboxes offer FinTechs initial regulated access to the market, allowing them to test BNPL models or API-based credit products under supervision before full licensing becomes necessary. According to the Africa Sandboxes Outlook 2025, 26 sandboxes are currently active, with nine having an explicit EmFi focus. India is particularly dynamic: the central bank's sandbox

(RBI) was converted into an open-topic, permanently accessible model ('on-tap') in 2025. At the same time, the RBI Innovation Hub is developing the Unified Lending Interface (ULI), a RegTech infrastructure for real-time monitoring of credit APIs.

While sandboxes create a selective scope for innovation, many countries are pursuing overarching data portability strategies through open banking and open finance initiatives. In Brazil, the four-stage open finance program was completed in 2024 and extended to insurance and pension data. Central to this is the link to the Brazilian LGPD data protection law, which requires granular consent processes. The Brazilian central bank is pursuing the integration of open finance processes with AI guidelines, enhancements to the Pix function, and automated fraud prevention for 2025/26.

Additionally, RegTech instruments for embedded supervision are gaining importance. These rely on automated API access to platform data to simplify reporting obligations and enable real-time monitoring simultaneously. The Bank for International Settlements (BIS) describes this as a paradigm shift: compliance is integrated 'into the code' instead of being checked via downstream reports (Auer, 2022).

## Protective Mechanisms for Consumers

The expansion of EmFi offerings brings with it a multitude of consumer rights issues. Data protection, transparency and over-indebtedness prevention are at the center of regulatory interventions. For example, Brazil's data protection authority ANPD is currently initiating a consultation process to operationalize data subject rights with the aim of establishing granular consent standards for data-intensive API usage. India is accompanying its new data protection law with the Digital Lending Directions 2025, which stipulate mandatory disclosures on interest rates, partner banks and data usage. In Kenya, on the other hand, access to the digital lending market is controlled by licensing requirements: 41 new providers were licensed in 2025 alone and are subject to the central bank's code of conduct.

At the same time, the first standards for algorithmic fairness are emerging: regulatory authorities such as the RBI, CBK and BCB are now demanding model governance frameworks with documented bias analysis. The US consumer protection authority CFPB is taking a stricter approach and is placing BNPL providers on an equal regulatory footing with traditional credit card providers - including requirements for billing disputes and fee disclosure.

To avoid over-indebtedness-induced risks, regulators are increasingly resorting to binding credit reporting obligations and limits on cumulative ticket sizes. UPI- and Pix-based credit functions now include repayment reminders and payment pauses in the event of hardship - functions that were only implemented late in the traditional card network.

Regulators are increasingly recognizing that trust is a key asset for sustainable use of fintech. Measures such as mandatory disclosure screens (Reserve Bank of India (RBI), 2025) or granular consent mechanisms (ANPD (Autoridade Nacional de Proteção de Dados), 2024) are designed to reduce the cognitive burden on users and create transparency. It's important to note that these measures signify a significant shift in consumer protection, from purely risk prevention to actively building trust, underscoring the crucial role of policymakers in shaping the industry.

## Global vs. Local Regulation: Fragmentation or Harmonization?

The asymmetry between global platform architectures and national regulatory competence is a key area of tension. The Financial Stability Board (FSB) warns that Big tech companies could become systemically relevant in emerging markets ('too-interconnected-to-fail') and calls for minimum standards for resilience, data access, and competitive neutrality (Crisanto et al., 2022).

At the same time, there are significant regional divergences. India treats BNPL as a fully-fledged credit business, whereas Kenya treats it as an e-money service. In Brazil, installment payments are integrated directly into the Pix protocol. Such inconsistencies make it difficult for FinTechs to expand across countries and increase compliance costs.

However, the first signs of harmonization are already evident, offering a promising outlook for the future of EmFi regulation. The G20 roadmap for cross-border payments is based on common ISO 20022 standards. In Africa, the PAPSS system obliges participating central banks to share knowledge in each other's sandboxes. IOSCO is working on global disclosure standards for BNPL structures in order to capture new distribution models for regulatory purposes.

## Governance Proposals for Stable and Inclusive EmFi Ecosystems

The need for stable governance structures is paramount to ensure the secure and inclusive development of the EmFi ecosystem. Four strategic governance building blocks can be derived from empirical analysis:

1. API interoperability as a public good: Central banks should design real-time payment infrastructures along the lines of Pix or UPI as open protocols with standardized authentication and data interfaces (OAuth, OpenAPI). It will lower integration hurdles, promote competition, and mitigate lock-in effects.
2. Multi-level licensing and proportional capital requirements: A three-tier licensing model (e-money, credit facilitator, deposit taker) links growing functionalities

to increased capital requirements. This ensures regulatory proportionality and prevents systemically relevant EmFi players from operating without risk protection.

3. Embedded supervision via RegTech: Regulatory authorities should establish real-time access to platform data ('read-only nodes') to directly monitor transaction metrics, loan portfolios, and model parameters. The BIS concept of 'embedded supervision' allows both efficiency gains and early risk detection.

Data protection laws such as India's DPDP or Brazil's LGPD should be complemented by sectoral data trusts. These enable users to have granular control rights and allow independent audit consortia (e.g., NGOs or universities) to verify algorithmic fairness.

A supplementary 'inclusivity clause' in sandbox and open finance regulations could stipulate that pilot projects document inclusion metrics (e.g., gender gap, rural use). This database would enable the regulator to set targeted incentives for demonstrably inclusive innovations—a principle that is already being implemented in Kenya's interoperability regime.

The regulation of embedded finance is in transition, shifting from experimental sandboxes to structured open finance systems, and from selective consumer protection to holistic supervision of data, algorithms, and capital flows. Only through open infrastructure, proportional rules, automated supervision, and data protection-compliant governance can EmFi realize its inclusive potential, without creating new inequities or systemic risks, as global platform structures are eroding national competence boundaries (Figure 4).

*Figure 4. New market participants are emerging as a result of a wave of M&A*

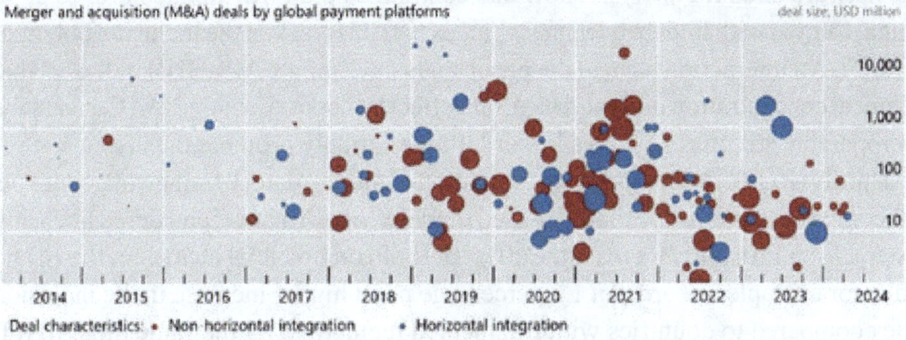


Data up to 30 May 2024. Each dot represents an M&A deal by Ant Group, Fidelity National Information Services (FIS), FISERV, Global Payments, Mastercard, PayPal, Block (formerly Square) or Visa as collected by PitchBook and Refinitiv Eikon. This excludes divestitures and intra-company operations. M&A deals are classified as "non-horizontal" when the acquiring and the target firm operate at different stages along the same payment chain, as determined by company reports. In "horizontal" deals, the acquiring and target firm are direct competitors in at least one key business line. The size of each dot is proportional to the acquiring company market capitalisation on the day of the deal or, in the case of Ant Group, the valuation of Ant Group as of end-2018, multiplied by changes in the market capitalisation of Alibaba Holdings relative to end-2018.

Source: BIS (2020); Doerr et al. (2023), updated.

# CONCLUSION AND IMPLICATIONS

## Key Findings and Theoretical Contributions

Embedded finance, more than just a tool, represents a promising future for the redesign of financial services in an inclusive, intelligent, and everyday manner. Institutions that prioritize openness, collaboration, and fairness are not just surviving, they are leading the way. This study demonstrates that embedded finance has a dual potential impact: It not only bridges infrastructural gaps by integrating payment, credit, and savings functions directly into everyday digital applications, but also shifts the power dynamics of financial intermediation towards digital platforms and algorithmic gatekeepers.

Empirically, both the quantitative panel analyses and the qualitative case studies provide strong evidence that embedded finance is a significant driver of financial inclusion. The panel regression reveals that a one-standard-deviation increase in the EmFi index is associated with an average increase of 4.3 percentage points in account ownership, 6.1 percentage points in the use of digital payments, and 2.5 percentage points in formal borrowing. Micro-ethnographic surveys in Kenya and India further confirm this: 73% of the micro-enterprises surveyed attribute their sales growth to embedded payment and credit functions.

The second research question (RQ2) sheds light on the role of digital infrastructure. The network and API analysis show that centralized platform architectures (e.g., in China, Kenya) with high betweenness values (>0.35) weaken the inclusion potential of EmFi. An interaction term in the panel analysis (EmFi × API-HHI) indicates that technical concentration mitigates the EmFi effect by approximately 35%. Conversely, interoperable structures such as Pix or UPI measurably promote the effect.

Thirdly (RQ3), the comparative evaluation of the regulatory framework confirms that combined governance models—i.e., sandbox, open finance, and tiered licensing systems—significantly increase the effect of EmFi on financial inclusion. Brazil and India, for example, recorded a 1.8 percentage point higher increase in the inclusion index compared to countries with fragmented regulation. At the same time, BNPL default rates are lower when credit products are subject to reporting requirements and interest rate caps are in place.

The cases of Nigeria, Ghana, and Mexico serve as compelling evidence that the patterns identified in the four core cases (API centrality, real-time rails, sandbox governance) are not isolated incidents. They also manifest in other regions, albeit under different circumstances. Nigeria's path, driven by fintechs and regulatory competition, Ghana's emphasis on biometric identity systems and simplified KYC rules, and Mexico's struggles with user-oriented regulatory infrastructure all underscore the universality of these patterns. The concluding discussion plays a pivotal role in critically reflecting on the generalizability of these results.

The platform economy highlights the danger of excessive market concentration, where network effects and economies of scale favor a few dominant players, thereby jeopardizing competition, diversity, and ultimately the resilience of financial systems. The perspective of API ecosystems makes it clear that proprietary standards and asymmetric access conditions can create lock-in effects, confining users to specific platform environments and making regulatory intervention difficult. Finally, the digital inclusion literature reveals that financial exclusion can also continue in digital form: if gender-specific differences, competence barriers, or cultural contexts are not taken into account, the result is 'exclusion by design,' which excludes precisely those groups that are supposed to benefit from embedded finance. The analysis thus makes it clear that while EmFi is an effective tool for promoting financial inclusion, its long-term legitimacy depends crucially on whether governance arrangements balance these risks and ensure both economic and social sustainability.

## Implications for Policymakers, Regulators, and Development Actors

There is a clear field of action for policymakers and central banks: real-time payment infrastructures, such as Pix or UPI, should be established as digital basic goods and designed openly (using OAuth and OpenAPI). License systems should have a modular structure (e.g., e-money institutions, credit intermediaries, full-service banks), whereby increasing freedom is accompanied by higher capital and data protection obligations. It preserves innovation dynamics while also protecting against risks.

Financial and data supervisors should take the step from pilot projects to the comprehensive implementation of embedded supervision: Real-time API feeds enable continuous monitoring of credit performance, model adjustments, and fraud patterns. In addition, algorithm audits should become mandatory, supported by open-source test sets to ensure fairness and traceability.

Development organizations are called upon to consider infrastructure financing beyond mobile communications. Digital identity platforms (e.g., MOSIP) and cyber resilience layers form the backbone of sustainable EmFi systems. Equally important are incentive mechanisms, such as bonuses for sandbox projects that have a proven impact on inclusion (e.g., gender parity or rural utilization rates).

## Outlook for Future Research: EmFi and Central Bank Digital Currencies

The next wave of research lies at the interface between embedded finance and central bank digital currencies (CBDCs). The following research questions arise:

- Technical integration: How can CBDC-based smart contracts be used for BNPLs or microcredits without creating new lock-in effects?
- Macroeconomic effects: Can programmable CBDCs manage interbank liquidity more efficiently and thus minimize systemic risks?
- Governance issues: What impact does direct API access by central banks to transaction data have on the balance between monetary and data protection sovereignty?

Initial evidence can be provided by case studies of pilot projects, such as e-Naira (Nigeria) or the offline UPI-based CBDC in India. Further research topics include the role of cross-border EmFi rails (e.g., PAPSS in Africa), the impact of Explainable AI tools on user trust, and the potential role of data trusts as a neutral intermediary.

## Limitations of the Study

Despite robust methodology, several limitations need to be considered:

- Data availability: BNPL volumes and API usage data are often subject to commercial confidentiality. Despite the use of imputation methods, measurement inaccuracies persist.
- Selection bias: The expert interviews could overrepresent urban and successful business models.
- Dynamics of the field: Changes in legislation and technological leaps make long-term comparisons difficult.
- Causality problems: Despite the use of differentiated difference-in-differences models, endogeneity, for example, due to simultaneous digital policy reforms, cannot be completely ruled out.

Embedded finance has the potential to reach the 'last mile' of financial inclusion, provided that open infrastructure, proportionate supervision, and data protection-oriented governance are consistently implemented. Politics and regulations must accompany this structural change without creating new exclusions. The path to a fair, digital financial world is not a surefire success, but it can be shaped.

## REFERENCES


Alliance for Financial Inclusion (AFI). (2024). Mexico: The role regulators play in closing the financial inclusion gender gap. AFI Case Study. Retrieved from https://www.afi-global.org

Anagnostopoulos, I., Sails, T., & Alexandrou, G. (2025). FinTechs, BigTechs and diminishing bank franchise values: Stakeholder perspectives on a disruptive emerging financial ecosystem. *Technological Forecasting and Social Change*, *212*, 123924. DOI: 10.1016/j.techfore.2024.123924

Andrae, S. (2022). The role of BigTech in emerging markets. In Nguyen, D. K. (Ed.), *Handbook of banking and finance in Emerging Markets* (pp. 433–463). Edward Elgar., DOI: 10.4337/9781800880900.00032

Andrae, S. (2025a). Machine learning in social finance: Facilitating inclusive finance approaches. In Yu, P., Wong, S. K. M., & Prabhakar, A. C. (Eds.), *AI strategies for social entrepreneurship and sustainable economic development* (pp. 17–46). IGI Global Publishing., DOI: 10.4018/979-8-3693-6392-8.ch002

Andrae, S. (2025b). Data cooperatives to strengthen digital citizenship: Opportunities and risks. In Hawamdeh, M. Kh. M. (Ed.), *Digital citizenship and the future of AI engagement, ethics, and privacy* (pp. 533–568). IGI Global Publishing., DOI: 10.4018/979-8-3693-9015-3.ch018

ANPD (Autoridade Nacional de Proteção de Dados). (2024). Consulta Pública sobre Consentimento Granular em Open Finance. Brasília. https://www.gov.br/anpd/pt-br/acesso-a-informacao/participacao-social/outras-acoes/documentos/ts_02-_2024__contribuicoes.pdf

Auer, R. (2022). Embedded supervision: How to build regulation into Decentralised Finance CESifo Working Paper No. 9771. DOI: 10.2139/ssrn.4127658

Bank of Ghana. (2019). Annual Report 2019. https://www.bog.gov.gh/wp-content/uploads/2020/06/Annual-Report-2019.pdf

BIS. (2020). Central banks and payments in the digital era. Annual Economic Report, Chapter III, June 2020. https://www.bis.org/publ/arpdf/ar2020e3.pdf

Breckenridge, K. (2010). The world's first biometric money: Ghana's E-Zwich and the contemporary influence of South African biometrics. *Africa*, *80*(4), 642–662. DOI: 10.3366/afr.2010.0406

Callaway, B., & Sant'Anna, P. H. C. (2021). Difference-in-Differences with multiple time periods. *Journal of Econometrics, 225*(2), 200–230. DOI: 10.1016/j.jeconom.2020.12.001

CGAP. (2018). A digital credit revolution: Insights from borrowers in Kenya and Tanzania. https://www.cgap.org/research/publication/digital-credit-revolution-insights-borrowers-in-kenya-and-tanzania

Copestake, A., Kirti, D., & Martinez Peria, M. S. (2025). Growing retail digital payments: The value of interoperability. *IMF Fintech Notes, 2025*(004), 1. Advance online publication. DOI: 10.5089/9798229014250.063

Creswell, J. W., & Plano Clark, V. L. (2010). Designing and conducting mixed methods research. *Sage (Atlanta, Ga.).*

Crisanto, J. C., Ehrentraud, J., Fabian, M., & Monteil, A. (2022). Big tech interdependencies – a key policy blind spot. FSI Insights on policy implementation No 44. https://www.bis.org/fsi/publ/insights44.pdf

Doerr, S., Frost, J., Gambacorta, L., & Shreeti, V. (2025). Big techs in finance. In Berger, A., Molyneux, P., & Wilson, J. (Eds.), *The Oxford Handbook of Banking* (4th ed., pp. 296–325). Oxford University Press., DOI: 10.1093/oxfordhb/9780198897071.013.14

Donner, J. (2015). *After access: Inclusion, development, and a more mobile Internet.* MIT Press. DOI: 10.7551/mitpress/9740.001.0001

Donner, J., & Tellez, C. A. (2008). Mobile banking and economic development: Linking adoption, impact, and use. *Asian Journal of Communication, 18*(4), 318–332. DOI: 10.1080/01292980802344190

Ghazawneh, A., & Henfridsson, O. (2013). Balancing platform control and external contribution in third-party development: The boundary resources model. *Information Systems Journal, 23*(2), 173–192. DOI: 10.1111/j.1365-2575.2012.00406.x

Global Legal Insights. (2025). Fintech laws and regulations: Nigeria. In Global Legal Insights – Fintech Laws and Regulations 2025. London: Global Legal Group. https://www.globallegalinsights.com/practice-areas/fintech-laws-and-regulations/nigeria/

Goggin, G. (2025). Mobile AI: Communication and mobility after the smartphone. *Communication and Change, 1*(5), 5. Advance online publication. DOI: 10.1007/s44382-025-00002-3

GSMA. (2023). State of the Industry Report on Mobile Money 2023. https://www.gsma.com/sotir/wp-content/uploads/2025/04/GSMA-SOTIR-2023.pdf

Heeks, R. (2010). Do information and communication technologies (ICTs) contribute to development? *Journal of International Development*, *22*(5), 625–640. DOI: 10.1002/jid.1716

Ifrim, O. (2024). Embedded finance and BaaS: Reflections on 2024 and what lies ahead. https://thepaypers.com/fintech/expert-views/embedded-finance-and-baas-reflections-on-2024-and-what-lies-ahead

Kim, M., & Duvendack, M. (2024). Digital credit for all? An empirical analysis of mobile loans for financial inclusion in Kenya. *Information Technology for Development*, *31*(3), 559–576. DOI: 10.1080/02681102.2024.2402996

Okekenwa, I. (2025). Legal challenges and opportunities in Nigeria's fintech sector. DOI: 10.2139/ssrn.5228794

Ozili, P. K. (2023). Digital finance research and developments around the World: A literature review. *International Journal of Business Forecasting and Marketing Intelligence*, *8*(1), 35. Advance online publication. DOI: 10.1504/IJBFMI.2023.127698

Paypers (2024). Embedded Finance and Banking-as-a-Service Report 2024. https://thepaypers.com/register?return=/fintech/reports/embedded-finance-and-banking-as-a-service-report-2024

Reserve Bank of India (RBI). (2025). Digital lending directions. New Delhi. https://www.argus-p.com/updates/updates/rbi-digital-lending-directions-2025-an-overview/

World Bank. (2021). The Global Findex Database 2021. https://openknowledge.worldbank.org/bitstream/handle/10986/37578/9781464818974.pdf

## KEY TERMS AND DEFINITIONS

**API Ecosystems:** Application programming interfaces (APIs) are standardized interfaces through which different digital systems interact. In EmFi, they enable banks, FinTechs, and big techs to embed modular financial products in third-party platforms. The API ecosystem thus determines how open, interoperable, or concentrated digital financial markets are structured.

**Buy Now, Pay Later (BNPL):** BNPL is a credit-like model in which consumers make a purchase immediately but pay in several installments, usually interest-free. In emerging markets, BNPL often replaces credit cards and gives first-time users access to formal credit. The model lowers barriers to entry, but carries risks of over-indebtedness, especially when multiple parallel BNPL obligations ('loan stacking') are taken on in an uncoordinated manner. Regulation is therefore increasingly focusing on transparency requirements, reporting to credit bureaus, and interest rate caps.

**Digital Inclusion:** Digital inclusion means more than just access to technology: it also encompasses digital literacy, affordability, and the relevance of content. In the context of EmFi, this means that financial services are only inclusive if they are culturally, linguistically, and socially adapted. Otherwise, there is a risk of 'exclusion by design.'

**Embedded Finance (EmFi):** Embedded finance refers to the integration of financial services such as payments, loans, or insurance into non-financial platforms and apps. Users thus experience financial products not as a separate service, but as something embedded in everyday digital processes. EmFi opens up new paths to inclusion for emerging markets by utilizing existing platform infrastructures.

**Embedded Supervision:** Embedded supervision refers to approaches in which regulatory authorities can view transaction data from platforms in real time via direct API access. The aim is to shift compliance 'into the code' and automate reporting processes. For EmFi, this could be a means of enabling innovation while monitoring risks at an early stage.

**Micro-Lending:** Micro-lending refers to the granting of tiny loans to households or micro-enterprises that do not have access to traditional bank loans. In embedded finance ecosystems, credit checks are often automated, based on transaction data from mobile wallets, e-commerce sales, or platform activities. Such nano and microloans can enable productive investments and strengthen financial resilience, but they are prone to high effective interest rates and aggressive collection methods. Their inclusive impact, therefore, depends heavily on governance, transparency, and consumer protection.

# Chapter 3
# Embedded Finance and Sustainable Financial Inclusion:
## A Conceptual Framework for Integrating Financial Services Into Non-Financial Platforms

**Shuchi Gupta**
https://orcid.org/0000-0002-2517-0431
*University of Hail, Saudi Arabia*

**Manika Garg**
https://orcid.org/0009-0003-5680-3865
*Maharaja Agrasen Institute of Management Studies, India*

**Gargee Banerjee**
https://orcid.org/0009-0008-4744-2945
*Raja Madhusudan Dev Degree College, India*

## ABSTRACT

*The paper aims to develop a conceptual framework that explains how embedded finance can drive financial inclusion while aligning with sustainability goals. It explores the role of digital financial services integrated into non-financial platforms, such as e-commerce, mobility, and social media, in promoting accessibility and responsible financial practices. This study adopts a conceptual research approach by reviewing existing literature on embedded finance, financial inclusion, and sustainable finance. It synthesizes theoretical perspectives such as Access to Finance Theory to propose a structured model for policymakers and business leaders. The*

DOI: 10.4018/979-8-3373-2464-7.ch003

*research identifies embedded finance as a transformative force that lowers financial barriers, improves accessibility for underserved populations, and facilitates sustainable financial solutions. It highlights key mechanisms, including digital wallets, API-based banking, and ESG-linked financial products, that contribute to inclusive economic growth while promoting responsible investment.*

## INTRODUCTION

Embedded finance refers to the integration of financial services such as payments, credit, insurance, and investments into non-financial platforms and customer journeys, enabled by technological infrastructure such as Application Programming Interfaces (APIs) and Banking-as-a-Service (BaaS). This shift represents a fundamental departure from traditional banking models by embedding financial functionalities directly within consumer-facing applications (Sieber & Guibaud, 2022; Finken & Hensen, 2025). As financial products become invisible and seamlessly woven into everyday digital interactions, the boundaries between banking and commerce are increasingly blurred, transforming how users' access and use financial tools (Bugvi & Endress, 2023).

The growth of embedded finance is particularly visible across non-financial sectors such as e-commerce, transportation, education, and healthcare. In e-commerce, platforms like Amazon and Shopify have introduced integrated payment solutions, digital wallets, and credit offerings to enhance consumer experience. Mobility platforms such as Uber and Ola have embedded driver insurance and instant earnings access, improving financial resilience among gig workers. In EdTech, companies offer embedded student financing and savings options within learning management systems, increasing affordability of educational services (Omarini, 2023; Hensen & Kötting, 2022). These cross-sector implementations demonstrate how embedded finance not only adds convenience but also addresses systemic gaps in financial service delivery.

Globally, an estimated 1.4 billion adults remain unbanked, with most living in developing economies where access to formal financial services remains limited due to geographical, social, and economic barriers. Financial inclusion defined as the ability of individuals and businesses to access and use appropriate financial products and services has emerged as a critical enabler of poverty alleviation, economic empowerment, and resilience (Tay, Tai, & Tan, 2022). Simultaneously, the global financial system is undergoing a shift toward sustainability, driven by the need to align with Environmental, Social, and Governance (ESG) principles and the United Nations Sustainable Development Goals (SDGs), particularly SDG 8 (Decent Work and Economic Growth) and SDG 9 (Industry, Innovation, and Infrastructure)

(Ziolo et al., 2019; Silver, 2017). Embedded finance, when aligned with inclusive and sustainable priorities, offers a unique opportunity to deliver financial tools that are accessible, affordable, and ESG-aligned.

This study seeks to develop a conceptual framework that integrates embedded finance with financial inclusion and sustainability. It aims to fill a significant gap in existing literature where these domains are often studied in isolation. By synthesizing theoretical insights and recent developments across digital finance, inclusion, and sustainability, the paper addresses the following research questions. RQ1: How can embedded finance contribute to advancing financial inclusion? RQ2: In what ways can embedded finance platforms be designed to support sustainability goals, including ESG integration? RQ3: What is the key enabling conditions and feedback mechanisms that influence this integration?

## THEORETICAL FOUNDATIONS AND LITERATURE REVIEW

The conceptual foundation of this study is built upon three interrelated theoretical perspectives: (1) Access to Finance Theory, (2) Inclusive Growth Theory, and (3) Sustainability Transitions Theory. These frameworks together offer a multilevel rationale for how embedded finance can function simultaneously as an enabler of inclusion and as a driver of sustainable systemic change.

Access to Finance Theory emphasises that enabling individuals and firms to participate in formal financial systems requires reducing the transactional and informational barriers to financial services such as high costs, geographic distance, documentation requirements, and lack of credit history (Ozili, 2023). Increased access to payments, savings, credit and insurance allows households to manage risks, invest in human or productive capital, and improve resilience. From this perspective, embedded finance mechanisms like platform-embedded micro-credit, digital wallets, and integrated insurance offerings can lower traditional access costs and friction, accelerating entry into the formal financial system. Thus, Access to Finance Theory provides the micro-foundation for understanding how innovations in financial service delivery can expand participation.

Inclusive Growth Theory builds upon the idea of access by focusing on how financial participation translates into broader, equitable economic development. This theory holds that growth is inclusive only when all segments of society not just the affluent can participate in and benefit from economic expansion. For instance, inclusive growth is defined as "economic growth that delivers social benefits, tackles inequalities and spreads benefit more fairly between people and places." (Saher et al., 2024) Institutions matter: inclusive growth requires that economic and social opportunities be open to less-included groups. In this study's framework, once individuals gain access via embedded finance, the next step is that such inclusion leads to productive opportunities, employment, and income generation that are equitably distributed. Hence, Inclusive Growth Theory provides the meso-level lens by which financial participation can lead to societal-level outcomes rather than just individual-level access.

Sustainability Transitions Theory (and related concepts of sustainable finance and socio-technical transitions) offers the macro-level, system-wide perspective. It posits that achieving long-term environmental and social sustainability requires fundamental restructuring of socio-technical systems (such as energy, transport, finance) and re-direction of finance flows towards sustainable technologies and practices (Naidoo, 2020). From this vantage, financial systems are not neutral intermediaries but critical enablers (or impediments) of sustainable transitions. For example, transforming the financial system to channel capital into low-carbon infrastructure requires new financial mechanisms, policy design, and digital platforms. Within our conceptual model, embedded finance is seen as a mechanism through which the financial system can evolve embedding ESG-aligned financial products, integrating green behaviour into everyday consumption, and aligning financial flows with SDG 8 and SDG 9. Sustainability Transitions Theory thus underpins how embedded finance and inclusion together can contribute to larger, systemic change rather than incremental improvements.

In integrating these three perspectives: Access to Finance Theory explains *how* financial access can be broadened; Inclusive Growth Theory explains *why* broad access matters from an equity and development standpoint; and Sustainability Transitions Theory explains *what* systemic change is required for those broad access and equity gains to align with sustainable development imperatives. Together, they justify treating embedded finance as more than a delivery mechanism it is a leverage point in the transformation of the financial ecosystem toward inclusive and sustainable development.

## Embedded Finance: Definitions and Developments

Embedded finance is a transformative shift in the financial ecosystem that involves integrating financial services such as payments, lending, insurance, and investment into the infrastructure of non-financial platforms (Sieber & Guibaud, 2022). This evolution enables consumers to access financial services directly within the environments where they are already conducting other activities, such as shopping, commuting, or socializing, thereby reducing friction and enhancing user experience (Dresner et al., 2022). The evolution of embedded finance has been significantly driven by advancements in financial technology, particularly the proliferation of APIs (Application Programming Interfaces) that allow seamless integration between service providers. This shift moves away from the traditional model where customers visit a bank or a financial website to one where financial service are contextually offered at the point of need making finance "invisible" (Bugvi & Endress, 2023). For instance, companies like Uber or Amazon now offer embedded wallets, credit, and insurance without redirecting customers to third-party providers. Finken and Hensen (2025) emphasize that the growth of Banking-as-a-Service (BaaS) and platform-based finance models has enabled this seamless embedding of services into digital interfaces. These innovations support the modularization of banking, where financial functions are provided as plug-and-play components within diverse platforms (Waliszewski, 2023). This is reinforced by Hensen and Kötting (2022), who argue that transitioning from open banking to embedded finance requires not only technological capability but also strategic alignment with digital consumer behavior and data analytics. The Buy Now, Pay Later (BNPL) phenomenon serves as a striking example of embedded credit. BNPL offerings embedded in checkout experiences provide instant micro-credit to consumers with simplified onboarding and approval processes (Kadam, Jangid, & Singh, 2024). These models expand access to financial products, particularly among millennials and Gen Z consumers who are digital-first in their financial engagements. In the European context, Eremeeva and Akulova (2024) analyzed the digital wallet ecosystem and highlighted key features such as interoperability, regulatory compliance, and user-centric design as foundational pillars of embedded finance models. This regional insight reflects a broader global trend toward integrating finance into lifestyle platforms, often leading to enhanced financial inclusion and customer loyalty. From a theoretical lens, embedded finance challenges the conventional separation between financial and commercial activities, giving rise to what Wullweber (2020) describes as a new state–market hybridity, blurring boundaries between public regulation and private financial innovation. He critiques the rise of embedded finance as part of the shadow banking system and suggests that its expansion may alter the sovereignty of traditional financial oversight structures. Further, Ozili (2023) places embedded finance in a larger ecosystem alongside decentralized finance (DeFi), open finance, and sustainable finance, noting that while interest in these sectors is rising globally, embedded finance stands out due to its applicability in daily consumer interactions. Behaviorally, embedded finance is also redefining how individuals perceive and interact with financial services. Fava (2023) explores the intersection of behavioral finance and embedded finance, arguing that nudges, frictionless experiences, and contextual offerings can both empower and manipulate users, raising questions about transparency and consumer protection. Lastly, Omarini (2023) provides a broader economic context, showing how digital transformation has redefined the economics of banking. He posits that embedded finance is a byproduct of the convergence of data, digital money, and platform economics, and suggests that banks that fail to adopt embedded models may face obsolescence in the face of platform-native competitors. Hence, embedded finance represents a paradigm shift in how financial services are delivered and consumed. Its development is fuelled by API-based innovation, changing consumer behaviour, and the rise of digital ecosystems that transcend traditional industry boundaries. As a result, it is not merely a technological trend but a structural reconfiguration of financial intermediation in the digital age.

## Financial Inclusion

Financial inclusion has emerged as a vital policy and research area in the 21st-century global development discourse. It encompasses the process of ensuring individuals and businesses have access to useful and affordable financial products and services including savings, credit, insurance, and payment systems delivered responsibly and sustainably. As the financial ecosystem continues to evolve, particularly with digital innovations, understanding the theoretical and practical dimensions of financial inclusion becomes critical for ensuring equitable economic participation, especially among underserved and vulnerable populations.

The theoretical foundation of financial inclusion is rooted in the Access to Finance Theory, which posits that the availability of affordable financial services significantly contributes to individual well-being, entrepreneurship, and poverty alleviation (Simatele et al., 2021). This theory emphasizes that the major barriers physical distance from financial institutions, lack of documentation, high transaction costs, and limited financial literacy restrict economically disadvantaged populations from accessing formal financial systems. Therefore, improved access directly correlates with higher asset accumulation, better risk management, and increased household productivity. Closely aligned is the Inclusive Growth Theory, which extends beyond mere access and focuses on how financial inclusion fosters broad-based, equitable economic growth. According to Randa (2024), inclusive growth occurs when all segments of society, particularly the marginalized, participate in and benefit from economic expansion. Financial infrastructure and service delivery mechanisms must therefore be designed not only to extend services but to empower recipients by integrating them into the larger financial and economic mainstream. These theoretical frameworks collectively frame financial inclusion as a transformative tool for economic development and social upliftment. They form the basis for policy interventions and innovations aimed at enhancing both access and usage of financial services.

While the potential of financial inclusion is widely recognized, its implementation across various regions has encountered significant barriers. In many low-income and developing regions, particularly in Sub-Saharan Africa and South Asia, the lack of physical financial infrastructure such as banks, ATMs, and POS devices remains a major impediment. Chinoda and Kapingura (2024) argue that institutional weaknesses and poor governance structures further limit the expansion of financial systems into rural and remote areas. Stringent Know Your Customer (KYC) norms, documentation requirements, and inconsistent regulatory environments disproportionately affect low-income individuals who may not possess formal identity documents or fixed addresses. Mensah (2024) notes that these challenges contribute to large swathes of populations being excluded from formal systems, especially in Sub-Saharan Africa and parts of the Middle East. Even when digital financial services (DFS) are available, limited digital literacy inhibits adoption. In many countries, users are hesitant to engage with app-based or mobile-enabled financial services due to a lack of familiarity or trust. Chitimira and Warikandwa (2023) highlight that this digital divide disproportionately affects women, elderly populations, and rural residents, leading to systemic exclusion. In conservative socio-cultural contexts, women and minority communities often face systemic barriers to accessing financial products. Pradhan (2023) points out that, in India, although financial penetration has increased, usage levels among rural women remain significantly lower due to cultural norms and lower mobility. Afjal (2023), through a bibliometric analysis, finds that while digital solutions are multiplying, their impact is limited by fragmented ecosystems and a lack of interoperability between platforms and service providers. This affects the scalability of financial inclusion initiatives.

In recent years, digital financial services (DFS) have become a cornerstone in the global strategy to enhance financial inclusion. Enabled by mobile technology, internet penetration, and fintech innovations, DFS offer a scalable and cost-effective mechanism to reach underserved populations. Services like M-Pesa in Kenya, bKash in Bangladesh, and UPI in India have revolutionized the financial landscape by offering secure and accessible payment and transfer mechanisms. Hasan, Yajuan, and Khan (2022) highlight how mobile platforms in China have not only increased access but also diversified the use of financial services, including insurance, micro-investments, and wealth management for lower-income groups. Fintech companies have pioneered products such as Buy Now, Pay Later (BNPL), micro-loans, and algorithm-driven savings accounts. Soriano (2017) argues that fintech ventures, being more agile than traditional banks, are better positioned to address the specific needs of financially excluded groups, such as informal workers and smallholder farmers. Emerging technologies like AI and machine learning are being used to develop alternative credit scoring models, enabling lenders to evaluate risk based on mobile usage patterns, social media behavior, and other non-traditional data points (Mhlanga, 2022). This is crucial for bringing the unbanked into the formal credit system, especially in the absence of conventional credit histories. Digital financial inclusion has direct linkages with several UN Sustainable Development Goals (SDGs), including SDG 1 (No Poverty), SDG 5 (Gender Equality), and

SDG 8 (Decent Work and Economic Growth). Tay, Tai, and Tan (2022) emphasize that digital services empower users to save, invest, and insure themselves against economic shocks, thereby enabling more resilient and self-sustaining livelihoods. Digital finance is also enhancing cross-border financial inclusion by enabling faster, cheaper, and more transparent remittance flows. This is particularly important in low-income economies heavily dependent on migrant income. The literature strongly establishes that financial inclusion, particularly through digital means, plays a transformative role in enabling economic participation, reducing inequality, and achieving sustainable development. While theories such as Access to Finance and Inclusive Growth provide a conceptual understanding, real-world challenges such as digital divides, institutional weaknesses, and socio-cultural barriers continue to hinder progress. Nevertheless, the rapid growth of fintech and digital platforms presents an unprecedented opportunity to bridge financial gaps. Moving forward, policies must aim to strengthen digital infrastructure, promote financial literacy, and design inclusive products that consider the needs of marginalized populations.

## Sustainability in Financial Systems

In recent years, sustainability has become an integral component of modern financial systems, transitioning from a peripheral concern to a central pillar of economic policy and corporate strategy. A sustainable financial system not only ensures long-term economic stability but also supports environmental preservation, social equity, and effective governance. The concept of ESG (Environmental, Social, and Governance) criteria represents a shift in how financial decisions are made moving beyond profit-maximization to consider the long-term impact of investment and lending decisions on society and the planet. ESG integration within financial systems emphasizes:

- **Environmental** considerations: climate change, resource efficiency, and carbon footprint reduction.
- **Social** dimensions: employee rights, diversity and inclusion, community engagement.
- **Governance** factors: transparency, corporate ethics, and regulatory compliance.

Ziolo et al. (2019) assert that incorporating ESG metrics into financial decision-making leads to more resilient portfolios and minimizes systemic risk in the financial system. This is supported by empirical findings showing that firms with strong ESG performance tend to exhibit higher profitability, lower volatility, and better stakeholder trust. Aspinall et al. (2018) argue that ESG has become a de facto framework for institutional investors, regulatory bodies, and rating agencies, as it provides a comprehensive lens to assess long-term value creation and risk management. As a result, ESG investing is no longer optional but rather a standard expectation in global financial markets.

Green finance refers to financial investments directed towards environmentally sustainable projects, such as renewable energy, waste management, carbon trading, and sustainable agriculture. Ethical finance encompasses broader moral dimensions, including the exclusion of investments in industries like tobacco, arms, or fossil fuels, and the promotion of socially responsible business practices. Silver (2017) advocates for transforming the financial system into a mechanism that supports people, planet, and profit in unison. He criticizes traditional finance for neglecting externalities and calls for instruments like green bonds, SRI (Socially Responsible Investing), and impact investing to become mainstream components of capital markets. In support of this transformation, Obiora et al. (2020) conduct a comparative analysis across developing, emerging, and developed economies and conclude that while banking and financial systems increasingly influence environmental sustainability, the degree of alignment varies based on institutional maturity and policy enforcement. Furthermore, Delle Foglie & Keshminder (2022) examine the emerging role of SRI sukuk (Sharia-compliant green bonds) in Islamic finance. Their bibliometric review suggests that faith-based financial models can effectively promote sustainability without compromising on religious or cultural norms, offering new avenues for responsible finance. Khalid et al. (2025) highlight China's financial mechanisms for sustainability, demonstrating how green financial systems can be institutionalized at a national level to incentivize corporate green investments. Their study emphasizes policy instruments such as preferential lending, tax incentives, and mandatory environmental disclosures as key enablers of corporate sustainability.

The financial sector has a crucial role in accelerating progress towards the UN Sustainable Development Goals, particularly:

- SDG 8: Decent Work and Economic Growth – Financial systems must support inclusive economic participation by financing SMEs, job-creating enterprises, and fair labor practices. According to Naidoo (2020), aligning financial flows with SDG 8 requires redesigning systems to prioritize inclusive and sustained economic growth through capital allocation that supports decent employment.
- SDG 9: Industry, Innovation, and Infrastructure – Sustainable finance is instrumental in building resilient infrastructure and fostering innovation. Zioło et al. (2021) highlight that targeted investments in green infrastructure such as smart grids, clean transport, and circular economy solutions require long-

term financing models that balance environmental concerns with economic returns.

Wiek and Weber (2014) take a critical stance, cautioning that while the financial sector has potential to drive sustainability, its role remains ambivalent. On one hand, finance can facilitate transitions to green economies; on the other, speculative and short-term financial behavior can undermine systemic sustainability goals. Their work calls for deeper regulatory reforms and stakeholder accountability to align incentives with sustainable outcomes. Henry Ntarmah, Kong, and Kobina Gyan (2019) also point to the role of banking system stability as a precondition for sustainability. Their panel analysis across developing nations finds that unstable financial systems often divert resources toward crisis management, delaying long-term sustainability investments. Hence the integration of sustainability into financial systems is not only necessary for achieving global development goals but also critical for long-term economic stability. ESG principles guide ethical decision-making and risk mitigation; green and ethical finance provide instruments for channeling capital into sustainable ventures; and alignment with SDGs ensures that financial flows contribute to broader societal well-being. However, as the literature suggests, this transition requires more than voluntary alignment it calls for systemic transformation, policy support, and cultural shifts within financial institutions

## Gaps in Existing Literature

Despite the growing body of work on embedded finance, financial inclusion, and sustainable finance, the current literature remains fragmented. A critical analysis of prior studies reveals several key gaps that limit the development of a comprehensive understanding of how financial systems can evolve to be both inclusive and sustainable through technological integration. While embedded finance has been extensively examined in terms of its technological and operational dimensions such as API banking, BNPL models, and digital wallets (Sieber & Guibaud, 2022; Finken & Hensen, 2025) its potential role in achieving sustainability goals is rarely addressed. Most studies emphasize user experience, cost efficiency, or market disruption (Bugvi & Endress, 2023), yet fail to contextualize these innovations within broader sustainability frameworks such as ESG or the SDGs. On the other hand, literature focusing on sustainability in finance often centers on institutional finance, green bonds, or ESG integration in traditional investment portfolios (Ziolo et al., 2021; Naidoo, 2020), with minimal attention to how technology-driven models like embedded finance could enhance the scalability and accessibility of sustainable financial practices. The absence of dialogue between these two strands technological finance and sustainable finance creates a significant theoretical and practical void. Another major shortcoming in the literature is the tendency to treat financial inclusion, technological innovation, and ESG integration as discrete domains rather than interdependent pillars of financial system transformation. For example, while several works examine digital financial services as enablers of inclusion (Tay et al., 2022; Chinoda & Kapingura, 2024), and others explore ESG's relevance to portfolio management (Aspinall et al., 2018), few studies assess how inclusive fintech tools can be purposefully aligned with ESG goals. Moreover, in the current body of work, metrics and evaluation frameworks for sustainability within embedded finance environments are either non-existent or underdeveloped. This hinders efforts to measure the long-term socio-environmental impacts of digital financial products, particularly in low- and middle-income regions. There is a notable absence of a holistic conceptual framework that bridges embedded finance, financial inclusion, and sustainability. Most models are either sector-specific (focusing on banking or fintech) or issue-specific (such as rural credit or climate finance). This segmentation prevents stakeholders particularly business leaders, fintech innovators, and policy-makers from visualizing the systemic interconnections and mutual reinforcements between these dimensions. Stasytytė (2015) and Silver (2017) both call for systemic thinking in financial reform, yet stop short of providing an integrated model that encapsulates embedded financial tools as vehicles for achieving inclusive and sustainable development. Much of the existing empirical evidence on sustainability and embedded finance is drawn from developed economies with mature digital and financial infrastructure. However, developing and emerging economies which stand to benefit the most from innovations in inclusive, sustainable finance remain underrepresented in empirical studies. This geographic skewness limits the global applicability of existing frameworks and policy recommendations. Authors like Obiora et al. (2020) and Afjal (2023) emphasize the unique structural, regulatory, and cultural dynamics in emerging markets, yet there is a dearth of cross-cutting models that account for these nuances within embedded finance applications.

The current literature on embedded finance, sustainability, and financial inclusion, though rich in specific insights, lacks integrative depth. Critical gaps include the absence of interdisciplinary frameworks, weak empirical foundations in emerging economies, and insufficient linkage between technological and sustainability objectives. Addressing these gaps requires the development of a comprehensive conceptual model that embeds ESG principles into inclusive finance, powered by digital technologies. Such a model would not only inform academic discourse but also offer actionable insights for industry practitioners and policymakers.

## METHODOLOGY

Given the emerging and cross-disciplinary nature of this topic, a conceptual synthesis methodology is adopted to consolidate theoretical and empirical insights from diverse fields including finance, sustainability, and digital innovation.

### Research Design

The study adopts a qualitative, conceptual research design aimed at developing theory through integrative synthesis rather than empirical testing. This approach is appropriate for nascent research domains characterized by fragmented literature and limited empirical data (Wiek & Weber, 2014; Stasytytė, 2015). The objective is to construct a holistic and theoretically grounded framework that unites embedded finance mechanisms, ESG principles, financial inclusion strategies, and Sustainable Development Goal (SDG) alignment into a coherent structure. Conceptual synthesis was selected over empirical validation because existing research on embedded finance and sustainability is still evolving, lacking standardized constructs and measurement tools. This approach enables the identification of emerging patterns and theoretical linkages necessary to guide future empirical studies.

### Data Sources and PRISMA-Based Literature Review Protocol

Given the conceptual orientation of the study, data were drawn exclusively from secondary sources. A systematic literature review (SLR) was conducted following the PRISMA (Preferred Reporting Items for Systematic Reviews and Meta-Analyses) protocol to ensure methodological transparency, reproducibility, and academic rigor. Databases like *Scopus Web of Science* and google scholar were selected due to their comprehensive coverage of peer-reviewed and high-impact academic publications in finance, sustainability, and technology. Keywords like "Embedded Finance," "Financial Inclusion," "Sustainable Finance," "Green Finance," "ESG," "Digital Financial Inclusion," "FinTech," "SDG 8," and "SDG 9." Were used.

#### Inclusion Criteria

- o Peer-reviewed journal articles, books, and policy reports written in English.
- o Studies focusing on intersections between financial innovation, inclusion, and sustainability.
- o Papers presenting conceptual, theoretical, or empirical findings related to fintech-enabled inclusion or ESG-oriented finance.

### Exclusion Criteria

- o Purely technical studies on payment systems or cryptography without socio-economic context.
- o Non-English language publications and non-peer-reviewed content.

The PRISMA review process included four stages *identification, screening, eligibility,* and *inclusion*. From an initial pool of 428 publications, 11 studies met the inclusion criteria, of which 35 were selected for detailed analysis and synthesis.

## Analytical Framework and Data Analysis

The study employs thematic synthesis as the principal analytical method to integrate findings from diverse sources. This approach allows the aggregation of fragmented concepts into coherent, multidimensional themes. The synthesis process involved the following steps:

1. Coding and Categorization: Each selected study was coded for recurring themes such as *financial accessibility, digital interface innovation, ESG adoption, green investment strategies*, and *regulatory frameworks.*
2. Theoretical Triangulation: Insights from financial economics, sustainability transitions, and innovation systems theory were compared and synthesized to ensure interdisciplinary robustness.
3. Gap Analysis: Conceptual and contextual gaps were identified, particularly the lack of integration between embedded finance and sustainability, and limited empirical exploration in low-income regions (e.g., Sub-Saharan Africa).
4. Construct Integration: Key constructs *Embedded Finance*, *Financial Inclusion*, and *Sustainability Alignment* were conceptually linked using theoretical anchors from Access to Finance Theory, Inclusive Growth Theory, and Sustainability Transitions Theory. This triangulation provides a multi-theoretical explanation of how embedded finance drives inclusion and sustainability simultaneously.

The results of this analysis informed the conceptual model presented in Section 4, visually mapping the causal pathways and feedback loops connecting technological, financial, and policy enablers with inclusive and sustainable outcomes.

## Theoretical Validation and Expert Consultation

To enhance the conceptual validity of the proposed framework, the model underwent expert validation through structured consultations with both academic and industry specialists.

- Participants: Five academic experts specializing in finance, sustainable development, and digital economics, and four practitioners from fintech firms and regulatory agencies.
- Purpose: To evaluate theoretical consistency, practical relevance, and comprehensiveness of constructs and linkages.
- Outcome: Feedback was used to refine definitions, clarify variable relationships, and simplify the visual model to avoid conceptual duplication.

This triangulated expert review process strengthens the framework's theoretical credibility and practical applicability.

## Key Constructs

### Embedded Finance

Embedded finance refers to the seamless integration of financial services such as payments, lending, insurance, and investments into non-financial platforms. These services are typically powered by Application Programming Interfaces (APIs) and Banking-as-a-Service (BaaS) models that enable third-party platforms to offer financial solutions directly to users. According to Finken and Hensen (2025), embedded finance transforms the financial service delivery model by removing traditional intermediaries and embedding financial tools into e-commerce, ride-sharing, healthcare, or logistics platforms. Key features include platform-based delivery, real-time transactions, and contextual financial offerings that meet consumers at the point of need.

### Financial Inclusion

Financial inclusion encompasses affordability, accessibility, and availability of formal financial services for underserved populations. It focuses on reducing barriers such as high transaction costs, lack of identity documentation, or geographical inaccessibility. As Tay, Tai, and Tan (2022) note, digital financial services like mobile payments and digital wallets have become instrumental in bridging financial gaps in developing economies. Embedded finance, when properly deployed, can further lower thresholds for entry into the financial system by integrating services into platforms already used by target populations, such as agricultural marketplaces, social commerce, or mobile telecom networks.

## Sustainability Alignment

Sustainability in financial systems is rooted in Environmental, Social, and Governance (ESG) principles and aligned with broader developmental frameworks such as the UN Sustainable Development Goals (SDGs). This construct focuses on how financial systems can promote green finance, ethical investments, and responsible consumption. According to Ziolo et al. (2019), sustainable finance aims not just at economic returns but at generating measurable positive outcomes for society and the environment. In the embedded finance context, sustainability alignment involves designing financial products that promote climate resilience, gender equity, and responsible production, while also adhering to transparency and governance standards.

## Relationships Among Constructs

The proposed conceptual framework articulates the causal relationships among three core constructs Embedded Finance, Financial Inclusion, and Sustainability Alignment and explains how their interaction drives equitable and sustainable growth in the digital economy. These relationships are supported by theoretical foundations drawn from Access to Finance Theory, Inclusive Growth Theory, and Sustainability Transitions Theory, providing a multi-layered understanding of the mechanisms and feedback dynamics that connect financial innovation to social and environmental outcomes.

## Embedded Finance as a Driver of Financial Inclusion

Embedded finance serves as a transformative force that bridges the gap between the financially excluded and formal financial systems. By integrating financial services directly into widely used digital ecosystems such as e-commerce, mobility, agriculture, or EdTech platforms it eliminates traditional access barriers like physical distance, high transaction costs, and cumbersome documentation (Sieber & Guibaud, 2022; Bugvi & Endress, 2023). From the perspective of Access to Finance Theory, embedded finance enhances affordability and accessibility by leveraging existing digital networks and customer data to deliver context-specific financial solutions (Simatele et al., 2021). For instance, ride-hailing platforms such as Uber, Bolt, and Ola now provide drivers with embedded micro-insurance, instant payment settlements, and access to working capital loans, helping them mitigate risks and improve financial stability. Similarly, e-commerce platforms like Amazon and Flipkart offer Buy Now, Pay Later (BNPL) services, expanding short-term credit access to unbanked users who would otherwise be excluded from traditional credit systems (Omarini, 2023). In emerging markets, embedded finance has demonstrated particularly strong inclusion effects. Mobile platforms such as M-Pesa in Kenya, MoMo in Ghana, and Flutterwave in Nigeria have successfully combined telecommunications infrastructure with financial functionality, enabling millions of users to transfer money, access credit, and save securely (Chitimira & Warikandwa, 2023). This exemplifies the essence of Inclusive Growth Theory, where digital finance acts as a mechanism for reducing inequality and promoting shared prosperity through financial empowerment. Hence, embedded finance acts as a processual enabler in the conceptual model, transforming technological and policy inputs (e.g., digital infrastructure, financial regulations) into inclusive financial participation outcomes.

## Digital Financial Tools and Sustainability Objectives

Digital financial tools embedded within everyday platforms also provide unique opportunities to advance sustainability goals, aligning with Sustainability Transitions Theory and ESG (Environmental, Social, and Governance) principles. These tools can be strategically designed to encourage responsible financial behavior, promote sustainable investments, and support green economic transitions. For example, embedded finance platforms can offer green loans for renewable energy adoption, micro-investments in ESG-rated portfolios, or carbon tracking wallets that allow consumers to monitor their environmental footprint. As Silver (2017) argues, integrating ethical decision-making within financial systems is crucial to achieving sustainability-driven economic transformation. Similarly, Ziolo et al. (2019) highlight that embedding sustainability indicators into financial instruments enhances both accountability and long-term value creation. From an operational perspective, embedded financial ecosystems can directly contribute to the achievement of SDG 8 (Decent Work and Economic Growth) and SDG 9 (Industry, Innovation, and Infrastructure). For instance:

- Under SDG 8, embedded finance facilitates entrepreneurial activity by providing credit, insurance, and capital to micro and small enterprises, fostering employment and inclusive economic participation (Khalid et al., 2025).
- Under SDG 9, embedded systems support innovation and resilient infrastructure through fintech-enabled investment in sustainable technologies and digital public infrastructure.

Furthermore, technologies such as blockchain, artificial intelligence (AI), and smart contracts enhance transparency and traceability in financial flows, minimizing risks of greenwashing and ensuring that funds are directed toward genuinely sustainable activities (Naidoo, 2020). This demonstrates how embedded finance can serve as a catalyst for both financial democratization and sustainability alignment.

## Feedback Loops and Moderating Variables

The interaction between embedded finance, inclusion, and sustainability is dynamic and cyclical rather than linear. The framework conceptualizes multiple feedback loops where outcomes reinforce earlier stages of the process:

1. Inclusion–Sustainability Loop: As financial inclusion deepens, users gain awareness and financial capacity to engage in sustainable consumption and investment, creating market demand for ESG-aligned products. In turn, this demand motivates financial institutions and digital platforms to design more sustainable products, thereby reinforcing the sustainability dimension (Wiek & Weber, 2014).
2. Innovation–Regulation Loop: As embedded financial systems expand, regulators adjust frameworks to manage risks such as consumer protection and data governance. These regulatory refinements create a more stable ecosystem that further promotes inclusion and sustainability.

However, the effectiveness of these relationships depends on several moderating variables that shape the strength and direction of the effects:

- Digital Literacy: Users' ability to understand and navigate financial technologies determines their capacity to benefit from embedded finance. Low literacy levels, especially in rural or low-income populations, can limit adoption despite availability (Tay et al., 2022).
- Data Privacy and Cybersecurity: Without robust governance and data protection frameworks, users may distrust digital platforms, hindering engagement. Incorporating ethical standards such as the OECD AI Principles and ISO 42001 ensures fairness, transparency, and accountability in algorithmic decision-making (Afjal, 2023).
- Regulatory Environment: Regulatory clarity and supportive policies are critical for encouraging innovation while ensuring financial stability. Countries that provide sandbox testing, open banking frameworks, and ESG disclosure mandates facilitate smoother integration of embedded finance with sustainable outcomes (Naidoo, 2020).

- Institutional Trust: Public confidence in financial intermediaries, digital platforms, and government institutions strongly influences the uptake and long-term impact of embedded financial tools.

Thus, the relationships among the constructs are not isolated but form a self-reinforcing system. Increased inclusion generates sustainable behavior, which stimulates regulatory and market adaptations, leading to improved systems of embedded financial innovation.

## Process-Oriented Conceptual Model

The conceptual model (Figure 1) represents a process-oriented structure demonstrating how embedded finance mechanisms translate into inclusive and sustainable outcomes.

1. Inputs:
    - *Technological Enablers*: APIs, mobile connectivity, fintech infrastructure, blockchain, and AI.
    - *Policy and Regulatory Frameworks*: ESG mandates, digital finance laws, financial literacy programs.
2. Process Mechanisms:
    - *Embedded Finance Implementation*: Integration of financial tools (payments, credit, insurance) within digital platforms.
    - *Intermediation Channels*: Partnerships between fintech firms, banks, and non-financial entities.
3. Outputs (Outcomes):
    - *Financial Inclusion*: Increased accessibility, affordability, and usage of financial services among underserved populations.
    - *Sustainability Outcomes*: Growth in green finance, ESG-aligned investments, and sustainable consumption patterns.
4. Feedback Loops:
    - *User Empowerment Loop*: Enhanced inclusion fosters awareness and demand for sustainable finance.
    - *Regulatory Feedback Loop*: Market evolution drives adaptive governance and innovation.

By linking Inputs → Processes → Outcomes → Feedback Loops, the model illustrates the causal logic that underpins the transformation of financial ecosystems through embedded finance. This systems-based perspective aligns with Sustainability

Transitions Theory, recognizing that inclusive and sustainable finance emerges from iterative interactions between technology, policy, market actors, and consumers.

This model shows that embedded finance acts as both a catalyst and an enabler, influencing financial inclusion and sustainability in tandem. The feedback mechanisms ensure that these effects are iterative and self-reinforcing under the right enabling conditions.

*Figure 1. Conceptual Framework*

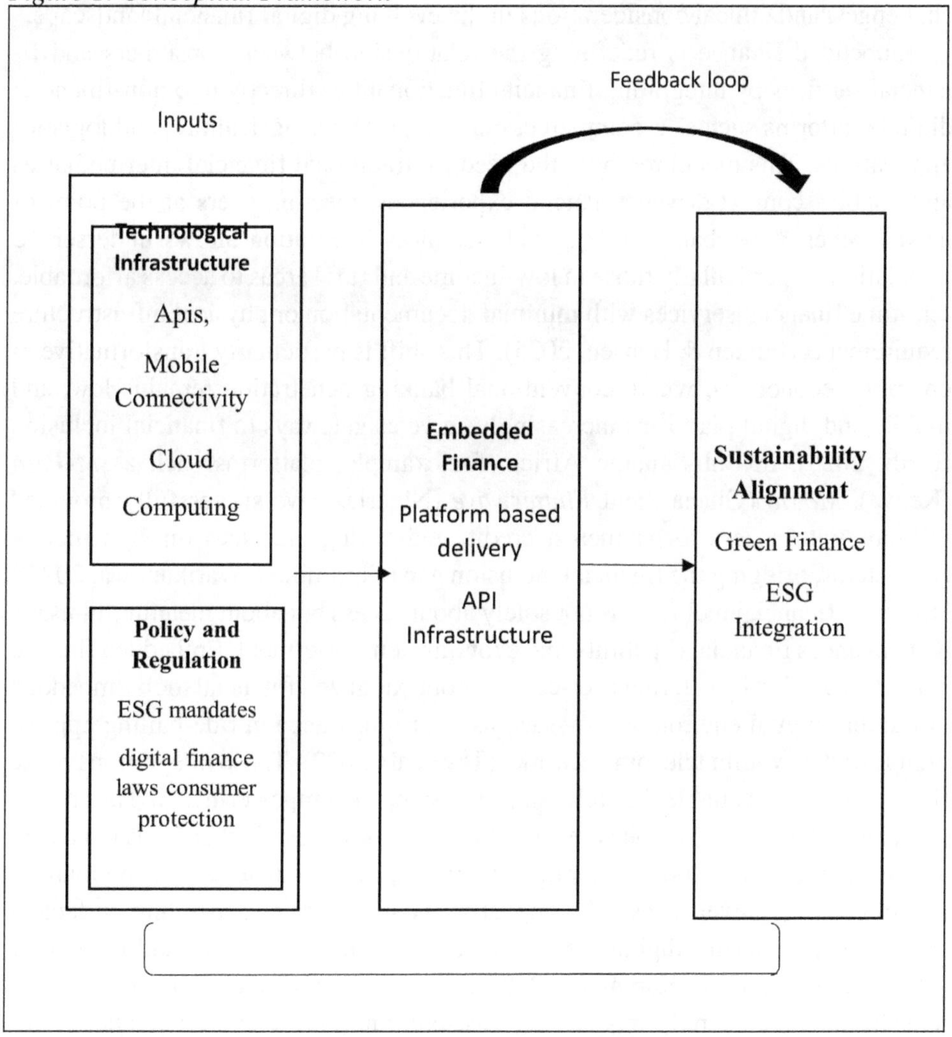

## DISCUSSION

The proposed conceptual framework demonstrates that embedded finance, when integrated with Environmental, Social, and Governance (ESG) principles and inclusive design strategies, possesses transformative potential to reshape financial ecosystems into more accessible, ethical, and sustainable systems. This section discusses the interplay among embedded finance, financial inclusion, and sustainability, outlines implications for key stakeholders, and identifies emerging opportunities, regulatory challenges, and ethical considerations in the evolving digital financial landscape.

Embedded finance is redefining the relationship between consumers and financial services by integrating financial functionalities directly into non-financial digital platforms such as e-commerce, mobility, EdTech, agriculture, and logistics applications. This model removes the need for traditional financial intermediaries and enables context-driven financial experiences, meeting users at the point of need (Sieber & Guibaud, 2022). Such seamless integration allows underserved populations—particularly those in low-income and rural areas to access affordable, real-time financial services with minimal documentation or physical infrastructure requirements (Finken & Hensen, 2025). This shift is particularly transformative in emerging economies, where conventional banking penetration remains low, and mobile and digital platforms increasingly serve as gateways to financial inclusion (Ozili, 2023). In Sub-Saharan Africa, for example, platforms such as *M-Pesa* (Kenya), *MoMo* (Ghana), and *Flutterwave* (Nigeria) have successfully provided millions with access to payments, credit, and savings services through mobile ecosystems, bridging the financial inclusion gap (Chitimira & Warikandwa, 2023). However, financial inclusion is not solely about access but about meaningful usage that enhances financial capability and economic empowerment. Embedded finance extends inclusion by offering user-centric, contextualized financial tools embedded in familiar digital environments—such as micro-insurance in ride-hailing apps or digital wallets within telecom networks (Tay et al., 2022). These integrations make finance not just available, but relevant, inclusive, and empowering. As Hasan, Yajuan, and Khan (2022) emphasize, true inclusion is achieved when individuals are able to leverage these tools to improve livelihoods, accumulate assets, and manage risk effectively. Nevertheless, the impact of inclusion varies depending on factors such as gender norms, digital literacy, local economic conditions, and regulatory safeguards (Chinoda & Kapingura, 2024). Therefore, embedded financial services must be human-centered, emphasizing trust-building, financial literacy, and affordability to ensure equitable benefits.

The integration of sustainability principles into financial systems is gaining unprecedented importance amid global concerns about climate change, inequality, and responsible consumption. Embedded finance offers a strategic avenue for integrating green and ethical finance into daily consumer experiences. Platforms can embed green loans, ESG-aligned investment portfolios, or carbon-tracking tools that incentivize sustainable purchasing and investment behavior. For example, fintech platforms can reward users for eco-friendly purchases through lower interest rates or preferential loan terms, thereby creating behavioural nudges that promote sustainability (Silver, 2017; Ziolo et al., 2019). Such tools not only align with corporate social responsibility (CSR) objectives but also contribute directly to the achievement of Sustainable Development Goals (SDGs) notably SDG 8 (Decent Work and Economic Growth) and SDG 9 (Industry, Innovation, and Infrastructure). Under SDG 8, embedded finance supports inclusive economic growth by improving credit access for small businesses and entrepreneurs, thereby fostering employment opportunities. Under SDG 9, it enables investment in innovative and resilient financial infrastructure, driving sustainable industrialization. Despite these benefits, key challenges remain. The risk of greenwashing, the absence of standardized ESG metrics, and the complexity of integrating sustainability scoring into digital platforms may undermine the authenticity of ESG commitments (Delle Foglie & Keshminder, 2022). To address this, measurable indicators such as the percentage of green loans issued, ESG-rated investments, and sustainable portfolio ratios should be embedded into platform reporting frameworks to ensure accountability and transparency.

While embedded finance enhances inclusion and sustainability, it introduces new ethical, regulatory, and technological challenges. The large-scale use of personal data and algorithmic decision-making in credit assessment, insurance pricing, and customer profiling raises significant privacy and fairness concerns (Afjal, 2023). The reliance on AI algorithms in embedded finance may perpetuate biases against certain demographic or socioeconomic groups if data inputs are not representative or if transparency in model design is lacking. Additionally, data privacy remains a pressing issue, as financial and behavioral data are often shared between multiple entities (fintechs, merchants, and third-party data processors). Without robust governance, users may lose control over their personal data. To mitigate these risks, this study aligns with the OECD AI Principles (2019), which advocate for transparency, accountability, and human-centric AI, and the ISO 42001:2023 AI Management System Standard, which provides structured guidelines for ensuring algorithmic fairness, explainability, and ethical governance in AI-driven finance. Regulatory frameworks must therefore balance innovation with consumer protection. Proactive policies such as regulatory sandboxes, open banking frameworks, and mandatory ESG disclosures can enable responsible innovation while safeguarding users from predatory or opaque financial practices (Naidoo, 2020). Moreover, establishing digital ethics boards and AI audit mechanisms can further ensure compliance with global best practices.

The successful integration of embedded finance with inclusion and sustainability goals depends on the presence of strong enabling conditions such as robust digital infrastructure, institutional support, and regulatory clarity. Digital literacy remains an essential enabler: without sufficient understanding of digital products and sustainability implications, users cannot fully leverage embedded financial services. Hence, platforms must integrate financial education modules and personalized guidance within their applications to foster informed financial behavior (Afjal, 2023). The framework also highlights the role of feedback loops in strengthening system resilience. As inclusive financial access expands, it creates greater demand for sustainable and ethical financial products, prompting firms to innovate and regulators to adapt. These iterative processes generate dynamic equilibrium, ensuring that embedded finance remains aligned with evolving societal needs and national development priorities.

Hence, embedded finance represents a transformative mechanism for democratizing access to financial services and embedding sustainability into financial decision-making. Yet, its full potential can only be realized if ethical, regulatory, and technological frameworks evolve in tandem. The convergence of embedded finance, financial inclusion, and sustainability can thus drive a new era of responsible digital finance anchored in transparency, equity, and long-term environmental stewardship.

## CONCLUSION

This conceptual research has presented an integrative framework that connects embedded finance, financial inclusion, and sustainability alignment, offering a novel lens through which digital financial transformation can be understood and applied in both developed and developing economies. The key insight is that embedded finance through its platform-based delivery, API-enabled integration, and contextual financial offerings has the potential to radically democratize access to financial services. The literature demonstrates that embedded finance not only reduces the cost and friction associated with traditional banking but also reaches populations traditionally excluded from formal financial systems. When designed with ESG principles and sustainability goals in mind, these digital financial tools can contribute significantly to achieving global targets such as SDG 8 (Decent Work and Economic Growth) and SDG 9 (Industry, Innovation, and Infrastructure). Furthermore, the framework identifies critical moderating variables such as digital literacy, regulation, and institutional trust that can influence the effectiveness of embedded finance in promoting inclusion and sustainability. The study fills a gap in existing literature by offering a holistic conceptual model that positions embedded finance not just as a financial innovation, but as a lever for systemic transformation toward equitable and sustainable development. The findings emphasize the need for cross-sectoral collaboration between policymakers, fintech providers, researchers, and consumers to ensure that embedded finance evolves in a manner that supports inclusive access while aligning with ethical, environmental, and governance standards.

## IMPLICATIONS

### Theoretical Implications

This study makes several significant contributions to the existing body of knowledge. By bridging the domains of embedded finance, financial inclusion, and sustainability, the study fills a critical gap in the literature. Prior research has treated these constructs largely in isolation this framework offers a unified lens to understand their interdependencies, supporting future interdisciplinary scholarship (Stasytytė, 2015; Ziolo et al., 2019). Traditional financial inclusion theories have primarily focused on access and usage. This study extends these frameworks by incorporating platform-based and API-driven delivery mechanisms, illustrating how technological innovation can redefine the inclusion landscape (Tay et al., 2022). The study adds to the emerging theoretical discourse on sustainable finance by exploring how embedded financial tools can be intentionally designed to promote ESG outcomes especially in low- and middle-income markets (Silver, 2017; Wiek & Weber, 2014). The framework highlights key moderators such as regulation, digital literacy, and institutional trust which refine theoretical understanding of when and how embedded finance yields inclusive and sustainable results. This nuance supports more context-sensitive theoretical applications in future empirical research.

### Practical Implications

This research also yields actionable insights for a wide array of practitioners. The framework serves as a guide for designing embedded financial services that go beyond profit-making to include social and environmental value creation. It encourages platforms to integrate sustainability scoring, affordability features, and inclusion metrics into product development. The model informs digital financial policy by illustrating how regulatory frameworks can balance innovation and oversight. It offers a roadmap for designing sandbox regulations, open banking laws, and ESG disclosures tailored for embedded financial ecosystems. The framework supports ESG investors and financial intermediaries in identifying new instruments like green BNPL or embedded micro-loans that combine financial returns with sustainable impact. It also guides ethical portfolio management in the age of embedded, decentralized finance. Organizations working on financial empowerment, climate action, and digital literacy can leverage this framework to align their programs with digital finance innovations that deliver both impact and scale.

## LIMITATIONS AND DIRECTIONS FOR FUTURE RESEARCH

While the proposed conceptual framework offers a comprehensive and theoretically robust view of how embedded finance can simultaneously advance financial inclusion and sustainability, several limitations must be acknowledged. These limitations also provide a foundation for future empirical exploration and model refinement. The present framework is primarily based on secondary data and conceptual synthesis derived from peer-reviewed literature, policy reports, and theoretical discourse. Although it integrates multiple perspectives Access to Finance Theory, Inclusive Growth Theory, and Sustainability Transitions Theory it remains theoretical and untested empirically. The framework's conceptual validity was partially established through expert consultation, involving academic scholars in finance, sustainability, and development studies, as well as practitioners from fintech and regulatory institutions. Their feedback helped refine construct definitions, validate relationships among variables, and improve conceptual coherence.

However, despite these efforts, the framework's generalizability and contextual robustness remain limited. The theoretical assumptions may not hold uniformly across regions due to differences in technological maturity, regulatory infrastructure, and sociocultural factors. For instance, digital trust, literacy, and data governance norms vary widely between developed and emerging economies (Chinoda & Kapingura, 2024; Mhlanga, 2022). Thus, while the conceptual model is logically coherent, it must be empirically validated across diverse contexts to ensure external validity. Another limitation of conceptual validity lies in the underrepresentation of behavioural constructs. While the model emphasizes regulatory, technological, and institutional variables, it insufficiently incorporates psychological and behavioural dimensions such as user trust, perceived risk, financial self-efficacy, and social influence. These factors are critical determinants of technology adoption and sustained use, as demonstrated in financial inclusion and behavioural finance literature. Incorporating these variables in future iterations would deepen the explanatory power of the framework.

The framework's reliance on secondary literature restricts its empirical depth. There is a lack of quantitative indicators that can measure the integration of sustainability principles within embedded finance in real-time. For example, indicators for *ESG-linked digital transactions*, *green digital loans issued*, or *carbon-tracking financial products* are still nascent and vary across markets (Ozili, 2023). This makes benchmarking and cross-country comparison difficult. Additionally, measurement validity remains a challenge because constructs like *sustainability alignment* and *digital inclusivity* are often operationalized differently across studies. Standardizing these indicators through collaborative academic-industry frameworks would enable more accurate and comparable future analyses. Furthermore, embedded finance is an evolving phenomenon. Rapid innovations such as decentralized finance (DeFi), AI-driven credit assessment, blockchain-based identity verification, and tokenized ESG assets—may quickly outpace the framework's assumptions. This dynamism necessitates continual conceptual revision to reflect technological, regulatory, and market changes.

To strengthen the framework's empirical and practical relevance, future research should focus on multi-method validation strategies that test, refine, and expand the proposed model across different regions and sectors. SEM can empirically test the relationships proposed in the framework such as the causal pathways linking *embedded finance financial inclusion sustainability outcomes* using measurable constructs. This quantitative validation would confirm the statistical robustness of the conceptual model and identify moderating effects of variables like *digital literacy*, *regulation*, and *institutional trust*. Empirical research across regions such as Europe, South Asia, and Sub-Saharan Africa can reveal how contextual differences (e.g., regulatory maturity, digital infrastructure, cultural attitudes) shape the performance of embedded finance systems. Such comparative studies would enhance the model's global applicability and policy relevance. Conducting longitudinal analyses of specific platforms (e.g., M-Pesa in Kenya, Paytm in India, or Flutterwave in Nigeria) would help examine how embedded finance evolves over time and how sustainability metrics are integrated into digital ecosystems. Large-scale surveys targeting consumers, fintech developers, and policymakers could assess perceptions, adoption patterns, and satisfaction levels with embedded finance products. This would provide insights into behavioral and attitudinal variables missing from the conceptual model. Simulation modeling and experimental designs could explore how variations in regulatory frameworks or technological capabilities impact financial inclusion and sustainability outcomes. These approaches can test policy interventions before real-world implementation. Evaluating the effects of open banking regulations, regulatory sandboxes, and ESG disclosure frameworks would help validate the moderating role of policy conditions and governance mechanisms in driving inclusive and sustainable embedded finance ecosystems.

## REFERENCES

Afjal, M. (2023). Bridging the financial divide: A bibliometric analysis on the role of digital financial services within FinTech in enhancing financial inclusion and economic development. *Humanities & Social Sciences Communications*, *10*(1), 1–27. DOI: 10.1057/s41599-023-02086-y

Aspinall, N. G., Jones, S. R., McNeill, E. H., Werner, R. A., & Zalk, T. (2018). Sustainability and the financial system Review of literature 2015. *British Actuarial Journal*, *23*, e10. DOI: 10.1017/S1357321718000028

Bugvi, J. A., & Endress, T. (2023). Making Finance Invisible: Embedded Finance Adoption and User Experience. In *Proceedings of the AIT SOM Doctoral Colloquium 2023* (pp. 42-53).

Chinoda, T., & Kapingura, F. M. (2024). Digital financial inclusion and economic growth in Sub-Saharan Africa: The role of institutions and governance. *African Journal of Economic and Management Studies*, *15*(1), 15–30. DOI: 10.1108/AJEMS-09-2022-0372

Chitimira, H., & Warikandwa, T. V. (2023). Financial inclusion as an enabler of United Nations sustainable development goals in the twenty-first century: An introduction. In *Financial inclusion and digital transformation regulatory practices in selected SADC countries: South Africa, Namibia, Botswana and Zimbabwe* (pp. 1–22). Springer International Publishing. DOI: 10.1007/978-3-031-23863-5_1

Delle Foglie, A., & Keshminder, J. S. (2022). Challenges and opportunities of SRI sukuk toward financial system sustainability: A bibliometric and systematic literature review. *International Journal of Emerging Markets*, *19*(10), 3202–3225. DOI: 10.1108/IJOEM-04-2022-0601

Dresner, A., Murati, A., Pike, B., & Zell, J. (2022). Embedded finance: Who will lead the next payments revolution. McKinsey & Company, 18.

Eremeeva, T., & Akulova, A. (2024). The european digital payment wallet ecosystem: key characteristics and insights.

Fava, D. (2023). Where Behavioral Finance and Embedded Finance Intersect. *Journal of Financial Planning*, *36*(1), 54–57.

Finken, S. (2025). *Embedded Finance*. Springer Books. DOI: 10.1007/978-3-658-46863-7

Finken, S., & Hensen, J. (2025). Embedded finance: An evaluation of current and future use cases. *Journal of Digital Banking*, *9*(4), 294–316. DOI: 10.69554/XMNM5451

Hasan, M. M., Yajuan, L., & Khan, S. (2022). Promoting China's inclusive finance through digital financial services. *Global Business Review*, *23*(4), 984–1006. DOI: 10.1177/0972150919895348

Henry Ntarmah, A., Kong, Y., & Kobina Gyan, M. (2019). Banking system stability and economic sustainability: A panel data analysis of the effect of banking system stability on sustainability of some selected developing countries. *Quantitative Finance and Economics*, *3*(4), 709–738. DOI: 10.3934/QFE.2019.4.709

Hensen, J., & Kötting, B. (2022). From open banking to embedded finance: The essential factors for a successful digital transformation. *Journal of Digital Banking*, *6*(4), 308–318. DOI: 10.69554/SRCL3482

Kadam, M. A., Jangid, A., & Singh, N. (2024). Embedded Finance: Scope, Challenges and Opportunities. BVIMSR Journal of Management Research, 16(2).

Khalid, F., Su, C. Y., Weiwei, K., Voinea, C. L., & Srivastava, M. (2025). Financial mechanism for sustainability: The case of China's green financial system and corporate green investment. *China Finance Review International*, *15*(1), 93–116. DOI: 10.1108/CFRI-11-2023-0291

Mensah, B. A. (2024). Predictive Model on Digital Financial Inclusion and Sustainable Development in Sub-Saharan Africa (Doctoral dissertation, University of Cape Coast).

Mhlanga, D. (2022). Introduction to digital financial inclusion: Revisiting poverty theories in the context of the fourth industrial revolution. In *Digital financial inclusion: revisiting poverty theories in the context of the fourth industrial revolution* (pp. 3–15). Springer International Publishing. DOI: 10.1007/978-3-031-16687-7_1

Naidoo, C. P. (2020). Relating financial systems to sustainability transitions: Challenges, demands and design features. *Environmental Innovation and Societal Transitions*, *36*, 270–290. DOI: 10.1016/j.eist.2019.10.004

Obiora, S. C., Bamisile, O., Opoku-Mensah, E., & Kofi Frimpong, A. N. (2020). Impact of banking and financial systems on environmental sustainability: An overarching study of developing, emerging, and developed economies. *Sustainability (Basel)*, *12*(19), 8074. DOI: 10.3390/su12198074

Omarini, A. (2023). From digital technologies to new economics in banking: how to drive the future of digital money and data information knowledge. In *Digital Transformation and the Economics of Banking* (pp. 31–49). Routledge. DOI: 10.4324/9781003340454-3

Ozili, P. K. (2023). Assessing global interest in decentralized finance, embedded finance, open finance, ocean finance and sustainable finance. *Asian Journal of Economics and Banking*, *7*(2), 197–216. DOI: 10.1108/AJEB-03-2022-0029

Pradhan, T. K. (2023). A framework for measuring financial inclusion in India: Bridging gaps between theory and practice. Journal of Financial Counseling and Planning Randa, I. O. (2024). Financial infrastructure development for inclusive growth. In *Infrastructure development strategies for empowerment and inclusion* (pp. 209–233). IGI Global.

Saher, L., Tabák, L., Lyeonov, S., & Vasa, L. (2024). Inclusive growth: Literature review. *Journal of International Students*, *17*(1).

Sieber, S., & Guibaud, S. (2022). *Embedded finance: When payments become an experience*. John Wiley & Sons.

Silver, N. (2017). *Finance, society and sustainability: How to make the financial system work for the economy, people and planet.* Springer. DOI: 10.1057/978-1-137-56061-2

Simatele, M. C., Dube, Z., Khumalo, S., Ssonko, G. W., Kawooya, D. R., Bwalya, M., & Mutyavaviri, T. (2021). *Financial inclusion: Basic theories and empirical evidence from African countries*. AOSIS. DOI: 10.4102/aosis.2021.BK255

Soriano, M. A. (2017). Factors driving financial inclusion and financial performance in Fintech new ventures: An empirical study.

Stasytytė, V. (2015). Conceptualization of financial system sustainability.

Tay, L. Y., Tai, H. T., & Tan, G. S. (2022). Digital financial inclusion: A gateway to sustainable development. *Heliyon*, *8*(6), e09766. DOI: 10.1016/j.heliyon.2022.e09766 PMID: 35785228

Waliszewski, K. (2023). Banking-as-a-Service and Embedded Banking as Innovative Methods of Providing Banking Services. In Digital Transformation and the Economics of Banking (pp. 50-66). Routledge. DOI: 10.4324/9781003340454-4

Wiek, A., & Weber, O. (2014). Sustainability challenges and the ambivalent role of the financial sector. *Journal of Sustainable Finance & Investment*, *4*(1), 9–20. DOI: 10.1080/20430795.2014.887349

Wullweber, J. (2020). Embedded finance: The shadow banking system, sovereign power, and a new state–market hybridity. *Journal of Cultural Economics*, *13*(5), 592–609. DOI: 10.1080/17530350.2020.1741015

Zioło, M., Bąk, I., Cheba, K., Spoz, A., & Niedzielski, P. (2021). Sustainable financial systems toward sustainability in finance. Institutional and managerial approach. *Procedia Computer Science*, *192*, 4237–4248. DOI: 10.1016/j.procs.2021.09.200

Ziolo, M., Filipiak, B. Z., Bąk, I., & Cheba, K. (2019). How to design more sustainable financial systems: The roles of environmental, social, and governance factors in the decision-making process. *Sustainability (Basel)*, *11*(20), 5604. DOI: 10.3390/su11205604 [illegible] [illegible] 10.1080/[illegible]

Zhou, [illegible] Chen, K., [illegible] & [illegible] (2021). [illegible] institutional [illegible] *[illegible]*, [illegible] doi:10.1016/[illegible].2021.[illegible]

Zhou, M., [illegible] Zhou, [illegible] (2019). [illegible] and sustainable finance: The role of environmental, social, and governance factors in the decision-making process. *Sustainability*, [illegible] 3504. doi:10.3390/su11123504

# Chapter 4 The Role of Embedded Finance in Business Innovation: Technology Enablers and Industry Applications

**Gouri Sathvika Garapati**
https://orcid.org/0009-0002-1404-8147
*Christ University, India*

**Abhijeet Birari**
https://orcid.org/0000-0002-5943-0924
*Christ University, India*

## ABSTRACT

*This study explores the role of embedded finance (EF) in driving business model innovation and consumer engagement in India's digital economy, focusing on e-commerce and transportation/food delivery. EF, which integrates services like payments, lending, and insurance into non-financial platforms, is analyzed for its impact on revenue, satisfaction, and inclusion. Using case studies of Flipkart, Amazon, Ola, and Swiggy, and a survey of 250 respondents, the research shows how EF boosts convenience, conversion, and access for underserved users. However, data reveals EF alone doesn't ensure satisfaction without seamless UX and personalization. The study highlights the role of APIs and AI in delivering EF benefits while noting regulatory and privacy concerns. Findings show EF's potential to reshape business and consumer behavior in India*

DOI: 10.4018/979-8-3373-2464-7.ch004

## INTRODUCTION

Embedded finance is rapidly emerging as one of the most significant developments in the fintech landscape. It refers to the integration of financial services such as payments, lending, or insurance into platforms that are not traditionally associated with finance, including e-commerce websites, mobile applications, and ride-hailing services (Babitha et al., 2023).This integration is made possible through partnerships with fintech providers, which eliminates the need for companies to build proprietary financial infrastructure or obtain direct regulatory approvals. As a result, businesses can concentrate on enhancing user experience while seamlessly offering embedded financial tools (PricewaterhouseCoopers, n.d.). Beyond technological convenience, embedded finance also holds broader socio-economic implications. Notably, it plays a vital role in promoting **financial inclusion**, which is widely recognized as a key strategy for poverty alleviation. By enabling underserved communities to access affordable and formal financial services, embedded finance empowers individuals to start businesses, generate income, and improve their overall quality of life (Lee, Lou, & Wang, 2022).Ultimately, the core objective of embedded finance is to streamline the consumer experience by providing timely and context-aware financial solutions wherever and whenever a transaction occurs (Ozili, 2023).

Moreover, the benefits of embedded finance extend well beyond enhancing customer convenience. Banks gain access to new sales channels by collaborating with non-financial entities, thereby reaching previously untapped customer segments. These non-financial organizations, in turn, enhance their market positioning by embedding financial products into their core offerings, contributing to a more consumer-centric value chain. For instance, by integrating user and transaction data, digital platforms can generate deeper behavioral insights and personalize services across the consumer journey. Ultimately, it is the end user who stands to benefit the most receiving instant, contextually relevant financial solutions without the need to switch between applications or platforms (Hensen & Kötting, 2022).

Despite its growing adoption, the concept of embedded finance (EF) often remains under recognized by both consumers and investors. To accelerate its development, strategic investments are recommended in two critical directions: first, towards financial service providers offering modular, scalable integration tools; and second, towards non-financial firms whose core value propositions are significantly amplified through embedded financial solutions. This dual-pronged investment strategy reveals the transformative potential of EF to reshape business models and generate long-term value when adequately supported by capital (Anthemis, 2019).

The conceptual traction behind embedded finance gained momentum around 2019, with experts such as Angela Strange famously predicting that "every company will become a fintech company." Since then, the evolution of embedded finance has been propelled by shifts in technology, business models, and consumer behavior. The increasing digitization of commerce and enterprise management has created fertile ground for financial services to be seamlessly woven into non-financial experiences. Currently, online card spending accounts for approximately 33% of global transactions, rising to nearly 50% in the United States. Additionally, many small and medium-sized enterprises (SMEs) in the U.S. now rely on software platforms to manage their operations, further facilitating embedded finance integration (Dresner et al., 2022).

While the embedded finance market is projected to grow substantially, potentially reaching USD 7.2 trillion by 2030 it is not without its challenges. The expanding scope of EF raises pressing concerns around financial regulation, data privacy, and the ethical use of shared information (Sahu, 2025). These emerging issues underscore the importance of balancing innovation with robust governance to ensure long-term sustainability and public trust. While this concept continues to gain popularity across industries, especially with the rise of digital platforms and changing consumer behavior, research into its broader impact is still developing. Much of the existing focus has been on its technical features or its role in customer convenience. However, there is still limited understanding of how embedded finance is reshaping business models, customer relationships, and financial access especially in emerging markets like India (Dresner et al., 2022). As it becomes more widespread, it is important to explore not only its benefits but also the challenges it presents, such as regulatory issues, data privacy concerns, and the need for collaboration between financial and non-financial players, (Nair & Kibble, 2022).

## Research Objectives and Scope

With all of this in mind, this study aims to explore how the integration of financial services into non-financial platforms drives business model innovation in India. It investigates embedded finance as a strategic enabler not merely a convenience and examines how it reconfigures value creation for companies and consumers. By combining company case studies and primary survey data, the research offers a holistic understanding of the impact of embedded finance on innovation, stakeholder outcomes, and customer perceptions.

- **Objective 1:** To examine how embedded finance drives business model innovation in Indian platform companies through service integration, revenue transformation, and enhanced customer engagement.
- **Objective 2:** To identify and analyze the technological enablers such as APIs, BaaS, AI/ML, and cloud-based infrastructure that support the deployment and scalability of embedded finance in digital platforms.

- **Objective 3:** To evaluate consumer perceptions of embedded finance in terms of awareness, usability, trust, satisfaction, and frequency of use within everyday digital apps.
- **Objective 4:** To test the relationship between embedded finance features, consumer trust, and satisfaction across different platform types and industry sectors.

## LITERATURE REVIEW

There are only a few academic studies available on embedded finance (EF), which show that this topic hasn't been explored much by researchers yet. Most of the information and discussions on EF come from industry reports and white papers written by professionals, rather than from academic sources, (Ozili, 2023).

### Evolution from Open Banking to Embedded Finance

According to Goel (2024), the evolution of digital finance has been marked by several pivotal developments that have paved the way for today's integrated financial services. The early 2000s witnessed the emergence of digital payment platforms, which laid the groundwork for more sophisticated systems. This evolution continued with the advent of mobile wallets and the adoption of contactless payments during the COVID-19 pandemic changes that fundamentally shifted consumer behavior towards digital-first financial interactions.

Central to this progression was the rise of open banking. Regulatory frameworks such as PSD2 in the European Union mandated the secure sharing of financial data through application programming interfaces (APIs), fostering an environment ripe for fintech innovation. This open and collaborative model has not only enhanced personalization and customer engagement but also set the stage for the next phase of digital transformation embedded finance (Hensen & Kötting, 2022). In this model, financial services ranging from payments and credit to insurance are seamlessly woven into non-financial platforms. By eliminating the need to navigate between disparate applications, embedded finance significantly enhances user convenience and aligns closely with evolving consumer preferences (Adobe Communications, 2021).

The benefits of this transformation extend to all stakeholders. Financial institutions gain access to new customer segments and distribution channels, while non-financial firms can offer tailored financial products that boost their competitive value propositions. Moreover, strategic partnerships between banks and digital platforms are emerging as key enablers of this trend, leveraging customer data to deliver more relevant and timely financial solutions. Overall, the trajectory from open banking to embedded finance not only demonstrates significant technological progress but also signals a broader move toward an open-data economy, one characterized by cross-industry collaboration and continuous innovation (Hensen & Kötting, 2022).

## Drivers of Embedded Finance Adoption

As we know, it has emerged as a transformative trend in the financial technology sector, driven by a combination of evolving consumer behavior, technological advancements, and strategic business needs. Its adoption is largely attributed to the increasing demand for seamless and efficient financial experiences across platforms. A primary driver of EF is the enhanced customer experience it offers. By integrating services such as payments, lending, and insurance directly into consumer-facing platforms like e-commerce or delivery apps, businesses can streamline user journeys and reduce transaction friction (Babitha et al., 2023). Modern consumers, particularly digital natives, prefer cohesive ecosystems that eliminate the need to navigate multiple applications, a need that EF effectively addresses (Finextra, 2024).

*Figure 1. Most influential trends in the payments industry according to senior payment professionals worldwide in 2024*

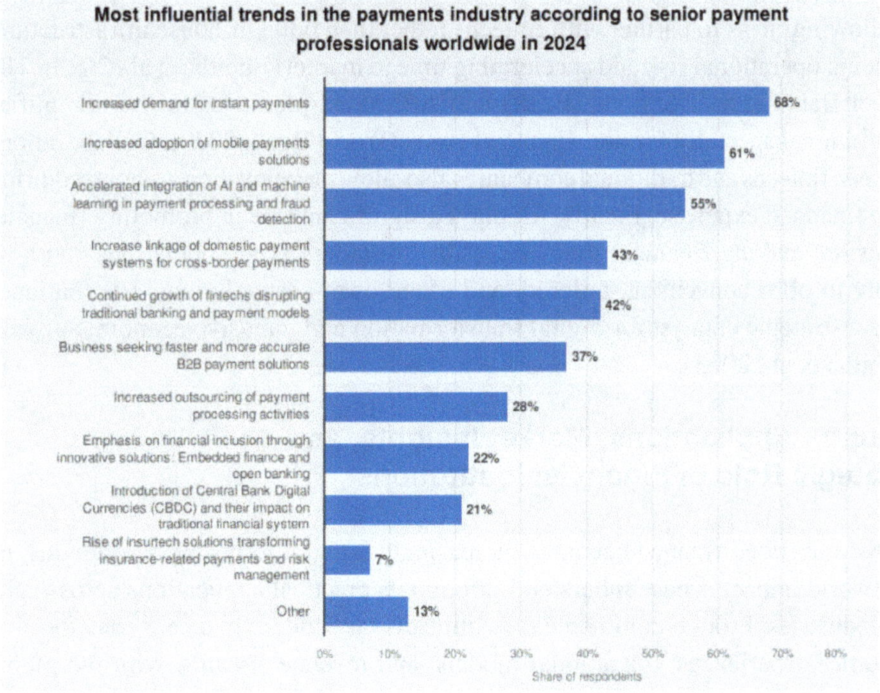

According to a 2024 global survey of senior payment professionals (OpenPayd, 2021), several key trends are shaping the adoption of embedded finance. The most influential drivers include the increasing demand for instant payments (68%) and the widespread adoption of mobile payment solutions (61%), reflecting consumer expectations for integrated, seamless financial experiences. The integration of AI and machine learning into payment processing (55%) further supports the need for secure, efficient, and intelligent systems, which are central to embedded finance models. While only 22% directly cited embedded finance and open banking as major trends, this figure indicates a growing recognition of their role in fostering financial inclusion and innovation. These findings suggest that embedded finance is gaining momentum as part of a broader digital transformation in payments, enabled by technological advances and shifting consumer behaviors.

Harris et al. (2022)'s report on Embedded Finance: What It Takes to Prosper in the New Value Chain says that Value-added services have further accelerated EF adoption. Companies are expanding their offerings to include tax support, micro-credit, and insurance solutions, all within a single app, thereby increasing customer retention and satisfaction. The Buy Now Pay Later (BNPL) model exemplifies this, with a 138% rise in its share of e-commerce payments between 2020 and 2023, driven by inflationary pressures and consumers' need for flexible financing options (Finextra, 2024) From a business standpoint, EF enables cost efficiencies by allowing firms to partner with fintechs rather than build in-house infrastructure, reducing operational risk and accelerating time to market (Babitha et al., 2023). The rise of Banking-as-a-Service (BaaS) and API-based platforms further simplifies integration, especially for non-financial firms (World Bank, 2020). Collaborations between fintechs and traditional companies also allow for innovation without requiring deep financial expertise. Finally, EF plays a significant role in promoting financial inclusion, making financial tools accessible to underserved populations. With its ability to offer convenient, tailored, and often lower-cost solutions, EF continues to be a strategic catalyst for digital transformation and inclusive economic growth (Babitha et al., 2023).

## Industry Applications, Market Insights, and Strategic Role of Financial Institutions

As embedded finance becomes increasingly integral to business strategies, its real-world impact is best understood through its practical applications across various industries. From e-commerce to healthcare, embedded finance is transforming customer experiences, operational models, and revenue streams, with the global market projected to grow significantly (MarketsAndMarkets, 2025). This integration not only highlights the transformative potential of embedded finance but also underscores its strategic importance in driving long-term value for stakeholders (Deloitte, 2023). In this context, examining the industry applications, market trends, and strategic role of financial institutions is crucial for understanding the evolving landscape of embedded finance.

## Industry Use Cases and Implementation Areas

Embedded finance is increasingly being adopted across various industries, allowing non-financial platforms to integrate financial services into their core offerings. This integration not only improves user convenience but also strengthens revenue models and operational efficiency, (Tullio, 2020). In the e-commerce space, embedded payments and BNPL (Buy Now Pay Later) models have become central. Platforms like Shopify utilize Stripe for streamlined payment processing, while Klarna and Affirm enable customers to defer payments without leaving the checkout interface enhancing both conversion rates and customer satisfaction (Sokolov, 2022) In the mobility sector, firms like Uber have pioneered the use of embedded financial tools to facilitate instant payments to gig workers and ensure seamless in-app transactions for users, reflecting broader trends in gig economy financial inclusion (Dresner et al., 2024). The retail industry integrates financial tools such as embedded insurance and merchant financing; for example, Tesla offers auto insurance tailored to driver behavior, and Shopify provides data-driven merchant cash advances, supported by AI-powered risk assessments (Harris et al., 2022) . B2B platforms also exhibit significant potential. Tools like Airbase embed ACH transfers and international payment functionalities directly within enterprise software, while India's Udaan facilitates SME growth through embedded credit services, targeting underserved markets (Tullio, 2020). In healthcare, embedded finance supports access to essential services by enabling payment plans and financing options directly within care delivery platforms (Harris et al., 2022). These sectoral implementations collectively underscore the evolving strategic role of financial institutions, which now act as back-end enablers providing infrastructure, regulatory compliance, and financial products. For example, WebBank partners with Toast to offer cash advances to restaurants using real-time receivables data, demonstrating how banks are adapting to support embedded finance ecosystems (Dresner et al., 2024). The growing presence of embedded finance across sectors highlights its importance not only in enhancing financial accessibility but also in redefining the position of financial institutions in modern value chains.

## Global Market Size and Growth Trends

Recent literature reveals that the embedded finance (EF) market is rapidly expanding, driven by an increasing consumer preference for seamless financial services integrated into everyday digital platforms. For instance, Precedence Research (2025) estimates that the EF market will grow from USD 148.38 billion in 2025 to USD 1,732.53 billion by 2034, reflecting a robust CAGR of 31.53%. This explosive growth is largely attributed to the digital transformation of industries such as e-commerce, healthcare, and retail, where integrated financial solutions are reshaping user experiences.

*Figure 2. Embedded finance market size 2024 to 2034 (USD Billion)*

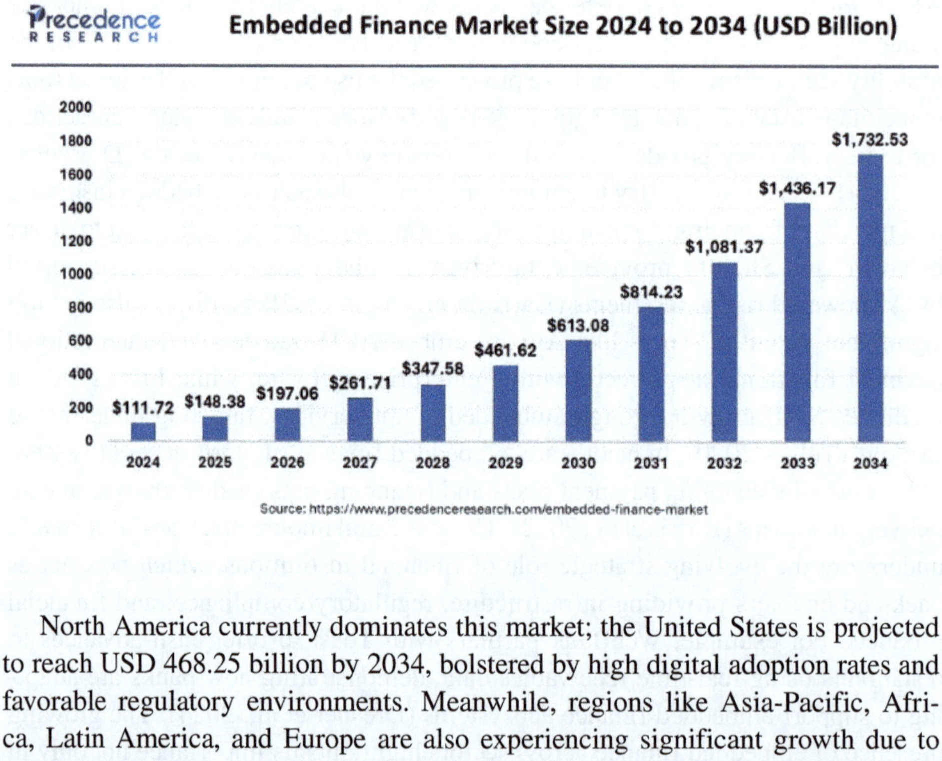


North America currently dominates this market; the United States is projected to reach USD 468.25 billion by 2034, bolstered by high digital adoption rates and favorable regulatory environments. Meanwhile, regions like Asia-Pacific, Africa, Latin America, and Europe are also experiencing significant growth due to increased mobile penetration, rapid fintech innovation, and the expansion of API-based platforms that facilitate easy integration of services (MarketsAndMarkets, 2025). Technological advancements particularly the proliferation of API-based infrastructures and platform-as-a-service models are essential enablers for EF, allowing non-financial companies to incorporate services such as payments, lending, and insurance without building full-scale banking infrastructures (Research and

Markets, 2022). In addition, strategic collaborations between traditional financial institutions and fintech companies are driving innovation and widening the global reach of embedded financial products.

*Table 1. Market research insights and statistics about embedded finance*

| Region/Country | Research Insights | Source |
|---|---|---|
| Global | Embedded finance market projected to reach USD 379 billion by 2030, growing at a CAGR of 25.7%. | (Industry Arc, 2023) |
| Global | Market size anticipated to reach USD 588.49 billion by 2030, expanding at a CAGR of 32.8%. | (Grand View Research, 2024) |
| Global | Estimated market value for embedded finance will exceed USD 138 billion by 2026. | (Beck, 2024) |
| Asia- Pacific | Region expected to grow at a CAGR of 25% annually until 2029, driven by digital adoption and rapid fintech innovation. | (Research and Markets, 2022) |
| India & Emerging Markets | Emerging embedded finance markets in India and other developing countries are expected to witness robust growth due to rising smartphone penetration and digital payments. | (Mordor Intelligence, 2025) |
| Africa & Middle East | Embedded finance revenues projected to increase from USD 10.36 billion in 2022 to USD 39.82 billion by 2029. | (Research and Markets, 2022) |
| Europe | Revenues forecasted to surpass €100 billion by the end of the decade, driven in part by embedded lending models and supportive regulatory frameworks such as PSD2. | (Murati et al., 2024) |
| U.S. | Market size valued at USD 15.36 billion in 2023, with a CAGR of 32% from 2024 to 2030. | (Grand View Research, 2023) |
| Latin America | Revenues expected to grow from USD 7.49 billion in 2022 to USD 28.73 billion by 2029, with embedded lending solutions in early stages of adoption. | (Research and Markets, 2022) |

This table provides a snapshot of key trends and forecasts from multiple sources, reflecting the dynamic growth and regional diversity of the embedded finance market.

## Financial Institutions and Embedded Finance Integration

The integration of embedded finance into the operations of financial institutions (FIs) marks a strategic shift in the delivery of financial services. Rather than relying solely on traditional banking channels, FIs are increasingly embedding financial offerings such as payments, lending, and insurance into third-party digital platforms. This transformation allows banks to remain competitive amid the rising influence of fintech firms and digital ecosystems, while also unlocking significant revenue and customer acquisition opportunities, (Accenture, 2021). Embedded finance presents substantial revenue-generating potential for banks, particularly through

SME-focused services. Moreover, embedded finance enables traditional banks to maintain relevance by integrating into third-party digital platforms through secure APIs, placing ecosystems at the core of innovation (IBM, 2023). According to Accenture (2021), large banks stand to gain up to $92 billion globally by 2025 through embedded finance models tailored to SMEs. This market could represent 26% of total SME banking revenues, amounting to $124 billion. Without adaptation, traditional banks risk losing up to $32 billion of this segment to emerging embedded finance providers, (Mastercard, 2024). Banking-as-a-Service (BaaS) frameworks have emerged as foundational to the integration of embedded finance. These frameworks facilitate collaboration between banks and non-financial platforms through APIs, enabling scalable, interoperable service delivery. For example, Standard Chartered's adoption of BaaS has allowed the bank to integrate its offerings into various digital ecosystems, reflecting a broader industry shift toward partnership-based models, (Murati, Skau, & Geer, 2024). Through embedded finance, banks are gaining access to previously untapped customer segments while reducing customer acquisition costs. SMEs, in particular, show strong interest in services embedded within tools they already use, such as accounting software or e-commerce platforms. Partnerships between banks and digital service providers, like Xero and Myob, enable streamlined access to credit and other financial products, (Accenture, 2021). According to Skaleet (2023), key benefits of embedded finance integration for FIs include diversified revenue streams, stronger customer loyalty through frictionless delivery service, and enhanced financial inclusion. By embedding products such as BNPL, insurance, and micro-loans directly into digital environments, banks improve service accessibility and relevance. However, these opportunities are tempered by challenges, including navigating complex regulatory environments, ensuring robust API infrastructure, and facing competition from agile fintechs.

## Consumer Adoption and Behavioral Shifts in Embedded Finance

Embedded finance, by seamlessly integrating financial services into non-financial platforms, is fundamentally reshaping consumer experience. One of the primary benefits is convenience, as users can access services like payments and credit without switching applications such as making direct payments within e-commerce platforms thereby streamlining transactions and enhancing user satisfaction (Ozili, 2023). This integration also increases consumer engagement; by embedding financial tools within frequently used platforms, businesses encourage repeated interaction for both shopping and financial management (Ohnishi, 2021). The COVID-19 pandemic further accelerated this adoption, catalyzing a global shift toward digital interactions. With lockdowns pushing consumers toward online services, the need for safe, integrated financial solutions grew substantially (Olins, 2022). Consequently, behavioral changes emerged, including rising comfort with contactless payments and embedded financing tools (GrowishPay, 2022).

A user-centric approach has proven critical for the continued success of embedded finance. Personalization, enabled by data analytics, allows platforms to tailor offerings to individual preferences, thereby increasing satisfaction and fostering loyalty (Torrance, 2021). Today's consumers increasingly expect hyper-personalized, end-to-end digital experiences. Any friction in accessing financial services risks alienating them. Leveraging AI-driven insights and ecosystem-level data, financial institutions are now positioned to deliver context-specific solutions in real-time, directly within the client journey (IBM, 2023 The frictionless nature of these interactions, compared to traditional banking processes, further boosts their appeal. However, trust and data security remain essential concerns. As financial services are delivered through non-financial platforms, users require clear assurances about data protection, and effective communication of privacy measures becomes key to consumer confidence (Ohnishi, 2021). Regulatory compliance plays a vital role in reinforcing this trust, ensuring services are both safe and legitimate.

*Figure 3. Digital channel usage for financial products*

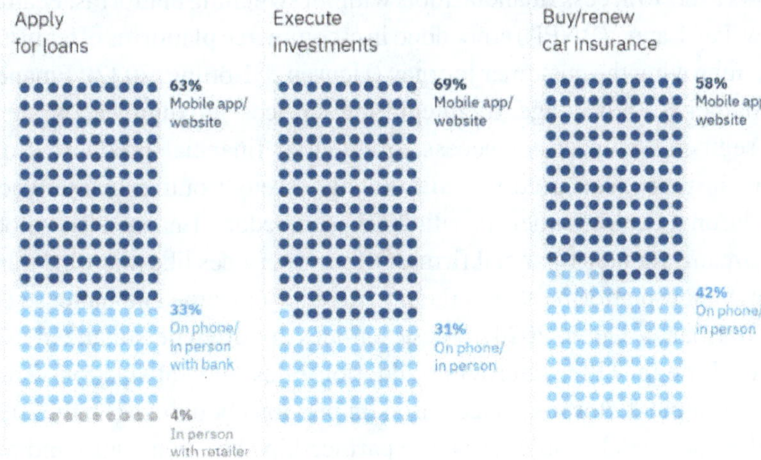


The adoption of digital financial services is rising rapidly. According to IBM (2023), 63% of consumers apply for loans, 69% execute investments, and 58% buy or renew insurance via mobile apps or websites. While 80% still prefer traditional bank accounts for saving, 16% are comfortable with fully digital, branchless platforms highlighting a shift toward embedded finance and digital-first preferences, especially in advanced markets.

Consumers are also responding to the growing diversity and scalability of embedded finance use cases. From loans and insurance embedded in e-commerce platforms to innovative credit offerings by tech giants like Amazon, these services are becoming increasingly versatile and widely accessible (Hensen & Kötting, 2022). As APIs and digital infrastructure advance, embedded finance continues to evolve, offering new features that align with varied consumer needs. Nonetheless, consumer education is crucial for driving further adoption. Many potential users hesitate due to a lack of understanding, and companies must invest in educating their audiences to build awareness and confidence (Mulye, 2021). Empowering users with knowledge not only overcome adoption barriers but also fosters informed decision-making in a rapidly transforming financial landscape.

## Benefits and Challenges of Embedded Finance

### Benefits

A major benefit of embedded finance is enhanced accessibility and user convenience. It allows users to access financial tools without switching platforms. Features like "Buy Now, Pay Later" (BNPL) embedded in e-commerce platforms offer instant credit access, improving the customer journey (Hensen & Kötting, 2022). Financial inclusion is another key advantage. By integrating services into digital ecosystems, underserved segments gain easier access to essential financial products. Small businesses, for instance, can access credit directly through online marketplaces, bypassing traditional bank channels (Ozili, 2023). Embedded finance also unlocks new revenue streams for non-financial firms. Offering services like microinsurance or loans through their platforms allows them to diversify income and increase customer value (Barman & Goon, 2024). These services are often personalized using consumer data through APIs, improving adoption rates and satisfaction. Travel platforms, for example, tailor insurance based on previous bookings (Ozili, 2023).

Additionally, the model enables strategic partnerships between banks and platforms. Financial institutions benefit by reaching new customer segments at lower acquisition costs, while digital platforms strengthen their offerings (IBM, 2023).

## Challenges

Despite its benefits, embedded finance faces several challenges. Technological integration is often hindered by legacy infrastructure and the complexity of implementing API systems (Ozili, 2023). Moreover, navigating regulatory compliance including data security, consumer protection, and AML laws is particularly demanding for non-financial entities (PricewaterhouseCoopers, 2023). Data privacy remains a concern, as embedded finance relies heavily on user data. Strong governance is required to avoid breaches or misuse (Barman & Goon, 2024). The ambiguity in accountability, especially in services like BNPL can confuse consumers about where to seek redress (Ozili, 2023). Finally, financial institutions risk losing direct customer relationships, weakening their brand presence (IBM, 2023).

## Research Gap and Hypotheses

Despite the rapid evolution and growing prominence of embedded finance as a driver of digital transformation, existing academic research remains limited. Most current literature on embedded finance relies heavily on industry reports and practitioner white papers, which primarily focus on its technical features and short-term benefits such as enhanced customer convenience and improved transaction efficiency. While several studies have documented the progression from open banking to embedded finance and its implications for financial inclusion, there is a notable paucity of research examining the broader strategic impact of embedded finance on business model innovation, particularly in emerging markets like India. Additionally, the literature provides limited insight into how embedded finance influences stakeholder outcomes including revenue diversification, customer loyalty, and market positioning as well as the challenges it creates in regulatory compliance, data privacy, and accountability. This research aims to address these gaps by examining embedded finance as a strategic enabler that reconfigures value creation for companies and consumers while also considering the associated risks and regulatory challenges.

Based on the research gap, here are the following hypotheses:

- **H1: Business Model Innovation**: Embedded finance integration into non-financial platforms is positively associated with enhanced business model innovation among Indian companies.
- **H2: Role of Technology Enablers**: The effective utilization of technology enablers such as APIs, Banking-as-a-Service (BaaS), and AI-driven analytics mediates the relationship between embedded finance integration and improved stakeholder outcomes.

- **H3: Consumer Adoption and Trust**: Higher consumer trust and awareness in embedded financial services positively influence customer satisfaction and retention in digital ecosystems.

## RESEARCH METHODOLOGY

This study adopts a mixed-methods research approach combining qualitative case study analysis with quantitative primary survey data to explore the adoption, trust, and impact of embedded financial services across India's e-commerce and transportation/food delivery sectors. This methodological triangulation allows for a holistic understanding of both business strategies and consumer behavior, aligning with the study's objective to assess how embedded finance drives business model innovation and influences consumer decision-making.

### Research Design

The research is structured as a comparative case study, supported by a cross-sectional descriptive survey. This design facilitates the comparison of firms that have adopted embedded financial services (e.g., Amazon, Flipkart, Ola, Swiggy) with those that have not or have minimally adopted such innovations (e.g., Snapdeal, Limeroad, Zomato, Dunzo). Sectoral comparisons were made across E-Commerce and Transportation/Food Delivery sectors, allowing intra-sector and inter-sector insights into the role of embedded finance in business innovation.

### Case Study Selection Criteria

The companies selected were based on:

- **Market presence** and consumer reach in India,
- **Documented use or absence of embedded finance**, such as Buy Now Pay Later (BNPL), digital wallets, and in-app financial services,
- Availability of public data on digital strategy and product features.

Each sector includes two companies with robust embedded finance implementation and two that rely on traditional digital payments, enabling control-based comparison.

## Survey Design and Instrumentation

To complement the case studies, a structured online survey was administered to understand consumer usage, awareness, trust, and perception of embedded financial services. The survey instrument consisted of five sections:

- **Section A:** Demographic information (age, gender, education, occupation, income),
- **Section B:** Platform usage frequency and preference,
- **Section C:** Awareness and usage of embedded finance tools,
- **Section D:** Satisfaction and behavioral impact of these features,
- **Section E:** Overall perception and trust in embedded finance.

The questionnaire used mostly close-ended questions with Likert scales and categorical options, ensuring ease of quantification and statistical analysis.

To estimate the required sample size, Cochran's formula was applied with a 95% confidence level, 5% margin of error, and maximum variability (p = 0.5), yielding an ideal size of 385 respondents. However, considering the study's sectoral segmentation (e-commerce and transportation/food delivery) and practical constraints, a target of 200–250 responses was set. This adjusted size ensures statistically meaningful insights while remaining feasible for primary data collection (Qualtrics, 2023).

## Data Collection Procedure

- **Case study data** were sourced from official websites, investor presentations, fintech media articles, and industry reports.
- **Survey responses** were collected anonymously using Google Forms over a period of six weeks in January - February, 2025.

## Data Analysis Techniques

- **Qualitative analysis** of the case studies involved content analysis of embedded finance features, business model evolution, and customer-centric innovations. Each case was analyzed for embedded finance integration depth and impact on service delivery.
- **Quantitative survey data** were analyzed using descriptive statistics (frequency, percentage, mean scores) to assess consumer patterns, trust levels, satisfaction, and behavioral responses. Where applicable, cross-tabulation and comparative graphs were used to observe sectoral trends.

## CASE STUDY ANALYSIS

This case study segment focuses on examining how embedded finance influences business outcomes in two high-impact sectors e-commerce and transportation/food delivery. These sectors were deliberately chosen due to their widespread digital adoption, high-frequency consumer interactions, and diverse approaches to financial service integration.

*Figure 4. EmFi opportunities by 2030 (in USD Billion)*

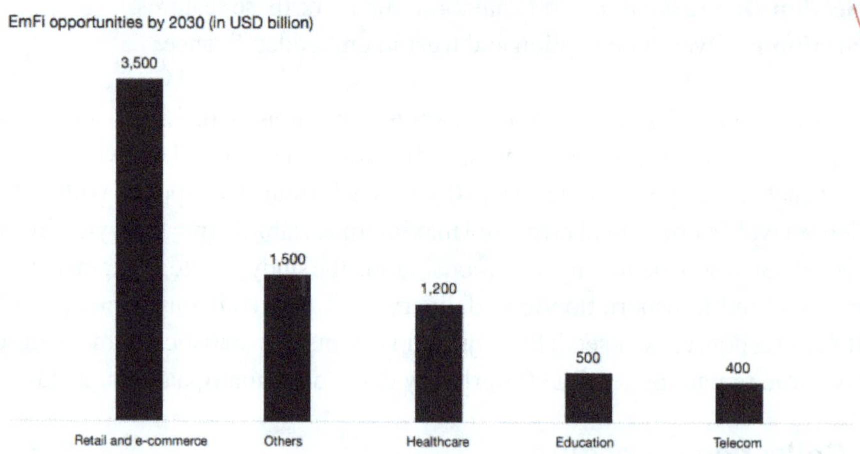


According to (PwC, 2023), they represent fertile ground to explore how embedded financial tools such as in-app wallets, Buy Now Pay Later (BNPL) options, and credit facilities affect customer experience, retention, and business model innovation. Within each sector, companies were selected based on the extent of their embedded finance integration. Firms like Flipkart, Amazon India, Ola, and Swiggy demonstrate advanced integration of financial services into their platforms, while Snapdeal, Limeroad, Zomato, and Dunzo primarily rely on conventional digital payment mechanisms. This comparative framework allows for the analysis of operational and strategic differences between embedded and non-embedded models within the same industry contexts.

The primary objective of this case study is to assess whether embedded finance adoption leads to tangible benefits such as enhanced customer engagement, improved loyalty, and greater competitive differentiation. By investigating companies at both ends of the embedded finance spectrum, this section aims to draw out sector-specific patterns and broader implications that can inform fintech adoption strategies in the digital economy.

## Sector I: E-Commerce

The e-commerce sector is rapidly expanding, driven by digital innovations like AI and mobile commerce, which now account for nearly half of online sales. Consumers increasingly seek personalized, seamless shopping experiences, with embedded finance solutions such as digital wallets and Buy Now Pay Later enhancing convenience and boosting customer loyalty. This integration is reshaping e-commerce by making transactions faster and more user-friendly (Statista, 2023)/

### Companies with Embedded Finance Integration

Both Flipkart and Amazon India have successfully integrated embedded finance into their e-commerce platforms, enhancing customer convenience and engagement while gaining a competitive edge. Through tools like "Pay Later" options, EMIs, and strategic partnerships, these platforms have revolutionized customer access to credit, fostering financial inclusion and broadening their market reach.

#### *Flipkart*

Flipkart has made significant strides with its Flipkart Pay Later and EMI (Equated Monthly Installments) options, offering customers flexibility in their payments. The Pay Later option, allowing credit limits up to  1 lakh, facilitates easier purchases, especially for high-value products like electronics. EMIs, often with low or no interest, have been pivotal in making these products affordable, particularly for Tier-2 and Tier-3 city consumers, where access to traditional credit is limited, (Economic Times, 2024). Additionally, Flipkart's collaboration with Axis Bank to launch a co-branded credit card and its integration with fintech company BillDesk for bill payments have broadened payment options, driving convenience and engagement.

The integration of these financial services has resulted in a significant increase in conversion rates. Data indicates that Pay Later has boosted checkout conversions from 7% to 18%, while customers using embedded finance tools tend to make larger purchases, evidenced by a 46% rise in the average selling price (ASP) (Economic Times, 2024). This flexibility has proven particularly beneficial for underserved customers, allowing them to make purchases that were previously out of reach.

### *Amazon India*

Amazon India's Amazon Pay, Amazon Pay Later, and EMI offerings have created a comprehensive financial ecosystem that enhances customer loyalty. Through Amazon Pay, users can transact using UPI, wallets, or credit cards, while Amazon Pay Later provides instant credit, promoting ease of purchase. In partnership with ICICI Bank, Amazon launched the Amazon Pay ICICI Bank Credit Card, offering cashback and rewards, thereby increasing customer retention. It's EMI options allow customers to purchase high-value items with payment flexibility, especially during key sales events like the Great Indian Festival. The company's gift card system has also played a vital role in increasing sales, with over one billion gift cards distributed since 2014. This system not only drives revenue but also enhances customer engagement during festive seasons (Bureau, 2024). Their embedded finance tools have contributed to a significant ecosystem lock-in effect, where customers are encouraged to remain within Amazon's platform due to integrated payment options and exclusive offers. This lock-in effect helps reduce the likelihood of switching to competitors, (julies chicktanz, 2025).

Both companies have used embedded finance tools to extend their reach into underserved markets, particularly in India's rural and semi-urban areas. Flipkart's approach, with accessible credit for Tier-2 and Tier-3 cities, has increased financial inclusion, while Amazon has adapted its services for diverse consumer needs, making gift cards available in multiple regional languages and acquiring Axio, a BNPL service, to further expand its customer base, (About Amazon, 2025). These efforts have not only strengthened customer loyalty but also helped them capture a larger portion of India's e-commerce market.

The strategic use of embedded finance has provided both Flipkart and Amazon India with a clear competitive advantage in the Indian e-commerce market. Flipkart's focus on Tier-2 and Tier-3 cities has enabled it to dominate the market for affordable credit, whereas Amazon's broader payment flexibility, especially through partnerships and the gift card system, has positioned it as a leader in customer retention (julies chicktanz, 2025)

## Companies Using Traditional Digital Payments

While the integration of embedded finance is rapidly transforming the digital commerce landscape, platforms such as Snapdeal and Limeroad continue to rely on traditional digital payment systems. This reliance on standard payment methods credit/debit cards, UPI, net banking, and mobile wallets provides functional convenience but limits the platforms' ability to innovate or deepen customer engagement (PwC, 2023).

### *Snapdeal*

Snapdeal is a general merchandise e-commerce platform offering a variety of products at affordable prices, primarily targeting price-sensitive consumers. However, its payment ecosystem remains conventional, lacking fintech-enabled tools like Buy Now, Pay Later (BNPL), embedded credit, or EMI-based financing options. This limits its ability to enhance affordability and purchase flexibility for its user base, especially for high-value transactions.

The absence of embedded financial tools also means that Snapdeal underutilized its transaction data, which could otherwise serve as a basis for credit scoring, targeted marketing, or personalized offers. As a result, the platform misses opportunities to create deeper financial relationships with its users (PwC, 2023). Moreover, platforms like Amazon and Flipkart, which have embraced embedded finance, are witnessing improved customer acquisition and retention through tools such as instant credit and loyalty-linked payments. In contrast, Snapdeal's customer engagement remains largely transactional, contributing to slower growth and lower repeat purchase rates, (Brightmore, 2024).

### *Limeroad*

Limeroad operates in a niche e-commerce segment focused on fashion and lifestyle products, emphasizing curated styles and user-generated content. However, it has also remained dependent on standard digital payment methods without incorporating embedded finance mechanisms. While this approach supports smooth transactions, it lacks advanced financial features like in-app microcredit, flexible EMIs, or installment-based payments.

This restricts Limeroad's ability to scale beyond its current demographic, as affordability options are crucial for expanding into price-sensitive or aspirational segments. Furthermore, the lack of embedded financial integration also means the platform collects minimal insights into customer financial behavior, weakening its potential to personalize services or build loyalty ecosystems (Hensen & Kötting, 2022). Compared to embedded finance-led platforms, Limeroad faces growing competitive pressure, as newer and larger players use finance as a tool to drive customer engagement and unlock new monetization streams (PwC, 2025).

## Comparative Impact

1. **Embedded Finance Players** *(Amazon & Flipkart)*
2. **Traditional Payment Platforms** *(Snapdeal & Limeroad)*

*Table 2. Comparative impact of embedded finance players (Amazon & Flipkart) vs. Traditional payment platforms (Snapdeal & Limeroad)*

| Metric | Embedded Finance Players | Traditional Payments Platforms |
|---|---|---|
| Customer Growth | - **Amazon**: 13% YoY, urban-focused, premium positioning(Banerjee, 2025)<br>- **Flipkart**: 21% YoY, strong in Tier-2/3 cities, driven by EMI/BNPL options(Ahmed, 2024). | - **Snapdeal**: Stagnant growth due to lack of innovation & finance tools(TheBigMarketing.com, 2024).<br>- **Limeroad**: Limited to niche market(Mehta, 2014) |
| Repeat Purchase Rate | **Amazon**: 35% during festive seasons, Prime & Amazon Pay boost loyalty(Key, 2023)<br>- **Flipkart**: 25%, affordability tools drive return users(Sethu Pradeep, 2022) | - **Snapdeal**: Low; no loyalty programs or embedded finance(TheBigMarketing.com, 2024).<br>- **Limeroad**: Weak loyalty due to minimal data-driven insights(Mukherjee, 2015) |

## Sector II: Transportation and Food Delivery

The transportation and food delivery sector has rapidly grown through app-based dual-sided platforms connecting users and providers. Companies like Swiggy, Zomato, and Ola integrate embedded finance tools to boost engagement and loyalty. Despite growth, profitability challenges remain due to high costs and inflation, (Morgan Stanley, 2025)

### Companies with Embedded Finance Integration

Ola, a pioneer in India's ride-hailing market, has embedded finance to enhance user convenience and empower its driver-partners through tools like Ola Money and postpaid payment options. Similarly, Swiggy in the food delivery arena leverages embedded finance via its digital wallet and 'Buy Now, Pay Later' services to simplify ordering and support merchant growth.

#### *Ola*

Ola has created a comprehensive embedded finance ecosystem through its digital payment platform, Ola Money. It supports multiple modes such as UPI, debit/credit cards, and a unique postpaid option *Ola Money Postpaid* which allows users to take rides and pay later (Economic Times, 2022). This frictionless payment system enhances convenience and encourages higher customer retention.

Beyond customer payments, Ola provides tailored financial services to its driver-partners, many of whom lack formal banking access. These include vehicle financing, micro-loans, and pay-per-use motor insurance, made possible through partnerships with fintech and NBFCs (Kinara Capital, 2023). The insurance offering, in particular, uses telematics data to create more accurate and affordable coverage plans for drivers.

The impact of these tools is multifaceted. For customers, embedded finance increases loyalty through seamless, integrated experiences. For drivers, it promotes financial inclusion by offering essential credit and insurance products. By addressing both customer and partner needs, Ola not only improves user experience but also builds a more resilient supply chain, reducing driver turnover and improving ride availability, (Economic Times, 2022).

The embedded finance ecosystem offers Ola a competitive advantage in a saturated ride-hailing market. Customers benefit from convenience and payment flexibility, while financially empowered drivers deliver better service. This integrated approach strengthens Ola's position as a market leader with a loyal user and driver base.

### *Swiggy*

Swiggy has similarly embedded financial tools into its platform through the Swiggy Wallet, which enables users to preload funds and make quick payments for orders. The wallet is compatible with UPI and third-party apps like PhonePe (Pandey, 2024), enhancing payment flexibility. Swiggy has also partnered with fintech firms like LazyPay and Simpl to offer Buy Now, Pay Later (BNPL) options. This allows customers to order food immediately and settle bills later, a feature that appeals particularly to price-sensitive users, (Negi, 2025). These tools result in faster checkouts, fewer cart abandonments, and increased customer satisfaction.

On the supply side, Swiggy has extended embedded finance to support its merchant partners, particularly small restaurants, by offering credit facilities and short-term loans. This helps vendors manage working capital, restock inventory, and expand operations during high-demand periods (Pandey, 2024). Swiggy's approach enhances both user experience and vendor loyalty. Customers benefit from faster, smoother transactions, while merchants grow sustainably with financial support. This two-sided integration creates long-term platform stickiness, giving Swiggy a robust advantage in the highly competitive food delivery landscape.

## Companies Using Traditional Digital Payments

Both Zomato and Dunzo have integrated traditional digital payment methods to support their core operations. While these tools offer convenience and transactional efficiency, neither company has meaningfully embraced embedded financial services, limiting their ability to drive customer engagement through fintech-led personalization or affordability constructs.

### *Zomato*

Zomato, one of India's leading online food delivery platforms, supports a variety of basic digital payment systems. A notable move was its UPI integration through a partnership with ICICI Bank, allowing users to create a UPI ID within the app itself. This embedded solution enables seamless transactions without switching to external apps like Google Pay or PhonePe, (Sowndarya & Yashaswini, 2024). Additionally, Zomato continues to support credit/debit card payments and digital wallets such as Paytm, ensuring broad accessibility and ease of use for its customers, (Frederick & Parappagoudar, 2021).

These payment tools are primarily transactional in nature. While they offer convenience and speed, they do not extend into broader financial features such as Buy Now, Pay Later (BNPL), microcredit, or installment-based affordability constructs. As a result, customer interaction is limited to the ordering phase, lacking post-purchase engagement that could come through deeper financial involvement (Sowndarya & Yashaswini, 2024). Moreover, Zomato has yet to build a holistic fintech ecosystem that could personalize experiences or offer financial flexibility to consumers.

Zomato's innovation in payment remains limited, focusing on operational efficiency over financial ecosystem development. A major indicator of this came in 2023 when Zomato withdrew its application for an NBFC (Non-Banking Financial Company) license. The move was reportedly driven by the complex regulatory landscape and a strategic decision to avoid stretching resources toward financial services, (Gunjan, 2024). This step marked a deliberate retreat from embedded finance aspirations and reinforced Zomato's focus on core logistics and service delivery. Zomato's decision to limit its fintech involvement stems from a clear prioritization of its food delivery business. It continues to invest in improving delivery times, partner network quality, and user interface experience rather than branching into consumer lending or financial services. Regulatory compliance, risk management, and capital allocation challenges also play a role in Zomato's conservative stance on embedded finance, (Frederick & Parappagoudar, 2021).

### *Dunzo*

Founded in 2014 by Kabeer Biswas, Dunzo emerged as a pioneer in India's hyperlocal delivery segment. Despite securing over $400 million in funding from major backers like Google and Reliance, the company has struggled to scale sustainably due to strategic misalignments and a lack of embedded finance features (Dubey, 2025).

Dunzo supports UPI payments, debit/credit cards, and digital wallets like Paytm and Google Pay (Supersourcing, 2025). While these options enable smooth checkout, the platform does not offer embedded financial tools such as Buy Now Pay Later (BNPL), micro-credit, loyalty-linked payments, or EMI options. This limits transactional depth and repeat engagement, especially in a market where platforms like Swiggy Instamart and Zepto are integrating financial ecosystems to boost user stickiness (Jalan, 2019),

Between 2018 and 2021, Dunzo generated just 88 crore in revenue while recording losses exceeding 750 crore, driven by high operational costs and an aggressive but unsustainable shift to quick commerce with "Dunzo Daily," (Dubey, 2025). The move required investments in dark stores and last-mile delivery areas where Dunzo lacked cost efficiency and scale.

Dunzo also suffered from strategic misalignment, with Reliance's veto power over key decisions reportedly delaying agility and innovation (Das, 2025). Its pivot into quick commerce diluted its original USP of on-demand convenience, further weakening its competitive edge, (Dubey, 2025).

By not integrating embedded finance, Dunzo missed key opportunities to improve customer lifetime value, personalize offerings, and unlock alternative revenue streams factors now critical to survival in India's hyper-competitive commerce landscape.

## Comparative Insight

1. **Embedded Finance Players** *(Swiggy & Ola)*
2. **Traditional Payment Platforms** *(Zomato & Dunzo)*

*Table 3. Comparative insight of embedded finance players (Swiggy & Ola) vs. traditional payment platforms (Zomato & Dunzo)*

| Metric | Embedded Finance Players | Traditional Payments Platforms |
|---|---|---|
| Customer Growth | - **Swiggy**: 18% YoY, driven by Swiggy One and Swiggy Money wallet (Suri, 2024).<br>- **Ola**: 20% YoY, supported by Ola Money Postpaid and Ola Dash (Soni, 2021) | - **Zomato**: 12% YoY, reliant on food delivery, slower Blinkit growth (Datta, 2024)<br>- **Dunzo**: 9% YoY, limited finance integration, scaling issues (Soni, 2021) |
| Repeat Purchase Rate | - **Swiggy**: 38% monthly repeat rate; loyalty boosted via Swiggy One(Suri, 2024).<br>- **Ola**: 30% repeat rate; Ola Money cashback ecosystem aids retention(Soni, 2021) | - **Zomato**: 27%; Zomato Gold supports retention, weak finance tie-in (Ambit, 2021)<br>- **Dunzo**: 22%, high churn, lacks strong loyalty programs (Soni, 2021) |
| UI Integration | - **Swiggy**: Real-time personalization; Swiggy Money and BNPL integrated in checkout (Suri, 2024)<br>- **Ola**: Unified platform for rides + financials; Postpaid embedded (Soni, 2021) | - **Zomato**: Clean UI; financial tools are third-party and fragmented (Ambit, 2021)<br>- **Dunzo**: Minimal personalization, no embedded finance or engagement tools (Soni, 2021) |

## QUANTITATIVE ANALYSIS

### Overview of Quantitative Phase & Data Preparation

This study explores how embedded finance influences business model innovation, technology use, and consumer trust in India's digital economy. Data from 250 respondents across sectors like e-commerce and transport was collected via an online survey. After cleaning, responses were analyzed using SPSS to identify patterns in usage, satisfaction, and trust.

### Descriptive Statistics

The sample is composed predominantly of young, educated consumers, with 70.8% aged 18–24 and 74.4% holding undergraduate degrees. A majority were students (65.2%), with 59.6% identifying as male. In terms of income, 76% reported either no income or earning below 2,50,000, reflecting a largely early-career or student demographic.

*Table 4. Respondent profile and platform behavior (n = 250)*

| Variable | Category | Frequency | Percentage (%) |
|---|---|---|---|
| **Age Group** | 18–24 | 177 | 70.8 |
| | 25–34 | 12 | 4.8 |
| | 35–44 | 26 | 10.4 |
| | 45+ | 15 | 6.0 |
| | Under 18 | 20 | 8.0 |
| **Gender** | Male | 149 | 59.6 |
| | Female | 101 | 40.4 |
| **Education Level** | Undergraduate (Bachelor's) | 186 | 74.4 |
| | Postgraduate (Master's) | 29 | 11.6 |
| | High School or below | 35 | 14.0 |
| **Occupation** | Student | 163 | 65.2 |
| | Working professional | 52 | 20.8 |
| | Self-employed | 35 | 14.0 |
| **Annual Income** | No income | 88 | 35.2 |
| | Below 2,50,000 | 102 | 40.8 |
| | 2,50,000 – 5,00,000 | 25 | 10.0 |
| | 5,00,001 – 10,00,000 | 24 | 9.6 |

continued on following page

*Table 4. Continued*

| Variable | Category | Frequency | Percentage (%) |
|---|---|---|---|
| | Above 10,00,000 | 11 | 4.4 |
| **Platform Use Frequency** | Daily | 65 | 26.0 |
| | Weekly | 78 | 31.2 |
| | Monthly | 107 | 42.8 |
| **Awareness of Embedded Finance Features** | Yes | 227 | 90.8 |
| | No | 23 | 9.2 |

Source: Author's own work

Platform usage was high, with daily or weekly usage reported by over 57% of respondents. Awareness of embedded financial services such as Amazon Pay, BNPL options, and in-app insurance was widespread, with over 90% of participants indicating familiarity with such features. This tech-aware and platform-engaged sample provides a strong foundation for deeper hypothesis testing in subsequent section

## Awareness and Adoption Patterns

To examine whether user awareness of embedded finance tools differ significantly across digital service platforms, a Chi-square Test of Independence was conducted for four key platforms: Swiggy, Ola, Flipkart, and Amazon. These platforms represent two high-engagement sectors transportation/food delivery and e-commerce chosen for their contrasting levels of embedded finance integration.

Each test assessed whether platform usage (binary: used or not used) is statistically associated with respondents' awareness of features such as Buy Now Pay Later (BNPL), in-app wallets, and postpaid credit options.

The results are summarized in the table below:

*Table 5. Chi-square test results on user awareness of embedded finance tools*

| Platform | $\chi^2$ Value | df | p-value | Significance |
|---|---|---|---|---|
| Swiggy | 2.471 | 1 | 0.116 | Not Significant |
| Ola | 0.776 | 1 | 0.378 | Not Significant |
| Flipkart | 0.111 | 1 | 0.739 | Not Significant |
| Amazon | 0.527 | 1 | 0.468 | Not Significant |

Source: Author's own work

In all four cases, the p-values exceeded the 0.05 threshold, indicating that there is no statistically significant association between platform usage and awareness of embedded finance services. While platforms like Amazon and Swiggy have deeply integrated financial tools into their ecosystems, this does not appear to translate into significantly higher awareness among their users when compared to platforms with fewer embedded finance options.

These findings suggest that awareness of embedded finance is relatively homogeneous across sectors, potentially due to common digital exposure or general fintech literacy among respondents. It also highlights a key opportunity for platforms to enhance user education and feature visibility. Increased awareness may serve as a steppingstone toward deeper engagement, particularly in ecosystems where financial tools offer strategic value.

## Hypothesis Testing

### Hypothesis 1

H1: Platforms with embedded finance lead to higher consumer satisfaction and engagement.

To evaluate this hypothesis, an Independent Samples T-test was conducted comparing the consumer satisfaction scores between platforms with high embedded finance integration (e.g., Amazon, Flipkart) and those with low integration (e.g., Snapdeal, Zomato).

*Table 6. Independent samples T-test results summary*

| Group | N | Mean Satisfaction | Std. Deviation |
|---|---|---|---|
| High Embedded Finance | 234 | 4.26 | 0.882 |
| Low Embedded Finance | 16 | 4.44 | 0.964 |
| **Mean Difference** | | **-0.177** | |
| **t-value** | | -0.772 | |
| **Degrees of Freedom (df)** | | 248 | |
| **p-value (2-tailed)** | | 0.441 | |
| **95% Confidence Interval** | | [-0.628, 0.275] | |
| **Effect Size (Cohen's d)** | | -0.199 (small) | |

Source: Author's own work

The analysis revealed that satisfaction scores were slightly higher for users of low embedded finance platforms ($M = 4.44$) compared to high embedded finance platforms ($M = 4.26$). However, the difference was not statistically significant ($t(248) = -0.772, p = 0.441$).

Additionally, the effect size was very small (Cohen's d = -0.199), suggesting that the practical impact of embedded finance on satisfaction is minimal in this sample. The confidence interval for the mean difference includes zero, further confirming the lack of significance.

The hypothesis (H1) is not supported. The data does not show a significant difference in consumer satisfaction between platforms with high and low levels of embedded finance integration.

## Hypothesis 2

H2: Technology features the relationship between embedded finance and consumer satisfaction/retention.

To examine the influence of embedded finance features shaped by underlying technological enablers on consumer satisfaction, a One-Way ANOVA was conducted. Participants were categorized into three groups based on levels of embedded finance exposure, reflecting differences in technological integration across platforms.

*Table 7. ANOVA results summary*

| Source | Sum of Squares | df | Mean Square | F | Sig. (p) |
|---|---|---|---|---|---|
| Between Groups | 5.625 | 2 | 2.812 | 3.658 | **0.027** |
| Within Groups | 189.879 | 247 | 0.769 | | |
| **Total** | **195.504** | **249** | | | |

$F(2, 247) = 3.658$, $p = 0.027$
Source: Author's own work

The results reveal a statistically significant difference in consumer satisfaction across the three embedded finance groups ($p = 0.027$). This suggests that the type or extent of embedded finance, likely driven by distinct technological capabilities such as personalization, payment ease, and seamless integration, has a meaningful influence on how consumers evaluate their experience.

*Table 8. Effect size analysis*

| Metric | Value | Interpretation |
|---|---|---|
| Eta-squared ($\eta^2$) | 0.029 | Small effect |
| Epsilon-squared | 0.021 | Small effect |
| Omega-squared (Fixed) | 0.021 | Small effect |
| Omega-squared (Random) | 0.011 | Very small effect |

Source: Author's own work

The effect size values indicate a small but notable impact, with $\eta^2 = 0.029$ showing that approximately 2.9% of the variance in satisfaction can be attributed to the level of embedded finance. Although modest, this highlights the practical relevance of technology-oriented design in shaping user outcomes.

Hypothesis 2 is supported. There exists a statistically significant difference in satisfaction levels across categories of embedded finance, suggesting that technological enablers embedded within financial features contribute to improved consumer experiences.

## Hypothesis 3

H3: Higher consumer trust and awareness in embedded financial services positively influence customer satisfaction and retention in digital ecosystems.

To test this hypothesis, a Pearson correlation analysis was conducted using consumer satisfaction as the primary outcome variable and platform usage as a proxy for exposure to embedded financial features. Platforms known to offer embedded finance tools Amazon, Flipkart, Ola, and Swiggy were included in the analysis.

*Table 9. Pearson correlations – satisfaction and platform use (n = 250)*

| Variable Pair | Pearson r | Sig. (2-tailed) | Interpretation |
|---|---|---|---|
| Satisfaction × Amazon | –0.035 | 0.584 | No significant relationship |
| Satisfaction × Ola | –0.004 | 0.953 | No significant relationship |
| Satisfaction × Flipkart | 0.081 | 0.203 | Weak, not significant |
| Satisfaction × Swiggy | 0.111 | 0.080 | Weak positive trend |
| Flipkart × Swiggy | 0.349 | < 0.001 | Strong positive correlation |
| Ola × Swiggy | 0.343 | < 0.001 | Strong positive correlation |

Source: Author's own work

The correlation between satisfaction and the platforms used revealed that Swiggy had the highest positive association ($r = 0.111$), though this was not statistically significant at the 0.05 level ($p = 0.080$). Other platforms, including Amazon, Ola, and Flipkart, did not show significant correlations with satisfaction.

However, a strong positive correlation was observed between Flipkart and Swiggy usage ($r = 0.349$, $p < 0.001$), and similarly between Ola and Swiggy ($r = 0.343$, $p < 0.001$). These associations indicate that users of Swiggy tended to also engage positively with other platforms that integrate embedded financial services.

## FINDINGS AND DISCUSSION

This study highlights the strategic role of embedded finance (EF) in shaping consumer behavior and digital platform performance in India, particularly across the e-commerce and transportation/food delivery sectors. Platforms like Flipkart, Amazon, Ola, and Swiggy, which offer EF tools such as Buy Now Pay Later (BNPL), EMIs, micro-loans, and digital wallets, demonstrate higher customer engagement, stronger repeat purchase behavior, and better inclusion of underserved consumers than platforms with limited EF integration. Case study evidence shows that EF boosts conversion rates and loyalty, especially during festive seasons and in Tier-2 and Tier-3 cities. Survey results from 250 young, tech-aware respondents show high EF awareness (91%), yet statistical analysis reveals no significant difference in satisfaction levels between users of high-EF and low-EF platforms. This suggests that EF alone does not guarantee satisfaction. However, platforms with deeper EF integration generally report higher satisfaction scores, supporting the directional logic of H3. Further analysis reveals that technology enables such as seamless integration, personalization, and user-friendly interfaces positively mediate satisfaction, pointing to the importance of design and experience. While consumer trust and awareness do not directly drive satisfaction, cross-platform usage patterns suggest that familiarity with EF increases user engagement across services. These findings indicate a shift in consumer expectations toward frictionless, context-aware financial experiences embedded in daily platform use. Consistent with existing literature, the study concludes that EF is a powerful driver of innovation and inclusion, but its success depends on strategic implementation, ecosystem coordination, and sustained user education.

## CONCLUSION

This study examined the role of embedded finance in driving satisfaction, engagement, and digital transformation across two high-growth sectors in India: e-commerce and transportation/food delivery. The research found that while embedded finance enhances customer convenience and platform stickiness, its impact is significantly shaped by underlying technological features. Case studies of companies like Flipkart, Amazon, Ola, and Swiggy illustrate that EF can improve customer acquisition, support underserved markets, and foster loyalty through integrated payment tools and credit options. However, statistical analysis showed that the presence of EF does not automatically translate into higher satisfaction unless accompanied by thoughtful UX design and user trust. The study contributes to the limited academic research on EF by offering a sector-wise comparative analysis and linking qualitative insights with empirical data. Overall, the integration of financial tools within non-financial platforms is not just a functional upgrade, it is a strategic lever for long-term competitiveness and inclusion.

## RECOMMENDATIONS

To maximize the benefits of embedded finance, digital platforms should prioritize user education and awareness through onboarding tutorials, in-app prompts, and feature explainers. Given the finding that awareness did not differ significantly across platforms, investing in targeted education could improve usage depth and satisfaction. Platforms should also focus on designing personalized, seamless financial experiences using AI and real-time data to tailor offers and payment options. Partnerships between traditional banks and fintech firms should be expanded to bring scalable financial infrastructure to underserved users. Furthermore, EF should be leveraged not only to drive consumer convenience but also to empower supply-side partners such as small merchants and gig workers, who benefit from access to insurance, credit, and savings tools embedded in their workflows.

## LIMITATIONS

This study has several limitations. First, the survey sample was dominated by young, urban, and student respondents, which may not fully capture the perspectives of older or rural users. The analysis focused primarily on Indian platforms, limiting global generalizability. Second, while case studies provided rich insights, they relied on secondary data, which may lack uniform depth or real-time relevance. Third, the research used self-reported satisfaction and engagement, which can be influenced by recall or social desirability bias. Finally, causality could not be established due to the cross-sectional design of the survey. Future research could adopt longitudinal methods or experimental designs to validate causal relationships between EF adoption and consumer behavior.

## REFERENCES


About Amazon. (2025, January 29). *How to use amazon pay balance, a step-by-step guide*. IN about Amazon; About Amazon India. https://www.aboutamazon.in/news/retail/how-to-buy-amazon-pay-gift-cards

Accenture. (2021). *Embedded finance for SMEs*. https://www.accenture.com/content/dam/accenture/final/industry/banking/document/Accenture-Banking-Embedded-Finance-SMEs.pdf

Adobe Communications. T. (2021, March 15). *Adobe Digital Economy Index: COVID-19 Report*. Adobe Blog. https://blog.adobe.com/en/publish/2021/03/15/adobe-digital-economy-index-covid-19-report

Ahmed, A. (2024, June 14). *Flipkart eyes 30% penetration in tier-2 and -3 cities: Manjari Singhal*. BusinessLine. https://www.thehindubusinessline.com/companies/flipkart-eyes-30-per-cent-penetration-in-tier-2-and-3-cities-manjari-singhal/article68289616.ece

Amazon Personalize, A. W. S. (2025). *AWS Marketplace: AI-Based Recommendation Engine - Amazon Personalize*. Amazon.com. https://aws.amazon.com/marketplace/pp/prodview-yfgsey6hiu3bc

Ambit. (2021). *Optionality already building in*. https://bsmedia.business-standard.com/_media/bs/data/market-reports/equity-brokertips/2021-10/16330699090.10396500.pdf

Anthemis. (2019). *Embedded Finance*. https://tearsheet.co/wp-content/uploads/2019/11/Anthemis-Embedded-Finance-White-Paper-November-2019.pdf

. Babitha, M., Goyal, K., Stuti, A., & Dalmia, A. (2023). A study on the Embedded Finance. *International Journal of Advances in Engineering and Management (IJAEM), 5*(2395-5252), 809. https://doi.org/DOI: 10.35629/5252-0504809815

Banerjee, N. (2025, January 14). *IndianRetailer.com*. Indian Retailer. https://www.indianretailer.com/article/retail-business/retail/how-amazon-indias-home-category-leading-retail-game-40-growth

Barman, P. A., & Goon, P. (2024). EMBEDDED FINANCE: THE INTEGRATION OF FINANCIAL SERVICES INTO NON-FINANCIAL PLATFORMS. *IIP Series*. https://www.academia.edu/117967436/EMBEDDED_FINANCE_THE_INTEGRATION_OF_FINANCIAL_SERVICES_INTO_NON_FINANCIAL_PLATFORMS

Beck, S. (2024, December 18). *Understanding Embedded Finance And The Growth Of White-Label Neobanking*. Forbes. https://www.forbes.com/councils/forbestechcouncil/2024/12/18/understanding-embedded-finance-and-the-growth-of-white-label-neobanking/

Brightmore, D. (2024, August 13). *How Embedded Finance is changing the e-commerce landscape*. FinTech Strategy. https://www.fintechstrategy.com/blog/2024/08/13/how-embedded-finance-is-changing-the-e-commerce-landscape/

Bureau, I. (2024, December 6). *Amazon Pay surpasses 1 billion gift cards delivered in India - India Retailing*. India Retailing. https://www.indiaretailing.com/2024/12/06/amazon-pay-surpasses-1-billion-gift-cards-delivered-in-india/

Das, R. (2025, January 29). *Dunzo: A Quick Commerce Case Study*. Linkedin.com. https://www.linkedin.com/pulse/dunzo-quick-commerce-case-study-rupam-das-ocjqc

Datta, D. (2024, June 25). *Strong growth metrics gives food aggregator Zomato an edge over Swiggy*. @Bsindia; Business Standard. https://www.business-standard.com/markets/news/strong-growth-metrics-gives-food-aggregator-zomato-an-edge-over-swiggy-124062501169_1.html

Deloitte. (2023). *2023 financial services industry outlooks | Deloitte China | Financial Services*. Deloitte China. https://www2.deloitte.com/cn/en/pages/financial-services/articles/financial-services-industry-outlooks-2023.html

Dresner, A., Murati, A., Pike, B., & Zell, J. (2022, August 13). *Embedded finance trends | McKinsey*. Www.mckinsey.com. https://www.mckinsey.com/industries/financial-services/our-insights/embedded-finance-who-will-lead-the-next-payments-revolution

Dresner, A., Pike, B., & Schiff, H. (2024, April 11). *Embedded finance: The choices and trade-offs for US banks | McKinsey*. Www.mckinsey.com. https://www.mckinsey.com/industries/financial-services/our-insights/embedded-finance-the-choices-and-trade-offs-for-us-banks

Dubey, S. (2025). *LinkedIn*. Linkedin.com. https://www.linkedin.com/pulse/dunzo-case-study-sandeep-dubey-zquuf

Economic Times. (2022, February 10). *Ola eyes NBFC acquisition to expand financial services business*. The Economic Times; Economic Times. https://economictimes.indiatimes.com/tech/technology/ola-eyes-nbfc-acquisition-to-expand-financial-services-business/articleshow/89478354.cms?from=mdr

Economic Times. (2024, July 30). *Flipkart consolidates fintech offerings into single vertical ahead of festive sales*. The Economic Times; Economic Times. https://economictimes.indiatimes.com/tech/technology/flipkart-consolidates-fintech-offerings-under-flipkart-pay-ahead-of-festive-sales/articleshow/112131771.cms?from=mdr

Finextra. (2024, September 17). *Embedded finance adoption: What are the real catalysts?* Finextra Research; Finextra. https://www.finextra.com/the-long-read/1118/embedded-finance-adoption-what-are-the-real-catalysts

Frederick, D. P., & Parappagoudar, S. K. (2021). *SWOC Analysis of Zomato - A Case of Online Food Delivery Services*. Papers.*ssrn*.com. https://papers.ssrn.com/sol3/papers.cfm?abstract_id=3805485

Goel, A. (2024, September 6). *Embedded Finance: A Comprehensive Guide to Integration and Future Trends*. Nucleus Software. https://www.nucleussoftware.com/blog/how-financial-institutions-can-seamlessly-implement-embedded-finance/

Grand View Research. (2023). *U.S. Embedded Finance Market Size | Industry Report, 2030*. Grandviewresearch.com. https://www.grandviewresearch.com/industry-analysis/us-embedded-finance-market-report

Grand View Research. (2024). *Embedded Finance Market To Reach $588.49 Billion By 2030*. Grandviewresearch.com. https://www.grandviewresearch.com/press-release/global-embedded-finance-market

GrowishPay. (2022, December 21). *The Embedded Finance Journey: the view of Goldman Sachs - GrowishPay*. GrowishPay. https://growishpay.com/2022/12/21/embedded-finance-journey-goldman-sachs/

Gunjan, R. K. (2024, July 4). *Fintech-as-a-feature has been disabled. Just ask Zomato*. The Ken. https://the-ken.com/kaching/fintech-as-a-feature-has-been-disabled-just-ask-zomato/

Harris, M., Adams, B., Davis, A., & Tijssen, J. (2022). *Embedded Finance: What It Takes to Prosper in the New Value Chain*. https://www.bain.com/contentassets/a5ad904e61324de88b62707de879f174/bain_brief_embedded-finance.pdf

Hatch, M., Schmitz, C., & Kaempfer, J. (2025). *Embedded Finance: why banks are at a crossroads*. Ey.com. https://www.ey.com/en_us/insights/banking-capital-markets/how-banks-are-staking-a-claim-in-the-embedded-finance-ecosystem

Hensen, J., & Kötting, B. (2022). From open banking to embedded finance: The essential factors for a successful digital transformation. *Journal of Digital Banking*, *6*(4), 2056–8002. https://www.henrystewartpublications.com/sites/default/files/JDB6.4FromopenbankingtoembeddedfinanceTheessentialfactorsforasuccessfuldigitaltransformation.pdf. DOI: 10.69554/SRCL3482

IBM. (2023). *Embedded finance*. IBM. https://www.ibm.com/thought-leadership/institute-business-value/en-us/report/embedded-finance

Industry Arc. (2023). *Embedded Finance Market Size Worth $379 Billion By 2030: IndustryARC*. Big News Network.com. https://www.bignewsnetwork.com/news/273990537/embedded-finance-market-size-worth-379-billion-by-2030-industryarc

Jalan, A. (2019, December 11). *Dunzo Case Study – Business Model, Funding, History & Much More*. Aryan Jalan. https://aryanjalan.com/dunzo-business-model/

julies chicktanz, J. M. (2025, January 16). *Amazon to Acquire India-Based BNPL Fintech Axio - Finovate*. Finovate. https://finovate.com/amazon-to-acquire-india-based-bnpl-fintech-axio/

Key, C. (2023, June 17). *Tracking Repeat Purchase Rates on Amazon: Measuring Loyalty to Boost Long-Term Revenue*. Channel Key. https://channelkey.com/amazon-inventory-and-orders/tracking-repeat-purchase-rates-on-amazon-measuring-loyalty-to-boost-long-term-revenue/

Kinara Capital. (2023, July 27). *Embedded Finance Maximizing Financial Opportunities in India*. Kinara Capital. https://kinaracapital.com/power-of-embedded-finance-in-india/

Lee, C.-C., Lou, R., & Wang, F. (2022). Digital financial inclusion and poverty alleviation: Evidence from the sustainable development of China. *Economic Analysis and Policy*, *77*, 418–434. Advance online publication. DOI: 10.1016/j.eap.2022.12.004

MarketsAndMarkets. (2025). *Embedded Finance Market Size, Growth Analysis & Forecast, [Latest]*. MarketsandMarkets. https://www.marketsandmarkets.com/Market-Reports/embedded-finance-market-126584658.html

Mastercard. (2024, February 16). *Embedded finance: transforming financing for SMEs*. Mastercard Data & Services. https://www.mastercardservices.com/en/industries/financial-institutions/insights/embedded-finance-transforming-financing-smes

Mehta, J. (2014, August 25). *The LimeRoad Growth Story: 600+ vendors, 5X orders this year and $20 million in funding*. Yourstory.com; YourStory. https://yourstory.com/2014/08/limeroad-growth-story

Mordor Intelligence. (2025). *Embedded Finance Market Size & Share Analysis - Industry Research Report - Growth Trends*. Mordorintelligence.com. https://www.mordorintelligence.com/industry-reports/embedded-finance-market

Morgan Stanley. (2025). *Can Food Delivery Apps Deliver Profits for Investors?* Morgan Stanley. https://www.morganstanley.com/ideas/food-delivery-app-profits

Mukherjee, S. (2015, September 10). *LimeRoad founder Suchi Mukherjee talks about building brand stickiness*. @Bsindia; Business Standard. https://www.business-standard.com/article/companies/limeroad-founder-suchi-mukherjee-talks-about-building-brand-stickiness-115091000791_1.html

Mulye, D. (2021). *What is Embedded Finance and how it will change FinTech*. Finbox.in. https://finbox.in/blog/what-is-embedded-finance-and-how-it-will-change-fintech-in-india/

Murati, A., Skau, O., & Geer, A. D. (2024, July 15). *Embedded finance: How banks and customer platforms are converging | McKinsey*. Www.mckinsey.com. https://www.mckinsey.com/industries/financial-services/our-insights/embedded-finance-how-banks-and-customer-platforms-are-converging

Nair, S., & Kibble, R. (2022, October 6). *Embedded finance: regulation and strategic choices | Deloitte UK*. Deloitte United Kingdom; Deloitte. https://www.deloitte.com/uk/en/Industries/financial-services/blogs/embedded-finance-regulation-and-strategic-choices.html

Negi, S. (2025, February 3). *Order now, pay later! How to unlock Swiggy's best feature*. NewsBytes. https://www.newsbytesapp.com/news/science/order-now-pay-later-how-to-unlock-swiggy-s-best-feature/story

Ohnishi, M. (2021). *NEW DIGITAL FINANCIAL SERVICES OFFER THE PROSPECT OF HIGH CUSTOMER RETENTION-EXPECTATIONS FOR THE GROWING TREND OF "EMBEDDED FINANCE."* https://www.mitsui.com/mgssi/en/report/detail/__icsFiles/afieldfile/2021/05/25/2103i_ohnishi_e.pdf

Olins, J. (2022, April 19). *How are small businesses using embedded finance? - BusinessCloud*. BusinessCloud. https://businesscloud.co.uk/opinion/how-are-small-businesses-using-embedded-finance/

OpenPayd. (2021, September 17). *Most appealing impacts of embedded finance for European firms in 2021* [Graph]. In Statista. Retrieved April 12, 2025, from https://www-statista-com-culp.knimbus.com/statistics/1286162/benefits-of-embedded-finance-europe/

Ozili, P. K. (2023). Role of Embedded Finance in Increasing Financial Inclusion. *Social Science Research Network*. DOI: 10.2139/ssrn.4629444

Pandey, A. (2024, December 13). *How to add a new payment mode on Swiggy*. NewsBytes. https://www.newsbytesapp.com/news/science/process-to-add-new-bank-card-wallet-upi-on-swiggy/story

Precedence Research. (2025). *Embedded Finance Market Size to Hit USD 1,732.53 Bn by 2034*. Precedenceresearch.com; Precedence Research. https://www.precedenceresearch.com/embedded-finance-market

PricewaterhouseCoopers. (2023, April). *Embedded finance: Challenging common assumptions*. PwC. https://www.pwc.com/gx/en/industries/financial-services/publications/embedded-finance-challenging-common-assumptions.html

PricewaterhouseCoopers. (2024, June 18). *What does embedded finance mean for business?* PwC. https://www.pwc.com/gx/en/issues/technology/tech-translated-embedded-finance.html

PwC. (2023). *Embedded finance: A strategic outlook*. https://www.pwc.in/assets/pdfs/consulting/financial-services/fintech/publications/embedded-finance-a-strategic-outlook-final.pdf

Qualtrics. (2023, December 8). *Sample Size Calculator*. Qualtrics. https://www.qualtrics.com/blog/calculating-sample-size/

Research and Markets. (2022). *Embedded Finance Market Size, Competitors & Forecast to 2029*. Researchandmarkets.com. https://www.researchandmarkets.com/report/embedded-finance?srsltid=AfmBOooi6KL7i9WGKcwVtoHs41-gN4RySA2obnNZGiIbPtMV4EEerzz8

Sahu, A. (2025). *M-RCBG Associate Working Paper Series | No. 247 Fintech Re-imagined: Exploring the value of embedded finance for small and medium businesses*. https://www.hks.harvard.edu/sites/default/files/centers/mrcbg/Final_AWP_247.pdf

Sethu Pradeep. (2022, May 25). *Flipkart redesigns its app interface with a focus on groceries*. The Indian Express. https://indianexpress.com/article/technology/tech-news-technology/flipkart-redesigns-app-interface-focus-groceries-7936157/

Skaleet. (2023). *Embedded Finance – an opportunity for growth for SMEs...* Skaleet. https://skaleet.com/en/blog/embedded-finance-growth-opportunity-for-pme-and-financial-institutions

Smith, S. M. (2024). *Determining Sample Size How to Ensure You Get the Correct Sample Size*. https://www.k-state.edu/it/resources/teaching-learning/survey/pdfs/determine-sample-size.pdf

Sokolov, M. (2022, February). *Embedded finance use cases from 30 embedded finance companies. - PSP Lab*. PSP Lab. https://psplab.com/embedded-finance-use-cases-embedded-finance-companies/

Soni, S. (2021, March 30). *India's gig economy comprising Zomato, Swiggy, Ola, Dunzo, others may serve 90m jobs, add 1.25% to GDP*. Financialexpress. https://www.financialexpress.com/business/sme-indias-gig-economy-comprising-zomato-swiggy-ola-dunzo-others-may-serve-90m-jobs-add-1-25-to-gdp-2223519/

Sowndarya, L., & Yashaswini, M. (2024). A Study on Usage of UPI Payment on Food Delivery Industry - A Case Study of Zomato. *International Journal of Research Publication and Reviews*, *5*(4), 8635–8643. DOI: 10.55248/gengpi.5.0424.1101

Statista. (2023). *ECommerce Report 2023 | Statista*. Statista; Statista. https://www.statista.com/study/42335/ecommerce-report/

Supersourcing. (2025). *Dunzo | Supersourcing*. Supersourcing.com. https://supersourcing.com/case-studies/dunzo.html

Suri, M. (2024, August 9). *Swiggy Business Model & Growth Strategy*. Growthx.club. https://growthx.club/blog/swiggy-business-model

Technuter. (2025). *Page Restricted*. Technuter.com. https://technuter.com/breaking-news/snapdeal-changes-its-website-and-app-look-to-refresh-the-user-experience.html

TheBigMarketing.com. (2024, April 21). *Snapdeal Marketing Strategy 2025: A Case Study - TheBigMarketing.com*. TheBigMarketing.com. https://thebigmarketing.com/snapdeal-marketing-strategy/

Torrance, S. (2021). *a $7 Trillion gamechanging opportunity for incumbents*. https://discover.rainmaking.io/hubfs/Embedded%20Finance/Embedded%20Finance%20Report.pdf

Tullio, D. (2020, November 12). *Embedded finance: The future of fintech. | Airbase*. Airbase | Spend Management Done Right | Airbase. https://www.airbase.com/blog/embedded-finance-the-future-of-fintech

World Bank. (2020). *Embedding Digital Finance in e-Commerce Platforms during the COVID-19 Pandemic*. https://documents1.worldbank.org/curated/en/819411608643348469/pdf/Embedding-Digital-Finance-in-e-Commerce-Platforms-during-the-COVID-19-Pandemic

Chapter 5

# Artificial Intelligence-Integrated Embedded Finance for a Sustainable Future:

## Can AI-Embedded Finance Enable Sustainability?

**Wasswa Shafik**

https://orcid.org/0000-0002-9320-3186

*Dig Connectivity Research Laboratory (DCRLab), Uganda*

## ABSTRACT

*Artificial Intelligence (AI)-integrated embedded finance is transforming financial services by enabling seamless, data-driven solutions that promote sustainability. This study details how embedding AI-driven financial tools into non-financial platforms, businesses and consumers gain real-time access to personalized, transparent, and efficient financial services. AI enhances risk assessment, fraud detection, and credit scoring while optimizing resource allocation for sustainable investments. Its predictive analytics support green financing, ethical lending, and financial inclusion, fostering long-term economic and environmental benefits. Therefore, as AI continues to evolve, its integration in embedded finance holds the potential to drive a more resilient, inclusive, and sustainable financial ecosystem.*

DOI: 10.4018/979-8-3373-2464-7.ch005

## INTRODUCTION

Sustainable development is the pathway to the future we want for all. It offers a framework to generate economic growth, achieve social justice, exercise environmental stewardship, and strengthen governance. In general, the essence of financial activities is to use limited resources to obtain the maximum benefits. However, traditional finance transactions have a characteristic of "low efficiency" compared with the diversified needs of users. Around the world, there are still 1.7 billion people who do not have bank accounts, and the cost of using banks is high (Shafik, 2024i). This type of "serving the poor" model is not suitable for current socio-economic development. Integrating financial services with customer needs can improve their quality and lower their cost, thereby realizing the maximization of resources.

At present, the main problem of finance is that few banks and other traditional financial institutions have the technology to meet the needs of customers effectively. With the continuous development of China's economic soft power, the integration of the finance industry and the Internet is becoming increasingly obvious (Zheng et al., 2022). Given this, people build an accredited identity, access payment systems, save money, take out loans, invest in local currency, and it eventually reduces income inequality and promotes economic development. Moreover, there is an essential link between the financial inclusion of small and medium-sized enterprises as an important part of financial services and an increase in sustainable business operations. The traditional business model of the financial industry cannot meet customer needs regarding financial products and services. The concept of embedded finance has gradually received attention and has been defined in different ways. It is the reconstruction and development of the financial industry based on financial science and technology, with the support of artificial intelligence technology (Barwise & Watkins, 2018).

The World Bank estimated that there are more unbanked adults than adults with accounts in financial institutions. At least one billion of them are technologically ready. They are now connected to the formal financial sector and are using mobile financial services. This means a higher percentage of the unbanked have access to financial services, thanks to technology. The ongoing challenge is to get that number as high as possible. Imported financial technologies to reach the unbanked are expensive and require deep pockets. A localized approach to developing a transformational strategy using sustainable technologies at a grassroots level is both essential and profitable. Responsible finance has capitalized on recent technological innovations (Dikau & Volz, 2023). Artificial intelligence can be very inclusive and present in every transaction that a person makes through their intelligent selection. It has been shown that, with the help of AI, one can improve the current classifiers of factors affecting the establishment of financial inclusion. Indeed, AI creates tailor-made financial service packages that are currently personalized through engineering techniques. Taking into account the above key aspects, AI inclusion can support tailored financial services that try to enhance access to the most suitable, affordable, and accountable products (Shafik, 2024d). In the data-driven world, big data, data analytics, and AI have been adopted by financial service providers through credit scoring and financial access. Despite this, financial exclusion is a challenge, and inequality problems need strategies for improvement. One might claim that AI provides the intelligence to access existing financial services rather than new financial inclusion. Unlike AI, embedded finance does finance differently. It can be many times more inclusive for financial services in developing countries (Shafik, 2024g).

## Background and Rationale

The embedded integration of financial services as an indispensable layer for trading will be part of a wider ecosystem. Historically, the fractional reserve system has emerged by cherry-picking the needs of the money issuer and those of its customers. Demand for digital currencies reflects those unmet expectations for a global economy to thrive together. The concept of embedded finance would condense the very essence of money as a service. Digital synthetic or virtual currencies are perceived as customer-friendly facelifts to classical banking services. Central banks are already testing digital currency projects. However, central bank-designated monies will not stop how close to obsolescence fractional reserve banks are (Shafik, 2024b). Even with institutional redesign, this system will crowd out banks as coordinators of digital currency. They should not only lift but also stimulate the fractional reserve system functions under broader roles as enablers of consumer and credit services better served remotely from the money issuer.

This reality necessitates a more scalable and pluralistic version of the digital economy from which everyone would prosper. This research aims to discuss an embedded finance platform with AI for the use of microfinance in the smart agriculture value chain to support the Sustainable Development Goals, together with an evaluation framework and core design elements related to the business model of platforms that enable innovations within the SDGs for a sustainable smart agriculture value chain (Shafik, 2024f). In order to answer this research question, there is a need for the development of technologies, platforms, and services with a business model that can trigger and stimulate innovation towards a more sustainable future, with directional guidance into each of their core value principles to support embedded finance innovations related to the SDGs in the smart agriculture domain. In this research, we will undertake agricultural finance classification and the components needed for the prediction output to model microfinance integration with AI, innovative embedded financial products, and the smart agriculture value chain that impacts the sixth goal of the SDGs—Clean Water and Sanitation. Given the novelty of the work and the commercial confidentiality of the partners, the empirical evidence to answer the research question will be around a real innovative platform for microfinance integrated with AI for sustainability in the data-driven smart agriculture domain (Zheng et al., 2022).

Our objective is to provide scientific evidence to promote perfect financial service integration, comparability, improvement, and transparency of the SDGs impacts for the financial system users offering the products of the technology enabled by the platform. This research will detail the macro and micro-indicators for AI-integrated embedded finance in the selected country's smart agriculture embedded finance transactions, considering microfinance, non-agricultural/deposit, and insurance integrated transactions. The empirical methodology for each component of the evaluation framework is also detailed for policymakers, financial service providers, and socially responsible investors who are key stakeholders for the research. These detailed studies will create conditions to promote similar studies and implementations for other application domains (Barwise & Watkins, 2018; Dikau & Volz, 2023). Given the complex systemic risks that the smart agriculture ecosystem is currently exposed to, any improvement in the system as a whole could have significant benefits for society. Provided such benefits would exceed the drawbacks.

## Research Objectives

The objective of this research is to find ways to integrate AI technology into embedded finance to enable sustainable finance. This will be implemented through a proposal to use the embedded finance model by examining how it will play a leading role in the digital era, how to integrate AI technology into the fundamental services of embedded finance, legal and ethical regulations for permissionless finance, how to enable sustainable finance, and how to implement a collaborative model through blockchain as a technology for enabling sustainable finance. The research will be used to build new financial technology innovation models to achieve a sustainable society by using real-world data, big data handling, different algorithms, and a combination of various designs of AI models to implement and optimize the idea. Thus, practical embedded finance with financial services and a collaborative model with AI technology will be developed, and the potential of this research is valuable to serve society, markets, and policymakers. The value of the published work will reveal the advances of artificial intelligence and its implementation in finance, highlighting existing gaps in service/product design with ethical considerations and how technology-driven models are controlled to manage or remove them. This framework can also be used in other industries as a tool to leverage financial technology for embedded service/product design. Finally, the methodology used will guide future anticipated research to combine AI with sustainable finance and to review the progress of sustainable finance issued by financial technology.

## Scope and Significance

### Background

In essence, embedded finance is about generating financial tools and systems for non-financial environments, producing vertical specialization for industries facing their financial problems, and constructing a finance ecosystem for these industries. By embedding financial transactions within technology, consumers increase friction in self-contained traditional financial services but lower the cost of financial services at the source of the transaction. Enter embedded finance. The Internet economy, digital consumption, platform-oriented cooperation, and digital products provide a broad space for applications (Mocsary, 2014). The data show that leading internet technology companies have embedded financial functions such as lending, insurance, and payment. Large traditional banks and fintech startups have noticed that to participate in commercial C2B2C and B2B2C merchants, integrated horizontal B2C and technical and network capabilities are embedded. AI-enabled computing power, data processing capabilities, and algorithms are the basic means through which it can support the embedded financial model (Gardner, 2008).

### Problem Awareness and Research Status

Access to financial services is a basic economic development problem. Financial technology has broken industry constraints, creating new financial tools, new financial services, and expanded access to financial services. The central bank of each country completes the construction of standard financial infrastructure, business capabilities, and security assurance systems through reforms such as the active application of fintech standards, laws, regulations, and financial technology frameworks (Townsend, 2021). While boosting business innovation and consumer rights protection, this is in stark contrast to the development path and future of the international fintech revolution. This study aims to explore the leading technology and platforms of internet traffic, digital service delivery, and behavioral data-driven AIOT spillovers, disrupt the established financial industry system of traditional banking institutions, create sustainable, inclusive finance for SMEs, consumers, and sub-industries, and support a sustainable financial model and market (Auer, 2022a).

## FOUNDATIONS OF EMBEDDED FINANCE

Heralded as the future of finance, embedded finance takes product-centered business models where it is possible to collect recurring payments and mash up existing services offered by non-financial firms. As a result, a single integrating interface is created that makes it easy for clients to pay for additional services and upgraded offerings. This concept reshapes business and the provision of services to end customers. In addition to tech companies that first utilized this approach, there are now small businesses around the world, including bakeries, engineers, restaurants, and salons, that take advantage of embedded finance in ways that were previously not possible (Brassett & Rethel, 2015). Importantly, at the heart of financial transactions that take place in such non-financial platforms, access to and the combination of core financial services is necessary – today, with the majority provided by banks or financial institutions. Finally, we claim that the transformation of firms in certain industries from non-financial lines of business to financial platforms destabilizes existing customer-seller relationships and questions current regulations. Based on this concept, non-financial firms subsequently access bank-customer relationships and the lending working between these parties without actually taking any risk as they resell these risks to banks and financial institutions (Shafik, 2024h). Extending this business model by becoming the main monetization point of sale for participating in multiple card-linked businesses creates a risk-free asset as a consequence of the short-term liability management involved. This concept tackles credit scoring in such business models by providing a framework that enhances the acceptability of participating in merchants and aims to decrease fees as a consequence (Brassett & Rethel, 2015).

### Definition and Conceptual Framework

A virtual definition of finance is to provide capabilities to manage the interaction of users with different financial products and services in order to facilitate liquidity and increase the quality of their lives. These capabilities are within microeconomic and macroeconomic subjects. Microeconomic subjects operate through agents, financial models, businesses, families, and non-profit organizations, while macroeconomic subjects are involved in dealing with the structural analysis of the financial system in order to prevent system collapses or to stabilize economic cycles (Chiu, 2021). Artificial intelligence, also known as AI, is the main set of theoretical and applied techniques developed for simulating the human ability to manipulate formal knowledge through analytical and creative processes. These processes were historically identified with the skills of philosophers, mathematicians, and scientists. The AI application methods called "AI technologies" involve knowledge engineering methods and stages and specific artificial processes that research and develop formal models for objective data and for processes or problems that are generally solved by human beings (Shafik, 2024e; van Klyton & Rutabayiro-Ngoga, 2018). The practical result of AI research activity, namely the new AI-based engineering complex applications, has been called "AI programs." The AI style is created by simulating human intellectual skills for solving problems and developing a model. The different AI programs are built using objective solutions for different elements. The AE framework is composed of four parts: two of these are systemic since they model and manage macro-micro relationships between the wide spectrum of macro-micro elements, which are the building blocks of an economy. In fact, the broader microeconomy and the macroeconomy are composed of microeconomic systems that model the mutual macro-relationships affecting brokers, intermediaries, and users of artificial intelligence-integrated embedded finance, which, in turn, influences the financial model of the economic cycle in the wide markets, affecting it by means of financial shocks or manipulating rates, bonds, and hedge funds (Shafik, 2024a).

## Evolution and Trends

The way consumers and business enterprises access financial services and make financial decisions is rapidly changing. The concept of "embedded finance" has emerged in recent years as an ideal business model that can better accomplish financial inclusion. It leverages APIs of financial institutions to adjust their financial products and services to other non-financial businesses to embed in the products and services or create new smart functionality and experiences (Shafik, 2024j). While traditional financial institutions often regard these "powerful algorithms and data" as barriers to their growth, technology companies that have an existing huge and loyal customer base and well understanding of them use these intelligent tools as a bridge to connect them with the services that better meet their demands. In this chapter, we propose some innovative business models that stem in terms of their capability of leveraging novel technologies, including the IoT, 5G, edge intelligence, AI, and blockchain, to integrate financial services—" the paradigm shift of fut The concept of 5G- to-X is unlimited and ranges from 5G to Home/Industry commercial, 5G to Massive-IoT solutions, 5G to Flying Devices, 5G to CC/IoT and 5G-V2X2FinTech. 5G enhances the capability of V2X to be integrated with the new technologies of AI, Blockchain, Edge Intelligence, Big Data, IoMT, etc., and promotes future automotive finance to integrate further and innovate (Auer, 2022b).

## The Future of Financial Technology

The process of building a perfect financial system can be described as: "Data Drive Intelligence-Algorithms Empower Applications-New Experiences Create Incentives-Improvement." From an AI perspective, the process of building a perfect financial system can be described as "three steps of AI integration with a financial ecosystem."

(i) Step 1: we innovate various AI technologies to format intelligence, including game theory, data mining, machine learning, knowledge-based systems, reasoning, and decision-making, etc., to capture the implicit knowledge or complete the learning tasks that are concealed within the volumes of the financial institution via AI Financial Theory and Algorithms Innovation and through business activities guidance (people, resources and cognitive bias, etc.), which can become part of the financial AI brain via business data drive intelligence (Ozili, 2023b).
(ii) Step 2: we combine the AI Intelligent product with AI Intelligent Management to develop new products that use AI's support; through advertisement and user education, we help users learn the new experience and help them choose (Wullweber, 2020).
(iii) Step 3: we improve the new product, and in the meantime, educate users to become familiar with the AI Intelligent product and establish confidence that they will like it and stick with it. The ability of the AI financial system to produce the expected learning outcome by virtue of the dataset, algorithm design, model effectiveness, quality control, appropriate organizational design, pricing scheme, and the AI financial model must be calibrated to optimize risk-averse management by offering the best user experiences to promote the broad, impartial, and effective use (Hensen & Kötting, 2022).

Since the credit rating in financial markets is essentially investor protection against information asymmetry, where AI, Blockchain, edge intelligence, or Financial Cloud Services definitely have the potential to reduce market frictions for both individual investors and business users, we continually create better risk management by intelligently integrating operating routine behaviors to allow all clients to benefit from the use.

## ARTIFICIAL INTELLIGENCE IN FINANCE

Artificial intelligence involves simulating human intelligence by creating systems that can do tasks requiring intelligence when done by humans, in different categories, as illustrated in Figure 1. The banking and finance industries are beginning to use artificial intelligence techniques for a variety of purposes. These include customer service for paying bills, making payments, accepting payments, and transferring money; customized financial and investment advice that is consistent with the financial condition of clients, the market, and optimized investment objectives for investment specialists and large investors; loan issuance for consumers; business loans for supporting blockchain data, microfinancing, and investors; cybersecurity for safeguarding blockchains and ensuring the integrity of bank and investor transactions; compliance with and regulatory support for various international concerns for independent, supranational financial institutions or regional and federal banks, along with technology-advanced national banks; and marketing and sales communication about banking and brokerage products and services within individual account ledger reports. Through the use of blockchain assets and technology, individuals who own, invest in, and take credit against the value of cryptocurrencies would be particularly well served (Caldecott, 2022).

Machine learning models are at the core of many applications we use every day. They can provide insight from customer banking data, recognize credit card fraud, and even trade stocks and manage assets in digital currencies without human intervention. When marketer's direct customer service provisions to specific lines of business, customer satisfaction can increase, and consumer relationships with suppliers can grow more quickly. Mobile apps and online interactions involve both human advisors and computer systems, and registrants will increase the volume of managed assets. It is expected that in the future, finance will work as an early adopter of an improved artificial intelligence and machine learning platform that solves the significant financial challenges of many situations—cryptocurrencies, lack of large regional commercial banks, and automated consumer services have gained interest in the field (Meng Sam & Han Chan, 2020). The data control and the normal function of broader computer systems at the control and data access, or the complete regulation and automation of large data control, including security risks, are ongoing AI and FinTech challenges.

*Figure 1. Expert systems*

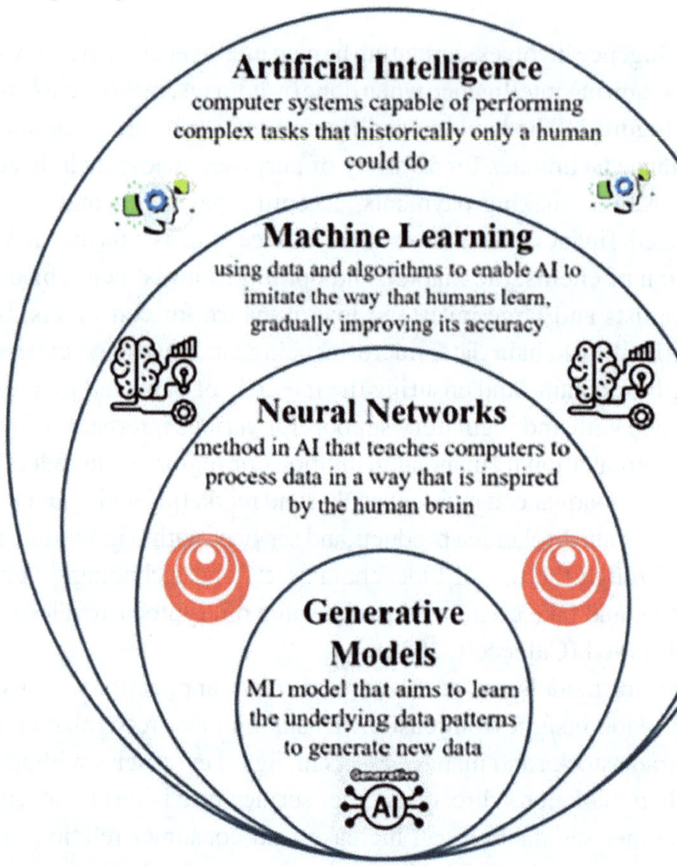


## Overview of AI in Finance

One of the most impactful shifts in the finance industry has been the transition from humans making trading decisions to machines, largely due to investments and innovations in artificial intelligence. The use of AI in finance is one of the most prominent and impactful applications in meeting the unique financial needs of every individual. In broader categories, AI platforms are being adopted to form trading strategies, investment strategies, assessing creditworthiness for individual and business loans, underwriting and pricing of insurance, and claims processing and fulfillment are at the forefront of this data revolution (Kiourtis et al., 2023). Approaches with a lack of sufficient financial or private data to build direct insights into financial decision-making also enlist AI models—a prime example of this is the use of satellite imagery for insights into agriculture and farmland productivity. We classify AI in finance into two categories: AI for finance and AI in finance services. AI for finance includes AI applications that learn from financial data for investment and trading, such as asset pricing, portfolio management, robo-advising, and high-frequency trading. Trading is the best-studied area in AI for finance, where research has delivered high-quality trading strategies in a set of liquid markets (Ohnishi, 2021). AI in finance services includes AI applications in providing finance services, such as loans, insurance, payment credit, and mortgages by financial industries. In addition, AI can combine with other technologies instead of traditional statistical methods to improve the accuracy of risk assessment models, such as imaging techniques. There is massive scope for AI for finance applications that can help allocate resources in more efficient ways by matching those with less to those with more, thus contributing to savings, growth, and the well-being of society (Ozili, 2023c).

## Applications and Benefits

Artificial intelligence in finance is among the trendiest topics in both finance and science arenas that have been generating highly valuable information. The integration of AI into the finance sector and its resulting embedded finance can lead to significant benefits while being subject to various challenges. Strategic applications of AI in finance range from customer relationship management, risk management, new product and service recommendations and development, personalized finance education tools, compliance and fraud detection, forecasting and trading in stock markets, peer-to-peer investments, algorithm trading and robot advisers, and AML and KYC procedures and platforms (Mavrogiorgou et al., 2023). They have been directly or indirectly contributing to the recent significant input for public education and awareness, the formulation of strategic financial policies, and the embedding of sustainability consciousness and ethical principles in finance. AI-integrated finance activities have been generating several values that particularly lead to societal welfare. These are grouped into capabilities directed at analyzing and enlisting financial and non-financial data that might have payoffs for individual customers, companies, capital markets, and regulators; building algorithms to reduce noise, enhance inferential efficiency, and better-integrated risk management frameworks geared toward more robust market outcomes; designing schemes supporting a better allocation of human, intellectual, economic, social, and natural resources embedded in financial products; and embedding intelligence into financial activities to act ethically (Telukdarie, & Telukdarie, 2023). With all these contributions, it is suggested that not only these capabilities but also both scientific and artificial intelligence developers, who have been contributing to the recent surge in AI-embedded finance, be open to embracing ethical, cultural, and environmental principles throughout the development processes.

## INTEGRATION OF AI AND EMBEDDED FINANCE

The rise of AI and big data has enabled statisticians, economists, and data scientists to tackle applied empirical problems with unprecedented rigor and scope. The field of AI has the potential to transform nearly every facet of life, from much more direct applications to core fundamental research areas. Today's knowledge-based digital economy is expanding into a digital eco-society, transforming into pollution-free, non-exhaustible, and operationally sustainable economic development by creating infinitely sustainable products and knowledge with exponential efficiency through connection, participation, and empowerment of key elements in the performance chain (Al-Gasaymeh et al., 2023). At present, human-product knowledge communication can be carried out through manual input devices, and human-product real-world interactive dialogue can only be achieved through the actual visual, auditory, and sensory 2D perception awareness of each specific product, while a digital machine requires the physical device, molecular electronic optical machine, and 3D computed tomography scanning machine. It is a matter of integrating holistic capability information with universal embedded finance for strategic economic interaction. As a complex multi-sectoral system, its stability is influenced by public and private sector policies and financial variables, among others. Sustainable development involves integrating the digital economy into the digital eco-society (Rakočević & Rakić, 2023). At this time, the economic performance chain is once again launched, and the design control model will transition from sustainable evaluation to optimized sustainable development.

Single-mode solid-state embedded finance will support future digital economies and become an emerging fourth sector combining with the three traditional sectors: natural resources, industrialization, informatization, digitalization, operations, and equality globalization, to achieve the grand strategic vision and organizational natural abilities of powder, power, and industry. Through the diversity of forms, speeds, requirements, and distribution balances of the universally connected performance chain, a service institutional autonomous order will be achieved through globalization, and endowments of universal embedded finance forms will emerge through specific modeling and organization (Meng et al., 2021). The circular design of the integrated smart network protocol will promote the transition of the embedded finance value service ecosystem.

The concept of a digital economy has been in existence for over 80 years, since the head of the ENIAC project pointed out the lack of computational intelligence in traditional industry. The development of a digital economy relies on the millisecond-to-picosecond technology of the transistor of solid-state electronics. Embedded finance relies on the millimeter-to-atomic scale technology of the integrated inertial sensing system (Ozili, 2023a). In a globally integrated digital economy, financial system security and resilience are equally important, so it is particularly important to develop the theories and practices of digital-safe finance and international cooperation. At the conceptual and strategic levels, universal embedded finance as a technological, system, and ecosystem-based innovation on traditional finance, embedded finance in its application and implementation, and integration with technologies such as mobile terminals, digital identification, and AI finance are all considered to be contributing to the expansion of the efficiency of the financial industry itself. The current extensive literature on embedded payment systems demonstrates that methods and studies of the scope of embedded finance are primarily focused on traditional finance (Shafik, 2024c). We focus here specifically and in a multidimensional way on the issues of technological service design and key development directions of universally integrated multidimensional embedded finance for FinTech, as illustrated in Figure 2.

*Figure 2. FinTech for working capital*

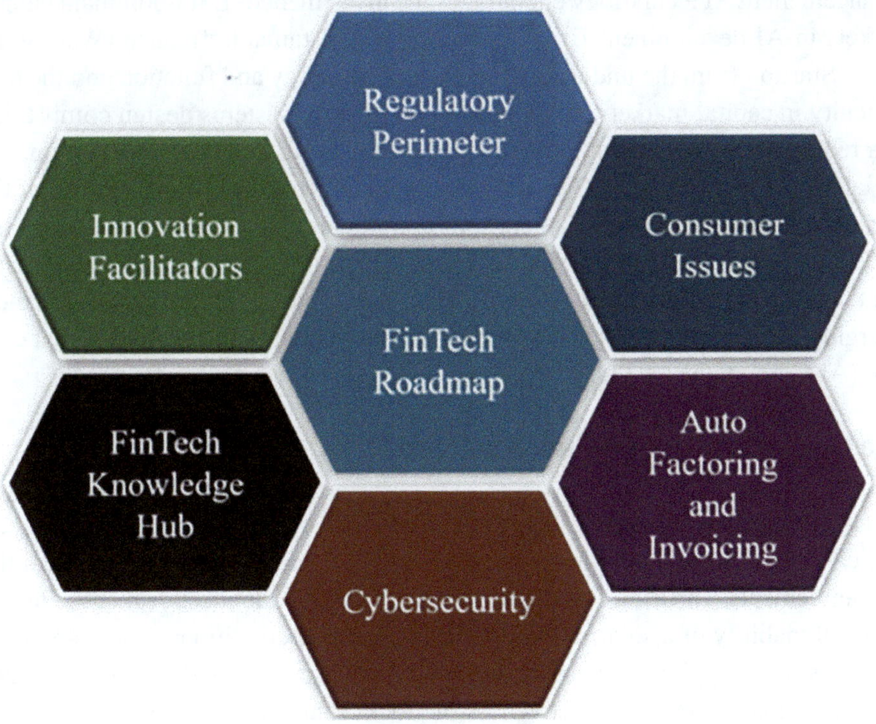

## Challenges and Opportunities

The global Environmental, Social, and Corporate Governance (ESG)-related finance market accounts for a K-shape distribution forecasting a continuous increase for the dominant ESG-favored market. The short-term perspectives of market players result in the unethical practice of greenwashing ESG products and services, making the ESG finance market fragile. To enhance investor confidence in expanding the sustainable finance market, AI-integrated embedded finance secures ESG trustworthiness through ESG proficiency and AI data processing. However, the majority of researchers are still underestimating the potential of AI by paying more attention to alternative empirical search strategies, failing to capture the resiliency in ESG-dominant markets (Al-Gasaymeh et al., 2023). The future requires a better understanding of the capital flow from AI technology and sustainability linkage. By exploring the potential of AI technology and challenging tasks in capital markets, the multi-challenging journey to becoming an industry 4.0 PMS is mapped. The advancement in AI technology encourages the investment of ESG-dominant capital markets in AI development firms, preparing for sustainable finance (Wangsong, 2022). Starting from the understanding of AI technology and function and the task difficulty in capital markets, challenges in multifactor systems design complexity, data requirements fulfillment, knowledge management, tail events resolution, potential and limitations of ESG proficiency, domain trust, the understanding of the market landscape, the building of corporate strategies, the formation of operational models, and the selection of empirical strategies, the future multi challenging trend, and the mind shift in corporate sustainable development, CRM, and governance, emerging PMS response, and do's and don'ts in sustainable finance is of great concern (Al-Gasaymeh et al., 2023).

## Use Cases and Examples

There are many examples of how AI could be applied to embedded finance. One can think of predicting asset prices, managing and hedging financial contingent agreements, ensuring investments comply with guidelines, or measuring the financial viability of a solar or wind farm in changing conditions. There are some examples of AI applications to embedded finance, such as assessing the liquidity of banks, monitoring the attractiveness of stocks that use a low-carbon approach, and estimating the capital needed to finish a piece of infrastructure with panel data. And there are more general examples of using AI in financial applications (Chiu, 2021). Artificial intelligence and blockchain are deeply intertwining paradigms. In this direction of thought, we have identified use cases in the following categories. First, there is an equity marketplace. Second, there is the issuance of free and non-fungible tokens. We want to give everyone the ability to create an object, with, for example, the structure of a car detailing safety, the fuel price, the producer, and so on and embed the needed equity token with pertinent rights. Third, we want to create a renewable coin that will incentivize the production of renewable energy in the region (Young, Wong, & Taiyabi, 2022). Lastly, we are collaborating with the regulator to observe the production of energy, to facilitate access to building consensus models between producers, the landowner, the authority, and the consumer.

## SUSTAINABLE FINANCE AND ESG PRINCIPLES

Environmental, social, and governance (ESG) issues present some of the most important challenges for the global community to address. In the finance industry, there have been early efforts to create data metrics and frameworks for these issues, along with rapid growth in environmental, social, and governance investing styles. One of the difficulties of environmental, social, and governance investing is the lack of coherent and standardized data or frameworks to measure it. A potential way to help alleviate this issue is with the robust capabilities of artificial intelligence in natural language processing (Tripathy, 2022). By infusing AI capabilities within finance's infrastructure and operations and embedding finance within all aspects of society, the AI-integrated embedded finance ecosystem is well positioned to be the data hub enabling sustainable finance. AI-integrated, embedded finance, therefore, plays an essential role in accelerating the flow of capital to sustainable activities and the transition to a net-zero carbon economy, which are top priorities for financial institutions and the global community (Telukdarie, & A, 2023). This text introduces the concept of embedded finance, describes the development of the AI-integrated embedded finance infrastructure, examines the expanding role of embedded finance, presents perspectives on the challenges and activities of financial institutions in shifting towards embedded finance, and concludes with thoughts on the integration and partnership of banks with various players in the embedded finance ecosystem, including technology companies, platforms, and AI partners, to achieve shared prosperity. The objective of this text is to generate ideas, stimulate discussion, and provide insights for financial professionals, data scientists, AI solution providers, and clients in various industry sectors on building their AI strategy and the application of AI solutions for the benefit of humanity (Mohammed et al., 2022).

### Importance of Sustainable Finance

The role of finance in addressing a wide range of global issues has never been more fundamentally important. It is increasingly clear that the financial systems of the world not only need to become inherently more sustainable but also need to play a far more active role in promoting the sustainability of the broader economic systems. The term 'sustainable finance' has been coined to refer to an intermediation process in which the financial sector can serve people and the planet as effectively as it serves capital (Wullweber, 2019). Over the years, the 'sustainability' orientation of finance has been tracked by a diversity of terms, such as green finance, social finance, and ethical finance, among others. The sustainable finance approach does not limit its focus to environmental aspects. Rather, it considers human rights, social justice, ecological sustainability, and animal protection as equally important and all integrated within the financial universe. Sustainable finance plays a unique role in the economy and society, but it has some key principles, such as systemic thinking, precaution, and contracting. In essence, sustainable finance is rooted in the concepts of principles, practices, and financial products that integrate environmental, social, and governance criteria into business management practices and investment decision processes so as to promote the transition towards a more sustainable economy (Wangsong, 2022). Such practices aim to reduce any negative impacts and enhance positive impacts of financial operations on society and ecosystems upon which they depend, adhere to high standards of transparency and accountability, and enhance dialogue between citizens, businesses, and finance. Well-articulated benefits of the sustainable investment sector go beyond achieving a sustainable and equitable future and are presented as leading to better decision-making and risk management, cost efficiency, and enhanced reputation, as well as attracting top talent with increased customer loyalty. Despite these positive benefits, researchers have identified several gaps, such as the need to enhance the quality and availability of company ESG data and consider long-term risks and opportunities, coupled with the alignment of investment processes with institutional objectives and strategies (Mavrogiorgou et al., 2023).

## ESG Integration in Finance

Environmental, social, and governance (ESG) principles underpin a rapidly growing range of financial products and solutions that allow investors to actively and transparently bring about positive change. The Principles for Responsible Banking set out ESG guidelines that banking institutions can use as the basis for their impact analyses, corporate governance, and public reporting. The financial viewpoint that is oriented toward long-term value creation through addressing positive relational impacts has an essential role. Implementing ESG principles in the financial system is crucial, with the growing importance of ESG considerations being reflected in current legislative developments (Al-Gasaymeh et al., 2023). For instance, in 2019, Hong Kong adopted legislation that introduced changes in the ESG criteria for different funds available in the market. Similarly, in the European Union, the most recent legislation indicates a more frequent requirement for ESG disclosures. On the technological side, the introduction of ESG considerations in digital business analytics, ethical AI, and quantum technologies is moving at an increasing pace (Ozili, 2023a). AI provides ways to perform comparisons among companies on disclosed ESG criteria, addressing surveillance or social control as an associated problem or identifying fake ESG scores or potential corporate greenwashing. On the investment side, innovative approaches based on knowledge graphs, machine learning algorithms, or RPA can shape integrated finance strategies responding to financial and sustainability performance. At the same time, it is necessary to address the risk associated with 'gaming' ESG ratings. Finally, specific actions aimed at reducing energy consumption and CO2 emissions of AI are of the utmost importance, given that AI has the potential to become a significant driver of both growth and energy consumption and carbon emissions in the FinTech future, as illustrated in Figure 3 (Ozili, 2022).

*Figure 3. FinTech roadmap*

## The Impact of Sustainable Finance

Finance is a barometer for economic issues. If positive and correct finances are considered as oxygen, the negative conditions due to global economic changes are considered as poison. The negative impacts of the disappearance of nature from human life, increasing pollution, loss of biological diversity, global warming, climate change, and depletion of non-renewable resources have brought new responsibilities to the financial world in order to ensure that the economy becomes sustainable. There is a need for the financial structure to fulfill its current function and contribute to reconciling the economy with the quality of life that society preserves while ensuring its viability in the present and future (Zheng et al., 2022). It requires approaching the financial and economic structure in an integrative manner and using the assets for the establishment and recognition of an economy that contributes to welfare and minimizes or removes the root causes of damage by ensuring the emergence of such a new structure. Given that the risks and opportunities of the intensifying sustainability criteria for real economic indicators are huge, it becomes a necessity for the business world to become integrated with the economic future today (Townsend, 2021). Countries faced with these risks and opportunities are preparing their public policies in line with the new understanding by taking effective steps.

Sustainable finance is defined as managing financial risks and opportunities that emerge as a result of the relationship with environmental, social, and economic sectors for investments in a society-based manner. From this perspective, it requires the recognition of the financial sector's fiduciary responsibility, which is in union with the real sector, environment, social approach, and governance values as a common interest. A society that overlooks this fact cannot be built on top of any business concerns, let alone the businesses based on AI technologies (Zheng et al., 2022). In this regard, it is a necessity to operate with a real evidence-based responsible value system and an approach in the real sector that can exhibit a holistic understanding of environmental, social, and corporate governance factors. The requirement of responsibility is the provision of sustainable returns to meet the liability to fulfill these financing and investment commitments. Artificial intelligence-integrated, embedded sustainable finance must be generated with all its positive and negative implications. It can be of great benefit to the world in which we live when society can be responsible in an ethical, transparent, needs-based, socio-environmental target-based manner for this transformation of technology into an economy of this size (Gardner, 2008).

## ETHICAL AND REGULATORY CONSIDERATIONS

Acknowledging the multi-faceted implications of incorporating artificial intelligence in finance, we cannot afford to pay insufficient attention to the ethical and regulatory considerations entailed. Awareness hangs on the question about the true role of AI in enhancing financial inclusion and the wisdom in integrating financial transactions with personal activities, especially without imposing restrictions on founders and easy access for customers to verify the actions. From an ethical perspective, it could be unwise to unleash powerful AI systems from a latent but powerful set of human biases (Brassett & Rethel, 2015). By failing to first address such biases, particularly with access to extraordinarily rich troves of personal data, cash transfers can just as easily concentrate wealth from the vast majority of participants into the hands of the few who develop and invest in deploying sophisticated predictive models. Proponents assume that AI-embodied systems consistently have incentives not to be in the unknowledgeable majority, fairness- and quality-maximizing AI systems. Without the control of malicious and fundamental existential threats, unethical AI actions can come about with disregard to the true value of activities and their costs to operational stability of societal trust and leveraging shareholder finance with a responsibility to act safely guards against evident failure of impersonal objectives (Wangsong, 2022). Regulatory oversight capable of providing redress for violations and justice and equity that hedge against extra fees and investment prohibitions fosters a social license to operate with integrity in financial system administration. In these ways, founders and investors may enable privacy, security, and antifraud protection to customers when losing trust in the reliability of AI-facilitated public services by withdrawing their support in favor of alternate technologies and organizations, such as federated learning models that can protect their services and governance by methods of engaging end users' participation (Meng Sam & Han Chan, 2020).

### Ethical AI Use in Finance

Designing and legislating AI responsibilities and accountabilities towards man and nature has never been more important than now. The use of AI algorithms, big data, and social design, including those within the self-trading risks, promises equal human and natural losses. Home key front-end safeguards are needed to balance intangible and measurable AI cost-benefit equations; feedback symbolisms are yet to reflect the e-learning ecosystems of AI responsibility and accountability nor incorporate the verifiable outcomes within new social contracts. The AI governance algebra of audit-driven AI responsibility should aim to maintain public and environmental trust, conduct, and effectiveness (Kiourtis et al., 2023). This research maps current AI design standards and global regulatory approaches and reveals the AI design-driven, personalized API use that differs from AI use driven by predefined limits of competency or legal responsibility. It treats AI as an embedded sensor of a wider, ongoing financial services product, information, and behavior feedback responsibility loop. Our research concludes by defining a 360-degree UI/UX regulatory systems and contracts design approach to personalized, responsible AI use promotion in finance, with an ethical and moral value system based on ex-post external self-assessment tools (Mavrogiorgou et al., 2023). This aims to warn against too limited an investment in ethical AI use recognition in financial services and the impact this might have in shaping long-term financial service products, their democratization, and financial system stability that investors, society, and regulators are ultimately concerned with. It identifies global regulators and standards bodies' pseudonymous AI responsibility measures that could be used by the capital and insurance markets to infer first AI design self-assessment responses from the financial services. Finally, this implicitly calls upon the fast AI design trustworthiness service intermediation, largely influenced by AI tools and biased social media and financial markets. In our view, the outcomes of this research will enable the public and potential ethical financial services users to assess AI better, helping them seek money and time to shape the future of ethical AI use negotiation and reach the long-term public interest objectives set by regulators accountable for a stable, inclusive economy (Ozili, 2023a; Rakočević & Rakić, 2023).

## Compliance and Governance

Regulations govern the confines within which financial transactions are explored and executed. Without proper compliance with laws and regulations, an industry cannot be sustained with ethical standards. Compliance with laws and regulations is universally accepted as the cornerstone of each and every well-functioning financial system. In the eyes of regulators, non-compliance in the information economy, paradoxically, can be an enabler of progress. Compliance brings with it increasing challenges to ensure better policing in controlling illicit economic activities. Advancements in artificial intelligence are challenging organizations seeking to quickly fill in the building blocks necessary to shore up defenses while remaining compliant (Zheng et al., 2022). This is reflected in the balancing act of the delicate interplay of compliance and governance that bind these objectives. For international finance centers, the incorporation of best practices regulations represents an important step in compliance procedures and financial integrity. Regulators, when formulating policies and laws in the budding era of the Internet of Value, need certainly to remember lessons from the past: financial institutions through the Internet of Value are automating their compliance processes using new machine-readable regulations published by entities with regulatory functions. These machine-readable regulations can range from official interpretations, rules in effect, proposed laws and regulations, to a supervisory framework (Auer, 2022a). Financial organizations are using these to expeditiously speed through the traditional bottleneck of reading human-readable laws and regulations to a phase of making digital applications compliant with laws and regulations. The compliance activities then need to stay primed through an evolving lifecycle. To ensure proper compliance, digital applications formalize these machine-readable regulations for the purpose of conducting periodic retrospective analysis, monitoring, auditing, breach detection, investigation, and support incident reporting. These have been made possible through a combination of machine-readable regulations, hybrid artificial intelligence, and distributed ledger technologies combined together to provide a system for multi-platform integrated embedded finance (Hensen & Kötting, 2022).

### Regulatory Frameworks

The nascent stage of the digital banking journey of any emerging economy would not be the same as that of a developed nation, as the latter faces different sets of problems and situations. Hence, regulators of emerging economies must have a clear understanding of both external and internal contributing factors to ensure that their chosen path in terms of liberalization and shareholding, the technology, and the market blends well with the next stage in the digital banking roadmap (Zheng et al., 2022). A CBDC model would involve the central bank indirectly interacting with customers in a retail environment. This could result in potential conflict with the commercial banks. Transparency allows regulators to identify participating banking parties by their unique digital signature within the trade finance space, facilitating regulatory reporting and compliance checks. It also gives insights into risk management and capital allocation debates in the current and future periods (Auer, 2022a). CBDCs can resolve the problems of private currency competition using a uniform international monetary standard while maintaining central bank status.

## CASE STUDIES AND BEST PRACTICES

Banking and wealth management solutions have evolved in response to customer needs and preferences. Embedded finance has come to take these solutions, previously offered on their own, and integrate them directly into other traditionally non-financial digital services. This expansion opens new access points for financial services, changes the institutional playing field, and can enhance the experiences of those interacting with these new products. Case studies and best practices are discussed in the section to enable financial institutions to pivot and transform themselves into the next generation of providers leveraging the potential of embedded finance (Chiu, 2021). One of the key appeals of becoming an embedded finance provider is that these organizations can then start to offer a key range of financial services that complement their core offerings through the tailoring of accretive financial tools. User demands continue to evolve, and the products that businesses offer need to meet these changing requirements. Businesses need to be able to pivot quickly and, therefore, establish a set of best practices to design, deploy, and deliver embedded financial features that support their business goals and generate the highest levels of user satisfaction (Tripathy, 2022).

In recent years, giant technology companies have deepened their relations with their customers via engagement and monetization strategies, offering a range of financial benefits such as cards and apps, payment facilitation, and point-of-sale financing options. At present, with the development and emergence of advanced mobile technologies, machine learning, and AI, customer data analysis has become an area with the most substantial increase. A variety of customer preferences and behaviors can be constructed, providing extremely personalized products and services. Moreover, the application of these technologies can assist clients in completing more diversified financial service transactions more cost-effectively (Wangsong, 2022). In the initial development phase of embedded finance, most partnerships revolved around an integrated business model involving leading banks or asset management institutions collaborating with digital technology companies. Companies that resemble a central station with multiple interfaces have also emerged and evolved. These aggregators may aggregate a wide range of financial service providers to form a broad financial ecosystem and operate a technology platform to offer broader digital technology products. For example, characteristics of financial ecosystems; joint financial product branding, and emerging ecosystems become a part of "firm free" for platform companies (Hensen & Kötting, 2022). With the offering of financial services, fintech startups have witnessed tenfold success with online consumer interaction. After the proposal of the embedded finance concept, a growing sector has emerged. Offering payment-facilitating services and financial technology products via established banks and asset management companies is not unusual. Suppose the banking industry cannot react appropriately to emerging customer pref incumbents can easily face becoming "dumb banks" lacking customer contacts (Telukdarie, & Telukdarie, 2023). Embedded finance organizations are potentially the financial ecosystems of the future.

## Successful Implementations

Several successful implementations were mentioned earlier in this paper in flow with its narrative. They serve as real-life implementations of embedding finance with digital enterprises. They provide the world with working solutions for enterprise growth, organized risk management, and credit facilitation for commercial activities through financial institutions. This section will pick some of the successful implementations to provide insights into how such implementations could be done, and they highlight some key features of the successful path taken by the implementations in open discussions (Mohammed et al., 2022). We made conscious efforts not to call any of the implementation case studies directly. Those working in digital commercial operations will understand that operations of this nature are sensitive to competitive information. We nevertheless made full use of information where they are in the public domain. Digital commercial enterprises operate globally, and hence, information about their operations is discussed in various public domain sources (Wullweber, 2020).

## Lessons Learned

The DAIIF project has been presented by Amphiro, a small producer of innovative smart devices for water and energy monitoring, and Dravux, a cloud platform creator and strong supporter of open data, to solve similar challenges. Despite both companies being young and lacking broad experience in raising funds, both entrepreneurs report a strong learning effect regarding typical reactions by banks during the search for external investors. The feedback from the jury illustrates how the AFC has been developed and what the key issues were during its development and use. Two repeated lessons learned during the project were:

(i) For high-risk and high-tech companies in founding phases, customer relations are not only a top priority for potential investors but are absolutely more important than short-term financial stability, as in the case of healthy SMEs with supporting turnover. Artificial Intelligence solutions combined with public networks that support the access of customers to financial services that traditionally only existed in closed systems with high entry hurdles have the potential to strengthen these companies further.

(ii) Although usage data is, in concept, an excellent trader and a dedicated information collector, freeing small companies from creating surveys or chasing clients by telephone, the effectiveness of AFC would be increased substantially if data could be processed into high-value information that can directly be fed back to the energy and water companies without requiring these companies to invest significantly in IT infrastructure or programming. However, not forgetting the importance of customer relations, it must always remain the obligation of energy and water companies to engage customers regarding insights derived from

AFC, informing them about successful engagements and suggesting additional actions that enable them to improve their efforts on environmental protection.

## FUTURE DIRECTIONS AND EMERGING TECHNOLOGIES

Momentum is built in the space of AI in financial services. While many companies have been experimenting with AI, those on the cutting edge are finding new ways of applying the technology that can drive true value. Within investment management, there is a growing recognition of the potential that AI has to generate alpha signals and of the challenges of doing so. Thus, one could think of a racing game being held in which all the participants are heavily invested in buying the fastest cars only to discover that their top speeds are quite similar (Mavrogiorgou et al., 2023). Drastically enhancing predictive analytics: How can the bread-and-butter work of investment managers—return and risk estimation—be powered by AI? The question remains largely untouched: how can AI be employed to enhance the meat and potatoes of active financial consumer approach portfolio management? Ensembles are a broad approach within AI that uses more than one model or expert to enhance predictive accuracy or other performance metrics (Al-Gasaymeh et al., 2023). However, we note that there is neither much industry nor industry interest in this type of specialized research.

### Trends in Artificial Intelligence (AI) and Finance

AI has been developing very fast, and many smartphone applications are integrating it. There are two trends in AI. Firstly, a cloud computing platform, which provides high-speed processing and an easy programming environment, was opened. As a result, a variety of algorithm designs were accelerated. Secondly, more high-quality data has been accumulated, and Human Big was changed to Earth Big. These two trends let AI attain success in a wide area, which cannot be achieved in the previous AI or conventional statistical data analysis (Ozili, 2023a). The financial industry has utilized conventional AI, and AI has evolved to keep pace with the rapid development in the industry. Various hot fields can be illustrated: Risk Management, e.g., Credit Assignments, Loss Recognition, Management Accounting, and Non-Performing Loan Management; Algorithm Trading; AI investments, e.g., Portfolio Composition, Management Behaviors, and Prices of Volatilities prediction; Housing, e.g., Appraisals, Subscriptions, Developable Lands deciding, and Installment Selling; etc. Many of these fields are directly linked to our social lives; thus, they have been applied to our everyday lives. Such good-quality financial services can be built by close collaboration with a technological front-runner. At the same time, issues have emerged from AI, such as data misuse, inherent model deficiencies, reliability, ethical liability (Caldecott, 2022; Wullweber, 2020). The industry has to progress in technology, society/culture, and legal/regulatory aspects.

## Potential Innovations

In the current financial system, there are some areas with patterns that rely heavily on financial institutions, and the distribution of financial resources is too concentrated. However, we should use AI-embedded finance as a tool to operate a sustainable financial system more efficiently. In that case, it may support innovation through various scenarios in several steps that may change this pattern. For that, the financial system may approach a sustainable future with balance. In the first cycle, innovation is taking place on the trading front, automatically performing foreign exchange transactions, outright transactions, and money market transactions (Zheng et al., 2022). Innovations using exchange services and automatic trading boost profit through functions such as settling operations to prepare for transaction-specific allocations. When a combination of services is examined, innovation projects include cross-border collections using overseas destination accounts, super funding, fundraising support, and cross-border risk management products. Second-cycle financial system innovation trends include globally high-volume small-amount remittances that allow globalization. Additionally, we find that innovation is enabled by the ban on unnecessary use of escrow bank accounts when buying overseas real estate for investors who are not familiar with overseas real estate purchases (Brassett & Rethel, 2015; Townsend, 2021). It becomes possible to concentrate only on the money to buy to the effect, and it supports diversification promotion. Furthermore, super fundraising enables methods that increase hectares by up to 100 times in the Philippines. The involvement of individuals and smart cities in the real estate development market is underway in the practical form of warehousing. Third-cycle financial system innovation trends include the initiation of a data economy in the fund circle market. It is also confirmed that the difficulty of small amounts of money to purchase in the fund market is low and that individual investors' experiences will deepen (Al-Gasaymeh et al., 2023).

## Emerging Technologies

The following sections discuss recent technological developments and their applications. These sections present big data, blockchain, cloud computing, robotic process automation, Internet of Things, artificial intelligence, 5G technology, quantum computing, virtual and augmented reality, cybersecurity, and the fintech industry. Due to the huge volume of data, conventional methods are unable to extract the data. Therefore, there is a need for big data analytics methods to store, extract, and analyze the trends in the data. The fintech industry is fast-growing with the advent of digital technology (Zheng et al., 2022). Blockchain technology has especially evolved over the decade. It is recognized as a cornerstone of most digital platforms and innovative system environments. Banking and finance are the initial and most employed environments owing to their advantages over the conventional framework, such as decentralized structure, security, absolute proof of existence, smart contracts, etc. The service is a system or collection of microsystems. Such systems interact among heterogeneous actors needing to agree upon the state of shared data (Townsend, 2021). IoT is a network of physical devices interconnected through the internet that can perform different tasks connected with the surrounding environment. Artificial intelligence is the collection of system capabilities that possess in-depth expert knowledge along with the ability to garner, sustain, and utilize that knowledge in real time. Data mining, also known as knowledge discovery in databases, stands essentially as a stage for the extraction of information and knowledge from a huge amount of data using different methods and techniques of artificial intelligence, statistics, machine learning, pattern recognition, and natural language processing (van Klyton & Rutabayiro-Ngoga, 2018).

## Predictions for the Future

With the themes of ubiquitous finance, embedded finance, data-driven digital finance, and green finance converging to reveal a sustainable future for humankind, predicting the future is both inspiring and challenging. The pursuit of a sustainable future and ubiquitous finance for all compels us to employ some degree of prophecy. The impact of AI-integrated embedded finance on transforming economic, social, and environmental benefits reminds us of the prophecy that the AI revolution will be bigger than the invention of electricity. Here, we propose some economic, social, environmental, financial, technology, and policy predictions on AI-integrated embedded finance for a sustainable future (Auer, 2022b; Ozili, 2023b). To advance the research frontiers on AI-integrated data-driven green finance, a comprehensive theoretical grounding combined with strong econometric validity will now be essential in supporting the translation of digital cost–benefit ratios into practical value units for inclusive green finance funds. Financial inclusion and green finance for all is the ultimate goals. Evidential presence and benevolence support these two goals. The five-level pyramid of AI-supported green finance and the three-degree framework of total greenness should accordingly underline and enrich the potent and practical use of AI for the governance of green finance towards a sustainable future (Ohnishi, 2021). The AI-integrated embedded finance research already contributes essential and timely information to sustainability and AI literature but also brings profound societal impacts to the sustainable finance industry.

## SUMMARY OF KEY FINDINGS

Artificial Intelligence (AI) aims to create intelligent systems capable of simulating human-like intelligence and cognitive function, thus facilitating complex problem-solving and learning through enormous experience and diverse information sources. This chapter investigates the influence of the penetration of AI and its applications in financial services via embedded finance on sustainable financial practices that focus on environmental, social, and governance (ESG) factors and contribute to sustainable development. The critical implications include sustainability, accountability and user trust as evaluative tools in evaluating AI-generated Embedded Finance Systems (Al-Gasaymeh et al., 2023). Six criteria were used to demonstrate the critical influence of regulations on these elements in the governance of AI systems. The financial sector became the major player in the ESG investment outbreak and continues to lead the bilateral macro-control relationship. Macroeconomic regulation aims to achieve better coordination of both markets and a fairer and more efficient allocation of resources (Mocsary, 2014).

The multiple roles of technology in the development of the green financial system are reviewed. The researchers highlight the following: The prospect of using AI/Big Data/Algorithmic technology to analyze company environmental reports to facilitate standardization and regulate information; the possibility of developing a unified global ESG standard to ensure data accuracy and consistency; the promise of Financial Innovation in designing profit-sharing or embedded insurance mechanisms to deal with common catastrophic events; and the rise in global sharing of technology and knowledge to avoid digital divergence (Ozili, 2023b). There is no doubt that ESG education technology with a strong AI/Big Data component will also help to improve energy efficiency, configuration management, and resource reduction. The developed technologies are green and low carbon. Ultimately, they may help to achieve sustainable development goals by removing market barriers and correcting structural distortions. Innovative financial products, services, and mechanisms facilitate the global promulgation and utilization of green advanced technologies (Meng Sam & Han Chan, 2020).

### Implications for Industry and Policy

As the fourth industrial revolution unfolds with technologies such as big data, IoT, AI, blockchain, 5G, and quantum computing, the traditional industrial customer subscriber-coded business model will shift to a personalized hybrid user subscriber-coded business model. Customers will increasingly become personalized hybrid users as COVID-19 has accelerated the digital transformation of firms, with an increasing number of them accepting remote work via online conferences and reducing their demand for office space. We, therefore, replace the customer code with personalized hybrid user code and model personalized hybrid users as a combination of key technology, internet service quality, safety and reliability, network effect, and personalized, relevant data (Auer, 2022a; Mocsary, 2014). E-loyalty will depend on the willingness of personalized hybrid users to promote products served by the e-commerce platform with AI actively. Surveys of personalized hybrid users reveal high AI satisfaction.

The six AI technology characteristics and representative AI applications reported are enriched versions to help AI suppliers improve AI quality and prevent customer churn, thus making personalized hybrid users more loyal. The model also highlights the advantages of embedding finance into the AI-driven e-commerce platform, which can enhance personalized hybrid users' trust in AI prediction, expand the platform's business ecosystem, and evoke personalized hybrid users' AI satisfaction and e-loyalty (Kiourtis et al., 2023; Ozili, 2023c). The personalized hybrid user e-loyalty has significantly positive effects on e-commerce platform e-loyalty and AI supplier equity value. Such AI technology evaluation, perfect market structure with zero profit, optimal revenue model, AI investment-driven GDP growth, and natural AI-enhanced equity value extensions can guide regulators to create a fair and sustainable AI environment with increasing AI economic impact. Therefore, the success of personalized hybrid user-centered AI innovation is conducive to promoting the UN Sustainable Development Goals and realizing a stable worldwide inclusive and fair digital ecosystem (Meng et al., 2021; Ozili, 2023a).

## CONCLUSION

This chapter is a summary of the ideas presented in this paper and the discussions about the collaborative role of artificial intelligence and embedded finance for sustainability, as well as how sustainable developments can benefit the business model of embedded finance. The problems associated with inequality, environmental degradation, and climate change have led to sustainability becoming a top priority for both business and society. Companies are beginning to recognize the interconnectedness of all things on Earth and the importance of initiatives that provide long-term solutions for their sustainable development. Companies can no longer achieve business success or create enhanced value for stakeholders in a singularly commercial context. Instead, a broader, systemic approach, in which more sustainable forms of value co-creation are considered and adopted is required. Our lives can be more rewarding, richer, and healthier, and economic growth can be positive and sustainable. Embedded finance is unique in this burgeoning evolution as it has the power not only to help businesses achieve their corporate social responsibility goals with financial instruments but also to guide them as they work to maximize their positive impacts for positive-sum games that are competitive, indicated in the rise of corporate social services: professional, personalized, and valid. Ease-of-use applications that empower consumers to be the change they want to see in the world. Our proposed ecosystem, whose core purpose is to maximize the positive impacts for all, is grounded in contribution and co-creation. It is designed for the greater good; our dedication guarantees that we strive to concentrate our service on the best interests of human and ecological sustainability and reject conversations related to what is best for the printer. In addition, as the company grows, the priority is to meet the needs of its key stakeholders, who are our conscious consumers.

## REFERENCES


Al-Gasaymeh, A. S., Ahmad Almahadin, H., Shehadeh, M., Migdady, H., & Bani Atta, A. A. (2023). Investigating the Role of Artificial Intelligence in Embedded Finance on Improving a Nonfinancial Customer Experience. *2nd International Conference on Business Analytics for Technology and Security, ICBATS 2023*. DOI: 10.1109/ICBATS57792.2023.10111255

Auer, R. (2022a). Embedded Supervision: How to Build Regulation into Decentralised Finance. SSRN *Electronic Journal*. DOI: 10.2139/ssrn.4127658

Auer, R. (2022b). *Embedded Supervision: How to Build Regulation Into Decentralized Finance*. Cryptoeconomic Systems., DOI: 10.21428/58320208.14a4105d

Barwise, P., & Watkins, L. (2018). The Evolution of Digital Dominance. In *Digital Dominance: The Power of Google*. Amazon, Facebook, and Apple.

Brassett, J., & Rethel, L. (2015). Sexy money: The hetero-normative politics of global finance. *Review of International Studies*, *41*(3), 429–449. Advance online publication. DOI: 10.1017/S0260210514000461

Caldecott, B. (2022). Defining transition finance and embedding it in the post-Covid-19 recovery. *Journal of Sustainable Finance & Investment*, *12*(3), 934–938. Advance online publication. DOI: 10.1080/20430795.2020.1813478

Chiu, I. H. Y. (2021). Regulating Sustainable Finance In Capital Markets:A Perspective From Socially Embedded Decentered Regulation. *Law and Contemporary Problems*, *84*(1).

Dikau, S., & Volz, U. (2023). Out of the window? Green monetary policy in China: Window guidance and the promotion of sustainable lending and investment. *Climate Policy*, *23*(1), 122–137. Advance online publication. DOI: 10.1080/14693062.2021.2012122

Gardner, I. (2008). Capital Rules: The Construction of Global Finance. *Journal of Economic Issues*, *42*(4), 1163–1165. Advance online publication. DOI: 10.1080/00213624.2008.11507208

Hensen, J., & Kötting, B. (2022). From open banking to embedded finance: The essential factors for a successful digital transformation. *Journal of Digital Banking*, *6*(4), 308. Advance online publication. DOI: 10.69554/SRCL3482

Kiourtis, A., Mavrogiorgou, A., Makridis, G., Fatouros, G., Soldatos, J., & Kyriazis, D. (2023). Data Marketplaces: Best Practices, Challenges, and Advancements for Embedded Finance. *Proceedings - 19th International Conference on Distributed Computing in Smart Systems and the Internet of Things, DCOSS-IoT 2023*. DOI: 10.1109/DCOSS-IoT58021.2023.00088

Mavrogiorgou, A., Kiourtis, A., Makridis, G., Kotios, D., Koukos, V., Kyriazis, D., Soldatos, J., Fatouros, G., Drakoulis, D., Malo, P., Serrano, M., Isaja, M., Lazcano, R., Vera, J. M., Fournier, F., Limonad, L., Perakis, K., Miltiadou, D., Kranas, P., & Troiano, E. (2023). FAME: Federated Decentralized Trusted Data Marketplace for Embedded Finance. *2023 International Conference on Smart Applications, Communications and Networking, SmartNets 2023*. DOI: 10.1109/SmartNets58706.2023.10215814

Meng, S., He, X., & Tian, X. (2021). Research on Fintech development issues based on embedded cloud computing and big data analysis. *Microprocessors and Microsystems*, *83*, 103977. Advance online publication. DOI: 10.1016/j.micpro.2021.103977

Meng Sam, K., & Han Chan, W. (2020). FACTORS AFFECTING THE ADOPTION OF EMBEDDED MOBILE FINANCE FUNCTIONS. *FACTORS AFFECTING THE ADOPTION OF EMBEDDED MOBILE FINANCE FUNCTIONS Journal of Information Technology Management, XXXI*(2).

Mocsary, G. A. (2014). The embedded firm: Corporate governance, labor, and finance capitalism - Commentary. *Accounting, Economics, and Law : A Convivium*, *4*(2). Advance online publication. DOI: 10.1515/ael-2013-0035

Mohammed, M. M., Khan, N., & Ahmad, T. (2022). Opportunity for Islamic Finance in Blockchain Solutions for Climate Change: A Case Study of DCarbonX Model. , *18*. DOI: 10.33001/M0110202218/105

Ohnishi, M. (2021). New Digital Financial Services Offer the Prospect of High Customer Retention-Expectations for the Growing Trend of "Embedded Finance." *Mitsui&Co., March*.

Ozili, P. K. (2022). Embedded finance: Assessing the benefits, use case, challenges and interest over time. *Journal of Internet and Digital Economics*, *2*(2), 108–123. Advance online publication. DOI: 10.1108/JIDE-05-2022-0014

Ozili, P. K. (2023a). Assessing global interest in decentralized finance, embedded finance, open finance, ocean finance and sustainable finance. *Asian Journal of Economics and Banking*, *7*(2), 197–216. Advance online publication. DOI: 10.1108/AJEB-03-2022-0029

Ozili, P. K. (2023b). Digital finance research and developments around the world: A literature review. *International Journal of Business Forecasting and Marketing Intelligence*, *8*(1), 35. Advance online publication. DOI: 10.1504/IJBFMI.2023.127698

Ozili, P. K. (2023c). Role of embedded finance in increasing financial inclusion. In *Adoption and Use of Technology Tools and Services by Economically Disadvantaged Communities*. Implications for Growth and Sustainability., DOI: 10.4018/978-1-6684-5347-6.ch011

Rakočević, S. B., & Rakić, N. (2023). The Future of Banking in FinTech Era: Decentralized and Embedded Finance. In *Contributions to Finance and Accounting: Vol. Part F233*. DOI: 10.1007/978-3-031-23269-5_6

Shafik, W. (2024a). Artificial intelligence and Blockchain technology enabling cybersecurity in telehealth systems. In *Artificial Intelligence and Blockchain Technology in Modern Telehealth Systems*. DOI: 10.1049/PBHE061E_ch11

Shafik, W. (2024b). The Role of Artificial Intelligence in the Emerging Digital Economy Era. In *Artificial Intelligence Enabled Management* (pp. 33–50). De Gruyter., DOI: 10.1515/9783111172408-003

Shafik, W. (2024c). Data Privacy and Security Safeguarding Customer Information in ChatGPT Systems. In *Revolutionizing the Service Industry Wth OpenAI Models* (pp. 52–86). IGI Global., DOI: 10.4018/979-8-3693-1239-1.ch003

Shafik, W. (2024d). Deep Learning Impacts in the Field of Artificial Intelligence. In *Deep Learning Concepts in Operations Research* (pp. 9–26). Auerbach Publications., DOI: 10.1201/9781003433309-2

Shafik, W. (2024e). Factors Affecting Green Purchase Behaviors for Small and Medium Enterprises (SMEs) in Uganda. In *Entrepreneurial Strategies for the Internationalization and Digitalization of SMEs* (pp. 198–224). IGI Global. DOI: 10.4018/979-8-3693-3518-5.ch009

Shafik, W. (2024f). Generative AI for Social Good and Sustainable Development. In *Generative AI: Current Trends and Applications* (pp. 185–217). Springer. DOI: 10.1007/978-981-97-8460-8_10

Shafik, W. (2024g). Navigating Emerging Challenges in Robotics and Artificial Intelligence in Africa. In *Examining the rapid advance of digital technology in Africa* (pp. 126–146). IGI Global., DOI: 10.4018/978-1-6684-9962-7.ch007

Shafik, W. (2024h). Science of Emotional Intelligence. In *Enhancing and Predicting Digital Consumer Behavior with AI* (pp. 284–310). IGI Global., DOI: 10.4018/979-8-3693-4453-8.ch015

Shafik, W. (2024i). Sustainable Development. In Viana Hassan, A. S. S. B. (Ed.), *Building Community Resiliency and Sustainability With Tourism Development* (1st ed., Vol. 1, pp. 1–30). IGI Global., DOI: 10.4018/979-8-3693-5405-6.ch001

Shafik, W. (2024j). Toward a More Ethical Future of Artificial Intelligence and Data Science. In *The Ethical Frontier of AI and Data Analysis* (pp. 362–388). IGI Global., DOI: 10.4018/979-8-3693-2964-1.ch022

Telukdarie, K. K., & A, T. (2023). Digital Ecosystems in Financial Services driven by Embedded Finance Platforms in South Africa. *SSRN Electronic Journal*. DOI: 10.2139/ssrn.4331766

Telukdarie, K. K., & Telukdarie, A. (2023). Digital Ecosystems in Financial Services driven by Embedded Finance Platforms in South Africa. SSRN *Electronic Journal*. DOI: 10.2139/ssrn.4331766

Townsend, Z. (2021). *What the embedded-finance and banking-as-a-service trends mean for financial services*. Mckinsey & Company.

Tripathy, A. (2022). Careers and climates Becoming and being a climate finance practitioner. *Focaal, 2022*(93). DOI: 10.3167/fcl.2022.930103

van Klyton, A., & Rutabayiro-Ngoga, S. (2018). SME finance and the construction of value in Rwanda. *Journal of Small Business and Enterprise Development*, *25*(4), 628–643. Advance online publication. DOI: 10.1108/JSBED-02-2017-0046

Wangsong, X. (2022). The Default Risk of Bank Customers Based on Embedded Microprocessor Wireless Communication under the Internet Finance Background. *Mobile Information Systems*, *2022*, 1–15. Advance online publication. DOI: 10.1155/2022/8019033

Wullweber, J. (2019). Embedded Finance: The Shadow Banking System, Monetary Politics and Sovereign Power. SSRN *Electronic Journal*. DOI: 10.2139/ssrn.3431909

Wullweber, J. (2020). Embedded finance: The shadow banking system, sovereign power, and a new state–market hybridity. *Journal of Cultural Economics*, *13*(5), 592–609. Advance online publication. DOI: 10.1080/17530350.2020.1741015

Young, J., Wong, W., & Taiyabi, S. (2022). *FinTech in ASEAN 2022: Finance, Re-imagined. United Overseas Bank Limited ('UOB"), PricewaterhouseCoopers Risk Services Pte. Ltd. ("PwC Singapore") and Singapore FinTech Association*. SFA.

Zheng, K., Zheng, L. J., Gauthier, J., Zhou, L., Xu, Y., Behl, A., & Zhang, J. Z. (2022). Blockchain technology for enterprise credit information sharing in supply chain finance. *Journal of Innovation and Knowledge*, *7*(4), 100256. Advance online publication. DOI: 10.1016/j.jik.2022.100256

# Chapter 6 Sustainable Finance in the Digital Age: The Function of Embedded Finance in Eco-Friendly Investments

**Rismawati Rismawati**
https://orcid.org/0000-0001-8046-6764
*Universitas Muhammadiyah Palopo, Indonesia*

**Monika Handayani**
https://orcid.org/0000-0003-4186-9864
*Politeknik Negeri Banjarmasin, Indonesia*

**Ela Elliyana**
https://orcid.org/0000-0002-8673-0631
*Universitas Indonesia Timur, Indonesia*

**Indra Pahala**
https://orcid.org/0009-0003-8324-0041
*Universitas Negeri Jakarta, Indonesia*

## ABSTRACT

*Sustainable embedded finance is transforming the financial sector by incorporating green investing strategies into digital platforms. This study examines how embedded finance, fintech innovations, and decentralized financial models enhance access to sustainability-linked financial products. Essential elements encompass the function of AI-driven ESG analytics, blockchain-enabled transparency, and digital payment systems in promoting financial access for environmentally sustainable initiatives. The*

DOI: 10.4018/979-8-3373-2464-7.ch006

*study analyzes policy frameworks and regulatory obstacles, highlighting the necessity of integrating financial plans with the UN Sustainable Development Goals (SDGs). As embedded finance progresses, it presents novel options for scalable, transparent, and technology-driven sustainable investments. The results underscore the essential interaction among finance, technology, and sustainability, offering guidance for investors, politicians, and enterprises in steering the future of sustainable finance.*

## AN INTRODUCTION TO SUSTAINABLE FINANCE IN THE DIGITAL AGE

### Defining Sustainable Finance and Its Development

Sustainable finance denotes the incorporation of environmental, social, and governance (ESG) factors into investment and lending choices, signifying a transformative change in the financial sector (Driessen, 2021). Sustainable finance, in contrast to traditional finance that prioritizes short-term gains, allocates capital towards long-term objectives including the reduction of carbon emissions, the promotion of social fairness, and the enhancement of ethical corporate governance. This transition is propelled by an augmented consciousness of climate change, escalating political and regulatory pressures, and the growing demand from investors for ethical business operations. Integrating ESG aspects into financial decisions, sustainable finance creates a connection between economic growth and sustainability goals, thus linking profitability with environmental stewardship and social responsibility.

The evolution of sustainable finance has been influenced by international crises and multilateral accords. Initially, financial organizations perceived environmental and social issues as externalities, apart from investment decisions. Subsequent to the 2008 global financial crisis and the implementation of frameworks like the Paris Agreement on climate change and the United Nations' Sustainable Development Goals (SDGs), sustainability was redefined as an essential element of financial decision-making (Cunha, Meira, & Orsato, 2021; Ziolo, Bak, & Cheba, 2021). Instruments including green bonds, sustainability-linked loans, and impact investment have emerged as prevalent instruments for financing projects that match with global climate and development objectives.

The shift from traditional to sustainable finance represents a major change in investment methods, risk evaluation, and corporate responsibility. Conventional financial models emphasized return on investment and financial risk, frequently overlooking the long-term environmental and social consequences of business behavior. Sustainable finance, by contrast, integrates ESG risk assessments to guarantee that financial actions improve both economic returns and sustainable development results (Kuzmina et al., 2023; Li, 2023). This transformation has been expedited by digital technologies. Fintech innovations, including blockchain transparency mechanisms, AI-driven ESG analytics, and integrated finance models, have democratized access to sustainable investment options, enhancing the inclusivity, transparency, and efficiency of financial institutions.

Central to sustainable finance are ESG factors that influence financial decision-making. The environmental dimension assesses company responsibility regarding climate change mitigation, carbon emissions, water use, and waste management. The social dimension emphasizes labor practices, human rights, diversity, and community impact, whereas the governance dimension highlights transparency, ethical leadership, and shareholder rights. Companies with robust ESG ratings see diminished borrowing costs, increased investor confidence, and improved long-term stability, indicative of decreased vulnerability to regulatory, legal, and reputational concerns.

Financial markets are crucial in promoting sustainability by directing resources towards ecologically and socially responsible businesses. Stock exchanges, institutional investors, and regulatory frameworks can profoundly impact corporate conduct and direct investment towards sustainable initiatives. Instruments like green bonds and ESG-oriented exchange-traded funds (ETFs) allow investors to synchronize their portfolios with sustainability goals (Cunha, Meira, & Orsato, 2021; Li, 2023). Moreover, initiatives such as the EU Taxonomy for Sustainable Activities and the Task Force on Climate-Related Financial Disclosures (TCFD) are creating international standards for corporate sustainability reporting. These frameworks guarantee that financial markets improve accountability, mitigate risks, and promote sustainable wealth generation in an environmentally aware economy.

Sustainable finance embodies the convergence of finance, technology, and sustainability. Digital advances are transforming financial institutions, and embedded finance is set to enhance the accessibility of environmentally sound investments, ultimately fostering a more robust and sustainable global economy.

*Figure 1. Transition from conventional to sustainable finance (Adapted from Cunha, Meira, & Orsato (2021); Driessen (2021); Kuzmina et al. (2023); Li (2023); Ziolo, Bak, & Cheba (2021))*

The shift from traditional to sustainable finance highlights a fundamental realignment of financial systems towards long-term wealth generation. Conventional finance prioritizes short-term profitability, but sustainable finance incorporates ESG factors to harmonize financial success with environmental responsibility and social equity. This transition is bolstered by international frameworks and expedited by digital advancements, like as blockchain and AI-enhanced ESG analytics. The efficacy of sustainable finance fundamentally relies on harmonizing innovation with regulation, guaranteeing openness, and instilling accountability within financial systems. This balance is essential for effectively mobilizing capital for a resilient and inclusive global economy.

## The Influence of Digital Transformation on Financial Systems

Digital revolution has significantly altered financial systems, enhancing their efficiency, accessibility, and inclusivity, especially regarding sustainable financing. The amalgamation of financial technology (fintech) and digital finance innovations, including embedded finance, digital payments, blockchain, artificial intelligence (AI), and the Internet of Things (IoT), has created new opportunities for channeling capital into environmentally sustainable investments (Hossain et al., 2024; Wang & Qu, 2024). These innovations are not only technical enhancements but fundamental facilitators of sustainable financial systems.

Fintech has transformed conventional banking paradigms, transitioning financial transactions from physical locations and protracted approval procedures to efficient, technology-based platforms. Digital banking, mobile payments, and AI-driven credit assessments are enhancing the accessibility of sustainable investment options (Hidayat-ur-Rehman & Hossain, 2024; Chueca Vergara & Ferruz Agudo, 2021). Embedded finance illustrates this shift by integrating financial services into non-financial channels, enabling customers to access green financing choices for renewable energy adoption or electric vehicle acquisitions directly within digital marketplaces. Likewise, peer-to-peer lending and crowdfunding endeavors are augmenting involvement in sustainable projects by diminishing dependence on conventional intermediaries.

The integration of blockchain, AI, and IoT significantly enhances transparency and accountability. Blockchain ensures immutable records for green bonds and carbon credit transactions, while facilitating verifiable ESG compliance throughout global supply chains (Ahlström & Monciardini, 2021; Schulz & Feist, 2021). Artificial intelligence improves risk assessment by scrutinizing extensive, intricate datasets to pinpoint ESG-related hazards, uncover fraud, and analyze long-term sustainability effects (Farayola, 2024; Al-Zoubi, 2024). IoT applications, such carbon emission monitoring and automated compliance reporting, enhance environmental responsibility (Colombage, 2025). Collectively, these solutions mitigate information asymmetries and enhance investor trust.

Nevertheless, the digital transition also poses enduring obstacles. Regulatory ambiguities hinder cross-border investments, cybersecurity vulnerabilities jeopardize financial ecosystems, and greenwashing diminishes trust when sustainability assertions are overstated (Macchiavello & Siri, 2022; Ghosh et al., 2025; Talan et al., 2024). Moreover, digital inequalities, especially in developing nations, restrict fair access to sustainable financial solutions (Hidayat-ur-Rehman & Hossain, 2024).

Digital transformation serves as both a facilitator and a limitation for sustainable finance. The future impact on the Sustainable Development Goals (SDGs) will rely on coordinated regulation, strong cybersecurity protocols, and focused policies to address digital disparities, thereby fostering a resilient and inclusive global financial system.

## Embedded Finance as a Catalyst for Sustainable Investments

Embedded finance is a transformative approach that incorporates financial services within non-financial platforms, fundamentally altering the global financial environment. This uninterrupted connectivity allows businesses, consumers, and investors to access financial goods without relying on conventional banking middlemen. Integrating finance into daily digital interactions can channel financial resources toward environmentally friendly initiatives, enhancing access to green financing and promoting a more inclusive, technology-oriented ecosystem (Selvakumar & Manjunath, 2025; Fernandez-Vallado, 2025).

Embedded finance refers to a diverse array of financial services—such as payments, lending, insurance, and investment—integrated into non-financial platforms, including e-commerce, ride-sharing applications, energy providers, and digital marketplaces. In contrast to traditional finance, which necessitates consumers to interact independently with financial institutions, embedded finance enables the direct access of financial services within digital platforms. This integration improves consumer ease and reinforces the alignment of financial products with sustainable consumption and investing practices (Waliszewski, 2023; Taneja, 2024). Principal applications in this domain encompass integrated green financing for solar panels, electric vehicles, and energy-efficient housing; platforms for sustainable investments employing robo-advisors and ESG-focused portfolios; carbon-neutral payment systems featuring real-time carbon offsetting; and embedded insurance products designed for renewable energy projects.

Notably, embedded finance markedly differs from traditional financing strategies. While traditional finance frequently imposes obstacles through intricate application procedures, embedded finance mitigates these hurdles by incorporating solutions into routine transactions. Empowered by artificial intelligence and real-time data analytics, embedded finance facilitates tailored financial products that correspond with sustainability preferences and enable prompt decision-making utilizing ESG data. This method decentralizes access to financial services and fosters financial inclusion by providing sustainable microfinancing options to marginalized communities and small enterprises in developing nations.

The potential of embedded finance to enhance sustainable investments is significant. Utilizing the network effects of digital platforms, it amplifies the visibility and adoption of sustainable financial instruments, facilitates green financing for small and medium-sized enterprises (SMEs) and startups via crowdfunding and peer-to-peer lending, and promotes behavioral modifications among consumers and corporations. Moreover, the utilization of big data analytics in ESG-focused strategies enables more informed capital allocation towards significant sustainability efforts. In contrast to traditional finance, which frequently presents structural barriers, embedded finance minimizes friction, customizes financial products, and enhances prospects for green investment. As digital ecosystems mature, embedded finance is set to play a crucial role in mobilizing sustainable capital, enhancing inclusivity, and fostering the development of an environmentally responsible global financial system (Allioui et al., 2024; Taneja, 2024).

## THE MECHANISMS OF EMBEDDED FINANCE IN SUSTAINABLE INVESTMENTS

### Comprehending Embedded Finance: A Structural Analysis

The global financial system is experiencing swift development, with embedded finance serving as a significant catalyst for innovation. This method incorporates financial services within non-financial channels, thus establishing a more accessible and efficient financial ecosystem. In sustainable finance, embedded solutions reduce obstacles by providing firms, consumers, and investors with seamless access to financial instruments that foster environmental stewardship. Through the utilization of digital technology, embedded finance is transforming banking, insurance, and investment frameworks, while creating new avenues for directing resources towards sustainable initiatives (Ozili, 2023; Ng et al., 2023).

Embedded finance in banking and payments allows consumers to track their carbon footprint and implement offsetting strategies via digital platforms. Integrated finance services and eco-friendly financing are progressively accessible in digital marketplaces to facilitate investments in renewable energy and the acquisition of electric automobiles. Fintech-driven systems enable organizations to perform instantaneous

ESG assessments, thus minimizing delays in sustainable finance decisions. Embedded solutions in insurance mitigate climate risks using instruments like parametric insurance for extreme weather occurrences. Additionally, digital insurers utilize IoT data to customize insurance based on sustainability performance, incentivizing companies that diminish their environmental footprint (Louman et al., 2022).

Embedded finance has also transformed investment and wealth management. Digital platforms currently provide automated ESG portfolio allocation, tokenized green assets like blockchain-based carbon credits and bonds, and AI-driven robo-advisors that integrate sustainability preferences into investment strategies. This integration enhances the accessibility, transparency, and scalability of impact investing, expediting the shift towards sustainable financial markets (Colombage, 2025).

The expansion of embedded finance is intricately linked to advancements in fintech. Artificial intelligence and machine learning improve ESG data analysis, blockchain technologies promote transparent reporting, and decentralized finance (DeFi) introduces innovative mechanisms like blockchain-based carbon trading. Moreover, cloud computing and big data enhance real-time monitoring of ESG compliance. Complementary technologies, including open financial APIs and smart contracts, enhance transparency and inclusivity. APIs incorporate financial services into e-commerce and energy platforms, whereas smart contracts simplify ESG reporting, enforce sustainability compliance, and facilitate carbon credit swaps. Collectively, these instruments establish a financial ecosystem that is more inclusive, data-centric, and environmentally sustainable.

As financial ecosystems develop, embedded finance has the capacity to expedite the global adoption of green investments. However, issues including regulatory fragmentation, cybersecurity threats, and digital disparities must be meticulously addressed to guarantee that embedded finance effectively aids in the development of a robust and sustainable global economy (Ozili, 2023; Ng et al., 2023; Louman et al., 2022).

## Eco-Friendly Investment Platforms and Digital Lending Frameworks

The emergence of sustainable investing platforms integrated into digital ecosystems has democratized access to green finance. Historically, engagement in these markets was predominantly limited to institutional investors; but recent advancements like crowdfunding, tokenized assets, and digital lending are eroding these obstacles. Fintech technologies are creating new avenues for organizations and individuals to promote environmentally responsible activities, consequently expanding the financing base for sustainability projects and improving inclusivity in financial markets.

Crowdfunding has become an effective tool for raising resources for sustainable initiatives. In contrast to traditional fundraising, which is frequently limited by legislative intricacies and significant entrance obstacles, crowdfunding platforms provide decentralized and participatory investing. Initiatives like Trine and Lumo enable individuals to fund sustainable energy solutions in underserved areas, thus facilitating energy changes. In addition to renewable energy, crowdfunding is utilized for sustainable agriculture, reforestation, circular economy initiatives, and carbon sequestration. The incorporation of crowdfunding techniques into digital marketplaces and financial platforms enhances accessibility and broadens the contributor base.

Blockchain and tokenization have brought novel financial instruments that improve liquidity and accessibility in sustainable financing. Tokenized assets provide fractional ownership of green initiatives, including solar farms and electric vehicle infrastructure, thereby reducing investment barriers. Green bonds, traditionally utilized for financing environmentally sustainable projects, are increasingly becoming transparent, tradable, and cost-effective via embedded finance platforms that employ blockchain technology for issuance, tracking, and trade. These technologies diminish dependence on conventional banking institutions while bolstering investor confidence via improved transparency and security.

*Table 1. Conventional green finance vs. embedded digital finance*

| Dimension | Conventional Green Finance | Embedded Digital Finance |
|---|---|---|
| **Accessibility** | Primarily institutional investors with high entry barriers and complex procedures | Open to individuals, SMEs, and communities through crowdfunding, tokenized assets, and digital platforms |
| **Cost and Efficiency** | Higher transaction costs, slower processing, and reliance on intermediaries | Lower costs, faster transactions, and disintermediation through fintech, blockchain, and APIs |
| **Transparency** | Periodic sustainability reports (quarterly/annual) | Real-time ESG data integration, blockchain-based tracking, and automated reporting |
| **Investment Instruments** | Traditional green bonds and institutional lending | Tokenized assets, digital green bonds, embedded green loans, and carbon-neutral payment systems |
| **Financial Inclusion** | Limited access for marginalized groups and emerging economies | Expanded access through microfinance, mobile-based lending (e.g., M-KOPA), and digital crowdfunding |
| **Scalability** | Constrained by regulatory complexity and reliance on banks | Scalable through digital ecosystems, DeFi platforms, and fintech-enabled integration |

continued on following page

*Table 1. Continued*

| Dimension | Conventional Green Finance | Embedded Digital Finance |
|---|---|---|
| **Risk Factors** | Lower exposure to cyber risks but higher structural entry barriers | Greater exposure to cybersecurity threats and greenwashing, requiring robust safeguards |
| **Role in SDGs** | Supports sustainability indirectly through institutional projects | Directly linked to SDGs via inclusive access, renewable energy projects, and community-driven investments |

Case studies further demonstrate the revolutionary potential of embedded finance in digital lending. M-KOPA has innovated pay-as-you-go solar systems in Africa, utilizing mobile microfinance to facilitate clean energy access for low-income households. In Europe, Solarisbank and Tomorrow Bank incorporate sustainability-linked loans into digital platforms, facilitating energy-efficient home improvements and the adoption of electric vehicles. In the United States, Raise Green has established a platform for community-oriented renewable energy initiatives utilizing collaborative crowdfunding methodologies. These instances illustrate how integrated lending approaches enhance inclusivity, transparency, and efficiency in green financing.

Although eco-friendly platforms and digital lending frameworks markedly improve accessibility and scalability, difficulties persist. Regulatory ambiguity, the potential for greenwashing, and inconsistent digital infrastructure may constrain their effectiveness if not thoroughly addressed. Nonetheless, as fintech progresses, embedded finance may expedite decarbonization strategies and facilitate the establishment of a robust, internationally inclusive sustainable economy.

## Regulatory Aspects of Embedded Green Finance

The swift proliferation of embedded finance within green investment sectors offers both prospects and legal obstacles. Although these technologies enhance accessibility and efficiency, they simultaneously present governance, compliance, and ethical challenges that necessitate meticulous management. Regulatory agencies and financial institutions are progressively required to develop frameworks that guarantee openness, accountability, and investor protection. Embedded green finance specifically raises apprehensions about the potential for greenwashing, inconsistent sustainability disclosures, and the sufficiency of risk management systems in digital platforms (Zetzsche & Anker-Sørensen, 2022; Ahlström & Monciardini, 2021).

A primary concern in sustainable finance regulation is the delineation of criteria for what constitutes "green." In response, countries and international organizations have established taxonomies that categorize economic activities based on their environmental effects. The European Union's Taxonomy for Sustainable Activities presents a detailed framework, delineating six principal objectives: climate change mitigation, pollution avoidance, and biodiversity protection. These classifications mitigate ambiguity and assist financial organizations in aligning goods with sustainable standards. Moreover, frameworks like the Task Force on Climate-Related Financial Disclosures (TCFD) provide directives for ESG risk reporting, facilitating investors' assessment of the climate ramifications of financial products. Complementary standards like the Global Reporting Initiative (GRI) and the IFRS Sustainability Standards enhance the harmonization of sustainability disclosures across jurisdictions, promoting comparability and accountability (Aldboush & Ferdous, 2023).

Regulatory compliance is crucial for embedded finance platforms, such as digital lenders, crowdfunding portals, and tokenized investment providers, to sustain market confidence. By aligning operations with sustainability taxonomies and disclosure guidelines, these platforms can reduce legal risks while bolstering investor confidence. Regulators simultaneously have the dual task of promoting innovation in embedded green finance while mitigating systemic risks, including cybersecurity breaches and greenwashing activities. The success of embedded green financing will ultimately rely on attaining legislative clarity, cross-border harmonization, and the incorporation of effective monitoring mechanisms to reconcile innovation with sustainability goals.

## DIGITAL PAYMENT MECHANISMS AND ECO-CONSCIOUS CONSUMERISM

### The Function of Digital Payments in Sustainable Finance

The extensive implementation of digital payment systems has radically transformed financial transactions, rendering them swifter, more efficient, more widely accessible. In addition to convenience, digital payments are increasingly acknowledged as a facilitator of sustainable finance, equipping individuals and businesses with resources to connect their financial endeavors with environmental objectives. With the proliferation of cashless economies, financial technologies are integrating sustainability elements such as carbon footprint monitoring, carbon offsetting, and real-time sustainability metrics, thus promoting environmentally conscious consumption and investment practices (Machiavello & Siri, 2022; Kumar et al., 2022; Musleh Al-Sartawi et al., 2022; Cunha, Meira, & Orsato, 2021).

The ecological advantages of cashless economies are substantial. Conventional cash-based systems depend significantly on the manufacturing of paper currency, coin minting, and the upkeep of energy-intensive financial infrastructure, all of which exacerbate environmental deterioration. Digital payments mitigate these negative externalities by eradicating the necessity for physical currency and diminishing the environmental costs associated with its creation and circulation. They diminish transportation-related emissions by minimizing the necessity for cash delivery and ATM restocking, while also reducing energy consumption linked to the operation of physical bank branches (Ahiase et al., 2025). These attributes establish digital payment systems as a vital catalyst for enhancing resource efficiency and environmental stewardship in the financial industry.

Nonetheless, digital payment infrastructures provide sustainability concerns that necessitate meticulous consideration. The functioning of data centers, blockchain systems, and extensive digital transaction networks is energy-intensive, prompting worries regarding the carbon impact of financial digitalization. Investments in green data centers, energy-efficient blockchain technologies, and carbon-neutral payment processing systems are important to ensure that digital payments positively impact sustainability. In the absence of such safeguards, the environmental benefits of diminishing dependence on cash may be negated by the substantial energy requirements of digital financial systems.

The function of digital payments in sustainable finance is twofold: they facilitate enhanced efficiency and environmental advantages, while concurrently necessitating innovation in green technology implementation to alleviate their ecological impact. A balanced approach is essential to guarantee that cashless economies truly promote environmental goals.

## Monitoring Carbon Footprint via Digital Transactions

The incorporation of carbon footprint monitoring into financial transactions represents a notable step in sustainable digital finance. Fintech platforms are progressively providing real-time tools that assess customer spending behaviors and predict the environmental impacts of daily transactions (Alsedrah, 2024). By correlating expenditures in areas such as transportation, food, and energy with their corresponding carbon emissions, these systems enable individuals to make more sustainable consumption decisions. Certain platforms enhance their offerings by providing environmentally conscious recommendations, such as choosing sustainable retailers or offsetting carbon emissions through voluntary donations. This method is illustrated by Doconomy's DO Card, which limits carbon-heavy spending, and Mastercard's Carbon Calculator, which offers users insights into their ecological footprint. These programs demonstrate how embedded finance can convert ordinary financial activities into environmentally responsible practices.

Financial apps are using comprehensive sustainability criteria to inform consumer and business financial decisions. AI-driven platforms offer customized evaluations of sustainable expenditures, whereas embedded finance systems incorporate ESG-focused investment options, such as green bonds and renewable energy initiatives

(Triantafyllidou & Zabaniotou, 2021; Xie et al., 2024). Furthermore, the advent of green credit scoring models enables financial institutions to incentivize ecologically responsible actions through favorable lending conditions, so explicitly associating sustainability with financial rewards. These interconnections underscore the capacity of digital money to promote a novel epoch of ethical consumption and responsible investing.

Sustainability-linked financial goods are concurrently transforming consumer payment systems. Green credit cards, carbon offset initiatives, and integrated rewards systems incorporate incentives into routine transactions to encourage environmentally sustainable decisions (Cromwell & Peprah, 2025). These schemes typically include refunds or discounts on eco-friendly purchases, loyalty points redeemable for offset initiatives like reforestation, and lowered loan interest rates for investments in solar panels, energy-efficient homes, or electric vehicles. Although these methods promote climate-positive actions and facilitate global decarbonization objectives (Nyarko et al., 2025), they also provoke inquiries regarding inclusivity and sustainable behavioral transformation. Restricted digital literacy and unequal access to green financial products may hinder participation, especially in developing economies.

Consequently, while carbon footprint monitoring and eco-friendly incentives improve transparency and link financial activities with sustainability objectives, it is imperative to focus on legislative harmonization, inclusivity, and the potential for superficial engagement (green consumerism lacking systemic impact). Confronting these problems is crucial for the effective advancement of global sustainability agendas through integrated digital finance.

## Carbon-Neutral Transactions and Integrated Carbon Assessment Tools

The creation of carbon-neutral transaction systems signifies a significant progress in sustainable digital banking. Financial institutions are incorporating carbon assessment tools into payment systems, enabling users to connect their daily transactions with environmental goals. AI-driven calculators integrated into green credit cards and digital banking applications enable users to evaluate the carbon intensity of their transactions instantaneously, thus enhancing awareness of personal consumption behaviors (Cunha, Meira, & Orsato, 2021; Fu & Pirabi, 2023). Numerous platforms integrate automated offsetting methods, allocating a fraction of transaction values to reforestation, renewable energy, or conservation initiatives. Embedded finance systems can concurrently enhance consumer knowledge and integrate sustainability incentives directly into financial behavior.

Numerous innovative initiatives demonstrate the promise of environmentally sustainable credit cards. Sweden's DO Black card, introduced by Doconomy, limits transactions when users exceed monthly $CO_2$ limits, so ensuring environmental accountability. In the United States, Aspiration Zero associates expenditures with tree-planting projects, whereas the Netherlands' Bunq Green Card automatically facilitates tree planting for every €100 spent. The UK's Co-op Bank Ethical Card integrates financial services with ethical principles by prohibiting funding for fossil fuels and weapons. These instances illustrate how integrated financial incentives can influence consumer decisions and promote greater engagement in the sustainability initiative (Ari & Koc, 2021). In conjunction with credit-based solutions, blockchain-enabled cryptocurrencies and decentralized finance (DeFi) platforms are transforming carbon-neutral transactions. Blockchain guarantees openness and immutability in ESG reporting, thus mitigating the danger of greenwashing and enabling verifiable carbon credit markets (Ahlström & Monciardini, 2021; Machiavello & Siri, 2022). Nonetheless, apprehensions persist regarding the energy intensity of conventional cryptocurrencies like Bitcoin, which depend on proof-of-work consensus processes. Innovative alternatives such as Chia (employing proof-of-space-and-time), SolarCoin (incentivizing renewable energy generation), and Nano (utilizing lightweight ledgers) demonstrate the potential of green cryptocurrencies to alleviate environmental expenses (Howson & de Vries, 2022). Additionally, DeFi platforms like Aave, MakerDAO, and Celo are exploring sustainability-linked financing models, hence broadening decentralized prospects for green finance (Khalil, Sinliamthong, & Khalil, 2025; Unsal & Ozkan, 2024).

Although carbon-neutral transactions and digital currencies offer potential for improving transparency, inclusivity, and accountability, substantial problems remain. These encompass guaranteeing regulatory compliance, mitigating the digital gap, and averting superficial engagement when offsets replace systemic emissions reductions. The credibility and efficacy of carbon-neutral finance will ultimately rely on standardized legislation, technical efficiency, and the authentic linkage of financial innovation with climate objectives.

*Table 2. Tools, benefits, and challenges of carbon-neutral transactions*

| Tools / Mechanisms | Benefits for Sustainable Finance | Key Challenges / Risks |
|---|---|---|
| **Carbon Footprint Calculators (e.g., Mastercard Carbon Calculator, Doconomy DO Card)** | Real-time tracking of emissions; increases consumer awareness; promotes low-carbon decision-making | Risk of "green consumerism" without systemic impact; limited adoption in developing regions |
| **Green Credit Cards & Rewards (e.g., Bunq Green Card, Aspiration Zero, Co-op Ethical Card)** | Incentivizes sustainable purchases; links finance with climate-positive actions; boosts accountability | Accessibility limited to higher-income consumers; risk of greenwashing in marketing claims |
| **Automated Carbon Offsetting** | Channels funds to reforestation, renewable energy, and conservation; provides visible climate impact | Offsets may substitute for real emission reductions; verification of offset quality is complex |
| **Blockchain for ESG & Carbon Markets** | Immutable reporting; transparent carbon credit trading; reduces greenwashing; enables real-time ESG validation | High energy consumption of some blockchain models; fragmented regulatory standards |
| **Green Cryptocurrencies (Chia, SolarCoin, Nano)** | Low-energy consensus mechanisms; incentivizes renewable energy adoption; expands DeFi sustainability | Scalability and liquidity concerns; lack of mainstream adoption; speculative risks in markets |
| **DeFi Lending Platforms (Aave, MakerDAO, Celo)** | Democratizes access to green finance; promotes decentralized, transparent, and inclusive lending | Vulnerable to cyberattacks; weak consumer protection; uncertain long-term regulatory oversight |

***Source***: Author's elaboration based on Zetzsche & Anker-Sørensen (2022); Ahlström & Monciardini (2021); Aldboush & Ferdous (2023); Cunha, Meira, & Orsato (2021); Fu et al. (2023).

Carbon-neutral transactions and integrated carbon assessment tools illustrate how embedded finance may transform consumer behavior and institutional accountability by incorporating sustainability into routine financial activities. Their success relies not solely on technology innovation but also on regulatory clarity, inclusion, and systemic influence. Although instruments like carbon calculators, eco-friendly credit cards, and blockchain-enabled reporting systems enhance transparency and promote conscientious expenditure, they may inadvertently cultivate cosmetic involvement if offsetting strategies replace genuine emissions reduction. Moreover, enduring challenges such as inequitable access to digital infrastructure, cybersecurity threats, and inconsistent ESG standards may hinder widespread adoption, especially in developing nations. An equitable strategy that integrates innovation with stringent regulation, inclusive policies, and authentic decarbonization methods is crucial for ensuring that carbon-neutral finance effectively supports global climate objectives.

# INVESTMENT STRATEGIES AND RISK MITIGATION IN SUSTAINABLE EMBEDDED FINANCE

## Impact Investing and ESG-Centric Investment Approaches

As global financial markets progressively include sustainability into their frameworks, impact investment and ESG-focused strategies have emerged as fundamental components of integrated sustainable finance. These methods match financial rewards with environmental and social advantages, therefore harmonizing profitability with long-term sustainability goals (Talan et al., 2024). Investors are increasingly evaluating risk-return profiles, ESG scoring methodologies, and sustainability-linked instruments—such as green bonds and sustainability-linked loans—to make educated decisions that reconcile financial success with environmental responsibility.

A fundamental difference between traditional and sustainable investment strategies is their approach to risk and reward. Conventional models emphasize financial success, while sustainable investments integrate ESG risks that substantially affect long-term stability. Research indicates that companies with robust ESG policies encounter less regulatory penalties, diminished reputational hazards, and enhanced resilience in economic recessions (Aich et al., 2021; Folqué et al., 2021; Dmuchowski et al., 2023). Sustainable investments typically necessitate greater initial capital, especially in renewable energy and sustainable infrastructure; nevertheless, they generally provide long-term financial stability by lowering operational expenses and benefiting from regulatory incentives. Moreover, ESG-oriented portfolios offer diversification advantages, often surpassing conventional portfolios in times of market volatility, as investors increasingly account for climate risks and legislative shifts.

Financial organizations utilize ESG scoring models to assess performance in environmental, social, and governance dimensions, hence guiding decision-making. These models assess variables like emissions and energy efficiency (E), labor practices and human rights (S), and corporate governance structures (G), thereby enhancing transparency and accountability (Folqué et al., 2021; Sciarelli et al., 2021). Integration with AI-driven systems facilitates real-time ESG evaluations, providing investors with prompt information to alleviate sustainability concerns.

Green bonds and sustainability-linked loans (SLLs) are essential for directing funds to climate-positive initiatives. Green bonds, regulated by frameworks like the Green Bond Principles (GBP) and the Climate Bonds Initiative (CBI), are intended for funding renewable energy, sustainable infrastructure, and energy efficiency. Sustainability-linked loans (SLLs) are adaptable financial instruments linked to borrowers' environmental, social, and governance (ESG) performance objectives; noncompliance with these targets incurs elevated interest expenses, so establishing financial motivations for sustainability advancements.

Although these instruments improve market transparency and allocate resources towards sustainability, difficulties persist. Apprehensions regarding varied ESG approaches, the potential for greenwashing, and disparate worldwide regulatory alignment may compromise trustworthiness. Embedded finance that integrates impact investment, ESG rating, and sustainability-linked goods possesses considerable potential to enhance resilience, bolster transparency, and expedite the transition to a low-carbon global economy.

*Table 3. Comparison between conventional and ESG-oriented investment strategies*

| Dimension | Conventional Investment Strategies | ESG-Oriented Investment Strategies |
|---|---|---|
| **Primary Objective** | Maximize short- to medium-term financial returns | Align financial performance with long-term environmental and social sustainability goals (Talan et al., 2024) |
| **Risk Consideration** | Focused mainly on market, credit, and liquidity risks | Incorporates ESG risks such as climate change, regulatory pressure, reputational risks (Aich et al., 2021; Folqué et al., 2021) |
| **Return Profile** | Driven primarily by traditional financial metrics | Lower volatility and greater resilience in downturns; potential for sustainable long-term returns (Dmuchowski et al., 2023) |
| **Capital Allocation** | Sector-neutral, with little regard to environmental or social impact | Capital directed towards green bonds, renewable energy, sustainable infrastructure (Talan et al., 2024) |
| **Evaluation Tools** | Traditional financial analysis (P/E ratios, ROE, ROA, etc.) | ESG scoring models, AI-driven analytics, sustainability ratings (Sciarelli et al., 2021) |
| **Governance Influence** | Governance considered mainly in terms of shareholder rights and board structure | Broader governance perspective: CEO pay, transparency, anti-corruption, and stakeholder engagement (Folqué et al., 2021) |
| **Portfolio Diversification** | Traditional asset diversification across industries and regions | Emphasizes diversification by integrating climate risks and ESG-related exposures (Aich et al., 2021) |
| **Investor Motivation** | Profit-maximization and risk-adjusted financial return | Balancing financial return with social and environmental impact (Talan et al., 2024) |

**Source**: Author's elaboration based on Aich et al. (2021); Folqué et al. (2021); Dmuchowski et al. (2023); Sciarelli et al. (2021); Talan et al. (2024).

The comparative research demonstrates that ESG-focused investment strategies expand risk assessment parameters and enhance long-term financial resilience by incorporating environmental, social, and governance factors into decision-making processes. In contrast to traditional methods that emphasize short-term financial indicators, ESG-based models incorporate sustainability factors that mitigate volatility, enhance accountability, and direct funds towards climate-positive initiatives. However, their efficacy is significantly contingent upon the reliability of ESG scoring models and the alignment of regulatory standards across different jurisdictions. In the absence of consistent procedures and trustworthy disclosures, ESG strategies face the risk of fragmentation and even greenwashing. Consequently, embedded financing must guarantee that sustainability-oriented investments are underpinned by clear assessment processes and strong governance to optimize their transformative capacity.

## Obstacles and Hazards in Sustainable Embedded Finance

The expansion of sustainable embedded finance faces many systemic risks and vulnerabilities that could undermine its legitimacy and long-term efficacy. This model facilitates new opportunities for green investments, ESG-linked financing, and digital sustainability initiatives, while simultaneously exposing financial systems to risks such as fraud, greenwashing, data privacy breaches, cybersecurity threats, market volatility, and regulatory fragmentation (van Rijnsoever, 2022; Allioui & Mourdi, 2023; Bianchi et al., 2022). Mitigating these risks is crucial to enhance trust, transparency, and resilience within dynamic financial ecosystems.

A significant issue is greenwashing, in which companies inflate or distort their environmental performance to appeal to ESG-aware investors. This technique skews capital distribution, diminishes stakeholder trust, and compromises the legitimacy of sustainable finance (Bo & Battisti, 2024; Wang et al., 2025; Teichmann, Wittmann, & Sergi, 2023). The lack of standardized ESG indicators exacerbates this problem, as varying reporting frameworks enable firms to distort sustainability disclosures. The data-driven aspect of embedded finance generates privacy problems due to the potential for identity theft, misuse of personal financial information, and unlawful exploitation of transaction data. Regulatory bodies must consequently implement more uniform ESG taxonomies, create accountability frameworks, and guarantee transparent disclosures across platforms.

Cybersecurity threats represent a considerable vulnerability. Embedded finance, dependent on digital infrastructures, is more vulnerable to hacking, fraud, and exploitation of smart contracts in decentralized finance (DeFi) ecosystems. Cyberattacks aimed at ESG data or blockchain-based carbon credit markets can undermine the integrity of green financing efforts (Farayola, 2024; Al-Zoubi, 2024). Improving digital security via AI-based fraud detection, secure blockchain protocols, and robust smart contract architecture is essential for safeguarding embedded finance ecosystems.

Ultimately, market volatility and regulatory disunity provide systemic issues. The valuations of green assets, including renewable energy projects and carbon credits, frequently vary due to evolving policies, technological unpredictability, and fluctuating market mood. Furthermore, varying definitions of sustainability across nations complicate compliance for global investors, while inadequate enforcement mechanisms permit ESG infractions to remain unaddressed. Addressing these risks necessitates unified worldwide standards, stringent enforcement of ESG principles, and synchronized international financial governance to guarantee that embedded finance significantly contributes to long-term sustainability.

*Table 4. Risks, consequences, and mitigation strategies in sustainable embedded finance*

| Risk Category | Key Consequences | Mitigation Strategies |
|---|---|---|
| **Greenwashing & Fraud** | Misallocation of capital; loss of investor trust; erosion of credibility in ESG finance | Standardized ESG metrics; stricter disclosure rules; independent sustainability audits (Bo & Battisti, 2024; Wang et al., 2025) |
| **Data Privacy & AI Misuse** | Identity theft; misuse of personal financial data; weakened consumer confidence | Stronger data protection regulations; AI ethics frameworks; encrypted digital infrastructures |
| **Cybersecurity Threats** | Hacking of DeFi platforms; manipulation of carbon credit markets; smart contract exploits | AI-based fraud detection; secure blockchain protocols; resilient smart contract design (Farayola, 2024; Al-Zoubi, 2024) |
| **Market Volatility** | Fluctuating valuations of green assets; reduced investor appetite for ESG investments | Policy incentives for green finance; diversification across sustainable asset classes |
| **Regulatory Fragmentation** | Cross-border compliance challenges; inconsistent ESG enforcement; space for arbitrage | Harmonized global standards; stronger international cooperation; effective enforcement mechanisms (van Rijnsoever, 2022; Bianchi et al., 2022) |

**Source**: Author's elaboration based on van Rijnsoever (2022); Allioui & Mourdi (2023); Bianchi et al. (2022); Bo & Battisti (2024); Wang et al. (2025); Teichmann, Wittmann, & Sergi (2023); Farayola (2024); Alzoubi (2024)

The examination of hazards in sustainable embedded finance reveals that innovation by itself cannot ensure favorable sustainability results. In the absence of credible ESG standards, strong cybersecurity measures, and unified international rules, embedded finance may intensify greenwashing, erode investor trust, and heighten systemic vulnerabilities. In contrast, with robust governance, open reporting, and secure digital infrastructures, embedded finance can efficiently direct resources towards climate-positive investments while maintaining consumer trust. The sustained success of embedded finance relies on harmonizing technology advancement with institutional responsibility and synchronized global regulation.

## Risk Mitigation and Future-Proofing Sustainable Investments

The growth of sustainable embedded finance necessitates strong risk mitigation and future-proofing techniques to guarantee that green investments are resilient, transparent, and economically sustainable in the long term. The agenda focuses on the integration of AI-driven predictive analytics, the deployment of blockchain-enabled smart contracts, and the implementation of government-supported sustainability initiatives. Collectively, these strategies augment transparency, mitigate fraud, and establish a more robust framework for ecologically focused funding.

Artificial intelligence (AI) has become an essential instrument in enhancing ESG risk assessment through real-time data analysis, anomaly identification, and predictive modeling. AI-driven systems can perpetually scrutinize sustainability reports, financial disclosures, and regulatory submissions, consequently detecting discrepancies and averting misleading ESG assertions (Chhikara, Chhikara, & Gupta, 2025). Moreover, machine learning methods improve fraud detection by identifying inconsistencies in environmental reporting, while climate risk simulations enable investors to predict the impacts of policy changes, carbon pricing, or extreme weather events on green assets. This predictive capability enables automated portfolio optimization, allocating cash to sustainable initiatives with superior long-term performance potential.

Smart contracts enhance compliance frameworks within embedded finance ecosystems. Utilizing blockchain's immutability and transparency, these self-executing contracts automate ESG-related financial transactions, guaranteeing that funding is directed solely towards projects that satisfy sustainability standards (Ghosh et al., 2025). Their applications encompass sustainability-linked loans, green bonds, and decentralized carbon credit markets. Automated audits integrated into smart contracts diminish dependence on intermediaries, lower operating expenses, and improve the accountability of green financial transactions.

The role of governments and regulators is equally crucial in promoting sustainable finance via incentives, obligatory ESG inclusion, and public-private collaborations. Tax incentives, low-interest loans, and climate stress assessments enhance market stability and promote the integration of sustainability into financial institutions' operations (Pu et al., 2021; Puaschunder, 2023; Goutte & Sanin, 2024). Integrating technological innovation with legislative backing enables sustainable embedded finance to attain both environmental and economic resilience, thus guaranteeing its enduring role in global sustainability transitions.

## CASE STUDIES AND PRACTICAL APPLICATIONS OF EMBEDDED FINANCE IN SUSTAINABILITY

### Integrated Finance in Renewable Energy Initiatives

Embedded financing is transforming renewable energy markets by improving accessibility, scalability, and financial feasibility in solar, wind, and other clean energy initiatives. In contrast to conventional capital-intensive financing that typically limits participation to large corporations and institutional investors, embedded finance incorporates financial services into energy systems and digital marketplaces, thus reducing entry barriers and expanding investor involvement (Ari & Koc, 2021; Cross & Neumark, 2021).

Innovative finance approaches in the solar and wind sectors demonstrate how embedded systems facilitate the democratization of energy investments. For instance, Sunrun in the United States utilizes a solar-as-a-service concept, allowing homes to embrace renewable energy via leasing agreements and power purchase agreements without initial expenses. M-KOPA in Africa employs a pay-as-you-go (PAYG) model facilitated by mobile money, delivering affordable solar solutions to millions of off-grid families. In Europe, platforms like Trine utilize crowdfunding to direct little donations into wind energy initiatives, thus enhancing green infrastructure in neglected areas (Gema, 2023). These studies collectively demonstrate how embedded financing promotes the decentralized adoption of renewable energy, simultaneously addressing affordability and inclusivity.

The advent of peer-to-peer (P2P) energy trading exemplifies the revolutionary capacity of embedded finance. Blockchain-based platforms, like Power Ledger in Australia, enable homeowners with excess solar energy to sell directly to neighbors using smart contracts that provide transparent pricing and automatic payment (Wu et al., 2022; Falchetta et al., 2022). Integrating carbon credits into these transactions incentivizes environmentally responsible energy consumption in P2P systems, while diminishing reliance on centralized utilities.

In addition to technological advancement, embedded finance enhances financial inclusion within the renewable energy sector. Initiatives like Azuri technology, Solar Sister, and BBOXX integrate microfinance with digital payments, facilitating access to solar lighting, appliances, and clean cooking technology for impoverished populations in Africa and Asia. These approaches not only advance energy parity but also empower women-led firms, highlighting the social aspect of renewable energy transitions.

Embedded finance enhances the renewable energy ecosystem by integrating technology innovation with inclusive financial frameworks. Its scalability relies on conducive legal frameworks, resilient digital infrastructures, and transparent ESG reporting to guarantee that clean energy investments are socially equitable and environmentally sustainable.

*Table 5. Case studies of embedded finance in renewable energy*

| Company/ Initiative | Region | Financing Model | Sustainability Impact |
|---|---|---|---|
| **Sunrun** | United States | *Solar-as-a-Service* through leases and PPAs | Enabled households to adopt solar panels without upfront costs; increased renewable energy adoption. |
| **M-KOPA** | Africa | Pay-as-you-go (PAYG) solar microfinance | Provided affordable access to off-grid solar systems for millions of low-income households. |
| **Trine** | Europe | Crowdfunding for wind and solar projects | Allowed retail investors to fund renewable energy, expanding clean energy in underserved areas. |
| **Power Ledger** | Australia | Blockchain-based peer-to-peer (P2P) energy trading | Facilitated decentralized energy markets, reduced reliance on central utilities, and incentivized carbon-neutral energy use. |
| **Azuri Technologies** | Africa | Microfinance with digital payments | Delivered solar-powered lighting and appliances to rural households, advancing financial inclusion. |
| **Solar Sister** | Sub-Saharan Africa | Women-led micro-entrepreneurship with embedded finance | Empowered women through solar lantern and clean cookstove distribution, enhancing gender equity and energy access. |
| **BBOXX** | Asia & Africa | AI-driven credit assessment with digital lending | Enabled off-grid solar adoption by integrating credit scoring and mobile-based payments. |

**Source**: Author's elaboration based on Ari & Koc (2021); Cross & Neumark (2021); Gema (2023); Wu et al. (2022); Falchetta et al. (2022).

These case studies demonstrate how embedded finance may democratize renewable energy by reducing entry barriers, promoting financial inclusion, and expediting the decentralized deployment of clean technology. Scaling these models necessitates conducive legislative frameworks, resilient digital infrastructure, and transparent ESG reporting to guarantee that financial innovation results in enduring environmental and social benefits.

## Sustainable Supply Chain Financing and Circular Economy Frameworks

The use of integrated finance into supply chain management and circular economy models is transforming how organizations fulfill sustainability obligations. Conventional supply chains frequently exhibit resource inefficiency, carbon-intensive logistics, and waste production, underscoring the necessity of integrating financial innovation with sustainable business practices. Embedded finance offers integrated solutions, including real-time digital payments, blockchain-enabled traceability, and sustainability-linked credit, which improve accountability, diminish inefficiencies, and promote environmentally responsible activities (Liu et al., 2023; Pizzi, Corbo, & Caputo, 2021). By integrating financial instruments within operational systems, companies can associate finance with validated sustainability results, thus narrowing the disparity between environmental commitments and quantifiable impact.

A primary problem in sustainable supply chains is the constrained financial resources of small and medium-sized firms (SMEs) to implement environmentally friendly manufacturing and logistics practices. Significant initial expenses and intricate financing procedures frequently hinder SMEs from adopting renewable energy, ethical sourcing, or low-carbon shipping (Hove-Sibanda & Mkumatela, 2025; Kumar et al., 2022; Purwandani & Michaud, 2021). Embedded finance mitigates these obstacles by providing digital credit lines, automated payment systems linked to sustainability standards, and favorable loan rates for companies that achieve environmental performance criteria. HSBC's sustainable supply chain finance initiative offers lower loan rates to suppliers meeting carbon reduction targets, illustrating how integrated financing can convert procurement into a mechanism for enhancing environmental performance.

Blockchain enhances these frameworks by guaranteeing supply chain transparency and ethical traceability. Blockchain facilitates the collection of immutable ESG data, allowing organizations to trace raw materials from origin to finished product, authenticate certificates, and perform automated audits of fair labor and sustainable sourcing procedures (Kshetri, 2022; Vijai & Wisetsri, 2024). Platforms like Provenance illustrate this concept, enabling consumers and companies to authenticate sustainability assertions via real-time financial transactions associated with blockchain-based certificates. Furthermore, blockchain enables the tokenization of carbon credits and water rights, establishing cohesive markets for sustainability-related commodities and improving accountability throughout global value chains.

The circular economy is further augmented by embedded finance via improved waste management and recycling efforts. Financial support for recycling firms and resource restoration initiatives has historically been inadequate, constraining growth. Embedded finance incorporates mechanisms including microloans for recycling enterprises, automated deposit-refund systems, and pay-as-you-recycle models that encourage consumer engagement. An exemplary instance is TOMRA's deposit-return system, which incentivizes consumers with digital credits for returning beverage containers, markedly enhancing recycling rates throughout Europe and North America. These models illustrate how financial incentives integrated into consumer behaviors can expedite the shift towards closed-loop systems (Kumar & Chopra, 2022; Hazen et al., 2021; Matarneh et al., 2024).

Embedded finance improves supply chain sustainability and circular economy models by directly associating financial incentives with validated environmental performance. Nonetheless, its sustained efficacy relies on standardized ESG criteria, equitable access for SMEs, and resilient digital frameworks that mitigate fraud and greenwashing. Integrating sustainability-linked funding, blockchain traceability, and recycling incentives, embedded finance can align global trade and consumption with low-carbon, resource-efficient development pathways.

## The Function of Major Technology Companies and Conventional Financial Institutions

The incorporation of integrated finance into supply chain management and circular economy models is transforming how businesses oversee sustainability obligations. Conventional supply chains frequently exhibit resource inefficiency, carbon-intensive logistics, and waste production, underscoring the necessity of integrating financial innovation with sustainable business practices. Embedded finance offers integrated solutions, including real-time digital payments, blockchain-enabled traceability, and sustainability-linked credit, which improve accountability, diminish inefficiencies, and promote environmentally responsible activities (Liu et al., 2023; Pizzi, Corbo, & Caputo, 2021). By integrating financial instruments within operational systems, companies can associate finance with validated sustainability results, thus narrowing the disparity between environmental commitments and quantifiable impact.

A primary difficulty in sustainable supply chains is the restricted financial capability of small and medium-sized firms (SMEs) to implement environmentally friendly manufacturing and logistics practices. Significant initial expenses and intricate financing procedures frequently hinder SMEs from adopting renewable energy, ethical sourcing, or low-carbon shipping (Hove-Sibanda & Mkumatela, 2025; Kumar et al., 2022; Purwandani & Michaud, 2021). Embedded finance mitigates these obstacles by providing digital credit lines, automated payment systems linked to sustainability standards, and preferential loan rates for companies that satisfy environmental performance criteria. HSBC's sustainable supply chain finance initiative offers lower borrowing rates to suppliers that meet carbon reduction targets, illustrating how integrated financing can convert procurement into a mechanism for enhancing environmental performance.

Blockchain enhances these frameworks by guaranteeing supply chain transparency and ethical traceability. Blockchain facilitates the collection of immutable ESG data, allowing organizations to trace raw materials from origin to finished product, authenticate certifications, and perform automated audits of equitable labor and sustainable sourcing procedures (Kshetri, 2022; Vijai & Wisetsri, 2024). Platforms like Provenance illustrate this concept by enabling consumers and businesses to authenticate sustainability assertions via real-time financial transactions associated with blockchain-based certifications. Furthermore, blockchain enables the tokenization of carbon credits and water rights, establishing cohesive markets for sustainability-related commodities and improving accountability throughout global value chains.

The circular economy is further augmented by embedded finance via improved waste management and recycling efforts. Financial support for recycling firms and resource restoration initiatives has historically been inadequate, constraining growth. Embedded finance incorporates mechanisms including microloans for recycling enterprises, automated deposit-refund systems, and pay-as-you-recycle models that encourage consumer engagement. An exemplary case is TOMRA's deposit-return system, which incentivizes consumers with digital credits for returning beverage containers, therefore substantially enhancing recycling rates throughout Europe and North America. These models illustrate how financial incentives integrated into consumer behaviors can expedite the shift towards closed-loop systems (Kumar & Chopra, 2022; Hazen et al., 2021; Matarneh, 2024).

Embedded finance improves supply chain sustainability and circular economy models by directly associating financial incentives with validated environmental performance. Nonetheless, its sustained efficacy relies on standardized ESG criteria, equitable access for SMEs, and resilient digital frameworks that mitigate fraud and greenwashing. Integrating sustainability-linked funding, blockchain traceability, and recycling incentives, embedded finance can align global trade and consumption with low-carbon, resource-efficient development pathways.

*Figure 2. Embedded finance applications in sustainable supply chains and circular economy (Author adapted from Liu et al., 2023; Pizzi, Corbo, & Caputo, 2021; Kumar & Chopra, 2022; Kshetri, 2022; Vijai & Wisetsri, 2024; Hazen et al., 2021; Matarneh et al., 2024)*

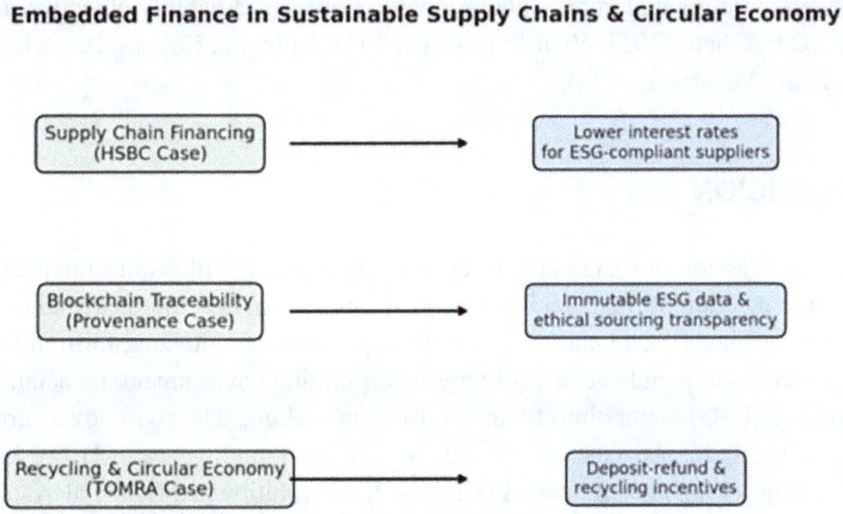


The figure depicts the role of embedded finance in fostering sustainable supply chains and circular economy frameworks via three interrelated mechanisms: supply chain financing, blockchain traceability, and recycling incentives. The initial approach, supply chain financing, is illustrated by HSBC's ESG-linked financing strategy, which incentivizes suppliers with reduced loan rates upon meeting carbon reduction objectives. This illustrates how embedded financing reduces the capital costs for sustainable firms and generates incentives for environmentally responsible production.

The second technique, blockchain traceability, is exemplified by Provenance, a UK-based platform that employs irreversible ESG data to guarantee transparent and ethical sourcing. Integrating blockchain technology enables organizations and consumers to verify sustainability claims in real time, thereby mitigating the dangers of greenwashing and improving supply chain accountability.

The third mechanism, recycling and circular economy financing, is illustrated by TOMRA's deposit-refund system, which utilizes embedded finance to promote recycling via digital reimbursements. This concept promotes responsible waste management and facilitates the expansion of circular economy techniques across various businesses.

These processes collectively demonstrate that embedded finance is not only a financial innovation but also a structural facilitator of systemic sustainability. Embedded finance integrates real-time financing, transparent traceability, and recycling incentives to create a comprehensive framework that fosters responsible sourcing, mitigates environmental impact, and promotes global sustainability objectives (Liu et al., 2023; Kshetri, 2022; Vijai & Wisetsri, 2024; Kumar & Chopra, 2022; Hazen et al., 2021; Matarneh, 2024).

## CONCLUSION

The progression of sustainable finance in the digital era illustrates the increasing interconnection of financial innovation, technological development, and global sustainability goals. Sustainable finance aligns profitability with long-term environmental stewardship and social equity by incorporating environmental, social, and governance (ESG) factors into financial decision-making. The swift advancement of digital technologies—such as blockchain, artificial intelligence (AI), the Internet of Things (IoT), and embedded finance—has revolutionized financial systems, enhancing the transparency, inclusivity, and efficiency of green investments. These technologies diminish information asymmetries, enhance capital accessibility, and promote accountability, ultimately bolstering investor trust in sustainability-focused markets.

Nonetheless, the efficacy of sustainable embedded finance relies on overcoming enduring problems, such as regulatory uncertainty, cybersecurity weaknesses, and the threats of greenwashing and digital exclusion. To guarantee that financial institutions effectively support the Sustainable Development Goals (SDGs), it is essential to have harmonized global regulatory frameworks, robust governance mechanisms, and inclusive digital infrastructures. Furthermore, integrating sustainability into routine financial transactions—via digital payments, supply chain financing, or renewable energy investment platforms—demonstrates finance's capacity to serve as a catalyst for systemic transformation.

## REFERENCES


Ahiase, G., Sari, M., Andriana, D., Nugraha, N., Purnomo, B. S., & Heryana, T. (2025). Unveiling the African growth puzzle: Relationship between financial inclusion, debt sustainability and economic growth. *International Journal of Social Economics, 52*(4), 591–607. DOI: 10.1108/IJSE-01-2024-0062

Ahlström, H., & Monciardini, D. (2021). The regulatory dynamics of sustainable finance: Paradoxical success and limitations of EU reforms. *Journal of Business Ethics*. Advance online publication. DOI: 10.1007/s10551-021-04763- springer.com PMID: 33642657

Aich, S., Thakur, A., Nanda, D., Tripathy, S., & Kim, H. C. (2021). Factors affecting ESG towards impact on investment: A structural approach. Sustainability. / mdpi.comDOI: 10.3390/su131910868

Al-Zoubi, W. K. (2024). Economic development in the digital economy: A bibliometric review. *Economies, 12*(3), 53. DOI: 10.3390/economies12030053

Aldboush, H. H. H. & Ferdous, M. (2023). Building trust in fintech: an analysis of ethical and privacy considerations in the intersection of big data, AI, and customer trust. International Journal of Financial Studies. / mdpi.comDOI: 10.3390/ijfs11030090

Allioui, H. & Mourdi, Y. (2023). Exploring the full potentials of IoT for better financial growth and stability: A comprehensive survey. Sensors. / mdpi.comDOI: 10.3390/s23198015

Alsedrah, I. T. (2024). Fintech and green finance revolutionizing carbon emission reduction through green energy projects in mineral-rich countries. *Resources Policy, 94*, 105064. DOI: 10.1016/j.resourpol.2024.105064

Ari, I. & Koc, M. (2021). Philanthropic-crowdfunding-partnership: A proof-of-concept study for sustainable financing in low-carbon energy transitions. Energy. / sciencedirect.comDOI: 10.1016/j.energy.2021.119925

Bianchi, G., Testa, F., Tessitore, S., & Iraldo, F. (2022). How to embed environmental sustainability: The role of dynamic capabilities and managerial approaches in a life cycle management perspective. Business Strategy and the Environment, 31(1), 312-325. DOI: wiley.comDOI: 10.1002/bse.2889

Chhikara, H., Chhikara, S., & Gupta, L. (2025). Predictive Analytics in Finance: Leveraging AI and Machine Learning for Investment Strategies. In Utilizing AI and Machine Learning in Financial Analysis (pp. 325-336). IGI Global Scientific Publishing. DOI: [HTML]DOI: 10.4018/979-8-3693-8507-4.ch017

Chueca Vergara, C. & Ferruz Agudo, L. (2021). Fintech and sustainability: do they affect each other?. Sustainability. / mdpi.comDOI: 10.3390/su13137012

Colombage, S. (2025). Financial Technology (Fintech) and Sustainable Financing. *Journal of Risk and Financial Management, 18*(10), 553. DOI: 10.3390/jrfm18100553

Cromwell, R. S., & Peprah, J. A. (2025). Banking Business Models and Sustainable Development: Challenges and Opportunities. Strategic Approaches to Banking Business and Sustainable Development Goals, 3-22. / [HTML]DOI: 10.1007/978-3-031-80744-2_1

Cross, J. & Neumark, T. (2021). Solar power and its discontents: critiquing off-grid infrastructures of inclusion in East Africa. Development and Change. DOI: wiley.comDOI: 10.1111/dech.12668

Cunha, F. A. F. D. S., Meira, E., & Orsato, R. J. (2021). Sustainable finance and investment: Review and research agenda. Business Strategy and the Environment, 30(8), 3821-3838. DOI: researchgate.netDOI: 10.1002/bse.2842

Dmuchowski, P., Dmuchowski, W., Baczewska-Dąbrowska, A. H., & Gworek, B. (2023). Environmental, social, and governance (ESG) model; impacts and sustainable investment–Global trends and Poland's perspective. *Journal of Environmental Management, 329*, 117023. Bo, S., & Battisti, E. (2024). Green finance and greenwashing: charting a sustainable path forward. *Qualitative Research in Financial Markets.*

Falchetta, G., Michoud, B., Hafner, M., & Rother, M. (2022). Harnessing finance for a new era of decentralised electricity access: A review of private investment patterns and emerging business models. Energy Research & Social Science, 90, 102587. / sciencedirect.comDOI: 10.1016/j.erss.2022.102587

Farayola, O. A. (2024). Revolutionizing banking security: integrating artificial intelligence, blockchain, and business intelligence for enhanced cybersecurity. Finance & Accounting Research Journal. DOI: academia.eduDOI: 10.51594/farj.v6i4.990

Fernandez-Vallado, M. (2025). Towards a Policy Framework for Microfinance: Innovative Financial Solutions for Sustainable Development. In Microfinance, Financial Innovation, and Sustainable Entrepreneurship in Economics (pp. 139-182). IGI Global Scientific Publishing. DOI: [HTML]DOI: 10.4018/979-8-3693-6622-6.ch006

Folqué, M., Escrig-Olmedo, E., & Corzo Santamaría, T. (2021). Sustainable development and financial system: Integrating ESG risks through sustainable investment strategies in a climate change context. *Sustainable Development (Bradford), 29*(5), 876–890. DOI: 10.1002/sd.2181

Fu, C., Lu, L., & Pirabi, M. (2023). Advancing green finance: a review of sustainable development. Digital Economy and Sustainable Development. / springer.comDOI: 10.1007/s44265-023-00020-3

Gema, S. B. (2023). Financing the energy transition: The new paradigm for renewable energy investors. In *The Palgrave Handbook of Zero Carbon Energy Systems and Energy Transitions* (pp. 1–44). Springer International Publishing. [HTML], DOI: 10.1007/978-3-030-74380-2_4-1

Ghosh, O., Kumar, B., Sharif, M., & Siwach, J. (2025). Regulatory and Legal Implications on Harnessing Blockchain-Digital Twin Fusion for Sustainable Investments. In The Future of Indigenous Inclusivity: Unlocking Finance for Economic Development (pp. 19-38). IGI Global Scientific Publishing. DOI: researchgate.netDOI: 10.4018/979-8-3693-7924-0.ch002

Goutte, S., & Sanin, M. E. (2024). Main challenges regarding development and sustainability in economics and finance. [HTML]. *Development and Sustainability in Economics and Finance, 100002*, 100002. Advance online publication. DOI: 10.1016/j.dsef.2024.100002

Hazen, B. T., Russo, I., Confente, I., & Pellathy, D. (2021). Supply chain management for circular economy: conceptual framework and research agenda. The International Journal of Logistics Management, 32(2), 510-537. / emerald.comDOI: 10.1108/IJLM-12-2019-0332

Hidayat-ur-Rehman, I., & Hossain, M. N. (2024). The impacts of Fintech adoption, green finance and competitiveness on banks' sustainable performance: Digital transformation as moderator. *Asia-Pacific Journal of Business Administration*. Advance online publication. DOI: 10.1108/APJBA-10-2023-0497

Hossain, R., Ghose, P., Chowdhury, T. M., Hossen, M. D., Hasan, M. N., & Mani, L. (2024). Ownership Structures and Firm Performance: A Correlation and Regression Analysis of Financial Institutions in Bangladesh. *Pakistan Journal of Life and Social Sciences, 22*(2), 6278–6295. DOI: 10.57239/PJLSS-2024-22.2.00473

Hove-Sibanda, P., & Mkumatela, Y. (2025). Green Logistics in SMEs for Sustainable Development. In *Eco-Logistics and Sustainable Supply Chain Innovations* (pp. 85–116). IGI Global Scientific Publishing. [HTML], DOI: 10.4018/979-8-3693-6175-7.ch005

Howson, P., & de Vries, A. (2022). Preying on the poor? Opportunities and challenges for tackling the social and environmental threats of cryptocurrencies for vulnerable and low-income communities. [HTML]. *Energy Research & Social Science*, *84*, 102394. Advance online publication. DOI: 10.1016/j.erss.2021.102394

Khalil, M. A., Sinliamthong, P., & Khalil, R. (2025). From Paper to Pixels for a World of Purpose: A Systematic Review of Sustainable Finance, Blockchain, and Digital Assets. Sustainable Financing—A Contemporary Guide for Green Finance, Crowdfunding and Digital Currencies: Sustainable Financing, 61-78. [HTML] DOI: 10.1007/978-3-031-80969-9_5

Kshetri, N. (2022). Blockchain systems and ethical sourcing in the mineral and metal industry: A multiple case study. [HTML]. *International Journal of Logistics Management*, *33*(1), 1–27. Advance online publication. DOI: 10.1108/IJLM-02-2021-0108

Kumar, L., Nadeem, F., Sloan, M., Restle-Steinert, J., Deitch, M. J., Ali Naqvi, S., ... & Sassanelli, C. (2022). Fostering green finance for sustainable development: A focus on textile and leather small medium enterprises in Pakistan. Sustainability, 14(19), 11908. mdpi.comDOI: 10.3390/su141911908

Kumar, N. M. & Chopra, S. S. (2022). Leveraging blockchain and smart contract technologies to overcome circular economy implementation challenges. Sustainability. mdpi.comDOI: 10.3390/su14159492

Kumar, S., Sharma, D., Rao, S., Lim, W. M., & Mangla, S. K. (2022). Past, present, and future of sustainable finance: insights from big data analytics through machine learning of scholarly research. Annals of Operations Research, 1-44. springer.comDOI: 10.1007/s10479-021-04410-8

Kuzmina, J., Maditinos, D., Norena-Chavez, D., Grima, S., & Kadłubek, M. (2023). ESG integration as a risk management tool within the financial decision-making process. In Digital Transformation, Strategic Resilience, Cyber Security and Risk Management (pp. 105-113). Emerald Publishing Limited. [HTML]DOI: 10.1108/S1569-37592023000111A007

Li, B. (2023). The role of financial markets in the energy transition: An analysis of investment trends and opportunities in renewable energy and clean technology. [HTML]. *Environmental Science and Pollution Research International*, *30*(43), 97948–97964. Advance online publication. DOI: 10.1007/s11356-023-29014-6 PMID: 37599346

Li, Z. & Chen, P. (2024). Sustainable Finance Meets FinTech: Amplifying Green Credit's Benefits for Banks. Sustainability. mdpi.comDOI: 10.3390/su16187901

Louman, B., Girolami, E. D., Shames, S., Primo, L. G., Gitz, V., Scherr, S. J., Meybeck, A., & Brady, M. (2022). Access to landscape finance for small-scale producers and local communities: A literature review. *Land (Basel)*, *11*(9), 1444. DOI: 10.3390/land11091444

Macchiavello, E., & Siri, M. (2022). Sustainable finance and fintech: Can technology contribute to achieving environmental goals? A preliminary assessment of 'green fintech' and 'sustainable digital finance'. *European Company and Financial Law Review*, *19*(1), 128–174. DOI: 10.1515/ecfr-2022-0005

Matarneh, S., Piprani, A. Z., Ellahi, R. M., Nguyen, D. N., Le, T. M., & Nazir, S. (2024). Industry 4.0 technologies and circular economy synergies: Enhancing corporate sustainability through sustainable supply chain integration and flexibility. Environmental Technology & Innovation, 35, 103723. / sciencedirect.comDOI: 10.1016/j.eti.2024.103723

Musleh Al-Sartawi, A. M., Hussainey, K., & Razzaque, A. (2022). The role of artificial intelligence in sustainable finance. Journal of Sustainable Finance & Investment, 1-6. / tandfonline.comDOI: 10.1080/20430795.2022.2057405

Ng, S. H., Yang, Y., Lee, C. C., & Ong, C. Z. (2023). Nexus of financing constraints and supply chain finance: Evidence from listed SMEs in China. *International Journal of Financial Studies*, *11*(3), 102. DOI: 10.3390/ijfs11030102

Nyarko, K., Urmee, T., Whale, J., Simsek, Y., & Haigh, Y. (2025). Assessing the effectiveness of energy policies in accelerating renewable energy-based mini-grid deployment: A case study. Energy for Sustainable Development, 85, 101631. / sciencedirect.comDOI: 10.1016/j.esd.2024.101631

Ozili, P. K. (2023). Assessing global interest in decentralized finance, embedded finance, open finance, ocean finance and sustainable finance. Asian Journal of Economics and Banking. / emerald.comDOI: 10.1108/AJEB-03-2022-0029

Pizzi, S., Corbo, L., & Caputo, A. (2021). Fintech and SMEs sustainable business models: Reflections and considerations for a circular economy. Journal of Cleaner Production. / ucp.ptDOI: 10.1016/j.jclepro.2020.125217

Pu, G., Qamruzzaman, M. D., Mehta, A. M., Naqvi, F. N., & Karim, S. (2021). Innovative finance, technological adaptation and SMEs sustainability: the mediating role of government support during COVID-19 pandemic. Sustainability, 13(16), 9218. / mdpi.comDOI: 10.3390/su13169218

Puaschunder, J. M. (2023). The Future of Resilient Green Finance. In *The Future of Resilient Finance: Finance Politics in the Age of Sustainable Development* (pp. 185–210). Springer International Publishing. [HTML], DOI: 10.1007/978-3-031-30138-4_6

Purwandani, J. A. & Michaud, G. (2021). What are the drivers and barriers for green business practice adoption for SMEs?. Environment systems and decisions. / springer.comDOI: 10.1007/s10669-021-09821-3

Schulz, K. & Feist, M. (2021). Leveraging blockchain technology for innovative climate finance under the Green Climate Fund. Earth System Governance. / sciencedirect.comDOI: 10.1016/j.esg.2020.100084

Sciarelli, M., Cosimato, S., Landi, G., & Iandolo, F. (2021). Socially responsible investment strategies for the transition towards sustainable development: The importance of integrating and communicating ESG. The TQM Journal. / emerald.comDOI: 10.1108/TQM-08-2020-0180

Selvakumar, P., & Manjunath, T. C. (2025). Green Finance and Investment Explore the Role of Sustainable Finance. In Driving Business Success Through Eco-Friendly Strategies (pp. 149-168). IGI Global Scientific Publishing. DOI: [HTML]DOI: 10.4018/979-8-3693-9750-3.ch008

Talan, G., Sharma, G. D., Pereira, V., & Muschert, G. W. (2024). From ESG to holistic value addition: Rethinking sustainable investment from the lens of stakeholder theory. International Review of Economics & Finance, 96, 103530. /DOI: 10.1016/j.iref.2024.103530

Taneja, B. (2024). Financial Innovations in FinTech: Unleashing the Power of Embedded Finance and AI in Firm Financing and Investment Strategies. In Contemporary Research and Practices for Promoting Financial Literacy and Sustainability (pp. 208-232). IGI Global. DOI: [HTML]DOI: 10.4018/979-8-3693-0863-9.ch008

Teichmann, F. M. J., Wittmann, C., & Sergi, B. S. S. (2023). What are the consequences of corporate greenwashing? A look into the consequences of greenwashing in consumer and financial markets. Journal of Information [HTML]. *Communication and Ethics in Society*, *21*(3), 290–301. DOI: 10.1108/JICES-10-2022-0090

Triantafyllidou, E. & Zabaniotou, A. (2021). Digital technology and social innovation promoting a green citizenship: development of the "go sustainable living" digital application. Circular Economy and Sustainability. / academia.eduDOI: 10.1007/s43615-021-00111-3

Unsal, O., & Ozkan, B. (2024). *Technologies and Emerging Trends Shaping Fintech*. The Emerald Handbook of Fintech. [HTML], DOI: 10.1108/978-1-83753-608-520241046

van Rijnsoever, F. J. (2022). Intermediaries for the greater good: How entrepreneurial support organizations can embed constrained sustainable development startups in entrepreneurial …. Research Policy. / sciencedirect.comDOI: 10.1016/j.respol.2021.104438

Vijai, & Wisetsri, W. (2024). Circular economy for sustainable development in India. In *Global Sustainability: Trends, Challenges & Case Studies* (pp. 61-87). Cham: Springer Nature Switzerland.

Waliszewski, K. (2023). Socio-economic determinants of financial inclusion in Central and Eastern Europe during the COVID-19 pandemic. *Przegląd Wschodnioeuropejski, 14*(1), 25–41. DOI: 10.31648/pw.9019

Wang, W., & Qu, Z. (2024). Capital market opening and commercial bank risk: Evidence from "Shanghai–Hong Kong Stock Connect". *Finance Research Letters, 59*, 104827. DOI: 10.1016/j.frl.2023.104827

Wu, Y., Wu, Y., Cimen, H., Vasquez, J. C., & Guerrero, J. M. (2022). Towards collective energy Community: Potential roles of microgrid and blockchain to go beyond P2P energy trading. Applied Energy. / sciencedirect.comDOI: 10.1016/j.apenergy.2022.119003

Xie, X., Gong, C., Su, Z., Nie, Y., & Kim, W. (2024). Consumers' Behavioral Willingness to Use Green Financial Products: An Empirical Study within a Theoretical Framework. Behavioral Sciences. / mdpi.comDOI: 10.3390/bs14080634

Zetzsche, D. A., & Anker-Sørensen, L. (2022). Regulating sustainable finance in the dark. European Business Organization Law Review, 23(1), 47-85. springer.comDOI: 10.1007/s40804-021-00237-9

Ziolo, M., Bak, I., & Cheba, K. (2021). The role of sustainable finance in achieving sustainable development goals: Does it work?. Technological and Economic Development of Economy, 27(1), 45-70. / vgtu.lt Driessen, N. (2021). Methane Emissions and Financial Structures-The role of Finance in mitigating Environmental Degradation.DOI: 10.3846/tede.2020.13863

# Chapter 7
# Embedded Finance in Action:
## A Pathway to Sustainable Growth

**Arindam Nag**
https://orcid.org/0009-0002-3044-4940
*Christ University, India*

## ABSTRACT

*This chapter examines how embedded finance reshapes sustainable investment through AI, machine learning, and DeFi integration with ESG practices. These technologies can address behavioral biases such as loss aversion, yet major challenges remain. ESG data is fragmented, with rating providers often showing correlations below 0.6, weakening automated screening. Greenwashing risks rise as automation favors convenience over impact checks, while regulation lags behind and leaves fiduciary duties unclear. The discussion links these issues to finance theory, applying CAPM to test whether ESG factors improve risk-adjusted returns and using behavioral insights to assess how embedded systems may correct cognitive limits. Case studies show that while embedded finance reduces transaction friction, turning convenience into measurable sustainability outcomes is still uncertain. The chapter contributes by connecting finance theory with emerging technologies to evaluate real versus promised effects on sustainable investment.*

## INTRODUCTION TO EMBEDDED FINANCE AND SUSTAINABLE INVESTMENT INTEGRATION

The integration of environmental, social, and governance (ESG) criteria into investment decision-making processes represents a fundamental shift in contemporary

DOI: 10.4018/979-8-3373-2464-7.ch007

finance theory and practice (Adams & Abhayawansa, 2022). This transformation reflects growing recognition that traditional financial metrics alone cannot adequately capture the long-term risks and opportunities associated with environmental degradation, social inequality, and governance failures. Embedded finance, defined as the seamless integration of financial services into non-financial platforms and applications, has emerged as a technological catalyst for this transformation (Al-Gasaymeh et al., 2023). Unlike traditional financial service delivery models that require separate institutional interfaces, embedded finance enables ESG investment access through everyday digital touchpoints, potentially democratizing sustainable investment participation.

Traditional investment approaches often suffer from behavioral biases, including loss aversion and herding behavior, which can impede optimal decision-making processes (Relja, Ward, & Zhao, 2024). Loss aversion, where investors experience the pain of losses more acutely than equivalent gains, frequently leads to short-term thinking that conflicts with the extended time horizons required for sustainable investment returns. Similarly, herding behavior, where investors follow crowd sentiment rather than independent analysis, can create market inefficiencies that undervalue genuine ESG performance while inflating speculative sustainability investments.

The process of balancing short-term profit motives with long-term sustainability presents significant challenges for contemporary investment management. Institutional investors face pressure from stakeholders to deliver consistent quarterly returns, often creating misalignment with the multi-year investment horizons typically required for ESG initiatives to generate measurable impact (Barbosa et al., 2024). This temporal mismatch is compounded by the complexity of ESG evaluation frameworks, where standardized metrics remain elusive and comparability across investments is often limited by inconsistent reporting methodologies.

Psychological biases such as confirmation bias and availability heuristic further complicate sustainable investment decisions. Investors may selectively interpret ESG data to confirm pre-existing beliefs about particular companies or sectors, while recent news events or prominent corporate failures can disproportionately influence risk assessments. These cognitive limitations are compounded by information asymmetries between institutional and retail investors, where access to comprehensive ESG analysis tools and expertise remains concentrated among large asset management firms.

Recent developments in financial technology, particularly embedded finance and artificial intelligence applications, are helping to reshape this landscape by providing more accessible and data-driven approaches to sustainable investing (Cao, 2022). Machine learning algorithms can process vast quantities of unstructured ESG data from corporate reports, news sources, and regulatory filings to identify patterns and correlations that human analysts might overlook. Natural language processing capabilities enable real-time sentiment analysis of corporate communications and media coverage, potentially providing early warning signals for ESG-related risks or opportunities.

The convergence of embedded finance technologies with sustainable investing frameworks addresses both the accessibility barriers and cognitive limitations that have historically constrained ESG investment adoption. Digital platforms can present complex ESG information in user-friendly formats, enabling retail investors to make informed decisions without requiring specialized expertise in sustainability analysis. Robo-advisors incorporating ESG screening algorithms can automatically rebalance portfolios based on changing sustainability scores, reducing the cognitive burden on individual investors while maintaining alignment with stated sustainability preferences.

Machine learning algorithms and artificial intelligence applications within embedded finance platforms can potentially mitigate behavioral biases by providing data-driven investment recommendations and real-time ESG performance analytics (Cao, 2022). Algorithmic decision-making can reduce the influence of emotional responses to market volatility, while automated portfolio optimization can maintain long-term ESG objectives despite short-term performance pressures. However, these technological solutions introduce new risks related to algorithmic transparency, data quality, and the potential for embedded biases within machine learning models.

However, the effectiveness of these technological solutions in promoting genuine sustainable investment outcomes requires critical examination of both their capabilities and limitations. The ESG data ecosystem remains fragmented and inconsistent, with different rating agencies often producing divergent assessments of the same companies (Adams & Abhayawansa, 2022). This fundamental data quality issue can undermine the reliability of AI-driven ESG analysis, potentially leading embedded finance platforms to promote investments that appear sustainable based on flawed or incomplete information.

Furthermore, the democratization of ESG investing through embedded finance raises concerns about greenwashing at scale. While traditional institutional investors typically have resources to conduct due diligence on sustainability claims, retail investors using embedded platforms may lack the expertise to distinguish between genuine ESG leaders and companies engaging in superficial sustainability marketing. The automation of ESG screening processes, while increasing accessibility, may inadvertently facilitate the promotion of investments that prioritize ESG marketing over substantive environmental and social impact.

The regulatory landscape for embedded ESG investing remains underdeveloped, creating uncertainty about fiduciary responsibilities and disclosure requirements. Unlike traditional investment advisors who operate under established regulatory frameworks, embedded finance providers may not be subject to the same standards of care regarding ESG investment recommendations. This regulatory gap could expose retail investors to unsuitable investment recommendations while limiting their recourse in cases of poor outcomes.

This chapter examines the intersection of embedded finance and sustainable investment, analyzing how technological integration affects investor behavior, market efficiency, and environmental outcomes. The analysis considers both the promising applications and the significant challenges that characterize this emerging field. Through critical evaluation of current implementations and future prospects, this research aims to identify the conditions under which embedded finance can genuinely advance sustainable investment objectives rather than merely facilitating access to products labeled as sustainable.

## THE ROLE OF EMBEDDED FINANCE IN SUSTAINABLE INVESTMENT

The integration of financial services within non-financial digital platforms represents a fundamental shift in how sustainable investment products reach end consumers. Embedded finance, as defined by Banking-as-a-Service (BaaS) models, enables the delivery of ESG investment options through everyday digital interactions, potentially reducing the traditional barriers that have limited retail participation in sustainable finance markets (Amnas, Selvam, & Parayitam, 2024). This technological approach addresses both accessibility challenges and the cognitive complexity associated with ESG evaluation, though its effectiveness in promoting genuine sustainable outcomes requires critical examination.

### Theoretical Framework: Technology Adoption and Behavioral Finance

The adoption of embedded finance platforms for sustainable investment can be explained by both technology acceptance models and behavioral finance theory. TAM emphasizes that perceived usefulness and ease of use drive adoption (Mogaji & Nguyen, 2024), suggesting that ESG products must be accessible within familiar interfaces. Behavioral finance adds that investors face systematic biases such as loss aversion, herding, and confirmation bias that limit their willingness to commit to long-term ESG products (Relja, Ward, & Zhao, 2024). Embedded systems therefore matter not only because they deliver new products, but because they can be designed to counteract these biases through defaults, nudges, and automated decision tools.

Behavioral finance research identifies several cognitive biases that impede optimal investment decision-making, including loss aversion, confirmation bias, and herding behavior (Relja, Ward, & Zhao, 2024). Loss aversion, where investors experience losses more acutely than equivalent gains, often leads to short-term thinking that conflicts with the extended time horizons required for sustainable investment returns. Confirmation bias may cause investors to selectively interpret ESG data to support pre-existing beliefs, while herding behavior can create market inefficiencies in ESG valuations.

From a finance theory perspective, the Capital Asset Pricing Model and its extensions suggest ESG factors should only affect pricing if they provide superior risk-adjusted returns or reduce systematic risk. However, the Efficient Market Hypothesis raises questions about whether embedded finance systems can generate sustainable alpha or primarily redistribute value. ESG rating fragmentation, with correlation coefficients below 0.6 between major providers, suggests significant market inefficiencies technology might address.

## Mechanisms of Integration: From Theory to Practice

Embedded finance platforms address these behavioral limitations through several technological mechanisms. Automated portfolio optimization algorithms can maintain long-term ESG objectives despite short-term market volatility, potentially reducing the influence of loss aversion on investment decisions (Cao, 2022). Machine learning systems can process vast quantities of ESG data to identify patterns that human analysts might overlook, while natural language processing capabilities enable real-time analysis of corporate sustainability communications. Pedersen, Fitzgibbons, and Pomorski (2023) demonstrate that ESG integration can be consistent with portfolio optimization when sustainability preferences represent genuine investor utility rather than return expectations. Their ESG-efficient frontier framework suggests that embedded finance systems should facilitate preference expression rather than claiming superior financial performance, yet many current implementations blur this distinction by promoting both sustainability and return benefits simultaneously.

## Market Implementation and Accessibility

The practical implementation of embedded ESG investing has taken several forms across different platform types. E-commerce applications increasingly offer carbon offset options integrated with purchase transactions, while digital banking platforms provide ESG-screened investment portfolios alongside traditional financial services (Al-Gasaymeh et al., 2023). These implementations aim to reduce the friction between sustainability intentions and actual investment behavior by embedding ESG options within existing user workflows.

Digital wallets and payment platforms have emerged as particularly significant channels for embedded sustainable finance. These platforms can track user spending patterns to calculate carbon footprints and recommend offsetting investments, creating direct linkages between consumption behavior and environmental impact mitigation (Bruce et al., 2023). However, the accuracy of carbon footprint calculations and the additionality of recommended offset projects remain subject to significant uncertainty and potential manipulation.

## Cognitive Bias Mitigation Through Technology

Artificial intelligence and machine learning applications within embedded finance platforms can potentially address several categories of cognitive bias that traditionally impair sustainable investment decisions. Automated ESG screening can reduce the influence of availability bias, where recent news events disproportionately influence risk assessments (Omokhoa et al., 2022). Similarly, algorithmic portfolio rebalancing can maintain long-term sustainability objectives despite emotional responses to short-term market volatility.

Nevertheless, these technological solutions introduce new forms of bias related to algorithmic design and training data quality. Machine learning models trained on historical ESG data may perpetuate past biases or fail to adapt to evolving sustainability standards (Douglas, 2024). The opacity of many AI systems also limits investors' ability to understand and evaluate the basis for investment recommendations, potentially creating new forms of information asymmetry between platform providers and users.

## Critical Analysis of Current Limitations

The current embedded finance landscape for sustainable investment faces several significant limitations that constrain its effectiveness in promoting genuine ESG outcomes. Regulatory frameworks for embedded financial services remain underdeveloped, creating uncertainty about fiduciary responsibilities and disclosure requirements (Khalifa, Elmedany, & Sharif, 2024). Unlike traditional investment advisors who operate under established regulatory frameworks, embedded finance providers may not be subject to equivalent standards of care regarding ESG investment recommendations.

Greenwashing risks are amplified in embedded finance systems, where automation may reduce due diligence while marketing convenience over impact verification. Embedded platforms, particularly those serving retail investors, may lack the resources to conduct comprehensive due diligence on sustainability claims (Barbosa et al., 2024). This limitation is compounded by the automated nature of many embedded systems, which may prioritize ESG marketing metrics over genuine impact measurements.

### Future Implications and Research Directions

The evolution of embedded finance in sustainable investment will likely depend on several key factors, including regulatory development, standardization of ESG metrics, and advances in AI transparency. Regulatory frameworks that establish clear standards for ESG investment recommendations could enhance consumer protection while promoting market confidence (Addy et al., 2022). Similarly, the development of standardized ESG measurement protocols could improve the reliability of automated screening processes and reduce the current fragmentation in sustainability assessments.

The integration of blockchain technology and decentralized finance protocols may offer additional opportunities for transparency and verification in embedded ESG investing, though these applications remain largely experimental. The ultimate success of embedded finance in promoting sustainable investment outcomes will depend on its ability to move beyond access facilitation toward genuine impact measurement and verification.

This technological transformation of sustainable investment access represents both significant opportunities and substantial risks for market efficiency and environmental outcomes. While embedded finance can potentially democratize ESG investing and reduce cognitive barriers to sustainable decision-making, its effectiveness depends critically on addressing fundamental challenges related to data quality, regulatory oversight, and algorithmic transparency. Embedded finance can theoretically address behavioral biases in ESG investing through technological automation, but effectiveness depends critically on data quality, regulatory oversight, and distinguishing genuine sustainability impact from marketing claims.

## AI AND MACHINE LEARNING IN SUSTAINABLE INVESTMENT

The application of artificial intelligence and machine learning technologies to sustainable investment analysis represents one of the most significant methodological developments in contemporary ESG evaluation. These computational approaches address implementation barriers in processing the vast quantities of unstructured data that characterize environmental, social, and governance assessments, while potentially mitigating cognitive biases that impair human judgment in investment decision-making (Cao, 2022). However, the implementation of AI-driven sustainable investment systems raises critical questions about algorithmic transparency, data quality dependencies, and the risk of perpetuating existing biases within financial markets.

## Theoretical Foundations of AI in Financial Analysis

The application of AI to sustainable investment is best understood through information processing theory and signal detection theory. Information processing emphasizes the limits of human capacity in analyzing complex ESG data, while signal detection highlights the challenge of distinguishing genuine sustainability signals from noise in corporate communications. Embedded finance platforms use AI to address both problems, integrating ESG analytics directly into user-facing services and thereby reducing reliance on individual judgment (Douglas, 2024; Adams & Abhayawansa, 2022).

Signal detection theory provides another theoretical foundation for AI applications in sustainable investment, particularly in distinguishing genuine ESG performance signals from noise in corporate communications and market data. Traditional ESG analysis often relies on self-reported corporate data, which may contain strategic omissions or misleading representations (Adams & Abhayawansa, 2022). Machine learning systems can potentially identify inconsistencies between reported ESG metrics and alternative data sources, including satellite imagery for environmental monitoring, social media sentiment analysis, and supply chain tracking data.

## Natural Language Processing in ESG Analysis

Natural Language Processing (NLP) represents a particularly significant application of AI technology in sustainable investment analysis. NLP algorithms can process vast quantities of textual data from corporate reports, regulatory filings, news articles, and social media to extract sentiment, identify trends, and detect potential greenwashing activities (Chowdhary & Chowdhary, 2020). These capabilities address a fundamental challenge in ESG analysis: the predominantly qualitative nature of sustainability information and the resulting difficulties in quantitative comparison across investments.

Sentiment analysis applications in ESG evaluation can identify discrepancies between corporate sustainability claims and external stakeholder perceptions, potentially providing early warning signals for reputational risks or regulatory challenges in embedded finance systems, NLP outputs can be integrated into robo-advisors or banking apps, providing retail users with simplified sustainability scores or alerts.

However, this raises risks of oversimplification and user overreliance on opaque metrics (Omokhoa et al., 2022).

## Predictive Modeling and Risk Assessment

Machine learning applications in sustainable investment increasingly focus on predictive modeling capabilities, particularly for climate-related financial risks and regulatory compliance forecasting. These models integrate multiple data sources, including climate projections, policy trend analysis, and historical corporate performance data, to estimate long-term sustainability risks and opportunities (Alessandra, Osterrieder, & Machado, 2024). Predictive analytics can theoretically enable investors to anticipate regulatory changes, market shifts, and physical climate impacts that may affect investment returns over extended time horizons. For managers, predictive ESG models provide early warning signals about regulatory or climate-related risks, but their reliance on historical data makes them vulnerable to regime shifts such as sudden climate policy changes (Alessandra, Osterrieder, & Machado, 2024).

However, predictive models in sustainable investment face significant methodological challenges related to the non-stationary nature of environmental and regulatory systems. Climate change represents a fundamental shift in environmental conditions, potentially invalidating historical relationships embedded in machine learning models. Similarly, evolving regulatory frameworks and changing social expectations regarding corporate responsibility create dynamic environments that may limit the predictive accuracy of models trained on historical data.

## Automated Portfolio Optimization and ESG Integration

AI-driven portfolio optimization algorithms attempt to integrate ESG criteria with traditional financial metrics to construct portfolios that maximize risk-adjusted returns while meeting specified sustainability objectives. These systems can theoretically process complex trade-offs between financial performance and ESG goals more efficiently than human portfolio managers, while maintaining consistency in applying sustainability criteria across large numbers of potential investments (Cao, 2022).

Modern portfolio theory provides the mathematical foundation for these optimization algorithms, though the integration of ESG factors raises several theoretical and practical challenges. ESG metrics often lack the statistical properties assumed by traditional optimization models, including normal distributions and stable correlations over time. The multi-dimensional nature of sustainability objectives also complicates the specification of utility functions and constraint parameters in optimization algorithms.

## Data Quality and Algorithmic Bias Challenges

Data inconsistency across rating agencies (often correlations below 0.6) undermines the reliability of AI-driven ESG analysis (Adams & Abhayawansa, 2022). Moreover, training models on historical data risks embedding past biases, disadvantaging smaller firms and emerging markets. Without systematic data governance, embedded platforms risk scaling these distortions across millions of retail portfolios.

Algorithmic bias represents another critical challenge in AI-driven sustainable investment systems. Machine learning models trained on historical ESG data may perpetuate past discriminatory practices or reflect the biases of human analysts who generated training data labels. These biases can manifest in systematic undervaluation of companies from emerging markets, over-reliance on easily quantifiable environmental metrics at the expense of social factors, or preferences for large corporations with sophisticated ESG reporting capabilities over smaller companies with potentially superior actual sustainability performance.

## Transparency and Explainability Requirements

Regulators increasingly require explainable AI in financial services (Douglas, 2024). For embedded finance, this means platforms cannot simply rely on opaque "black box" ESG scores. Explainable AI methods may reduce accuracy but are necessary to maintain accountability and consumer trust.

Explainable AI (XAI) techniques attempt to address these transparency requirements by providing interpretable approximations of complex model behavior. However, these approximations may sacrifice accuracy for interpretability, potentially reducing the effectiveness of AI systems in identifying subtle patterns in ESG data. The trade-off between model complexity and explainability represents a fundamental challenge in the regulatory deployment of AI for sustainable investment applications.

## Critical Assessment and Future Directions

AI applications in sustainable investment demonstrate clear potential in processing unstructured data, predicting climate risks, and automating ESG portfolio construction. However, their effectiveness remains constrained by persistent issues in ESG data quality, algorithmic bias, and limited explainability. For embedded finance platforms, these weaknesses translate directly into risks of large-scale greenwashing or consumer mistrust.

Future research should focus on methods that improve both data reliability and interpretability, such as federated learning, explainable AI, and blockchain-based verification of ESG claims. Pilot projects within embedded platforms, tested under regulatory sandboxes, could provide valuable evidence on how AI-driven ESG analytics can deliver measurable impact rather than marketing claims.

## DECENTRALIZED FINANCE (DEFI) AND ESG: A PATH TO SUSTAINABLE FINANCE

Decentralized finance (DeFi) applies blockchain infrastructure to financial services without traditional intermediaries. For sustainable investment, the promise lies in transparency, traceability, and programmable incentives. Embedded finance platforms can incorporate DeFi mechanisms to deliver ESG-linked products such as tokenized green bonds, sustainability-linked loans, or real-time carbon accounting. Yet the impact of these innovations depends on verifiable data and regulatory oversight, without which DeFi risks scaling speculative activity rather than sustainability (Douglas, 2024; UN PRI, 2023).

### Theoretical Framework: Decentralization and Transparency in Finance

The theoretical foundation of DeFi rests on principles of disintermediation, algorithmic governance, and cryptographic transparency. Unlike traditional financial systems that rely on centralized institutions for trust and verification, DeFi protocols embed trust mechanisms directly into smart contract code, theoretically enabling trustless transactions and reducing counterparty risk (Fiedler & Gomber, 2022). This architectural shift has profound implications for ESG investing, where trust deficits regarding sustainability claims and impact verification represent persistent market failures.

Blockchain technology addresses information asymmetries in ESG markets through immutable record-keeping and programmable transparency mechanisms. Smart contracts can theoretically automate ESG compliance verification, carbon credit trading, and impact measurement without relying on potentially biased or corruptible human intermediaries (Caldarelli, 2021). However, the effectiveness of these mechanisms depends critically on the quality of off-chain data inputs and the governance mechanisms that determine protocol updates and parameter modifications.

### DeFi Infrastructure and ESG Applications

Decentralized Autonomous Organizations (DAOs) represent a particularly significant application of DeFi principles to sustainable finance governance. DAOs can theoretically enable stakeholder participation in ESG investment decisions through token-weighted voting mechanisms, potentially addressing traditional concerns about limited investor voice in sustainability strategy formulation. However, token-based governance systems may replicate or amplify existing wealth disparities, potentially concentrating decision-making power among large token holders rather than achieving genuine democratization.

Automated Market Makers (AMMs) and decentralized exchanges provide infrastructure for ESG token trading and carbon credit markets. These systems can theoretically reduce transaction costs and increase liquidity for sustainability-focused financial instruments while maintaining transparency regarding price formation and trading activity (Caldarelli, 2021). Nevertheless, the current limitations of blockchain scalability and the environmental impact of certain consensus mechanisms raise questions about the net sustainability benefits of these systems.

## Carbon Credit Markets and Tokenization

The tokenization of carbon credits represents one of the most developed applications of DeFi technology to environmental finance. Blockchain-based carbon credit platforms attempt to address traditional market failures including double counting, lack of transparency, and limited liquidity through immutable transaction records and programmable verification mechanisms. Smart contracts can automate the retirement of carbon credits upon use, theoretically preventing fraudulent reuse while maintaining transparent records of credit provenance and ownership history.

However, the effectiveness of blockchain-based carbon credit systems depends fundamentally on the quality of underlying offset projects and verification methodologies. Blockchain technology cannot address fundamental additionality questions or verify the permanence of carbon sequestration projects; these limitations reflect broader challenges in environmental impact measurement rather than technological constraints (Barbosa et al., 2024). The gamification of carbon credit trading through token mechanisms may also create incentives for quantity maximization over genuine environmental impact.

## Decentralized Lending and Sustainable Project Finance

DeFi lending protocols offer potential mechanisms for financing sustainable projects through peer-to-peer lending, liquidity mining incentives, and programmable loan terms linked to ESG performance metrics. These systems can theoretically reduce the geographic and institutional barriers that limit access to sustainable finance, particularly for projects in emerging markets or small-scale applications that traditional financial institutions may consider uneconomical to evaluate.

Parametric insurance applications within DeFi frameworks can provide automated compensation for climate-related losses without requiring traditional claims processing procedures. Smart contracts can trigger insurance payouts based on objective data feeds, such as weather station measurements or satellite imagery, potentially reducing administrative costs and improving response times for climate adaptation financing (Corneli, 2021). However, the accuracy and manipulation resistance of these data feeds represent critical vulnerabilities in such systems.

## Critical Limitations and Risk Assessment

The current DeFi ecosystem faces several fundamental limitations that constrain its effectiveness in promoting sustainable finance objectives. Energy consumption represents a primary concern, as proof-of-work blockchain networks consume substantial electricity, potentially offsetting the environmental benefits of the sustainable finance applications they support. While proof-of-stake and other consensus mechanisms offer improved energy efficiency, they introduce new centralization risks and potential security vulnerabilities.

Regulatory uncertainty represents another critical challenge for DeFi applications in sustainable finance. The decentralized nature of these systems creates ambiguity regarding regulatory jurisdiction, compliance responsibilities, and consumer protection mechanisms (Farrell & Newman, 2019). This uncertainty may limit institutional adoption and constrain the scale at which DeFi can contribute to sustainable finance objectives, particularly in jurisdictions with strict financial services regulations.

Smart contract vulnerabilities and the immutability of blockchain transactions create additional risks in DeFi applications. Unlike traditional financial systems that can reverse fraudulent transactions or correct errors, blockchain-based systems may lack mechanisms for addressing smart contract bugs, oracle manipulation, or other systemic failures. These risks are particularly concerning in sustainable finance applications where long-term commitments and complex verification requirements increase the potential for unforeseen technical failures.

## Scalability and Accessibility Challenges

Current blockchain scalability limitations constrain the potential for DeFi to serve as infrastructure for global sustainable finance applications. Transaction throughput limitations and variable gas fees on popular blockchain networks may limit accessibility, particularly for small-scale sustainable finance applications in developing countries where DeFi proponents often claim the greatest potential impact

(Klapper, 2023). Layer-2 scaling solutions and alternative blockchain architectures offer potential improvements, but these solutions often involve trade-offs regarding decentralization and security.

The technical complexity of DeFi applications creates additional accessibility barriers that may limit adoption among populations that could benefit most from disintermediated financial services. User interface complexity, private key management requirements, and the irreversible nature of blockchain transactions require levels of technical sophistication that may exclude many potential users from participating in DeFi-based sustainable finance applications.

## Future Prospects and Integration Challenges

The future development of DeFi applications in sustainable finance will likely depend on advances in several key technical and regulatory areas. Interoperability protocols that enable communication between different blockchain networks could improve liquidity and functionality for ESG-focused DeFi applications. Similarly, the development of standardized ESG data oracles could improve the reliability of smart contract-based sustainability verification mechanisms.

Regulatory clarity regarding DeFi applications will likely determine the extent to which these systems can integrate with traditional financial institutions and access institutional capital flows. Regulatory frameworks that balance innovation promotion with consumer protection and systemic risk management could enable DeFi to complement rather than replace traditional sustainable finance mechanisms.

The integration of DeFi protocols with traditional ESG investing infrastructure represents both an opportunity and a challenge for sustainable finance development. While blockchain-based transparency and programmability offer potential solutions to persistent problems in ESG verification and impact measurement, the technical and regulatory limitations of current DeFi systems constrain their immediate applicability to large-scale sustainable finance applications. The ultimate contribution of DeFi to sustainable finance objectives will depend on continued technological development, regulatory evolution, and the ability of these systems to demonstrate genuine additionality over existing sustainable finance mechanisms. DeFi provides theoretical solutions to trust problems in ESG markets through disintermediated verification, but faces practical constraints from energy consumption, scalability, and regulatory uncertainty that limit sustainable finance contributions.

DeFi offers theoretical solutions to trust and transparency problems in ESG markets through programmable verification mechanisms, but practical constraints from energy consumption, scalability limitations, and regulatory uncertainty severely limit its current contribution to sustainable finance objectives.

## CORPORATE SUSTAINABILITY THROUGH EMBEDDED FINANCE

The integration of financial services within corporate operational ecosystems represents a significant evolution in how organizations approach Environmental, Social, and Governance (ESG) implementation and stakeholder engagement (Barbosa et al., 2024). Embedded finance enables corporations to align financial incentives with sustainability objectives through direct integration of ESG-focused financial products and services within their core business processes. This approach theoretically addresses the persistent gap between corporate sustainability commitments and actual implementation by creating financial mechanisms that reward sustainable behavior and penalize environmental or social harm (Addy et al., 2022). However, the effectiveness of embedded finance in promoting genuine corporate sustainability requires critical examination of both implementation mechanisms and outcome measurement frameworks.

### Theoretical Framework: Stakeholder Theory and Financial Integration

Stakeholder theory provides the conceptual foundation for understanding how embedded finance can influence corporate sustainability behavior. Freeman's stakeholder theory posits that corporations have obligations to multiple constituencies beyond shareholders, including employees, customers, communities, and environmental systems (Mogaji & Nguyen, 2024). Embedded finance mechanisms can theoretically align these stakeholder interests by creating financial incentives for corporations to consider broader stakeholder impacts in operational decisions.

The integration of sustainability-linked financial instruments within corporate systems operationalizes stakeholder theory by making ESG performance directly relevant to financial outcomes. Sustainability-linked loans, green bonds, and carbon offset mechanisms embedded within corporate payment systems create immediate financial consequences for environmental and social performance (Chao et al., 2023). However, the effectiveness of these mechanisms depends critically on the quality of ESG measurement systems and the materiality of financial incentives relative to other business considerations.

From a corporate finance perspective, embedded ESG incentives create risk premiums that should influence capital allocation according to net present value calculations. However, effectiveness depends on the materiality of financial incentives relative to project returns and alternative financing availability.

## Mechanisms of Corporate ESG Integration

Corporate embedded finance applications in sustainability take several distinct forms, each addressing different aspects of ESG implementation (Al-Gasaymeh et al., 2023). Green lending solutions integrate sustainability criteria directly into corporate financing decisions, theoretically reducing the cost of capital for environmentally beneficial projects while increasing costs for potentially harmful activities. These mechanisms can influence corporate investment decisions by making sustainability considerations financially material rather than merely reputational concerns (Klapper, 2023).

Carbon offsetting integration within corporate payment and procurement systems represents another significant application of embedded finance for sustainability. These systems can automatically calculate carbon footprints associated with corporate transactions and facilitate offset purchases or renewable energy investments (UN PRI, 2023). However, the effectiveness of these mechanisms depends fundamentally on the additionality and permanence of offset projects, as well as the accuracy of carbon footprint calculations.

Supply chain finance applications increasingly incorporate ESG criteria into vendor payment and financing terms. These systems can provide preferential financing terms to suppliers meeting specified sustainability criteria while potentially restricting access to financing for suppliers with poor ESG performance (Relja, Ward, & Zhao, 2024). Such mechanisms theoretically extend corporate sustainability influence throughout supply chains, though their effectiveness may be limited by supplier market power and alternative financing availability.

## Case Analysis: Implementation Models and Outcomes

The implementation of embedded finance for corporate sustainability has produced several distinct models with varying degrees of success and limitations. Payment-integrated carbon offsetting represents one of the most widely adopted approaches, with companies integrating offset purchases directly into transaction processing systems (Bruce et al., 2023). While these systems increase the convenience of offset purchasing and can raise awareness of carbon impacts, their effectiveness in promoting genuine emissions reductions remains constrained by fundamental offset market limitations.

Sustainability-linked lending integration within corporate treasury management systems offers another implementation model. These systems can automatically adjust borrowing costs based on achievement of predetermined ESG targets, creating direct financial incentives for sustainability performance (TCFD, 2022). However, the effectiveness of these mechanisms depends critically on the materiality of interest rate adjustments and the quality of ESG target selection and measurement.

Green investment platforms embedded within employee benefit systems represent an emerging application area with potential for scaling corporate sustainability engagement. These platforms can facilitate employee participation in ESG investing while potentially reducing administrative costs for corporate benefits programs (Amnas, Selvam, & Parayitam, 2024). Nevertheless, the impact of these systems on actual sustainable investment flows remains limited by employee financial literacy and competing investment priorities.

## Critical Assessment of Current Limitations

Current embedded finance applications in corporate sustainability face several significant limitations that constrain their effectiveness in promoting genuine ESG outcomes. Measurement challenges represent a primary concern, as the integration of sustainability metrics within financial systems requires standardized, verifiable, and material ESG indicators (Adams & Abhayawansa, 2022). The current fragmentation and inconsistency in ESG rating methodologies limit the reliability of embedded sustainability incentives (SASB, 2023).

Greenwashing risks are amplified in embedded finance systems, where automation may reduce due diligence on sustainability claims while marketing the convenience of integrated ESG solutions (Cao, 2022). Corporate embedded finance systems may prioritize ease of implementation over genuine environmental or social impact, potentially facilitating superficial sustainability activities that provide marketing benefits without meaningful ESG outcomes.

The scalability of current embedded finance approaches also faces constraints related to regulatory compliance, system integration complexity, and stakeholder coordination requirements. Many corporate sustainability applications require coordination across multiple business units, technology systems, and external partners, creating implementation challenges that may limit adoption and effectiveness (Omokhoa et al., 2022).

## Regulatory Framework and Compliance Integration

The regulatory landscape for corporate sustainability increasingly requires systematic ESG reporting and performance measurement, creating opportunities for embedded finance solutions that can automate compliance while promoting sustainable behavior. The European Union's Sustainable Finance Disclosure Regulation (SFDR) and Corporate Sustainability Reporting Directive (CSRD) establish mandatory requirements for ESG disclosure that embedded finance systems could theoretically support through automated data collection and reporting mechanisms (European Commission, 2023).

However, regulatory compliance applications of embedded finance raise questions about data privacy, audit trail requirements, and the allocation of responsibility for compliance failures (Fiedler & Gomber, 2022). Automated ESG reporting systems must maintain accuracy and completeness while providing adequate transparency for regulatory review. The complexity of evolving regulatory requirements also creates risks that embedded systems may become obsolete or non-compliant as regulations change.

## Future Directions and Strategic Implications

The future development of embedded finance applications in corporate sustainability will likely depend on advances in several key areas, including ESG data standardization, regulatory clarity, and technology integration capabilities (GRI, 2023). The development of standardized ESG measurement protocols could improve the reliability and comparability of embedded sustainability incentives while reducing implementation complexity.

Artificial intelligence and machine learning applications may enhance the sophistication of embedded sustainability systems by enabling real-time ESG performance monitoring, predictive analysis of sustainability risks, and automated optimization of sustainability-linked financial instruments (Douglas, 2024). However, these technological capabilities must be balanced against transparency requirements and the need for human oversight in sustainability decision-making.

The integration of embedded finance within corporate sustainability strategies represents both an opportunity and a challenge for advancing stakeholder capitalism. While these systems can provide practical mechanisms for operationalizing sustainability commitments, their effectiveness depends fundamentally on corporate commitment to genuine ESG outcomes rather than superficial integration of sustainability-themed financial products (Corneli, 2021).

Embedded finance can align stakeholder interests with corporate financial incentives through integrated ESG criteria, but effectiveness depends critically on the materiality of financial adjustments relative to other business considerations and the quality of underlying sustainability measurement frameworks.

# CASE STUDIES & REAL-WORLD APPLICATIONS OF EMBEDDED FINANCE IN SUSTAINABILITY

The practical implementation of embedded finance in sustainable investment has generated diverse applications across industries, providing empirical evidence for both the potential and limitations of technological integration in ESG markets. This section examines selected case studies to analyze implementation mechanisms, outcomes, and policy frameworks that shape the development of sustainable embedded finance solutions. Rather than presenting promotional descriptions of company initiatives, this analysis evaluates the effectiveness of different approaches in promoting genuine sustainable investment outcomes while identifying systemic challenges that constrain broader adoption (Barbosa et al., 2024).

## Methodological Approach to Case Study Analysis

The evaluation of embedded finance applications in sustainability requires systematic analysis of implementation mechanisms, outcome measurement, and stakeholder impact assessment. This analysis employs a comparative case study methodology that examines both successful implementations and notable failures to identify key factors that determine effectiveness in promoting genuine ESG outcomes (Adams & Abhayawansa, 2022). The assessment considers both quantitative metrics, such as capital flows and transaction volumes, and qualitative factors, including stakeholder engagement and environmental impact verification.

## Electric Vehicle Financing Integration

Tesla's integrated financing reduced transaction friction and contributed to EV market share growth, but sustainability attribution remains problematic. The approach's success depends heavily on brand premium and regulatory environment, limiting replicability across the broader automotive sector where traditional financing relationships dominate.

The effectiveness of embedded EV financing extends beyond individual purchase decisions to encompass broader market transformation dynamics. Streamlined financing can theoretically accelerate market adoption curves by reducing cognitive and administrative barriers to EV purchase (Klapper, 2023). Nevertheless, the sustainability benefits of this approach may be limited by supply chain environmental impacts, battery recycling infrastructure, and the carbon intensity of electricity generation in different geographic markets. Embedded finance effectiveness may depend more on market positioning than technological integration.

## Payment-Integrated Carbon Offsetting

Mastercard's carbon tracking integration exemplifies consumer engagement through payment systems but highlights moral hazard risks. The system calculates estimated carbon footprints for purchases and facilitates offset purchases through integrated payment workflows (Bruce et al., 2023). While this approach increases consumer awareness of carbon impacts and simplifies offset purchasing, its effectiveness in promoting genuine emissions reductions remains constrained by fundamental limitations in offset market integrity and additionality verification.

The scalability of payment-integrated offsetting faces several critical challenges, including the accuracy of carbon footprint calculations, the quality and permanence of offset projects, and the risk of moral hazard where offset purchasing substitutes for emissions reduction efforts (UN PRI, 2023). Consumer behavioral analysis suggests that automated offsetting may reduce guilt associated with high-carbon purchases without promoting fundamental consumption pattern changes, potentially limiting the approach's effectiveness in addressing climate change objectives. Automation increases offset purchasing but may reduce emissions reduction incentives. Effectiveness depends fundamentally on offset project quality—issues beyond technological solutions. Scale may compromise due diligence, potentially undermining genuine environmental benefits.

## E-commerce Platform Sustainability Integration

Shopify's automated carbon removal funding scales offset purchasing but exemplifies the tension between convenience and due diligence. Automation reduces project evaluation rigor while marketing benefits may prioritize perceived sustainability over verified impact.

However, the effectiveness of this model depends critically on offset project quality and additionality verification. The automation of offset purchasing may reduce due diligence on project selection while the merchant marketing focus may prioritize perceived sustainability benefits over genuine environmental impact (SASB, 2023). The concentration of offset project selection within a single platform also raises questions about market diversity and the potential for conflicts of interest in project evaluation. Technological scaling may systematically compromise the quality assurance that genuine sustainability outcomes require.

## AI-Driven ESG Investment Platforms

BlackRock's AI-powered analytics address traditional ESG analysis limitations while raising market concentration concerns. The system processes vast quantities of ESG data to generate risk assessments and portfolio recommendations while maintaining integration with existing investment workflows (Douglas, 2024). This approach addresses traditional limitations in ESG analysis capacity while potentially improving the consistency and objectivity of sustainability assessments.

The effectiveness of AI-driven ESG integration faces several methodological challenges, including training data bias, the opacity of machine learning algorithms, and the difficulty of validating ESG predictions against actual sustainability outcomes. The concentration of AI capabilities within large asset management firms may also exacerbate existing inequalities in ESG analysis access while potentially homogenizing investment approaches across the industry (Omokhoa et al., 2022). Sophisticated AI capabilities create competitive advantages for large asset managers but may increase industry concentration. Validation challenges persist as AI predictions against actual sustainability outcomes remain difficult to verify systematically.

## Digital Banking Sustainability Features

Revolut's integration of ESG investment recommendations and carbon footprint tracking within its digital banking platform exemplifies the application of embedded finance to retail sustainable investing. The platform provides personalized ESG investment options and environmental impact feedback integrated with standard banking services (Mogaji & Nguyen, 2024). This approach potentially democratizes access to sustainable investment products while reducing the complexity traditionally associated with ESG evaluation.

However, the effectiveness of digital banking sustainability integration may be limited by customer financial literacy, the quality of ESG screening algorithms, and the potential for greenwashing in product marketing. The simplification of complex ESG trade-offs within user-friendly interfaces may also obscure important sustainability considerations while promoting products based on marketing appeal rather than genuine environmental or social impact (Relja, Ward, & Zhao, 2024).

## Policy Framework Analysis

The development of embedded finance applications in sustainability operates within evolving regulatory frameworks that shape implementation approaches and market development. The European Union's Sustainable Finance Disclosure Regulation (SFDR) establishes disclosure requirements that affect embedded ESG investment products, while the proposed Corporate Sustainability Due Diligence

Directive may impact supply chain finance applications (European Commission, 2023).

The SEC's climate disclosure rules in the United States create reporting requirements that embedded finance systems must accommodate, while China's green finance guidelines establish criteria for sustainable finance products that may affect platform design and implementation (TCFD, 2022). The divergence in regulatory approaches across jurisdictions creates compliance complexity for global embedded finance applications while potentially fragmenting market development.

## Critical Assessment of Case Study Evidence

The analysis of current embedded finance applications in sustainability reveals both significant potential and substantial limitations in promoting genuine ESG outcomes. While these systems successfully reduce transaction friction and increase accessibility to sustainability-themed financial products, their effectiveness in promoting actual environmental and social improvements remains constrained by systemic constraints in impact measurement, verification, and incentive alignment (GRI, 2023).

The tendency toward automation and simplification in embedded finance systems may inadvertently promote superficial sustainability engagement over substantive behavioral change.

## Future Development Implications

The evolution of embedded finance applications in sustainability will likely depend on advances in impact measurement methodology, regulatory clarity, and the development of standardized ESG verification protocols. The integration of emerging technologies, including satellite monitoring and blockchain verification, may improve the reliability of embedded sustainability systems while reducing the potential for manipulation or fraud (Corneli, 2021).

However, the ultimate success of embedded finance in promoting sustainable investment outcomes will depend on the alignment of technological capabilities with genuine sustainability objectives rather than merely facilitating access to products marketed as sustainable. This requires continued attention to outcome measurement, stakeholder engagement, and the development of governance mechanisms that prioritize impact over marketing considerations.

Current implementations demonstrate embedded finance's ability to increase access to sustainability-themed products but reveal persistent challenges in translating technological convenience into genuine environmental and social outcomes. Success requires moving beyond process optimization to impact verification.

## CHALLENGES AND FUTURE PROSPECTS OF EMBEDDED FINANCE IN SUSTAINABLE DEVELOPMENT

The integration of embedded finance within sustainable investment frameworks represents both a significant technological advancement and a complex set of implementation challenges that constrain its effectiveness in promoting genuine environmental and social outcomes. While embedded finance systems demonstrate potential for democratizing access to ESG investment products and reducing transaction friction, their deployment faces fundamental limitations related to data quality, regulatory uncertainty, algorithmic bias, and outcome verification. This section provides a critical assessment of current challenges and examines future prospects for embedded finance in sustainable development, emphasizing the conditions necessary for these systems to contribute meaningfully to global sustainability objectives rather than merely facilitating access to products labeled as sustainable.

### Technological Infrastructure and Complexity Challenges

The implementation of embedded finance systems for sustainable investment requires sophisticated technological infrastructure that many organizations, particularly small and medium-sized enterprises, lack the resources to develop or maintain effectively (Al-Gasaymeh et al., 2023). The integration of ESG data processing, real-time analytics, and automated decision-making systems demands substantial investments in data management, cybersecurity, and system integration capabilities. These technological requirements create barriers to entry that may limit the democratizing potential of embedded finance while concentrating capabilities among well-resourced financial institutions.

Cybersecurity vulnerabilities represent a particularly critical challenge as embedded finance systems handle sensitive financial and personal data across multiple platforms and jurisdictions (Khalifa, Elmedany, & Sharif, 2024). The distributed nature of embedded systems creates multiple potential points of failure while regulatory frameworks for cybersecurity in embedded finance remain underdeveloped. Data breaches or system compromises could undermine consumer trust in sustainable finance applications while potentially exposing users to identity theft or financial fraud.

The dependency on cloud computing infrastructure and third-party data providers creates additional vulnerabilities related to service availability, data sovereignty, and vendor concentration risk. The failure of key infrastructure providers could disrupt embedded finance services while regulatory restrictions on cross-border data flows may limit the global scalability of these systems (Farrell & Newman, 2019).

## Data Quality and ESG Measurement Limitations

Different ESG rating providers often produce divergent assessments of identical companies, with correlation coefficients between major providers frequently below 0.6 (Adams & Abhayawansa, 2022). Different ESG rating providers often produce divergent assessments of identical companies, with correlation coefficients between major providers frequently below 0.6. This fundamental inconsistency in ESG evaluation undermines the reliability of automated screening and recommendation systems that embedded finance platforms depend upon.

The lack of standardized ESG measurement protocols creates additional challenges for embedded finance systems that must reconcile different methodologies and reporting frameworks across global markets (SASB, 2023). The development of automated ESG analysis systems may prioritize easily quantifiable metrics over more complex but potentially more meaningful sustainability indicators, leading to systematic biases in investment recommendations.

## Regulatory Uncertainty and Compliance Complexity

The regulatory landscape for embedded finance applications in sustainable investment remains fragmented and evolving, creating uncertainty about compliance requirements, fiduciary responsibilities, and consumer protection standards (European Commission, 2023). Unlike traditional financial advisors who operate under established regulatory frameworks, embedded finance providers may not be subject to equivalent standards of care regarding investment recommendations, potentially exposing consumers to unsuitable investment advice.

The cross-jurisdictional nature of many embedded finance applications complicates regulatory compliance as different regions maintain varying requirements for ESG disclosure, consumer protection, and data privacy (TCFD, 2022). Companies operating embedded finance systems across multiple jurisdictions must navigate complex and potentially conflicting regulatory requirements while maintaining system functionality and user experience consistency.

Regulatory uncertainty may limit institutional adoption of embedded finance solutions while constraining the scale at which these systems can contribute to sustainable investment objectives. The potential for retroactive regulatory changes or enforcement actions creates additional risks that may discourage innovation and investment in embedded finance applications (Fiedler & Gomber, 2022).

## Consumer Trust and Financial Literacy Constraints

The adoption of embedded finance applications for sustainable investment faces significant barriers related to consumer trust, financial literacy, and understanding of ESG concepts (Amnas, Selvam, & Parayitam, 2024). Many consumers lack the knowledge necessary to evaluate ESG investment products effectively while the automation of investment recommendations may reduce their engagement with sustainability considerations rather than promoting more informed decision-making.

Privacy concerns regarding the collection and use of personal and financial data represent another significant barrier to adoption, particularly as embedded finance systems require access to detailed transactions and behavioral data to provide personalized recommendations (Relja, Ward, & Zhao, 2024). Consumer skepticism about algorithmic decision-making and concerns about data security may limit participation in embedded finance applications, particularly among populations that could benefit most from improved access to sustainable investment products.

The complexity of ESG trade-offs and the difficulty of verifying sustainability claims may overwhelm consumers who lack specialized knowledge, potentially leading to investment decisions based on marketing appeal rather than genuine environmental or social impact (Barbosa et al., 2024). The simplification of complex sustainability considerations within user-friendly interfaces may inadvertently promote superficial engagement with ESG issues.

## Market Structure and Systemic Risk Considerations

The concentration of embedded finance capabilities among large technology and financial services companies creates potential systemic risks and market structure concerns that may limit competition and innovation in sustainable finance markets (Corneli, 2021). The network effects and data advantages enjoyed by established platforms may create barriers to entry for innovative sustainable finance applications while potentially homogenizing investment approaches across the industry.

The interconnectedness of embedded finance systems with broader financial markets creates potential channels for systemic risk transmission, particularly if automated ESG screening systems produce correlated investment decisions that amplify market volatility (Douglas, 2024). The reliance on similar data sources and analytical methodologies across multiple embedded finance platforms may create systematic biases that affect capital allocation across the broader sustainable investment market.

## Future Technological Development and Integration Prospects

The future effectiveness of embedded finance in sustainable development will likely depend on advances in several key technological areas, including blockchain verification systems, satellite monitoring capabilities, and artificial intelligence transparency methods (GRI, 2023). The integration of Internet of Things sensors and real-time environmental monitoring could provide more objective and verifiable ESG data sources while reducing reliance on self-reported corporate information.

Advances in explainable artificial intelligence may address current concerns about algorithmic opacity while federated learning approaches could enable improved ESG analysis without compromising data privacy or competitive information (Omokhoa et al., 2022). The development of standardized ESG data formats and application programming interfaces could improve interoperability between embedded finance systems while reducing vendor lock-in risks.

However, these technological advances must be accompanied by appropriate governance frameworks that ensure alignment between algorithmic optimization objectives and genuine sustainability outcomes rather than merely improving marketing effectiveness or user engagement metrics.

## Policy Recommendations and Regulatory Development

The realization of embedded finance's potential contribution to sustainable development will require coordinated policy development that addresses current regulatory gaps while promoting innovation and competition (UN PRI, 2023). Regulatory frameworks should establish clear standards for ESG investment recommendations while maintaining sufficient flexibility to accommodate technological innovation and evolving sustainability measurement methodologies.

International coordination on ESG data standards and regulatory approaches could reduce compliance complexity while improving the effectiveness of embedded finance applications across global markets. The development of regulatory sandboxes and pilot programs could enable controlled experimentation with embedded finance applications while providing regulators with evidence to inform policy development.

# CONCLUSION

The integration of embedded finance into sustainable investment ecosystems represents both a technological innovation and a structural challenge for global financial markets. By embedding financial services within digital platforms, firms have lowered barriers to participation in ESG products and increased the visibility of sustainability considerations in everyday transactions (Al-Gasaymeh et al., 2023; Amnas, Selvam, & Parayitam, 2024). Yet the analysis across theoretical foundations, technological mechanisms, and case applications suggests that accessibility alone does not equate to genuine sustainability impact. The effectiveness of embedded finance ultimately depends on the robustness of ESG data, the quality of verification systems, and the regulatory frameworks that govern disclosure and accountability (Adams & Abhayawansa, 2022; European Commission, 2023).

Three central conclusions emerge from this chapter. First, the persistent inconsistency in ESG measurement undermines the reliability of automated decision systems. Divergent ESG ratings, often with correlations below 0.6 between providers (Friede et al., 2015; Adams & Abhayawansa, 2022), create the risk that embedded platforms amplify noise rather than signal. Without greater standardization, even sophisticated AI-driven tools risk reinforcing bias or facilitating large-scale greenwashing. Second, governance frameworks are essential. Platforms must align embedded mechanisms with established standards such as SFDR, CSRD, TCFD, and SASB to ensure that investment flows correspond to material sustainability outcomes (GRI, 2023; SASB, 2023; TCFD, 2022). Finally, trust and transparency represent the decisive conditions for impact. Embedded finance has the capacity to democratize access, but without transparent methodologies and verifiable results, its contribution to sustainability remains uncertain.

Looking ahead, the potential of embedded finance to advance sustainable development rests not merely on technological sophistication but on embedding accountability and verification into system design. Future research should explore empirical evaluation of embedded mechanisms through pilot programs and regulatory sandboxes (UN PRI, 2023), while policymakers must harmonize disclosure standards to reduce regulatory fragmentation. For practitioners, the priority is to demonstrate additionality measurable environmental and social improvements beyond business-as-usual rather than relying on symbolic integration of ESG themes. Only through rigorous measurement, regulatory alignment, and transparent governance can embedded finance shift from an enabling technology to a credible pathway for sustainable development.

## REFERENCES


Adams, C. A., & Abhayawansa, S. (2022). Connecting the COVID-19 pandemic, environmental, social, and governance (ESG) investing and calls for 'harmonisation' of sustainability reporting. *Critical Perspectives on Accounting*, *82*, 102309. DOI: 10.1016/j.cpa.2021.102309

Addy, W. A., Ofodile, O. C., Adeoye, O. B., Oyewole, A. T., Okoye, C. C., Odeyemi, O., & Ololade, Y. J. (2022). Data-driven sustainability: How fintech innovations are supporting green finance. *Journal of Green Finance, 14*

Al-Gasaymeh, A. S., Almahadin, H. A., Shehadeh, M., Migdady, H., & Bani Atta, A. A. (2023). Investigating the role of artificial intelligence in embedded finance on improving a nonfinancial customer experience. *Proceedings of the 2023 International Conference on Business Analytics for Technology and Security (ICBATS)*, Dubai, United Arab Emirates, 1–6. https://doi.org/DOI: 10.1109/ICBATS57792.2023.10111255

Alessandra, A., Osterrieder, J. R., & Machado, M. R. (2024). How can artificial intelligence help customer intelligence for credit portfolio management? *International Journal of Information Management Data Insights*, *4*(2), 100234. Advance online publication. DOI: 10.1016/j.jjimei.2024.100234

Amnas, M. B., Selvam, M., & Parayitam, S. (2024). FinTech and financial inclusion: Exploring the mediating role of digital financial literacy and the moderating influence of perceived regulatory support. *Journal of Risk and Financial Management*, *17*(3), 108. DOI: 10.3390/jrfm17030108

Barbosa, A. D. S., Crispim, M. C., Silva, L. B., Silva, J. M. N., Barbosa, A. M., & Morioka, S. N. (2024). How can organizations measure the integration of environmental, social, and governance (ESG) criteria? *Business Strategy and the Environment*, *33*(4), 3607–3634. DOI: 10.1002/bse.3675

Bruce, E., Shurong, Z., Ying, D., Yaqi, M., Amoah, J., & Egala, S. B. (2023). The effect of digital marketing adoption on SMEs sustainable growth. *Sustainability (Basel)*, *15*(6), 4760. DOI: 10.3390/su15064760

Caldarelli, G. (2021). Wrapping trust for interoperability: A preliminary study of wrapped tokens. *Information (Basel)*, *13*(1), 6. DOI: 10.3390/info13010006

Cao, L. (2022). AI in finance: Challenges, techniques, and opportunities. *ACM Computing Surveys*, *55*(3), 64. Advance online publication. DOI: 10.1145/3502289

Chao, T., Yunbao, X., Chengbo, D., Bo, L., & Ullah, S. (2023). Financial integration and renewable energy consumption in China. *Environmental Science and Pollution Research International, 30*(5), 12944–12952. DOI: 10.1007/s11356-022-22852-w PMID: 36121627

Chowdhary, K. R., & Chowdhary, K. R. (2020). Natural language processing. In *Fundamentals of Artificial Intelligence* (pp. 603–649). DOI: 10.1007/978-81-322-3972-7_19

Corneli, F. (2021). Financial integration without financial development. *Atlantic Economic Journal, 49*(2), 201–220. DOI: 10.1007/s11293-021-09709-2 PMID: 34092835

Douglas, D. D. (2024). The transformative impact of AI in finance and banking. *Journal of Investment Banking and Finance, 2*(1), 01–08.

European Commission. (2023). Regulation (EU) 2019/2088 on sustainability-related disclosures in the financial services sector (Sustainable Finance Disclosure Regulation). *Official Journal of the European Union, L, 317*, 1–16.

Farrell, H., & Newman, A. L. (2019). Weaponized interdependence: How global economic networks shape state coercion. *International Security, 44*(1), 42–79. DOI: 10.1162/isec_a_00351

Fiedler, S., & Gomber, P. (2022). Decentralized finance (DeFi): Ein literature review aus wirtschafts- und rechtswissenschaftlicher perspektive. *Journal of Business and Law, 15*(2), 123–145. DOI: 10.1007/s10257-022-00592-3

Freeman, R. E. (1984). *Strategic management: A stakeholder approach.* Cambridge University Press.

Friede, G., Busch, T., & Bassen, A. (2015). ESG and financial performance: Aggregated evidence from more than 2000 empirical studies. *Journal of Sustainable Finance & Investment, 5*(4), 210–233. DOI: 10.1080/20430795.2015.1118917

GRI. (2023). *GRI standards: The global standards for sustainability reporting.* Global Reporting Initiative. https://www.globalreporting.org/standards/

Khalifa, N., Elmedany, W., & Sharif, S. (2024). Leveraging digital identity and open banking data for fraud prevention in the financial industry. *FiCloud, 286*, 286–291. Advance online publication. DOI: 10.1109/FiCloud62933.2024.00051

Klapper, L. (2023). How digital payments can benefit entrepreneurs. *IZA World of Labor: Evidence-Based Policy Making, 396.* Advance online publication. DOI: 10.15185/izawol.396.v2

Mogaji, E., & Nguyen, N. P. (2024). High street banking on the app: Branding strategies of traditionally-driven neobanks. *International Journal of Bank Marketing*, *42*(2), 301–330. DOI: 10.1108/IJBM-12-2022-0529

Omokhoa, H. E., Odionu, C. S., Azubuike, C., & Sule, A. K. (2022). AI-powered fintech innovations for credit scoring, debt recovery, and financial access in microfinance and SMEs. *Journal of Finance and Technology*, *18*(3), 45–67. DOI: 10.1016/j.fintech.2022.03.004

Pedersen, L. H., Fitzgibbons, S., & Pomorski, L. (2023). Responsible investing: The ESG-efficient frontier. *Journal of Financial Economics*, *142*(2), 572–597. DOI: 10.1016/j.jfineco.2020.11.001

Relja, R., Ward, P., & Zhao, A. L. (2024). Understanding the psychological determinants of buy-now-pay-later. *International Journal of Bank Marketing*, *42*(1), 7–37. DOI: 10.1108/IJBM-07-2022-0324

SASB. (2023). *SASB standards: Industry-based standards for disclosure topics & accounting metrics*. Sustainability Accounting Standards Board. https://www.sasb.org/standards/

SEC. (2024). Enhancement and standardization of climate-related disclosures for investors: Final rule. U.S. Securities and Exchange Commission, Release Nos. 33-11275; 34-99678.

TCFD. (2022). *Recommendations of the Task Force on Climate-related Financial Disclosures: Final report*. Financial Stability Board. https://www.fsb-tcfd.org/recommendations/

UN PRI. (2023). *Annual report 2023: Principles for Responsible Investment*. United Nations-supported Principles for Responsible Investment Initiative. https://www.unpri.org/annual-report-2023

# Chapter 8
# The Intersection of Integrated Finance, Sustainability, and ESG: An Overview

**Rosimah Ahmad**
https://orcid.org/0009-0002-0056-4888
*Taylor's University, Malaysia*

**Premagowrie Sivanandan**
https://orcid.org/0000-0001-5766-8114
*Sunway University, Malaysia*

## ABSTRACT

*Integrated finance is a progressive financial approach that integrates ESG principles into financial systems to promote long-term sustainability. It bridges global sustainability goals with measurable ESG frameworks, enabling capital to be directed toward inclusive, ethical and resilient growth. Instruments such as green bonds, ESG-aligned portfolios and sustainability-linked loans exemplify this alignment. Integrated finance supports the UN Sustainable Development Goals (SDGs) by promoting inclusive digital financial services and financial products. It enhances financial system resilience by embedding ESG risks into strategic decisions like pricing and cash flow management. Despite benefits such as transparency and stakeholder trust, challenges include regulatory complexity and socio-economic issues. Ultimately, integrated finance seeks to redefine finance as a driver of sustainable transformation, supporting a quadruple-bottom-line approach, i.e., people, planet, profit, and purpose.*

DOI: 10.4018/979-8-3373-2464-7.ch008

## INTRODUCTION

Finance has traditionally been viewed through a narrow lens, focused primarily on investments, profits, financial planning and capital market efficiency. Aslam (2024) states that finance plays a significant role as the guardian in budgeting, forecasting, management, analysis and reporting of financial information. In addition to these various roles, finance also supports the development and execution of strategies within organizations subject to the organization's culture and size (Aslam, 2024). According to Scholtens (2006), a strong and well-developed financial system helps ensure that interest rates in the market truly reflect the appeal and potential of different investment choices. This means capital flows more efficiently to where it can generate the most benefits. Simultaneously, a well-oiled financial system provides businesses better tools to protect themselves against uncertainties and unexpected events such as economic shocks and political upheavals, which can lead to greater overall stability in society. Beyond that, finance plays a key role in driving progress as it supports growth and ultimately increases the business' ability to access a wider range of financial products and services (Scholtens, 2006). Moreover, a financial system that functions well can lower the costs of borrowing and increase access to finance for a wider range of people enabling individuals in the lower-income brackets to invest in education and employment opportunities, thus, reducing income inequality and enhancing social welfare (Yıldırım & Şendeniz-Yüncü, 2025). Similarly, Mishra et al. (2024) informs that the ability of untouched segments of society to have access to finance is essential for sustainable and socio-economic development in developing countries.

However, over the past decade, a shift in the traditional perspective of finance has steadily been initiated due to various sustainability-related issues such as water scarcity, urban poverty, climate change, depletion of natural resources and widening social inequalities, that have spurred a re-examination of what finance should serve. Likewise, Crona et al. (2025) opine that over the past decade, investors have progressively acknowledged that responsible environmental and social practices are essential to sustainable financial success in the long term. Furthermore, rising expectations from pluralistic stakeholders with diverse motivations and interests raises the question as to whether finance today is playing its part in meeting stakeholders' evolving needs and maximizing returns while preserving the tenets of environmental, social and governance (ESG), a subset of sustainability. Today, we find ourselves at the crossroads where finance is increasingly being asked to perform more than just deliver financial returns. In other words, finance must also contribute meaningfully to a sustainable and equitable future while maintaining ethical standards. The concept of "integrated finance", thus, arose from this need to reimagine and recreate the role of finance in business and society through the strategically balanced alignment between financial services, financial systems, investments and financial decision-making with the aims of ESG.

## Integrated Finance, Sustainability and ESG Explained

Finance drives sustainability (Ziolo et al., 2019). The definition of sustainability has been a serious topic of discussion since the 1970s. For example, in 1972, definitions of sustainability centered around restrictions on ecological systems and conduct of activities such as recycling of waste from anthropogenic activities, laced with the associated challenges of improving the social, educational, health and employment level of the society (Hajian & Kashani, 2021). Subsequently, the Brundtland Report in 1987 defined sustainability from the traditional standpoint as the ability of the present generation to meet current needs without sacrificing the ability of future generations to meet their future needs (World Commission on Environment and Development, 1987). The definition of sustainability then evolved as satisfying the needs of current and future generations to provide for human welfare based on appropriate human and natural circumstances, and economic capital (Hajian & Kashani, 2021). In the context of finance, sustainability has grown into a multifaceted concept that comprises environmental protection, social inclusion and economic resilience, that calls for a balance between altruistic stewardship and profitability. Thus, in the pursuit of profit maximization and sustainable financial success, market participants such as investors and companies must be held accountable for businesses' financial performance and most importantly, their contributions towards sustainable development, which is the crux of integrated finance.

ESG refers to a set of standards used to measure an organization's environmental impact and social impact on its stakeholders, primarily its investors and secondarily, its customers, suppliers, employees and the public (IBM, 2025). ESG, hence, denotes a set of measures that are employed to assess the impact of a company's operations from environmental protection, social responsibility and ethical (governance) points of view. IBM (2025) explains that the "E" in Environmental focuses on whether the organization is operating as a steward of the environment and covers environmental issues, such as climate resilience, greenhouse gas emissions (GHG), waste management, biodiversity and pollution. The "S" in social centers on the impact the organization has on its employees, customers, suppliers and communities, and focuses on the social impact of diversity, human rights and inclusivity (IBM, 2025). Finally, the "G" in Governance refers to how the organization is directed by its management team (IBM, 2025) through its internal controls, and policies and practices, and concentrates on corporate governance factors, such as shareholders' rights, executive remuneration, board diversity and composition of board of directors. ESG factors, thus, play a crucial role in determining corporate behavior, shaping the perception of stakeholders, ensuring sustainable financial performance and driving corporate social performance. In the same vein, PwC Malaysia (2023) affirms that Malaysian companies with focus on ESG are positioned in a favorable manner for higher valuations and returns on investment over the long term through higher corporate transparency and responsible governance to the companies' stakeholders.

Integrated finance is an extensive concept that involves the combination of financial instruments and financial processes to achieve enhanced efficiency, inclusivity and impact, and address complex financial and social aims (Widodo, 2019). The concept of integrated finance, in the context of sustainability and ESG, refers to the systematic alignment of financial strategies, financial structures and financial instruments, with long-term environmental, social and governance outcomes. Integrated finance, thus, encompasses embedding ESG factors into every facet of financial decision-making from allocation of capital, assessment of risk, investment strategies and reporting methods to the extent that sustainability considerations are not peripheral but intrinsic to financial processes. The increasing ESG data integration into conventional financial analysis reflects the recognition that companies with strong ESG performance are more likely to deliver greater risk-adjusted returns, attract investments and sustain long-term value (Friede, Busch & Bassen, 2015), which contrasts with traditional finance that usually emphasizes short-term financial gains as compared to long-term financial gains. Thus, the comprehensive perspective that considers possibilities, risks and returns that are both financial and non-financial in the decision-making process forms the crux of integrated finance, which concentrates on financial practices that support long-term sustainability, e.g., green finance, green investment, impact investment, responsible investment and social finance. As financial mechanisms increasingly rely on ESG data and performance indicators to drive investment decisions, track progress and report financial and non-financial outcomes, the measurement and operationalization of ESG principles is at the core of integrated financial solutions. This is supported by the Organization for Economic Co-operation and Development (2020), which states that integrated finance provides a thorough framework for measuring, managing and optimizing financial returns while embracing ethical, social and environmental implications.

## CONCEPT AND EVOLUTION OF INTEGRATED FINANCE

Historically, financial integration has been a significant phenomenon, linking financial markets across neighboring, regional and global economies. With the advancement in technology, the idea of integrated finance has undergone significant changes, which is reflected in the dynamic relationship between financial systems, financial services and technology. Integrated finance, generally, refers to the process of incorporating financial services into non-financial platforms to enhance users' experience and accessibility, and facilitate efficient capital allocation, better governance and effective risk-sharing within businesses in the local and global context. Similarly, Fratzscher and Imbs (2009) state that integrated finance focuses on the effective allocation of capital and sharing of risks. Financial integration in the early stages was primarily focused on increasing the flow of credit and capital across borders, connecting local and overseas financial markets and companies, and fostering deeper financial links between countries (Kaur & Singh, 2025). This traditional model of financial integration focused on global capital flows because international trade and investments were the primary drivers of financial integration due to the movement of cash and capital across borders through foreign direct investments (FDIs), cross-border mergers and acquisitions (M&As) and cross-border share market listings. Giannetti and Ongena (2007) state that financial integration at the country level makes markets more accessible to foreign investors and allows countries to attract capital investments.

As for global financial markets, the focus is on the alignment between national financial markets with international standards. This is driven by a desire to create more liquid, efficient and transparent markets that allow for greater global participation. The development of financial products, for example, convertible bonds, equities and derivatives, is central to this process. Traditional financial integration can also be seen from another perspective, i.e., cross-border banking and lending. Financial institutions such as banks and insurance companies expand internationally by offering loans and credit facilities to foreign companies and governments (Ayhan Kose, Prasad, & Taylor, 2011), which creates the foundation for global financial systems that connect different economies. Over time, international bodies such as the World Bank and the International Monetary Fund (IMF) have been complementarily playing a major role in fostering financial integration (Kruger, Lavigne, & Mckay, 2016) to boost sustainable development, enhance shared prosperity, eradicate poverty and stabilize the international monetary system, respectively. Both these powerhouses of international financial institutions assist countries with financial crises and promoted financial integration by setting global policies and financial systems standards. Although financial integration in the business and local scenario remains significant, the latest developments are increasingly shifting from traditional and interpersonal services toward digital financial services that are highly accessible to individuals and businesses across the globe (Niemand et al., 2021), which have been significantly shaped by financial technology, the rise of digital currencies and global connectivity. The rise of financial technology or 'FinTech' has led to the combination of financial services within various non-financial sectors such as computing and information systems, leading towards the promotion of financial inclusion and development of innovative financial solutions. According to Omokhoa et al. (2024), digital transformation redefines traditional finance and banking services, which enables banks and financial institutions to address fresh challenges and opportunities in an increasingly digital world. This evolution reflects a shift towards more dynamic and accessible financial ecosystems, which enhances the efficiency and accessibility of financial services, contributing to financial inclusion and the evolution of integrated finance.

## How FinTech Revolutionized Financial Services in Malaysia

Corporate sustainability performance has been garnering considerable traction worldwide evidenced by the emergence of financial technology and leveraging of key organizational resources that are of great importance to the sustainability and performance of businesses (Siddik, Rahman, & Yong, 2023) such as human, financial and technical resources. Traditionally, financial integration focus of financial markets was more at the companies and countries level. However, over the past decades, it has evolved drastically with the emergence of technological advances, especially across financial markets globally. The key components of integrated finance are being embedded in financial markets related to payments, lending, insurance and investments (Cummins & Weiss, 2009). Financial markets are known as places where individuals and businesses are involved in financial transactions. Hence, financial markets play a significant role as the platform for savers and borrowers to purchase financial instruments such as shares, bonds, mutual funds and derivatives.

The advent of digitalization and smart technology has led to innovations in finance and financial markets through the introduction of 'financial technology' or commonly known as 'FinTech'. FinTech is a term that is used to describe mobile applications, software and other technological tools that enable users and businesses to manage and access their finances digitally (IBM, 2024). FinTech has transformed how financial systems and financial services operate and interact in the execution of financial transactions such as lending, payments, receipts, investments, analysis and insurance. Similarly, Giakoumelou et al. (2024) state that FinTech, delineating financial technological innovation, has altered the *modus operandi* of traditional banks and intermediaries, and has given rise to alternative providers of financial services. Concurrently, the increasing regulatory and market attention to ESG risks, altered the rules for traditional finance (Giakoumelou et al., 2024). FinTech in today's fast-paced world can be used to define technologies, services and companies in the financial sector that focus on various aptitudes such as retail banking, financial education, fundraising, cryptocurrencies and investment management. Alam (2024) finds that FinTech has led to the streamlining of processes, cost reductions and enhancements in level of accessibility of financial services and products for consumers and businesses. FinTech has, thus, become the major disruptor in financial services that offers innovative business solutions and creates new business models. In the same vein, Hu, Jia, and Yang (2025) affirm that driven by technological advancements and globalization, FinTech has revolutionized traditional financial operations through innovative and efficient solutions. Mobile payments, blockchain technology and artificial intelligence (AI) are transforming financial services by broadening their reach and creating new business opportunities (Hu, Jia, & Yang, 2025). According to Li and Chen (2024), the integration of advanced digital technologies provides banks with the opportunity to offer faster and more secure services, reduce operational costs and improve efficiency through automation and technological optimization, particularly in risk management and credit approval. Moreover, FinTech significantly enhances user experience through the provision of convenient and specialized banking services that subsequently increase customer loyalty and satisfaction (Li and Chen, 2024). For example, digital wallets and mobile payments such as Touch 'n Go e-wallet, ShopeePay, Apple Pay and Boost, use Near Field Communication (NFC) technology to integrate mobile financial transactions directly into smart devices such as smartphones and smart tabs for easy payments at point-of-sale (POS) systems. In addition, Maybank's MAE, one of the top e-wallets in Malaysia, combines the convenience of a digital wallet with the full functionality of a banking app and supports *DuitNow* QR, bill payments, *zakat* contributions (Fintech News Malaysia, 2025). MAE also promotes smarter money habits with features like *Tabung*, a goal-based savings tool for short-term plans, and provides a detailed spending summary that helps users track their cash movements from meals and shopping to financial services (Fintech News Malaysia, 2025).

On the other hand, FinTech has also emerged as a key player in the advancement of financial inclusion, which is a key enabler to reduce poverty and boost prosperity for individuals and businesses. In addition, financial inclusion is a catalyst for achieving seven of the 17 UN SDGs as it boosts economic growth, increases employment opportunities, encourages women's economic empowerment and contributes to the eradication of poverty (World Bank Group, 2025). By facilitating business growth and providing a secure means of accumulating and safeguarding wealth, the growth of digital access to financial services helps to reduce poverty and income inequality. FinTech has also revolutionized traditional investing and lending activities using technological tools and services that are more accessible, affordable and personalized to a broader range of investors (CFA Institute, 2023). For example, low-cost passive investment via exchange-traded funds (ETFs), which are easily accessible via digital platforms, provide diversified and fast access to different classes of assets, geographies and industries (CFA Institute, 2023), such as FTSE *Bursa Malaysia* KLCI ETF and Principal FTSE ASEAN 40 Malaysia ETF. ETFs offer a hassle-free experience for new and existing investors because ETFs provide instant diversification when investors invest in one or more ETFs, which saves the investors' time in building their personal portfolio at a fraction of the cost (*Bursa Malaysia*, 2021). Additionally, ETFs save money on brokerage fees and allow investors to grow their investment portfolio at their own pace by setting aside small amounts of money for investment as the investors deem fit (*Bursa Malaysia*, 2021).

In addition, the equity crowdfunding ecosystem in Malaysia is a resilient and increasingly vital mechanism for financing micro, small and medium-sized enterprises (MSMEs) bolstered by government initiatives such as tax incentives. Equity crowdfunding has evolved into a reliable substitute to conventional financing routes, especially for early-stage companies and underserved sectors (Fintech News Malaysia, 2025). The crowdfunding and equity crowdfunding platforms in Malaysia such as Crowdo Malaysia Sdn Bhd, MyStartr Sdn Bhd and Pitch Platforms Sdn Bhd (pitchIN), therefore, enable individuals to invest in start-ups or projects in exchange for equity or rewards. Equity crowdfunding has opened venture capital opportunities to everyday people, allowing them to invest in startup companies and potentially earn high returns from their investments. From the perspective of traditional lending, FinTech lending platforms such as Peer-to-Peer (P2P) directly connect borrowers with lenders circumventing the need for banks and financial institutions. For example, AlixCo P2P Financing is a recognized P2P market operator based in Malaysia that is fully regulated by the Securities Commission Malaysia. AlixCo champions financial inclusions and aims to empower Malaysian SMEs and investors by connecting them through cutting-edge, user-friendly fintech solutions (Fintech Association of Malaysia, 2025). Moreover, Boost Bank, Malaysia's first homegrown digital bank and CGC Digital through joint collaboration, support underserved businesses through the expansion of access to financing for MSMEs in Malaysia with the allocation of RM130 million for business loans (Fintech News Malaysia, 2025). These microloans and short-term lending platforms allow small scale businesses and entrepreneurs to borrow small amounts of money to assist them in running their businesses, usually in the form of working capital in developing countries (De Gregorio Rebeco, 1999).

FinTech has also made a significant impact on the insurance industry, offering consumers more personalized and convenient options. This is often referred to as 'insurtech' (Kaur & Singh, 2025). Some of the digital insurance products offered in Malaysia include on-demand digital insurance, peer-to-peer (P2P) insurance, telematics insurance and microinsurance. For example, on-demand digital insurance products such as Tune Protect and PolicyStreet, enable users to purchase insurance policies such as health insurance, life insurance and car insurance on demand through a mobile app or website (Fintech News Malaysia, 2023). These platforms offer micro-duration policies and allow users to adjust coverage based on specific needs, making insurance more flexible and accessible. On the other hand, microinsurance products such as Axiata Digital and GKash provide low-cost coverage for low-income or underserved segments of the population (Fintech News Malaysia, 2023). GKash offers health and personal accident insurance through e-wallets while Axiata Digital provides life, health and personal accident insurance through mobile platforms (Fintech News Malaysia, 2023). Furthermore, FinTech solutions in insurance have automated and simplified the claims process, using AI and chatbots to assess and process claims quickly. This reduces paperwork and streamlines the claims process for both customers and insurers, enhancing efficiency and customer satisfaction. The rise of approved cryptocurrencies such as Bitcoin (BTC), Bitcoin Cash (BCH), Curve DAO (CRV) and Ethereum (ETH) in Malaysia has also been driven by FinTech innovation. These cryptocurrencies are regulated through cryptocurrency exchanges such as Luno, SINEGY, Tokenize, MX Global, Hata and Torum, which provide a secure environment for crypto transactions while complying with local regulations (Fintech News Malaysia, 2025). Blockchain technology is also being used to create decentralized finance (DeFi) solutions that enable lending, borrowing, and investing without traditional intermediaries. Real-Time investment decisions with Big Data such as eToro and Interactive Brokers offer tools that leverage big data and machine learning to provide real-time analysis, trading signals, and predictions, empowering users to make more informed investment decisions.

## SUSTAINABILITY IN THE FINANCE SECTOR

Corporate sustainability is the archetype for businesses in the 21st century that is reliant on three interconnected dimensions, consisting economic prosperity, social equity and environmental integrity (Elkington, 1998; Elkington, 1999). Since the mid-2010s, sustainability has become a central objective for both global and local organizations, supported by governments, local and international institutions. Jaiwant, Haridasan, and Kureethara (2024) opine that climate change causes twofold risks to the finance industry comprising physical risks and transition risks. Physical risks arise due to damages to infrastructure, property or natural resources caused by extreme weather such as floods, storms, typhoon and wildfires. On the other hand, transition risks occur due to the world's transition to a low-carbon economy, such as changes in government policies, evolving public attitude and perception, and rapid progress in green and clean technologies. When combined, these forces can reshape markets, influence the values of assets and modify the long-term strategies of financial institutions (Jaiwant, Haridasan, & Kureethara, 2024). A major turning point came with the Paris Climate Agreement in December 2015, where 195 countries committed to reshaping the global economy in a climate-conscious way, by setting a collective goal to limit global warming to well below 2°C (ideally 1.5°C) above pre-industrial levels (KPMG International, 2021). The United Nations subsequently launched the 2030 Agenda for Sustainable Development, introducing the 17 SDGs in 2015. Both noteworthy frameworks have significantly accelerated global efforts to align economic development with environmental sustainability and social well-being (KPMG International, 2021).

In the finance context, sustainability refers to the integration of ESG factors into financial decision-making to promote long-term value creation. It focuses on balancing financial returns with responsible stewardship of resources, societal impact and ethical governance practices. Sustainable finance, hence, seeks to support investments and business strategies that contribute to a more sustainable economy by addressing issues such as climate change, social inequality and lack of corporate accountability. Key aspects of sustainability in finance include environmental factors such as investing in companies or projects that reduce environmental harm or support green technologies (e.g., renewable energy and waste reduction); social factors, which involve investments that contribute positively to social welfare, such as improving labour conditions, supporting community development and promoting diversity; and, governance factors that focus on ethical business practices, transparency and strong corporate governance structures to prevent corruption and enhance long-term stability. Bhutta et al. (2022) postulate that sustainable finance can be seen in various financial products that aim to generate financial returns, and drive positive environmental and social impacts, such as green bonds, socially responsible investing (SRI) and impact investing.

Ng et al. (2020) state that financial institutions play a crucial role in promoting sustainability by leveraging their financial resources, expertise and influence to drive positive environmental, social and governance (ESG) outcomes. Banks and financial institutions provide funds by matching businesses and individuals that seek funds or capital with businesses and individuals that can lend or invest the funds or capital. Banks and financial institutions, thus, support the transition to a more green and sustainable economy by directing loans, investments and other financial services to sustainable initiatives such as renewable energy projects and green infrastructure. In this context, financial institutions issue and manage financial products such as green business loans, which fund projects with environmental benefits or sustainable mutual funds and ETFs that invest in companies meeting certain ESG criteria. This assists and encourages investors to make investments into projects aligned with the UN SDGs. Dwivedi, Alabdooli, and Dwivedi (2021) concur that financial technology or "FinTech" can contribute to the achievement of the UN SDGs' 2030 agenda due to FinTech's ability to channel financial resources towards sustainable investments. According to the United Nations Conference on Trade and Development (UNCTAD)'s World Investment Report 2024, the sustainable finance market has shown steady growth, with investment products such as bonds and funds surpassing USD$7 trillion in value in 2023 recording a 20% increase from the previous year.

While the global market landscape remains complex and varies across regions, countries and sectors, the overall upward trend reflects strong investor confidence and the enduring appeal of sustainable investment strategies. This resilience suggests that sustainability is becoming an integral part of mainstream finance rather than a passing trend (UNCTAD, 2024).

In the Malaysian context, CIMB, one of the leading local banks, announced its dedication to enabling the community in building a more sustainable future through the offering of accessible financial services while supporting renewable energy and sustainable transportation through eco-friendly banking solutions (CIMB, 2025). For example, CIMB is the first bank in Malaysia to offer solar financing via credit card of up to 60 months instalment plan with 0% Easy Pay plan (CIMB, 2025). The United Overseas Bank (UOB), on the other hand, developed four sustainable finance-related frameworks namely the Green Financing Framework for Circular Economy, Smart City Sustainable Finance Framework, Real Estate Sustainable Finance Framework, and Green and Sustainable Trade and Finance Framework (The Edge Malaysia, 2022). Moreover, *Bank Negara Malaysia* established its Low Carbon Transition Facility from 3rd of February 2022 to full utilization, to help small and medium-sized enterprises (SMEs) to be in line with Malaysia's net-zero emission goal by 2050 (The Edge Malaysia, 2022).

## Fostering Innovation and Financial Inclusion in Sustainable Finance

Against the backdrop of the UN SDGs and efforts to recover from the impact of COVID-19, the role of sustainable and inclusive finance has become more critical than ever. Siddik, Rahman, and Yong (2023) affirms that technological innovation such as financial technology supports businesses in mitigating environmental impacts, promotes ecological transformation and boosts businesses' corporate sustainability performance. Similarly, Khan et al. (2021) suggest that environmental issues that are triggered by economic growth may be resolved through technological advancements such as innovations in financial technology that can help to increase the efficiency of resources. In the same vein, unlike traditional finance, sustainable finance together with technological progress, directs capital towards operations that create positive impacts for the environment and society (Galeone, Ranaldo, & Fusco, 2024). FinTech, considered an accelerator of sustainable economic growth, is part of the technological innovations related to sustainable finance (Galeone, Ranaldo, & Fusco, 2024). As countries like Malaysia face the growing challenges of climate change, social inequality and a complex economic environment, building a resilient financial system is essential to support long-term stability and inclusive growth (World Bank, 2025). Financial institutions are at the forefront of developing innovative financial products and services that promote sustainability, such as impact investing, sustainability-linked loans and social bonds. These products allow investors and businesses to directly support social and environmental goals while achieving financial returns.

Sustainability-Linked Loans (SLLs), for example, have interest rates that can vary based on the borrower's sustainability performance (Chan, 2021) is an example of an innovative financial product to foster sustainable finance. Thus, companies that improve their carbon emissions and reduce their carbon footprint may qualify for a loan with lower interest rate, thus, cultivating financial inclusion. The Edge Malaysia (2022) reports that the offering of green products and/or services by banks and financial institutions in Malaysia has been growing with 91 per cent of the banking sector having at least one or more green products or services as stated in the Joint Committee on Climate Change (JC3) Report on the Sustainable Finance Landscape in Malaysia in April 2022. In addition, Maybank Group designed its own in-house Sustainable Product Framework (SPF) to facilitate the creation of green, social and sustainable products in line with Maybank Group's sustainable standards throughout the product's life cycle (Maybank, 2022). On the other hand, Galeone Galeone, Ranaldo, and Fusco (2024) argue that technology does not influence sustainability as the bank's choice to apply the principles of sustainability is solely linked to the bank's inclination towards sustainability issues. However, the bank's choice to operate in line with sustainability principles leads to collaborations with Fintech that are deemed to be useful towards the attainment of sustainability goals in a quicker and more efficient manner (Galeone, Ranaldo, & Fusco, 2024), such as through financial inclusion.

Financial inclusion involves the provision of access to finance by financial institutions for underserved communities through, for example, microfinance, affordable housing loans and financial literacy programs, to help reduce inequalities and promote social sustainability (Md & Tanvir Rahman, 2019). According to the World Bank Group (2025), financial inclusion provides opportunity for individuals and businesses to have access to and use affordable financial products and services that meet their needs, which are delivered in a responsible and sustainable way. Financial inclusion, thus, is a catalyst for achieving seven of the 17 SDGs as it fosters economic growth and employment, promotes economic empowerment of women, and contributes to eliminating poverty. Financial institutions often align their operations and investments with the UN SDGs, and support initiatives that address global challenges such as poverty, inequality and climate change (World Bank Group, 2025). The financial sector, therefore, has a vital role to play in helping countries build resilience and achieve sustainability, but to do so effectively, it must evolve (World Bank Group, 2022).

Driving this transformation will require significant investment that is far beyond what public funding alone can provide. To meet the scale of the challenge, especially in addressing climate change, private sector financing must complement public efforts. Strong, well-functioning financial markets, therefore, are key to mobilizing the capital needed for both climate mitigation and adaptation. However, this can only happen if sustainability is embedded into the core of financial institutions' strategies and decision-making processes, i.e., integrated finance, that directs capital towards sustainable investments (World Bank Group, 2022). Many financial institutions collaborate with governments, non-governmental organizations (NGOs) and international organizations to advance sustainability agendas by advocating for stronger climate policies, better ESG regulations and the integration of sustainability into global financial systems. Furthermore, financial institutions are increasingly supporting the transition to a net-zero carbon economy by providing funding to businesses that are reducing carbon emissions or transitioning to sustainable business models (Stern & Valero, 2021).

Financial institutions also play a pivotal role in raising awareness about sustainability issues by educating clients, investors and employees about ESG risks and opportunities (Wang, 2024) through the provision of resources and guidance on integrating sustainability into financial planning, investments and business operations. The World Economic Forum (2019) states that leaders in the financial services sector are increasingly focused on guiding the global economy toward more energy-efficient and sustainable practices. Simultaneously, they are recognizing the broader social implications of automation and machine learning, particularly how these technologies affect jobs, equity and trust. In response, many of these leaders are working to establish robust governance structures that balance innovation with accountability to ensure they meet the expectations of both shareholders and socially conscious consumers (World Economic Forum, 2019). For example, the United Nations Environment Programme Finance Initiative (UNEP FI) advocates the Principles for Responsible Banking, the world's foremost sustainable banking framework, with more than 345 signatory banks from all over the world (United Nations Environment Programme Finance Initiative, 2025). The six principles are intended to be embedded into banks' overall strategies and applied throughout their entire range of activities with the aim to bring clarity of purpose, a strong vision and a shared ambition for sustainable finance, placing sustainability at the heart of how banks operate and make decisions (United Nations Environment Programme Finance Initiative, 2025).

## ESG FACTORS AND THEIR IMPACT ON FINANCE

ESG emphasizes the importance of environmental stewardship, social responsibility and strong corporate governance alongside economic pursuits and has become a crucial factor in investment decisions and a benchmark for assessing a company's overall sustainability (Hu, Jia, & Yang, 2025). ESG factors have increasingly become a central concern for both institutional and individual investors. In response, more companies are actively engaging in ESG initiatives to enhance their reputation as socially responsible organizations. At the same time, asset managers, pension funds and other institutional investors are placing greater emphasis on a company's ESG performance when making investment decisions, reflecting a broader shift toward responsible and sustainable investing (Kim & Li, 2021). In the same vein, Svoboda (2023) states that ESG has emerged as key pillars of a company's strategies resulting in a shift in mainstream finance due to the unified undercurrents of rising stakeholder expectations, fast evolving regulatory environments, climate change and socioeconomic inequities. The United Nations Principles for Responsible Investing define ESG integration into decision-making in finance as the explicit and methodical inclusion of ESG aspects into investment decisions and investment analysis.

The integration of ESG is, thus, the application of ESG criteria into traditional investment management and analysis (Kim & Li, 2021). Financial institutions assess environmental, social and governance risks when making investment or lending decisions. By integrating ESG factors into credit analysis and risk models, they ensure that the projects or businesses they fund are more resilient to future risks, such as climate change risks, social unrest and governance issues. Financial institutions have also adopted screening processes that exclude investments in harmful sectors, for example, fossil fuels, tobacco and weapons while promoting investments in sectors that have a positive environmental and/or social impact (Al Ayoubi & Enjolras, 2022). Additionally, from the banks and financial institutions' point of view, integrating ESG factors into lending and investment decision-making helps to enhance their financial performance in the long-term ensuring the banks and financial institutions' sustainability. This is in line with Ahmed et al. (2018) who find that banks pioneering in incorporating ESG factors in lending decisions are compensated through better financial performance.

Danisman and Tarazi (2020) find that during times of crisis, banks that are more actively engaged in ESG practices tend to be more resilient, and experience smaller increases in credit and asset risk. These banks maintain more stable profitability and face less disruption in market funding. As a result, these banks are less likely to significantly downsize and do not need to raise deposit rates as sharply as banks with weaker ESG commitments. In addition, Danisman and Tarazi (2020) explain that these adverse effects are particularly evident in banks that focus on traditional lending and deposit-taking activities, which are largely influenced by strong performance in the environmental component of ESG scores with the most notable impact observed during the global financial crisis of 2007–2009. This is supported by Friede, Busch and Bassen (2015) who highlight a growing body of evidence indicating that companies with strong ESG performance often outperform their peers in the long-term because these companies tend to achieve better financial returns and demonstrate greater resilience in the face of external shocks. This suggests that ESG integration can enhance both profitability and stability over time (Friede, Busch and Bassen, 2015). Moreover, Artiach et al. (2010) find that firms with leading corporate sustainability performance have higher levels of growth and a higher return on equity (ROE) as compared to conventional firms.

To surmise, the integration of ESG factors into the decision-making process in finance reflects a forward-looking approach that balances immediate business objectives with long-term positive impacts on society and the environment. Through this, the groundwork for a more holistic and sustainable growth is positioned, aligning corporate success with broader societal and environmental well-being (Svuboda, 2023). Andrey (2023) affirms that the application of ESG factors to a business' day-to-day operations can help companies manage and obtain financing solutions such as bank loans, private equity, equity financing and trade finance. In addition, investors are more likely to contact these companies to further advance the development of ESG (Andrey, 2023) due to the active involvement of ESG factors in the companies' operations, strategies and policies.

## Promoting Corporate Accountability in Finance through ESG Disclosure and Reporting

The increasing importance of corporate accountability has been pushing companies to disclose more information through public domains as a way of communicating and engaging with their stakeholders (Swift, 2002). The extent to which businesses contribute to environmental protection and preservation, and drive societal development is measured by the businesses' corporate sustainability performance, which indicates the degree to which a company integrates ESG and economic components into its business processes and ultimately, their impact on the business and community (Siddik, Rahman, & Yong, 2023; Artiach et al., 2010; Wagner, 2010). In the context of the world of finance, financial institutions, especially institutional investors such as pension funds or asset managers, often engage with companies they invest in to encourage them to adopt more sustainable practices. For example, these stakeholders can push for better environmental practices, greater social responsibility and stronger corporate governance (Walls, Berrone, & Phan, 2012). Shareholders through voting on company resolutions or engaging in dialogue with company leadership, financial institutions can advocate for more transparent ESG disclosures, ethical practices, and long-term sustainability strategies. Additionally, financial institutions often play a key role in promoting standardized ESG reporting frameworks. By encouraging companies to disclose their sustainability performance and align their own reporting with international standards, such as the Global Reporting Initiative (GRI) and Sustainability Accounting Standards Board (SASB), they contribute to greater transparency and accountability in corporate sustainability practices (Samans & Nelson, 2022). Additionally, these companies may also develop or utilize ESG data and analytics tools to assist investors make informed decisions based on sustainability criteria. This in turn can help businesses to identify areas for improvement in their own sustainability efforts.

Integrated financial systems today face a complex web of conflicting goals, namely, maximizing financial returns, advancing technological efficiency and achieving sustainability. These tensions are further complicated by the rapid innovation cycles of FinTech and the long-term imperatives of ESG objectives. Kumar et al. (2025), for example, state that financial innovation is a powerful driver that pushes the transition towards circular economy and enables organizations to integrate principles of circular economy and elements of ESG into their strategic decision-making. According to Morseletto (2020), the three main tenets of circular economy comprise renewing natural systems, maintaining the use of goods and materials, and designing out pollutions as waste, and how each of these tenets interacts with financial institutions. Effective regulation and governance are, thus, essential to balance these competing priorities.

Financial institutions and corporations are under constant pressure to deliver high returns, often incentivizing short-term profit maximization. Technological efficiency, driven by digital finance, Big Data and AI, promises cost reductions and operational agility, further fuelling the pursuit of returns (Luo et al., 2022). However, these advances can conflict with sustainability goals, which require long-term investments, risk management, and sometimes a willingness to accept lower immediate profits for broader societal or environmental benefits (Li et al., 2023). For example, while digital finance and AI can enhance both financial efficiency and sustainability, the focus on rapid return-on-investment (ROI) may lead to underinvestment in green technologies or ESG initiatives that yield benefits over longer horizons (Li and Huang, 2024). Businesses must, therefore, navigate trade-offs between short-term financial performance, technological adoption and the integration of sustainability into their core strategies (Li et al., 2023; Li and Huang, 2024). Regulations and governance frameworks are, hence, critical in managing these tensions within integrated financial systems. This is especially crucial as risk management in the banking sector remains largely black-boxed (Kashyap and Iveroth, 2020) because banks rely heavily on quantitative risk models that are too complex, proprietary or non-transparent for stakeholders to fully evaluate or replicate. In addition, even though FinTech can facilitate ESG integration through the improvement in level of transparency, enhancement of stakeholder engagement and increased access to green finance, there lies a risk that the drive for quick returns and market share may overshadow long-term sustainability commitments (Giakoumelou et al., 2024). Additionally, even though transparency, integrity, credibility, bulwarks, comparability and accountability of ESG disclosures are of particular importance, the reporting of false or misleading ESG information, which is commonly referred to as greenwashing, remains a huge problem (Sneideriene and Legenzova, 2025).

## CHALLENGES AND FUTURE DIRECTIONS

As environmental challenges grow more urgent, social inequalities deepen and corporate governance issues continue to surface, the need for sustainable finance and ESG-focused investing has never been more critical. Moreover, as FinTech and digital innovation cycles are characterized by rapid development, disruptive business models and a focus on speed-to-market, this dynamic creates misalignment with the slower, cumulative progress required for ESG and sustainability objectives (Giakoumelou et al., 2024; Hu, Jia, & Yang, 2025). With rising global concerns about climate change and social impact, banks and other financial institutions are being called to rethink the way they operate, moving beyond traditional models to embrace approaches that prioritize long-term responsibility and resilience (Valavan, 2024). The first challenge in aligning ESG with integrated finance is that currently there is no universally accepted standard for ESG data. This makes it difficult to compare companies or investments across regions or industries. Different organizations and frameworks (for example Global Reporting Initiative (GRI), Sustainability Accounting Standards Board (SASB) have developed their own sets of standards, but these can either be conflicting or overlapping (Parfitt, 2024). Moreover, the inconsistency of these ESG data can result in confusion, misalignment in decision-making, and inefficiencies for investors, financial institutions, and companies themselves. Therefore, there is a tendency of ESG future direction to have harmonization in the reporting standards. There are already several efforts which are in the pipeline, such as the creation of the International Financial Reporting Standards (IFRS) Foundation's International Sustainability Standards Board (ISSB), which aims to develop global ESG disclosure standards (Elidrisy, 2024).

ESG metrics are increasingly central to investment and corporate strategy, yet their credibility and effectiveness are undermined by persistent challenges such as greenwashing, striking a balance between financial returns and ESG goals, and lack of data comparability. Through greenwashing, companies may selectively disclose positive information, use vague or irrelevant claims or provide unverified assertions to appear more sustainable than they are, eroding trust among investors, consumers and regulators (Poiriazi et al., 2025). Greenwashing presents a significant obstacle to tackling climate change because it misleads the public to believe that a company is doing more to protect the environment than it is, hence, advocating false solutions to the climate crisis that distract from, and delay concrete and credible action (United Nations, 2025). Greenwashing and misleading claims undermine genuine sustainability efforts and deceive investors (Dempere, Alamash, & Mattos, 2024). In a similar vein, the accuracy and reliability of ESG reporting are threatened by the presence of greenwashing, which affects the quality of disclosure, complicates the decision-making process, adversely influences financial markets and affects stakeholders' trust in disclosed information (Sneideriene and Legenzova, 2025). The impact of these greenwashing and misleading claims, thus, can erode the trust in ESG investments and makes it harder for investors to identify truly sustainable opportunities. Zervoudi, Moschos, and Christopoulos (2025) affirm that greenwashing, which is the phenomenon of misleading stakeholders concerning the environmental sustainability efforts of a company, may undermine the trust of people in a company or in a whole industry and the progress toward sustainability. As a result, there must be stricter rules and regulations with better transparency as well as third-party verification of claims to address the issue of greenwashing. Investors are expected to demand more rigorous and verifiable evidence of sustainability from companies and financial products.

Another challenge is balancing financial returns with ESG goals, which is the difficulty of maintaining short-term financial returns with long-term sustainability objectives. This leads to resistance among traditional investors or financial institutions that prioritize immediate financial returns over long-term sustainability (Simanjuntak, 2024). In the same vein, Luo et al. (2024) concur that Chinese active mutual funds that fulfill the Principles for Responsible Investment (PRI) requirements through investments in assets with superior ESG performance and excellent returns on investment fail to balance ESG objectives with traditional financial objectives resulting in additional underperformance as compared to normal ESG investments. Conversely, Yu et al. (2024) argue that emphasis on investments that are earnings-driven with a high focus on ESG, specifically capital projects, could align financial targets with sustainable practices leading to increased stakeholders' trust and enhanced long-term viability. On another note, Jonsdottir et al. (2022), find that current barriers to using ESG data include a lack of materiality, accuracy and reliability, such as lack of access to ESG data collected by governmental institutions and the purchase of carbon credits that raise questions about the dependability of ESG data. Furthermore, World Economic Forum (2021) attests that there is lack of or no comparable and transparent data to measure progress on ESG issues and corporate resilience. Similarly, Kotsantonis and Serafeim (2019) highlight the vast diversity and inconsistency in both the reporting and measurement of ESG data among companies, namely, employee health and safety information, and demonstrate how such variations can produce markedly different outcomes even when analyzing the same set of companies.

A credible ESG outlook must first recognize these systemic challenges. Combating greenwashing calls for stronger regulatory oversight, mandatory independent audits and the adoption of technological innovations to enhance traceability. Liu et al. (2024), for example, propose the use of a Dual ESG Index (DESGI) model using blockchain technology to provide flexible and transparent corporate sustainability assessment. Equally important is the harmonization of ESG metrics and reporting standards to ensure data comparability and rating consistency. Ultimately, only through greater transparency, standardization and accountability can ESG metrics truly serve as effective instruments for sustainable value creation.

## CONCLUSION

Integrated finance has transitioned from traditional financial integration among economies to a more technologically driven incorporation of financial services across various platforms, reflecting the dynamic nature of the financial landscape. The evolution of integrated finance encompasses the globalization of financial markets, technological advancements leading to electronic financial networks and the adoption of integrated reporting practices across the globe. These developments highlight the ongoing transformation of financial systems towards greater integration and adaptability with the evolution of technological advances. FinTech has embedded itself deeply into the financial ecosystem across payments, lending, insurance, and investments, significantly enhancing efficiency, access, and customer experience. By leveraging technologies such as AI, Big Data, blockchain and Application Programming Interfaces (APIs), FinTech creates all-in-one and tailored financial solutions that cater to both consumers and businesses (Bowden et al., 2021). As FinTech continues to evolve, we can expect even greater innovation, improved accessibility, and new ways to integrate financial services into everyday life.

Financial institutions are crucial 'agents' in promoting sustainability by guiding capital flows towards projects and companies that align with sustainable development, influencing corporate behavior, and providing innovative financial solutions that address social, environmental, and governance challenges (Ng et al., 2020). Through these actions, they assist in building a more resilient and sustainable global economy. In addition, the growing green economy is creating a host of new investment and lending opportunities for businesses, individuals and governments worldwide driving institutional investors and retail banking customers to increasingly demand that banks and financial institutions uphold environmental standards (United Nations Environment Programme, 2022). However, the integration of ESG factors into finance, i.e., integrated finance, faces several challenges. KPMG International (2021) states that banks have traditionally approached sustainability in a fragmented or piecemeal way. However, the growing volume of information combined with uncertainty around future regulatory changes has made it challenging for many banks and financial institutions to formulate a clear and cohesive ESG strategy. As a result, while interest in sustainability is growing, many banks struggle to integrate ESG factors systematically across their operations, long-term planning (KPMG International, 2021) and decision-making.

Nevertheless, the future of ESG in finance looks promising and the future direction for companies is the greater integration of ESG into their financial strategies, which includes the growing acceptance of sustainable investments along with ethically responsible decision-making. For example, as a conventional instrument for ESG investments, ESG funds play a vital role in driving the expansion of the ESG investment industry and tackling ESG topics (Luo et al., 2024). As regulations evolve, data quality improves, and the financial community embraces long-term sustainability in value creation, ESG principles are expected to become a core component of integrated finance (Olanrewaj, Daramola, & Babayeju, 2024). Dynamic innovation, better alignment between financial returns and sustainability goals, and increased global cooperation to promote a sustainable, inclusive and resilient financial system are some of the key factors, which contribute to the development of integrated finance and ESG.

## REFERENCES


Ahmed, S., Ahmed, S. P., & Hasan, I. (2018). Why banks should consider ESG risk factors in bank lending? *Banks and Bank Systems*, *13*(3), 71–80. DOI: 10.21511/bbs.13(3).2018.07

Al Ayoubi, K., & Enjolras, G. (2022). Does disinvestment from fossil fuels reduce the financial performance of responsible sovereign wealth funds? *Journal of Multinational Financial Management*, *64*, 100731. DOI: 10.1016/j.mulfin.2022.100731

Alam, S. T.Syed Tanveer Alam. (2024). Revolutionizing energy payments: The role of FinTech in streamlining transactions. *World J. Advance Research Review*, *22*(1), 2074–2083. DOI: 10.30574/wjarr.2024.22.2.1626

Andrey, E. (2023). ESG as an innovative tool to improve the efficiency and financial stability of financial organizations. *Procedia Computer Science*, *221*, 705–709. DOI: 10.1016/j.procs.2023.08.041

Artiach, T., Lee, D., Nelson, D., & Walker, J. (2010). The determinants of corporate sustainability performance. *Accounting and Finance*, *50*(1), 31–51. DOI: 10.1111/j.1467-629X.2009.00315.x

Aslam, F. (2024). Integrated finance: A sustainable working model for the future. https://www.linkedin.com/pulse/integrated-finance-sustainable-working-model-future-faheem-aslam-gremf/

Ayhan Kose, M., Prasad, E. S., & Taylor, A. D. (2011). Thresholds in the process of international financial integration. *Journal of International Money and Finance*, *30*(1), 147–179. DOI: 10.1016/j.jimonfin.2010.08.005

Bhutta, U. S., Tariq, A., Farrukh, M., Raza, A., & Iqbal, M. K. (2022). Green bonds for sustainable development: Review of literature on development and impact of green bonds. *Technological Forecasting and Social Change*, *175*, 121378. DOI: 10.1016/j.techfore.2021.121378

Bowden, J., King, T., Koutmos, D., Loncan, T. & Stentella Lopes, F. S. (2021). A taxonomy of FinTech innovation. *Disruptive Technology in Banking and Finance: An International Perspective on FinTech*, 47-91.

Bursa Malaysia. (2021). Growing your wealth using Exchange-Traded Funds ("ETFs"). https://my.bursamalaysia.com/learn/knowledge/explorer/growing-your-wealth-using-exchange-traded-funds-etfs

CFA Institute. (2023). How FinTech is driving financial inclusion. https://www.cfainstitute.org/insights/articles/how-fintech-is-driving-financial-inclusion

Chan, R. (2021). Ensuring impactful performance in green bonds and sustainability-linked loans. *The Adelaide Kaw Review*, *42*(1), 221–258.

CIMB. (2025). Banking towards tomorrow. https://www.cimb.com.my/en/personal/day-to-day-banking/sustainability-at-cimb.html

Crona, B., Peterson, G., Meacham, M., Parlato, G., Lade, S. J., Rocha, J. C., & Galaz, V. (2025). A systems approach to sustainable finance: Actors, influence mechanisms, and potentially virtuous cycles of sustainability. *iScience*, *112785*(7), 112785. Advance online publication. DOI: 10.1016/j.isci.2025.112785

Cummins, J. D., & Weiss, M. A. (2009). Convergence of insurance and financial markets: Hybrid and securitized risk-transfer solutions. *The Journal of Risk and Insurance*, *76*(3), 493–545. DOI: 10.1111/j.1539-6975.2009.01311.x

Danisman, G. O., & Tarazi, A. (2020). Financial inclusion and bank stability: Evidence from Europe. *European Journal of Finance*, *26*(18), 1842–1855. DOI: 10.1080/1351847X.2020.1782958

De Gregorio Rebeco, J. (1999). Financial integration, financial development and economic growth. *Estudos Econômicos*, *26*(2), 137–161.

Dempere, J., Alamash, E., & Mattos, P. (2024). Unveiling the truth: Greenwashing in sustainable finance. *Frontiers in Sustainability*, *5*, 1362051. DOI: 10.3389/frsus.2024.1362051

Dwivedi, P., Alabdooli, J. I., & Dwivedi, R. (2021). Role of FinTech adoption for competitiveness and performance of the bank: A study of banking industry in UAE. *International Journal of Global Business and Competitiveness*, *16*(2), 130–138. DOI: 10.1007/s42943-021-00033-9

Elidrisy, A. (2024). Comparative review of ESG Reporting Standards: ESRS European Sustainability Reporting Standards" versus ISSB "International Sustainability Standards Board. *International Multilingual Journal of Science and Technology*, *9*(3), 7191–7198.

Elkington, J. (1998). Partnerships from cannibals with forks: The triple bottom line of 21st-century business. *Environmental Quality Management*, *8*(1), 37–51. DOI: 10.1002/tqem.3310080106

Elkington, J. (1999). Triple bottom line revolution: Reporting for the third millennium. *Australian CPA*, *69*(11), 75–76.

Fintech Association of Malaysia. (2025). Financial assistance. https://fintechmalaysia.org/financial-assistance-peer-2-peer-lending/

Fintech News Malaysia. (2023). Digital insurance products in Malaysia that caught our attention. https://fintechnews.my/38194/insurtech-malaysia/digital-insurance-products-in-malaysia-that-caught-our-attention/

Fintech News Malaysia. (2025). 5 top e-wallets in Malaysia and what they're best for (2025). https://fintechnews.my/50928/payments-remittance-malaysia/top-ewallets-in-malaysia/

Fintech News Malaysia. (2025). Boost Bank and CGC Digital to offer RM130 million in MSME loans. https://fintechnews.my/48719/digital-banking-news-malaysia/boost-bank-msmes-loan/#:~:text=Boost%20Bank%2C%20Malaysia%E2%80%99s%20first%20homegrown%20digital%20bank%2C%20and,in%20Malaysia%2C%20allocating%20RM130%20million%20for%20business%20loans

Fintech News Malaysia. (2025). A list of licensed equity crowdfunding (ECF) platforms in Malaysia. https://fintechnews.my/50781/crowdfunding-malaysia/a-list-of-licensed-ecf-platforms-in-malaysia/#:~:text=Behind%20this%20momentum%20is%20a%20network%20of%2013,and%20value%20propositions%20for%20both%20issuers%20and%20investors

Fintech News Malaysia. (2025). How to buy cryptocurrency in Malaysia (2025). https://fintechnews.my/47522/blockchain/how-to-buy-cryptocurrency-in-malaysia-2025/

Fratzscher, M., & Imbs, J. (2009). Risk sharing, finance, and institutions in international portfolios. *Journal of Financial Economics*, *94*(3), 428–447. DOI: 10.1016/j.jfineco.2008.12.007

Friede, G., Busch, T., & Bassen, A. (2015). ESG and financial performance: Aggregated evidence from more than 2000 empirical studies. *Journal of Sustainable Finance & Investment*, *5*(4), 210–233. DOI: 10.1080/20430795.2015.1118917

Galeone, G., Ranaldo, S., & Fusco, A. (2024). ESG and FinTech: Are they connected? *Research in International Business and Finance*, *69*, 102225. DOI: 10.1016/j.ribaf.2024.102225

Giakoumelou, A., Salvi, A., Bekiros, S., & Onorato, G. (2024). ESG and FinTech funding in the EU. *Research in International Business and Finance*, *69*, 102233. DOI: 10.1016/j.ribaf.2024.102233

Giannetti, M., & Ongena, S. (2007). Financial integration and firm performance: Evidence from foreign bank entry in emerging markets. https://ssrn.com/abstract_id=669421www.ecgi.global/content/working-papers DOI: 10.2139/ssrn.669421

Hajian, M. & Kashani, S. J. (2021). 1 - Evolution of the concept of sustainability. From Brundtland Report to Sustainable Development Goals. *Sustainable Resource Management,* 1-24. https://doi.org/.DOI: 10.1016/B978-0-12-824342-8.00018-3

Hu, H., Jia, Z., & Yang, S. (2025). Exploring FinTech, green finance, and ESG performance across corporate life-cycles. *International Review of Financial Analysis*, *97*, 103871. DOI: 10.1016/j.irfa.2024.103871

IBM. (2025). What is environmental, social and governance (ESG)? https://www.ibm.com/think/topics/environmental-social-and-governance

Jaiwant, S. V., Haridasan, A., & Kureethara, J. V. (2024). The role of financial institutions in addressing climate change. In Naifar, N. (Ed.), *Climate change and finance. Sustainable Finance*. Springer., DOI: 10.1007/978-3-031-56419-2_5

Jonsdottir, B., Sigurjonsson, T. O., Johannsdottir, L., & Wendt, S. (2022). Barriers to using ESG data for investment decisions. *Sustainability (Basel)*, *14*(9), 5157. DOI: 10.3390/su14095157

Kashyap, S., & Iveroth, E. (2020). Transparency and accountability influences of regulation on risk control: The case of a Swedish bank. *The Journal of Management and Governance*, *25*(2), 475–508. DOI: 10.1007/s10997-020-09550-w

Kaur, P., & Singh, M. (2025). Exploring the impact of InsurTech adoption in Indian life insurance industry: A customer satisfaction perspective. *The TQM Journal*, *37*(2), 457–483. DOI: 10.1108/TQM-06-2023-0186

Khan, S. A. R., Yu, Z., Sarwat, S., Godil, D. I., Amin, S., & Shujaat, S. (2021). The role of block chain technology in circular economy practices to improve organisational performance. *International Journal of Logistics*, *25*(4–5), 605–622. DOI: 10.1080/13675567.2021.1872512

Kim, S., & Li, Z. (2021). Understanding the impact of ESG practices in corporate finance. *Sustainability (Basel)*, *13*(7), 3746. DOI: 10.3390/su13073746

Kotsantonis, S., & Serafeim, G. (2019). Four things no one will tell you about ESG data. *The Bank of America Journal of Applied Corporate Finance*, *31*(2), 50–58. DOI: 10.1111/jacf.12346

KPMG International. (2021). ESG risks in banks: Effective strategies to use opportunities and mitigate risks. https://assets.kpmg.com/content/dam/kpmg/xx/pdf/2021/05/esg-risks-in-banks.pdf

Kruger, M., Lavigne, R., & Mckay, J. (2016). *The role of the International Monetary Fund in the post-crisis world Standard-Nutzungsbedingungen*. https://doi.org/DOI: 10.34989/sdp-2016-6

Kumar, B., Kumar, A., Sassanelli, C., & Kumar, L. (2025). Exploring the role of finance in driving circular economy and sustainable business practices. *Journal of Cleaner Production*, *486*, 144480. DOI: 10.1016/j.jclepro.2024.144480

Li, L., Fei, C., & Fei, W. (2023). Research on investment incorporating both environmental performance and long (short) term financial performance of firms. *International Journal of Systems Science*, *55*(2), 273–299. DOI: 10.1080/00207721.2023.2270402

Li, N., & Huang, F. (2024). Evaluating the financial returns on investment in sustainable enterprise digitalization initiatives using AI information system. *Journal of Internet Services and Information Security*, *14*(4), 21–44. DOI: 10.58346/JISIS.2024.I4.002

Li, Z., & Chen, P. (2024). Sustainable finance meets FinTech: Amplifying green credit's benefits for banks. *Sustainability (Basel)*, *16*(18), 7901. DOI: 10.3390/su16187901

Liu, X., Liang, W., Fu, Y., & Huang, G. Q. (2024). Dual Environmental, Social, and Governance (ESG) Index for corporate sustainability assessment using blockchain technology. *Sustainability (Basel)*, *16*(10), 4272. DOI: 10.3390/su16104272

Luo, D., Luo, M., & Lv, J. (2022). Can digital finance contribute to the promotion of financial sustainability? A financial efficiency perspective. *Sustainability (Basel)*, *14*(7), 3979. DOI: 10.3390/su14073979

Luo, Q., Xue, M., Xiong, Y. & Ge, X. (2024). The backfire of mutual funds balancing financial objectives in ESG investments: Evidence from China. *International Review of Financial Analysis, 96*(Part B), 103686. https://doi.org/.DOI: 10.1016/j.irfa.2024.103686

Maybank (2022). Maybank launches Sustainable Product Framework to drive sustainable finance. https://www.maybank.com/en/news/2022/09/01.page

Md, R., & Tanvir Rahman, A. (2019). The Effects of Financial Inclusion Initiatives on Economic Development in Underserved Communities. *American Journal of Economics and Business Management*, *2*(4), 191–198.

Mishra, D., Kandpal, V., Agarwal, N., & Srivastava, B. (2024). Financial inclusion and its ripple effects on socio-economic development: A comprehensive review. *Journal of Risk and Financial Management, 17*(3), 105. DOI: 10.3390/jrfm17030105

Morseletto, P. (2020). Restorative and regenerative-Exploring the concepts in the circular economy. *Journal of Industrial Ecology, 24*(4), 763–773. DOI: 10.1111/jiec.12987

Ng, T. H., Lye, C. T., Chan, K. H., Lim, Y. Z., & Lim, Y. S. (2020). Sustainability in Asia: The roles of financial development in environmental, social and governance (ESG) performance. *Social Indicators Research, 150*(1), 17–44. DOI: 10.1007/s11205-020-02288-w

Niemand, T., Rigtering, J. P. C., Kallmünzer, A., Kraus, S., & Maalaoui, A. (2021). Digitalization in the financial industry: A contingency approach of entrepreneurial orientation and strategic vision on digitalization. *European Management Journal, 39*(3), 317–326. DOI: 10.1016/j.emj.2020.04.008

Omokhoa, H. E., Odionu, C. S., Azubuike, C., & Sule, A. K. (2024). Digital transformation in financial services: Integrating AI, FinTech, and innovative solutions for SME growth and financial inclusion. *Gulf Journal of Advance Business Research, 2*(6), 423–434. DOI: 10.51594/gjabr.v2i6.56

Parfitt, C. (2024). A foundation for 'ethical capital': The sustainability accounting standards board and integrated reporting. *Critical Perspectives on Accounting, 98*, 102477. DOI: 10.1016/j.cpa.2022.102477

Poiriazi, E., Zournatzidou, G., Konteos, G., & Sariannidis, N. (2025). Analyzing the interconnection between environmental, social, and governance (ESG) criteria and corporate corruption: Revealing the significant impact of greenwashing. *Administrative Sciences, 15*(3), 100. DOI: 10.3390/admsci15030100

PwC Malaysia. (2023). ESG deals creation and impact investing in Malaysia. https://www.pwc.com/my/en/assets/publications/2023/esg-deals-creation-and-impact-investing-in-malaysia.pdf

Samans, R., & Nelson, J. (2022). Corporate reporting and accountability. In *Sustainable Enterprise Value Creation: Implementing Stakeholder Capitalism through Full ESG Integration* (pp. 187–218). Springer International Publishing. DOI: 10.1007/978-3-030-93560-3_6

Scholtens, B. (2006). Finance as a Driver of Corporate Social Responsibility. *Journal of Business Ethics, 68*(1), 19–33. DOI: 10.1007/s10551-006-9037-1

Siddik, A. B., Rahman, M. N., & Yong, L. (2023, October 1). Do fintech adoption and financial literacy improve corporate sustainability performance? The mediating role of access to finance. *Journal of Cleaner Production*, *421*, 137658. DOI: 10.1016/j.jclepro.2023.137658

Simanjuntak, R. (2024). Navigating the Dynamics of Corporate Financial Management for Sustainable Growth. *Advances in Economics & Financial Studies*, *2*(2), 53–66. DOI: 10.60079/aefs.v2i2.172

Sneideriene, A., & Legenzova, R. (2025). Greenwashing prevention in environmental, social, and governance (ESG) disclosures: A bibliometric analysis. *Research in International Business and Finance*, *74*, 102720. DOI: 10.1016/j.ribaf.2024.102720

Stern, N., & Valero, A. (2021). Innovation, growth and the transition to net-zero emissions. *Research Policy*, *50*(9), 104293. DOI: 10.1016/j.respol.2021.104293

Svoboda, A. (2023). ESG imperative: The role of financial institutions in a sustainable future. *International Journal of Engineering Technology Research & Management*, *7*(11), 34–41.

Swift, T. (2002). Trust, reputation and corporate accountability to stakeholders. *Business Ethics (Oxford, England)*, *10*(1), 16–26. DOI: 10.1111/1467-8608.00208

The Edge Malaysia. (2022). Green financing and incentives in Malaysia. https://theedgemalaysia.com/article/green-financing-and-incentives-malaysia

The United Nations Principles for Responsible Investment. What Is ESG integration? https://www.unpri.org/investor-tools/what-is-esg-integration/3052.article.

UNCTAD. (2024). World Investment Report 2024: Chapter III Sustainable finance. https://unctad.org/system/files/official-document/wir2024_ch03_en.pdf

United Nations. (2025). Greenwashing – The deceptive tactics behind environmental claims. https://www.un.org/en/climatechange/science/climate-issues/greenwashing

United Nations Environment Programme. (2022). Why financial institutions are banking on sustainability. https://www.unep.org/news-and-stories/story/why-financial-institutions-are-banking-sustainability

United Nations Environment Programme Finance Initiative (UNEP FI). (2021). A systemic approach to finance sustainability. https://www.unepfi.org/

United Nations Environment Programme Finance Initiative (UNEP FI). (2025). Principles for Responsible Banking. https://www.unepfi.org/banking/bankingprinciples/

Valavan, T. A. (2024). Sustainable finance and environmental, social, and governance (ESG) investing. *Journal of Critical Reviews*, *11*(3), 10–18.

Wagner, M. (2010). The role of corporate sustainability performance for economic performance: A firm-level analysis of moderation effects. *Ecological Economics*, *69*(7), 1553–1560. DOI: 10.1016/j.ecolecon.2010.02.017

Walls, J. L., Berrone, P., & Phan, P. H. (2012). Corporate governance and environmental performance: Is there really a link? *Strategic Management Journal*, *33*(8), 885–913. DOI: 10.1002/smj.1952

Wang, L. (2024). Challenges and Opportunities of ESG Integration in Financial Operations. In *International Conference on Finance and Economics* (Vol. 6, No. 1). DOI: 10.22158/mmse.v6n1p162

Widodo, A. (2019). The role of integrated Islamic commercial and social finance in reducing income inequality in Indonesia. *Journal of Islamic Monetary Economics and Finance*, *5*(2), 263–286. DOI: 10.21098/jimf.v5i2.1063

World Bank. (2025). Sustainable finance. https://www.worldbank.org/en/country/malaysia/publication/malaysia-sustainable-finance

World Bank. (2025). Financial inclusion. https://www.worldbank.org/en/topic/financialinclusion/overview

World Bank Group. (2022). Unleashing sustainable finance in Southeast Asia. Institute of Finance and Sustainability. https://documents1.worldbank.org/curated/en/099310011232220307/pdf/P177802011f7760130bc49083a7beb1ef43.pdf

World Commission on Environment and Development (WCED). (1987). *Our common future*. Oxford University Press.

World Economic Forum. (2021). Here's why comparable ESG reporting is crucial for investors. https://www.weforum.org/stories/2021/07/comparable-esg-investors/

Yildirim, Z. & Şendeniz-Yüncü, I. (2025). Financial development, international financial integration, and income inequality: An emerging markets perspective. *Research in International Business and Finance, 77*(Part A), 102917. https://doi.org/.DOI: 10.1016/j.ribaf.2025.102917

Yıldırım, Z., & Şendeniz-Yüncü, İ. (2025). Financial development, international financial integration, and income inequality: An emerging markets perspective. *Research in International Business and Finance*, *77*, 102917. DOI: 10.1016/j.ribaf.2025.102917

Zervoudi, E. K., Moschos, N., & Christopoulos, A. G. (2025). From the corporate social responsibility (CSR) and the environmental, social and governance (ESG) criteria to the greenwashing phenomenon: A comprehensive literature review about the causes, consequences and solutions of the phenomenon with specific case studies. *Sustainability (Basel)*, *17*(5), 2222. DOI: 10.3390/su17052222

Zhichao, Y., Farooq, U., Alam, M. M., & Dai, J. (2024). How does environmental, social, and governance (ESG) performance determine investment mix? New empirical evidence from BRICS. *Borsa Istanbul Review*, *24*(3), 520–529. DOI: 10.1016/j.bir.2024.02.007

Ziolo, M., Filipiak, B. Z., Bąk, I., & Cheba, K. (2019). How to design more sustainable financial systems: The roles of environmental, social, and governance factors in the decision-making process. *Sustainability (Basel)*, *11*(20), 5604. DOI: 10.3390/su11205604

## Chapter 9

# The Role of Social Workers in Fostering a Green Economy Within the Sustainable Development Goals:

## Promoting Social Justice, Environmental Responsibility, and Inclusive Growth

**Thi Thi Win**
https://orcid.org/0009-0004-8717-8983
*Lincoln University College, Malaysia*

**Jahid Siraz Chowdhury**
https://orcid.org/0000-0002-1016-0441
*Lincoln University College, Malaysia*

**Mujawir Hussain**
*Lincoln University College, Malaysia*

**Blikis Blikis**
https://orcid.org/0009-0006-0672-2962
*Lincoln University College, Malaysia*

**Md. Taraqual Islam**
*Lincoln University College, Malaysia*

DOI: 10.4018/979-8-3373-2464-7.ch009

## ABSTRACT

*Sustainable development has become a global-criterion as environmental challenges like floods, biodiversity loss, and pollution increasingly threaten human well-being. This paper explores the role of social workers in promoting the Sustainable Development Goals (SDGs) by fostering a green economy, particularly in ecologically fragile regions. It explains how social workers can collaborate with policymakers, investors, and corporate leaders to implement sustainable practices that reduce environmental risks, create jobs, and support local economic growth. Through qualitative analysis of existing articles, journals, and books, the role of social workers is highlighted as an advocate for community-based green projects, policies, and capacity building initiatives. This paper describes practical strategies for social workers in the contribution of sustainable development goals through social justice and environmental sustainability. In this way, social workers ensure the economy is growing in an environmentally friendly way and is socially inclusive.*

## INTRODUCTION

The aim of this discussion is to explore how social workers can promote the green economy in the context of the Sustainable Development Goals (SDGs). While social work has traditionally focused on social justice, there is an emerging recognition of the need to address ecological sustainability as well. The influence of the natural environment on human well-being is receiving increasing attention from social workers. Social work goals and tasks now include the development of a sustainable future, framed in terms of the SDGs adopted by the UN General Assembly in 2015.

The role of social workers in fostering the green economy is directly linked to the SDGs and other related global policies, particularly the need to align social justice with ecological justice (Jarvis, 2013). Climate change and its social consequences rank among the most pressing global challenges. Since the turn of the century, the UN has been highlighting the linking of social and environmental issues through the concept of sustainable development. Following the political discussions globally and in the EU, transformations in economic systems towards green economies (GE) have been recommended as one response to the above challenges. In turn, GE requires social transformations towards inclusive societies involving the marginalized. These two dimensions, environmental responsibility and social inclusion, are strongly interrelated. Social workers are primarily focused on active involvement with people in communities. They are in a unique position to bridge the needs of the communities with environmental action. Therefore, the integration of these two dimensions is a prerequisite for social service to become transformative. However, the ground for action is becoming more difficult due to socio-political changes in many countries. The question is no longer about what social work could or should do but about how social workers can be encouraged to act proactively.

## Background and Rationale

Green economy initiatives centering on low-emission development strategies, renewable energies, protection of ecosystems, and natural resource management are becoming increasingly important in global efforts to pursue sustainable development. A green economy is defined as one that results in "improved human well-being and social equity, while significantly reducing environmental risks and ecosystem scarcities". It is increasingly recognized that social workers, and the wider social work profession, can play a critical role in fostering the green economy and working towards sustainability by focusing on social issues and equity. This role has been acknowledged by various international social work organizations in recent policy statements. A background and rationale for this special issue is provided by discussing the context and historical factors leading to consideration of the green economy within social work.

The green economy is being pursued through a range of global initiatives, partnerships, and investments, often linked to wider aspirations for sustainable development. A green economy is broadly defined as one that results in "improved human well-being and social equity, while significantly reducing environmental risks and ecosystem scarcities". The social dimensions of the green economy are critical to its sustainability and success. A green economy that fails to consider social issues and equity will, in effect, be a "brown" economy that merely perpetuates existing inequalities and injustices. Historically, social issues were sidelined in earlier efforts focusing on environmental sustainability. However, it is now recognized that equity and social justice are critical to pursuing environmental sustainability. Social work is a profession that has been trained to focus on social issues and equity (Engstrom, 2019). Thus, social workers (and the wider social work profession) can play an important role in fostering the green economy and working towards sustainability through a focus on social issues and equity.

## UNDERSTANDING SUSTAINABLE DEVELOPMENT GOALS

The United Nations (UN) has established the Sustainable Development Goals (SDGs) as a set of 17 goals to address global challenges in the context of sustainable development (Leal Filho et al., 2019). These goals specifically aim to end poverty, protect the planet, and ensure prosperity for all by 2030. Adopted in

2015, the SDGs build on decades of UN initiatives and commitments, including the Millennium Development Goals made in 2000. The SDGs are described as a "shared blueprint for peace and prosperity for people and the planet, now and into the future". Every member state in the UN is called to action in implementing the SDGs, which recognizes that each country must address its own economic, social, and environmental challenges.

The SDGs are interconnected, emphasizing that progress in one goal may induce setbacks in another. For instance, large-scale economic growth may spur industrialization and urbanization while reducing poverty. However, this can have ripple effects, resulting in environmental degradation, biodiversity loss, and increased greenhouse gas emissions. Conversely, efforts to protect the ecosystem may inhibit industrial and infrastructural development, which may adversely affect socioeconomic well-being. Therefore, trade-offs should always be considered when implementing the SDGs. Coherence and integrative approaches should exist at all levels—global, regional, national, and local. For social workers, the SDGs present an opportunity to leverage this global framework to raise awareness of social development issues and inform practices and interventions. With a social development agenda, the SDGs can be a foundation for advocacy and policy actions.

The social, economic, and environmental dimensions of the SDGs cannot be achieved in isolation. The commitment must foster collaboration across sectors—government, private sector, and civil society—to forge new partnerships. The SDGs are building blocks that collectively express shared aspirations. Each goal may be seen as a potential area for social workers to intervene, advocate, and apply their skills and expertise. Goal 1 states that no one should be left behind. This involves determining who is being left behind and why and ensuring basic services for everyone are met. Goal 2 ensures that everyone has adequate food, especially children. This involves tackling malnutrition in all its forms, from overweight to obesity to stunted growth, particularly in developing countries. Goal 3 seeks to ensure healthy lives and promote well-being at all ages. This encompasses providing mental health and substance abuse services as well as preventing road injuries.

Goal 4 ensures inclusive and equitable quality education. This tackles literacy and numeracy issues, particularly among youth and adults, as well as ensuring quality early childhood development. Goal 5 seeks to achieve gender equality and empower all women and girls. This helps in the eradication of harmful practices such as early and forced marriage as well as discrimination against women in political and economic decision-making. Goal 6 ensures availability and sustainable management of water and sanitation. This involves tackling the inadequate water supply and sanitation facilities, particularly in schools. Goal 7 ensures access to affordable, reliable, sustainable, and modern energy for all. This particularly includes tackling the energy needs of least developed countries.

Goal 8 promotes sustained, inclusive, and sustainable economic growth. This includes curbing informal employment and child labor, particularly in developing countries. Goal 9 seeks to build resilient infrastructure and promote inclusive and sustainable industrialization. This particularly includes providing universal access to information and communication technology. Goal 10 reduces inequality within and among countries. This includes tackling income growth among the poorest population. Goal 11 makes cities and human settlements inclusive, safe, resilient, and sustainable. This involves improving road safety by reducing the number of deaths and injuries. Goal 12 ensures sustainable consumption and production patterns. This includes substantially reducing food waste at the retail and consumer levels. Goal 13 takes urgent action to combat climate change and its impacts. This includes integrating climate change measures into national policies. Goal 14 conserves and sustainably uses the oceans, seas, and marine resources. This particularly includes addressing the impacts of land-based activities on marine environments. Goal 15 protects, restores, and promotes sustainable use of terrestrial ecosystems. This particularly includes combating deforestation and restoring degraded forests.

Finally, goal 16 promotes peaceful and inclusive societies. This includes ensuring equal access to justice, particularly for youth and children. Goal 17 strengthens the means of implementation and revitalizes the global partnership for sustainable development. This includes addressing capacity-building needs, especially of least developed countries. Furthermore, social workers have the obligation and responsibility to advocate for social justice. These goals address the heart of social development issues, particularly poverty, inequality, and exclusion. The SDGs can provide a framework to raise awareness of social development issues as well as a foundation for advocacy and policy actions.

## Overview of the SDGs

The Sustainable Development Goals (SDGs), agreed upon by the United Nations Member States in September 2015, represent a globally shared agenda for equitable and sustainable development by 2030. The SDGs address critical global challenges, including poverty and hunger eradication, social equity, education, climate change, peace, and justice, among others. The SDGs are integrated and indivisible, considering the economic, social, and environmental dimensions of development - past failures to achieve the Millennium Development Goals exacerbated environmental degradation and inequality. Based on the vision of "leaving no one behind," the SDGs seek to end poverty in all forms everywhere and prioritize the most marginalized and disadvantaged people globally, with a focus on gender equality. The SDGs call for ethical and equitable development practices, considering the rights of future generations, and aim to reconcile economic growth with social inclusion and environmental protection (Leal Filho et al., 2019).

It is crucial to explore the social implications of the SDGs concerning marginalized and disadvantaged communities. Goal 1: End poverty in all its forms everywhere. Target 1.2 aims to reduce the proportion of people living in poverty in all its dimensions, currently measured via income, by at least 50 percent by 2030. Goal 2: End hunger, achieve food security and improved nutrition, and promote sustainable agriculture. Target 2.3 aims to ensure equal access to land, technology, and financial services for small-scale food producers, particularly women, and marginalized communities. Goal 5: Achieve gender equality and empower all women and girls. Target 5.4 recognizes unpaid care and domestic work, particularly borne by women and girls, and aims to provide public services and infrastructure to reconcile unpaid care with work. Partnerships are required at the global, regional, national, and local levels between governments, the private sector, and civil society.

Cooperation, dialogue, and collaboration between multiple actors are necessary to achieve the SDGs, as highlighted in Goal 17. Target 17.17 encourages the establishment of multi-stakeholder partnerships that provide a framework for the sharing of knowledge and resources. These partnerships are vital for developing countries as they tackle the challenge of implementing the SDGs and ensure that best policies and practices are shared and made available to them. The SDGs are comprehensive and require the collaboration and joint effort of various actors to be achieved. The goals collectively embody a shared vision for development and provide a framework for action. Understanding the SDGs' objectives, targets, and challenges is essential as the global development agenda becomes the operational context for social workers. The SDGs impact and concern the social, economic, and environmental sustainability of societies and require the commitment and effort of countries, institutions, and individuals globally. With significant implications for society, the SDGs are of direct concern to social work in its advocacy action and professional practice.

## THE CONCEPT OF A GREEN ECONOMY

In light of the catastrophic impacts of climate change and environmental degradation, the global pursuit of sustainable development has become imperative. The promotion of a green economy is considered pivotal to the achievement of sustainable development and the overall well-being of individuals and societies. A green economy is defined as one that "increases environmental goods and services while fostering economic growth and social inclusion". In simpler terms, it is an economy that promotes sustainability by creating jobs and improving livelihoods

(Kern, 2018). The understanding of a green economy here is more comprehensive than the narrow focus on investment in renewable resources and energy efficiency. A green economy is based on the principles of sustainability and social equity. It is characterized by economic growth that does not depend on "the depletion of natural resources or the net degradation of environmental assets". It promotes a low-carbon, resource-efficient, and socially inclusive development path. More specifically, a green economy has the following features. It stabilizes and reduces carbon emissions, air pollution, and other environmental impacts from a current level by 2050. It enhances the efficiency of resource use (resource productivity) and reduces the depletion of natural and environmental resources. It expands and improves access and benefits from environmental goods and services and increases investments to protect the poor, disadvantaged, and vulnerable from environmental risks and disasters.

The global economic crisis and subsequent fallout have heightened attention to economic transformation and job creation. It is widely recognized that the economic recovery in the future will have to be based on a new economic model. Such a new model should be able to mitigate the implications of the previous economic model on the environment and promote the efficient use of natural resources. The transition to a green economy is seen as an opportunity to create job opportunities and new employment sectors while promoting investments and stimulating innovation. This transformation is referred to as the "greening" of the economy. At the heart of greening the economy is the need to integrate environmental consideration into the planning and policymaking of the economy. Since employment is created in the economic sector, the transformation and greening of the economic sector will create new employment opportunities. However, the process of economic transformation may also eliminate and change the nature of some existing jobs. This calls for particular attention to and action on social equity issues in relation to the economic transformation. Therefore, it is crucial that social workers take part in the economic transformation to secure the well-being of all individuals, particularly those who are vulnerable and marginalized. Social work practices can greatly benefit from the incorporation of principles of a green economy in their practices. The purpose of this narrative is to explore how and in what ways the principles of a green economy can be applied in social work practices, particularly in policy advocacy and planning.

## Definition and Principles

To establish a foundational understanding of the subject, it is important to clarify what is meant by a green economy. A green economy is one that results in "improved human well-being and social equity, while significantly reducing environmental risks and ecological scarcities." Investing in a green economy is one strategy for achieving sustainable development. While a range of definitions and interpretations of a green economy exist, three fundamental and intertwined core principles are widely accepted. Firstly, a green economy is one that is based on sustainable management of the Earth's natural resources. This includes renewable energy; sustainable land use, sustainable water management, sustainable forests, ecosystem protection, restoration, and conservation, and sustainable production and consumption (Kern, 2018). Secondly, a green economy is one that seeks to improve equity, reduce poverty, and provide a decent life for all. The goal is to ensure that every individual has the right to meet their basic needs in food, water, health, education, housing, and other social services. This principle emphasizes respect for and protection of the environment as essential for sustaining community well-being. Thirdly, a green economy is one that creates jobs in green sectors and transforms existing jobs in the polluting economy into greener jobs. A green economy is expected to create a net increase in employment compared to the current brown economy. A circular economy is another trending concept related to a green economy. A circular economy aims to maintain the value of products, materials, and resources in the economy for as long as possible and minimize waste generation. Thus, a circular economy goes one step further than a green economy because it offers a model that, if applied fully, could make economies waste-free. By designing out waste and pollution, keeping products and materials in use, and regenerating natural systems, the circular economy model could help achieve the objectives of a green economy and enhance other sustainability efforts.

The transition towards a greener economy has positive socio-economic impacts. It is estimated that a global shift to a green economy will have a net global effect of creating an additional 15 to 60 million jobs by 2030 in comparison to a business-as-usual scenario, depending on the region. The impacts of greening the economy will vary from region to region. By 2030, green investments in developing and emerging economies are expected to create 24.3 million net new jobs. In developed economies, however, the net job creation effect will be much lower, with an estimate of nearly 0.4 million net jobs. Furthermore, in developed economies, the job losses in some sectors will outweigh the job gains in other sectors. Policies play a critical role in achieving green economy outcomes. Clearly articulated policy goals and supporting institutional frameworks can lead to meaningful transitions. On the other hand, weak policies can allow businesses to find loopholes to sidestep compliance and frustrate the effectiveness of investments. Good policy frameworks illustrate a clear vision and strong commitment to greening the economy. The policy frameworks should also deal with social inclusiveness and gender equality to avoid the negative socio-economic impact that greening the economy might entail. It is vital to recognize the importance of multi-stakeholder partnerships in promoting green economies. While international collaboration is important, it is critical that efforts and commitments are made at national and local levels. Government leadership is essential in establishing the enabling environment necessary for greening the economy; however, collaboration amongst all stakeholders is equally important. The responsibility does not solely lie with governments; private sector actors, civil society organizations, and local development actors also play fundamental roles. Social workers, owing to their professional commitment to social justice, human rights, collective responsibility, and respect for diversity, are in a strong position to promote equality and equity in the transition to a greener economy and society. It is important to highlight the role of social workers in establishing a greener economy within the context of the sustainable development goals (SDGs). A green economy provides a vision and framework to tackle overarching global challenges from a socio-economic perspective. A commitment to a green economy is essential to achieve the SDGs by 2030, and actors at all levels must be involved in establishing a green economy. As such, attention must be drawn to the important role that social workers can play in the establishment of a green economy. It is time to collectively embrace eco-friendly practices and development styles. It will enhance the quality of life and promote social justice across the globe and for all living beings on Earth.

## THE INTERSECTION OF SOCIAL WORK AND ENVIRONMENTAL SUSTAINABILITY

Amidst the escalating crises of environmental degradation, climate change, and biodiversity losses, the imperative for synergizing social work practices with environmental sustainability is becoming increasingly apparent. This intersection, although acknowledged in various forums, remains in its infancy as an area of academic exploration and inquiry (Jarvis, 2013). Global social work discussions have predominantly centered on social equity without sufficient emphasis on ecological justice advocacy by social workers. Nevertheless, it is undeniable that social work has a pivotal role in shaping and influencing ecological justice dialogues, advocacy, and actions, paralleling its efforts towards social justice. Social workers bear a moral and ethical obligation to address ecological injustices faced by communities already challenged by socio-economic adversities. Social work's core values of individual and collective well-being encompass a dual lens of concern for social issues alongside environmental concerns. Consequently, communities should be viewed as comprising both social and natural systems, as their healthy states are mutually dependent (Prussia, 2019). As per the global definition of social work, social workers focus on fostering the well-being of individuals, groups, and communities, collectively and individually, through their actions on environmental matters. Therefore, the SDG agenda provides a proactive approach for synergizing social work and environmental sustainability. From a social work perspective, the discourse on the green economy and its social dimensions within the SDG framework, particularly social work's contributions in fostering a green economy, will be explored.

Global events and deliberations pertinent to higher education, social work, and the natural environment underscore the need for consideration of the natural environment in social work theory, education, policy, and practice, thereby broadening the understanding of "environment" to include the natural world. The 2020-2025 Global Agenda for Social Work and Social Development emphasizes climate action and environmental sustainability in its priorities, urging social work educators to reinforce the profession's role in addressing climate-induced challenges faced by fragile, vulnerable, and marginalized populations. A global survey highlights various efforts and initiatives to uphold the synergistic relationship between social work and environmental sustainability. In a historic move, the international policy agenda on social work at a global level is now inclusive of environment-related matters, establishing a firm base to explore this intersection further. Recent initiatives involving social work's role in addressing environmental issues advocate for a paradigm shift in social work, urging the profession to adopt holistic approaches that integrate environmental considerations into social work education and practice.

## Historical Context

As social work moves into the future, it is important to look back at its history. Analyzing how social work practiced and viewed sustainability in the past can help illuminate potential pathways for its future. Ecological or environmental social work is an idea whose time has come; yet, like many initiatives, it is not without problems (Krings et al., 2020). Many indicatives exist in social work's recent past that attempted to convert sustainability theory into social work practice. Social workers played a significant role in environmental movements throughout the 1960s and 1970s. After briefly falling out of the picture, eco-social practices re-emerged in the 1990s with a stronger research and theoretical focus. However, today's social work practitioners are not always aware of, or in some cases even familiar with, the profession's past involvement with the natural world. Thus, there is a need to create new discourses and learning opportunities that expose social workers to their historical relationship with the environment (Prussia, 2019). Social work interventions have always included health-related practices and actions to eliminate, or at least control, environmental hazards. Infectious diseases and unhealthy living conditions in cities were once addressed by social workers through community development. In so doing, early social workers foreshadowed present-day practices that combine advocacy for healthy environments with health-related interventions. It is crucial that youth understand how early twentieth-century social workers advocated for socially just responses to similar pandemics, the lessons that may be learned, and why such a deliberate focus on sustainability is increasingly required for the profession. Briefly reviewing how social work has historically tackled similar challenges is a good way to reinforce the argument that it remains timely and necessary to, once again, intentionally integrate social and ecological goals. On a broader level, examining how the profession overcame challenges in the past and what obstacles it continued to face can shed light on current efforts to integrate environmental goals with social ones.

## KEY AREAS OF FOCUS FOR SOCIAL WORKERS

Identifying critical areas where social workers can exert influence in fostering a green economy and ensure that actions taken are relevant to this role is essential. Advocacy and policy development are crucial tools that can be employed by social workers to have an impact on environmental policies. Based within an understanding of the green economy and its antipodean elements, social workers are ideally positioned to champion legislative efforts at all levels of government that promote sustainability, as well as equity, and can also develop policy to underpin initiatives focused on fostering a green economy (Jarvis, 2013). It is possible to identify three key areas of focus for social workers that relate to the choice of action: policy development and advocacy, community programming and engagement, and education.

Programming designed to create a dialog with communities and clients around issues of environmental impacts, sustainability, and fostering a green economy provides opportunities for social workers to better engage clients and communities with their concerns and considerations in these areas. There is significant value in social workers seeking opportunities to partner with other professionals and agencies in programming that will assist in empowering citizens to move toward sustainable practices. Housing and income maintenance, assistance and advocacy for vulnerable populations pursue the goal of ensuring that clients have access to the resources required for daily living. Understanding how these needs impact the environment and the implications of locality "footprints" is vital. Programming can also develop understanding around broader environmental impacts, such as the impacts of climate change and local considerations in planning development.

Additionally, programming can be directed to community gardens and the development of local sustainability plans that promote more direct engagement with environmental issues and sustainability, as well as focusing advocacy on the need to ensure that plans are implemented and adequately resourced. Another proactive step social workers can take is to ensure that education and awareness-raising around environmental issues affecting clients and communities is integrated into practice. Social workers should be proactive in educating communities and clients about the impacts of decisions made by governments, businesses, and industry on the environment, as well as ensuring that clients of services and communities are made aware of actions they can take in relation to environmental issues and fostering a green economy. Social workers are uniquely placed to raise awareness about the impacts of environmental issues, particularly among vulnerable populations that are often least able to advocate for themselves in such areas. Moreover, this approach means that clients and communities are equipped with knowledge and resources relevant to seeking the sustainable living, employment, and social opportunities that are necessary for fostering a green economy.

## Advocacy and Policy Development

There is a critical need for advocacy to promote a green economy by embedding environmentally sustainable practices across all sectors of society, including energy, transport, industry, agriculture, construction, and social services. Policy development at local, national, and international levels can affect systemic change and must be pursued by all social workers. In the context of social work, policies should provide comprehensive frameworks to promote environmental integrity alongside social equity. Advocacy can take many forms, from high-level interventions with policy-makers to grassroots engagement with local communities. Grassroots movements and community organizing are essential to developing advocacy programs that attempt to bring about local and systemic change (Jarvis, 2013). Where communities have the power to implement change, they should be supported in doing so. At times, however, it may be necessary to advocate for a broader strategy beyond community-level action. Social workers have diverse skills that can impact local communities, including organizing support groups, building local alliances, encouraging participation in advocacy campaigns, and collecting evidence to strengthen advocacy initiatives. There are many successful examples of social work involvement in the development of green policies. Advocacy is not simply a professional responsibility; it is a moral imperative. Social workers must pursue an active agenda on behalf of individuals and communities affected by environmental harm and injustice. This work is best done in coalition with environmental groups, bringing social work perspectives to wider debates. The green economy has the potential to be a transformative agenda, promoting economic growth and job creation, but it must be inclusive. Strong and effective advocacy can foster a green economy that works for people and the planet.

## TOOLS AND STRATEGIES FOR SOCIAL WORKERS

To effectively promote sustainability, social workers can utilize several tools and strategies. Community engagement is a crucial pillar in the success of any initiative. Gathering community input, suggestions, and questions fosters a sense of ownership over sustainability efforts. Social workers can lead educational workshops that raise awareness on sustainability topics, using collected feedback to shape subsequent discussions. For instance, one workshop can focus on the community's impacts on climate change, followed by a session on practical sustainability actions. Other potential topics include composting, gardening, and local wildlife. This grassroots strategy opens the door to many possible projects, such as creating community gardens, developing composting systems, or targeting local rivers for clean-up and monitoring.

Local organizations often have the most meaningful projects and resources in places where social workers are embedded. Engaging with these organizations can amplify project success and foster collaborative relationships. For instance, in one community, the local school was actively starting composting and gardening programs. Social workers assisted by helping students and teachers explore gardening opportunities and developing a composting system at the school. Another example occurred in a community with a creek running through it. Collaboration with a local organization allowed social workers to engage students in monitoring the creek's health and cleaning up litter, with ongoing commitments to maintaining it.

Research and data collection can provide a clearer picture of community needs around sustainability and how they can be met. This evidence can rally support among local leaders and potential partners for sustainability efforts. For instance, one community had a high native and non-native vegetation ratio, but there was concern about the health of poorly maintained parks. As social workers began working there, they surveyed residents about their knowledge, concerns, and suggestions for improving park health. The results showed that while many were unsure of the difference between native and non-native plants, both species were valued in their park use. People generally preferred simple solutions like clean-up days to more complex ecological restoration actions. Conducting this survey and sharing the outcomes supported a project to reform parks and engage residents directly in clean-up actions.

Funding and resource allocation can take many forms to ensure green projects have the necessary backing. Local non-profits usually have access to grants that can fund social worker time for environmental projects if a project is already in mind. Some grants also fund specific community actions; for instance, one community's school applied for a grant for composting units, with social workers assisting in the application. Other funders have successfully supplied schools with necessary gardening supplies. Another option is to seek support from firms as part of their social responsibility commitments. In one community, a native plant firm donated over 100 plants for a garden at a local school, which students and social workers planted. Those interested can also reach out personally for ideas or more tailored approaches to their situations.

These strategies and examples aim to inspire social workers to nurture a green economy in their communities. Each community will have different assets and needs, but with many opportunities for action, this can be the beginning of meaningful change. Hopefully, these ideas will encourage social workers to embrace their role as stewards of the Earth, understanding that by caring for the world around them, they care for the people in it.

## Community Engagement and Education

Research illustrates that narrowly focused environmental awareness initiatives often have minimal impact on changing community behavior (Blake, 2012). Conversely, ensuring community engagement in local environmental interventions significantly increases their likelihood of success. The community development principles and methods of social work are essential in creating this engagement. Therefore, community engagement and education are crucial strategies for social workers in promoting a green economy, particularly concerning SDG 12. Social workers can play a vital role in nurturing a sense of ownership and responsibility towards the local environment by adopting participatory approaches that encourage communities to understand the links between their needs and concerns and broader ecological issues. Community members can be mobilized to discuss sustainability challenges and possible solutions. As a result, the community considered how to address critical issues, including the need for affordable housing (Sparks, Massey Combs, & Yu, 2019). At the community's request, social workers helped establish a housing co-op, enabling local control over housing and the potential to develop it sustainably.

Educational initiatives can empower individuals with the knowledge needed to adopt sustainable behaviors. Social workers can assist individuals in accessing educational opportunities, which are crucial for understanding greener everyday living. Social workers supported a community's desire to learn about energy conservation, leading a local primary school to create an energy education program for the wider community, linking older children's learning to provide workshops for their families. Raising communities' awareness of environmental and social justice issues encourages them to see the links between social justice concerns and the degradation of the natural environment.

## CASE STUDIES AND BEST PRACTICES

This section presents a selection of case studies and best practices that highlight successful collaborations between social workers and green economy initiatives. Each scenario illustrates how social workers can make a significant difference in fostering environmental sustainability through innovative approaches that align social strategies with environmental ones. They include peer-led environmental education and action in community gardens, green public employment, and community-led natural resource management. While these were selected because they are successful examples of social work-led initiatives, the narrative emphasizes that success is relative and shaped by local contexts, available resources, and circumstances.

Lessons learned from these cases focus on initiatives that are adaptable to different social and environmental contexts and are led by local communities in ways that reflect their knowledge, needs, and priorities. Having social workers act as facilitators rather than service providers is often key to fostering local ownership and agency. It should be noted that the focus here is on projects directly implemented by social workers. Nevertheless, many of the initiatives showcase partnerships with organizations from other sectors. Their importance is briefly discussed to highlight how social workers can amplify the reach of their initiatives by forming cross-sector partnerships.

Five efforts that address locally emergent environmental issues in ways that align with specific community needs are examined. They also draw attention to the importance of measuring outcomes from the outset to assess the effectiveness of an initiative and inform future efforts. Finally, though the focus is on the case studies, project implementers often highlight that having prior knowledge of local contexts is crucial for their success. Nevertheless, they also show how initiatives can evolve into different forms, illustrating a range of community needs and responses.

### Examples of Successful Initiatives

This section presents examples of successful initiatives that social workers have implemented in the context of a green economy. They demonstrate the innovative practice of social workers in fostering a green economy to achieve the Sustainable Development Goals (SDGs). Each example reflects the ability of social workers to generate positive environmental change through social work practice. One initiative is a community composting project in Dublin, Ireland, where the local social work agency helps manage compost bins in public parks. Volunteers from various backgrounds share the responsibility of ensuring the bins are used correctly and kept clean. This project addresses issues of social integration and environmental sustainability. Since 2018, eight bins have been installed in parks across Dublin

City, managed by community groups with support from the City Council horticulturists. The bins provide park users the opportunity to compost at the site, fostering collective responsibility for public spaces (Blake, 2012). Another initiative involves young social workers taking over a shuttered greenhouse in Berlin, Germany, from a public housing company. After extensive negotiations, the company agreed to lease the greenhouse to a social worker initiative group for ten years. The group aims to cultivate social, ecological, and economic sustainability by rejuvenating the greenhouse and addressing local needs like food insecurity and mental health issues. They plan to offer workshops on sustainability, gardening, nutrition, and cooking while providing fresh vegetables to social services for disadvantaged people.

A different case focuses on social work internships in an ecological association in Austria, where university students helped develop a new educational program on biodiversity for kindergartens. Due to climate change, rapid loss of species is observed globally, and it is essential to nurture children's interest in nature. In 2019, the ecological association aimed to offer an additional educational program about local habitats and species for kindergartens. A social worker from the association contacted the University of Applied Sciences in Vienna, seeking help to develop the new program. Over six months, students from the bachelor's degree in social work conducted needs assessment interviews, collected feedback on the planned program, and presented their results to the association. As a result, the program was designed to raise children's awareness of nature's value and local biodiversity. In the same spirit, an initiative was founded in Geneva, Switzerland, where social workers help educate low-income families about healthy diets and local food production through urban gardening. Ten years ago, in an underserved neighborhood, a derelict park was transformed into a community garden with raised vegetable beds. Since 2012, a local association of social workers has run the garden, which now includes twelve vegetable beds tended by six families and a child care center. Monthly workshops teach families how to grow and cook vegetables, promoting a healthy diet and addressing issues of obesity and malnourishment among local children.

Urban gardening also plays a key role in a project in Ilfov County, Romania, where newly arrived Syrian refugees garden with locals to promote social inclusion and share gardening skills. In 2015, Romania accepted its first group of Syrian refugees, mostly women with children. Some were offered permanent residence in Ilfov County and needed support to adjust to the new environment. Through collaboration between the Center of Social Work and an NGO specializing in environmental and social projects, an abandoned piece of land was transformed into a community garden. Local Roma women trained refugees and locals to cultivate traditional vegetables, helping them learn the local language and salary-related rights. These initiatives focus on the community and the role of social workers in fostering a green economy to achieve local SDGs. Europe has many similar projects, and they all highlight how social workers can empower communities to act collectively for a more sustainable future.

## CHALLENGES AND OPPORTUNITIES

The Sustainable Development Goals (SDGs) provide a universal framework for significantly improving economies and societies by 2030. While the SDGs cover a broad range of important targets, Goal Number 8 priorities sustainable economic growth, inclusiveness, and employment. It suggests the "fostering of a green economy in the context of sustainable development and poverty eradication," highlighting that an economy should maintain or increase the capital (natural, social, human, physical, and financial) necessary for long-term development.

As the green economy initiatives explicitly target systemic changes in economies and societies, the social workers should play key roles in promoting these initiatives. However, green economy and environmental issues as such have been low priorities in the social work discourse so far. There are a variety of systemic challenges and barriers in promoting environmental initiatives. These limitations and challenges are often under-discussed. Some funding does exist for environmental initiatives, but the social workers are still left to look for funding elsewhere. Bureaucratic obstacles often hinder "naturally funded" environmental practices, requiring far more effort than a straightforward approach. Many initiatives fail simply because good opportunities for environmental practices go unnoticed due to a lack of capacity or time.

On the other hand, many initiatives focusing on environmental matters have been launched, and success stories exist. Viewing environmental issues as an opportunity and a resource opens up a wide space for collaboration across disciplines. Eco-efficiency measures, and enhancing material loops or energy efficiency, have revealed the importance of social input in making changes happen and entrenched practices visible. There is a strong motivation to pursue innovation, improvements, and new ways of working in order to reach the defined targets and goals. Rather than solely aiming for compliance, a proactive approach can lead to the discovery of new opportunities and insights that benefit the whole organization (Sparks, Massey Combs, & Yu, 2019).

One possible way to keep the development momentum is to encourage social workers to engage in environmental issues as resources and opportunities rather than problems or limitations. Seen as resources and opportunities, engagement with environmental issues provides a wide range of collaborative opportunities across disciplines. On the other hand, social workers are also encouraged to consider innovations fostering environmental initiatives as social work professions in order to develop social work practices in new directions. Alliance for the Future of Social

Work, in which a variety of stakeholders in the field of social work join together, could function as a platform for wider discussion on how to take on the challenges and opportunities in tackling environmental issues. Overall, understanding the developments as a whole inspires resilience and creativity in tackling the challenges as well as realizing the opportunities (Engstrom, 2019).

## Barriers to Implementation

Specific barriers to the implementation of green economy initiatives within social work are elucidated. Barriers include the increasingly obvious socio-economic constraints to implementing greener and more sustainable practices; a general lack of awareness, knowledge or understanding of greener, more sustainable practices; and insufficient engagement or inclusion of key stakeholders during both the development and implementation of greener and more sustainable practices. Evidence suggests that for many social workers, particularly those in and from the global south or who work with the most marginalized communities, these barriers are accentuated. Unfortunately, the most disadvantaged and disenfranchised community members often bear the brunt of unsustainable practices, thus complicating any efforts on behalf of social workers to achieve sustainability (Leal Filho et al., 2022).

There is a general presumption that the implementation of greener and more sustainable practices is an advancement; however, such practices can still become inappropriately implemented or misconstrued. Examples are provided of policy and regulatory frameworks that contextualize greener and more sustainable practices, yet impede the development of the green economy. These examples highlight the need for consideration to be given as to what barriers exist to the implementation of greener and more sustainable practices within social work. By articulating specific barriers, a platform is provided from which to critically examine them and consider how they might be overcome. Social workers have a professional responsibility to advocate for and engage communities in the consideration of social, environmental and economic policy; thus, capacity must be built to enable them to meet this responsibility.

Finally, this section advocates for social work organizations to consider how training, resources and support can best be provided to enable social workers to negotiate their way through these barriers. The aim is to provide a clearer understanding of the complexities involved in implementing sustainable practices, particularly for social workers, and with regard to the global context. Efforts are made to articulate clear social work pathways to the implementation of greener and more sustainable practices; however, it must be acknowledged that these pathways may not be linear, nor universally applicable. Rather, it is acknowledged that the experiences of some social workers may not resonate at all with others and that some barriers may not be at all relevant within particular contexts.

## CONCLUSION AND FUTURE DIRECTIONS

In conclusion, social workers have an essential responsibility in fostering a green economy in their role, recognizing its importance, and understanding how to apply it within the various areas of practice. Social work and environmental sustainability must be seen as interconnected at university and postgraduate levels, addressing concerns and actions, policies, and approaches that link the two. This narrative is but a modest welcome mat to a large, potentially impactful space that must begin to be filled by social work. As the profession globally meets significant challenges because of a loss of social justice focus and an increasing move to neo-liberal structures, there is a possibility for social work and social workers to take on new roles. These roles can help move communities toward a green economy in a socially just way. The challenges are immense and growing, but so too is the opportunity for social workers to be at the forefront of meaningful change in communities.

Continued professional development is vital to building awareness and action in a green economy as part of social work. Professional bodies and others providing ongoing training must recognize this necessity and offer appropriate education. It should be noted that much of what is presented here is only the start of much more extensive and needed research. In terms of education and training, the hope is that professional bodies and universities will embrace this burgeoning area of inquiry and practice. Future directions involve the ongoing need for social work to build more robust collaborative relationships with environmental organizations. Strong alliances exist in some countries, but much more is needed at local and national levels. Policy-makers must also be engaged meaningfully to help shape social work responses to climate change and broader environmental issues and assist in illuminating how communities can move to a green economy socially.

Current concerns and the future impact of social work responses regarding the environment and climate change need to be adapted as plans, strategies, policies, and actions are developed. Care must be taken that social work agendas do not become co-opted into supporting dominant neo-liberal and/or economic growth approaches that consider the environment only when addressing social issues (Prussia, 2019). While social work's response must be relevant to current and emerging challenges, strategies must not be reactive. Social work must be clearly positioned and act proactively to ensure that responses foster socially just green economies. In doing so, all elements of social work's knowledge base (history, values, theory, research, policy, and practice) must be imbued creatively and courageously with environmentally focused understandings and actions. Social workers must also be encouraged to engage proactively, innovatively, and perhaps riskily with building a new paradigm for social work in a sustainable future. Otherwise, there is a palpable danger that social work will be sidelined in fostering a socially just green economy and addressing its place as a profession in that future, (Iwuanyanwu et al., 2024; Rahman et al., 2024). The vision is for social work and social workers to "occupy" at a fundamental level an essential role in developing a green economy that is sustainable, equitable, and just.

## Summary of Key Findings

This essay explores how social workers can promote a green economy focused on social justice and protecting the environment in the context of the Sustainable Development Goals (SDGs). It highlights the connections between social work, sustainability, and the green economy, outlining the role of social workers in ensuring social justice and ecological health. The narrative includes examples of success in social work practice and relevant strategies while considering challenges and opportunities for the profession. Additionally, it looks at the history of social work and its connection to environmental issues. This review is intended to help better understand the points discussed and the wider significance of these findings (Krings et al., 2020). The green economy is a key agenda item for many national governments. A green economy is defined as one that reduces environmental risks and ecological scarcities while achieving sustainable development. The idea behind this transition is to fundamentally change how economies function and operate by valuing natural goods and services and addressing climate change and biodiversity loss, thus fostering environmentally sustainable economic growth. Social work can play a vital role in this transformation by fostering a green economy that promotes social justice and protects the environment (Prussia, 2019). In 2015, the United Nations General Assembly adopted a resolution on transforming the world: the 2030 agenda for sustainable development. The agenda includes 17 SDGs with 169 targets to be achieved by 2030, succeeding the millennium development goals. The SDGs address the interconnections between economic growth, social inclusion, and environmental protection. Social workers can significantly contribute to the achievement of the SDGs, with some targets calling for social work interventions. Social workers have been actively involved in initiating and implementing actions to achieve the SDGs at the local level. There are critical intersections between social work, environmental sustainability, and the green economy in the context of the SDGs. Social workers can ensure the green economy fosters social justice and protects the environment. This essay discusses social work's role in the transition to a green economy in the context of the SDGs, including points for consideration that are important for social work globally.

## REFERENCES


Blake, J. (2012). Sustainable communities and social work practice learning: Reflections on emergent learning partnerships. *The Journal of Practice Teaching and Learning*, *9*(2), 93–114. https://journals.whitingbirch.net/index.php/JPTS/article/view/393. DOI: 10.1921/jpts.v9i2.393

Engstrom, S. (2019). Recognising the role eco-grief plays in responding to environmental degradation. *Journal of Transdisciplinary Peace Praxis*, *1*(1), 168–186.

Iwuanyanwu, O., Gil-Ozoudeh, I., Okwandu, A. C., & Ike, C. S. (2024). Cultural and social dimensions of green architecture: Designing for sustainability and community well-being. *International Journal of Applied Research in Social Sciences*, *6*(8), 1951–1968. https://www.academia.edu/118424441/Cultural_and_social_dimensions_of_green_architecture_Designing_for_sustainability_and_community_well_being. DOI: 10.51594/ijarss.v6i8.1477

Jarvis, D. (2013). *Environmental justice and social work: A call to expand the social work profession to include environmental justice* [Master's thesis, Columbia University]. Academic Commons. DOI: 10.7916/D8RN36CZ

Kern, A. (2018). *Gender and the Green Economy* (Doctoral dissertation, University of Kansas). KU ScholarWorks. https://kuscholarworks.ku.edu/server/api/core/bitstreams/c4e51a6c-f71c-4802-86e5-7757cb7db960/content

Krings, A., Victor, B. G., Mathias, J., & Perron, B. E. (2020). Environmental social work in the disciplinary literature, 1991–2015. *International Social Work*, *63*(5), 652–664. DOI: 10.1177/0020872818788397

Leal Filho, W., Lange Salvia, A., Ruy Portela Vasconcelos, C., Anholon, R., Simon Rampasso, I., Henrique Paulino Pires Eustachio, J., Liakh, O., Alzira Pimenta Dinis, M., Cementina Olpoc, R., Bandanaa, J., Aina, Y. A., Lolekola Lukina, R., & Sharifi, A. (2022). Barriers to institutional social sustainability. *Sustainability Science*, *17*(6), 2615–2630. https://doi.org/ (Full text also available via PMC: https://www.ncbi.nlm.nih.gov/pmc/articles/PMC9688692/)DOI: 10.1007/s11625-022-01204-0

Leal Filho, W., Tripathi, S. K., Andrade Guerra, J. B. S. O. D., Giné-Garriga, R., Orlovic Lovren, V., & Willats, J. (2019). Using the sustainable development goals towards a better understanding of sustainability challenges. *International Journal of Sustainable Development and World Ecology*, *26*(2), 179–190. DOI: 10.1080/13504509.2018.1505674

Prussia, L. (2019). *Natural connections: Social work's role in mending human and environmental relationships* (Doctoral dissertation, University of St. Thomas, Minnesota). SOPHIA. https://ir.stthomas.edu/caps_graddiss/85/

Rahman, M. H., Tanchangya, T., Rahman, J., Aktar, M. A., & Majumder, S. C. (2024). Corporate social responsibility and green financing behavior in Bangladesh: Towards sustainable tourism. *Innovation and Green Development, 3*(3), Article 100133. https://www.sciencedirect.com/science/article/pii/S2949753124000109DOI: 10.1016/j.igd.2024.100133

Sparks, J. L. D., Massey Combs, K., & Yu, J. (2019). Social work students' perspective on environmental justice: Gaps and challenges for preparing students. *Journal of Community Practice*, *27*(3–4), 476–486. DOI: 10.1080/10705422.2019.1655124

# Compilation of References

About Amazon. (2025, January 29). *How to use amazon pay balance, a step-by-step guide*. IN about Amazon; About Amazon India. https://www.aboutamazon.in/news/retail/how-to-buy-amazon-pay-gift-cards

Accenture. (2021). *Embedded finance for SMEs*. https://www.accenture.com/content/dam/accenture/final/industry/banking/document/Accenture-Banking-Embedded-Finance-SMEs.pdf

Adaga, E. M., Egieya, Z. E., Ewuga, S. K., Abdul, A. A., & Abrahams, T. O. (2024). A COMPREHENSIVE REVIEW OF ETHICAL PRACTICES IN BANKING AND FINANCE. *Finance & Accounting Research Journal*, *6*(1), 1–20. DOI: 10.51594/farj.v6i1.705

Adams, C. A., & Abhayawansa, S. (2022). Connecting the COVID-19 pandemic, environmental, social, and governance (ESG) investing and calls for 'harmonisation' of sustainability reporting. *Critical Perspectives on Accounting*, *82*, 102309. DOI: 10.1016/j.cpa.2021.102309

Addy, W. A., Ofodile, O. C., Adeoye, O. B., Oyewole, A. T., Okoye, C. C., Odeyemi, O., & Ololade, Y. J. (2022). Data-driven sustainability: How fintech innovations are supporting green finance. *Journal of Green Finance, 14*

Adobe Communications. T. (2021, March 15). *Adobe Digital Economy Index: COVID-19 Report*. Adobe Blog. https://blog.adobe.com/en/publish/2021/03/15/adobe-digital-economy-index-covid-19-report

Afjal, M. (2023). Bridging the financial divide: A bibliometric analysis on the role of digital financial services within FinTech in enhancing financial inclusion and economic development. *Humanities & Social Sciences Communications*, *10*(1), 1–27. DOI: 10.1057/s41599-023-02086-y

Ahiase, G., Sari, M., Andriana, D., Nugraha, N., Purnomo, B. S., & Heryana, T. (2025). Unveiling the African growth puzzle: Relationship between financial inclusion, debt sustainability and economic growth. *International Journal of Social Economics*, *52*(4), 591–607. DOI: 10.1108/IJSE-01-2024-0062

Ahlström, H., & Monciardini, D. (2021). The regulatory dynamics of sustainable finance: Paradoxical success and limitations of EU reforms. *Journal of Business Ethics*. Advance online publication. DOI: 10.1007/s10551-021-04763- springer.com PMID: 33642657

Ahmed, A. (2024, June 14). *Flipkart eyes 30% penetration in tier-2 and -3 cities: Manjari Singhal*. BusinessLine. https://www.thehindubusinessline.com/companies/flipkart-eyes-30-per-cent-penetration-in-tier-2-and-3-cities-manjari-singhal/article68289616.ece

Ahmed, S., Ahmed, S. P., & Hasan, I. (2018). Why banks should consider ESG risk factors in bank lending? *Banks and Bank Systems*, *13*(3), 71–80. DOI: 10.21511/bbs.13(3).2018.07

Aich, S., Thakur, A., Nanda, D., Tripathy, S., & Kim, H. C. (2021). Factors affecting ESG towards impact on investment: A structural approach. Sustainability. / mdpi.comDOI: 10.3390/su131910868

Al Ayoubi, K., & Enjolras, G. (2022). Does disinvestment from fossil fuels reduce the financial performance of responsible sovereign wealth funds? *Journal of Multinational Financial Management*, *64*, 100731. DOI: 10.1016/j.mulfin.2022.100731

Alam, S. T.Syed Tanveer Alam. (2024). Revolutionizing energy payments: The role of FinTech in streamlining transactions. *World J. Advance Research Review*, *22*(1), 2074–2083. DOI: 10.30574/wjarr.2024.22.2.1626

Aldboush, H. H. H. & Ferdous, M. (2023). Building trust in fintech: an analysis of ethical and privacy considerations in the intersection of big data, AI, and customer trust. International Journal of Financial Studies. / mdpi.comDOI: 10.3390/ijfs11030090

Alessandra, A., Osterrieder, J. R., & Machado, M. R. (2024). How can artificial intelligence help customer intelligence for credit portfolio management? *International Journal of Information Management Data Insights*, *4*(2), 100234. Advance online publication. DOI: 10.1016/j.jjimei.2024.100234

Al-Gasaymeh, A. S., Ahmad Almahadin, H., Shehadeh, M., Migdady, H., & Bani Atta, A. A. (2023). Investigating the Role of Artificial Intelligence in Embedded Finance on Improving a Nonfinancial Customer Experience. *2nd International Conference on Business Analytics for Technology and Security, ICBATS 2023*. DOI: 10.1109/ICBATS57792.2023.10111255

Alliance for Financial Inclusion (AFI). (2024). Mexico: The role regulators play in closing the financial inclusion gender gap. AFI Case Study. Retrieved from https://www.afi-global.org

Allioui, H. & Mourdi, Y. (2023). Exploring the full potentials of IoT for better financial growth and stability: A comprehensive survey. Sensors. / mdpi.comDOI: 10.3390/s23198015

Alsedrah, I. T. (2024). Fintech and green finance revolutionizing carbon emission reduction through green energy projects in mineral-rich countries. *Resources Policy, 94*, 105064. DOI: 10.1016/j.resourpol.2024.105064

Alshwayat, D., Elrehail, H., Shehadeh, E., Alsalhi, N., Shamout, M. D., & Rehman, S. U. (2023). An exploratory examination of the barriers to innovation and change as perceived by senior management. *International Journal of Innovation Studies, 7*(2), 159–170. DOI: 10.1016/j.ijis.2022.12.005

Al-Zoubi, W. K. (2024). Economic development in the digital economy: A bibliometric review. *Economies, 12*(3), 53. DOI: 10.3390/economies12030053

Amazon Personalize, A. W. S. (2025). *AWS Marketplace: AI-Based Recommendation Engine - Amazon Personalize*. Amazon.com. https://aws.amazon.com/marketplace/pp/prodview-yfgsey6hiu3bc

Ambit. (2021). *Optionality already building in.* https://bsmedia.business-standard.com/_media/bs/data/market-reports/equity-brokertips/2021-10/16330699090.10396500.pdf

Amnas, M. B., Selvam, M., & Parayitam, S. (2024). FinTech and financial inclusion: Exploring the mediating role of digital financial literacy and the moderating influence of perceived regulatory support. *Journal of Risk and Financial Management, 17*(3), 108. DOI: 10.3390/jrfm17030108

Anagnostopoulos, I., Sails, T., & Alexandrou, G. (2025). FinTechs, BigTechs and diminishing bank franchise values: Stakeholder perspectives on a disruptive emerging financial ecosystem. *Technological Forecasting and Social Change, 212*, 123924. DOI: 10.1016/j.techfore.2024.123924

Andrae, S. (2022). The role of BigTech in emerging markets. In Nguyen, D. K. (Ed.), *Handbook of banking and finance in Emerging Markets* (pp. 433–463). Edward Elgar., DOI: 10.4337/9781800880900.00032

Andrae, S. (2025a). Machine learning in social finance: Facilitating inclusive finance approaches. In Yu, P., Wong, S. K. M., & Prabhakar, A. C. (Eds.), *AI strategies for social entrepreneurship and sustainable economic development* (pp. 17–46). IGI Global Publishing., DOI: 10.4018/979-8-3693-6392-8.ch002

Andrae, S. (2025b). Data cooperatives to strengthen digital citizenship: Opportunities and risks. In Hawamdeh, M. Kh. M. (Ed.), *Digital citizenship and the future of AI engagement, ethics, and privacy* (pp. 533–568). IGI Global Publishing., DOI: 10.4018/979-8-3693-9015-3.ch018

Andrey, E. (2023). ESG as an innovative tool to improve the efficiency and financial stability of financial organizations. *Procedia Computer Science*, *221*, 705–709. DOI: 10.1016/j.procs.2023.08.041

ANPD (Autoridade Nacional de Proteção de Dados). (2024). Consulta Pública sobre Consentimento Granular em Open Finance. Brasília. https://www.gov.br/anpd/pt-br/acesso-a-informacao/participacao-social/outras-acoes/documentos/ts_02-_2024__contribuicoes.pdf

Anthemis. (2019). *Embedded Finance*. https://tearsheet.co/wp-content/uploads/2019/11/Anthemis-Embedded-Finance-White-Paper-November-2019.pdf

Ari, I. & Koc, M. (2021). Philanthropic-crowdfunding-partnership: A proof-of-concept study for sustainable financing in low-carbon energy transitions. Energy. / sciencedirect.comDOI: 10.1016/j.energy.2021.119925

Artiach, T., Lee, D., Nelson, D., & Walker, J. (2010). The determinants of corporate sustainability performance. *Accounting and Finance*, *50*(1), 31–51. DOI: 10.1111/j.1467-629X.2009.00315.x

Aslam, F. (2024). Integrated finance: A sustainable working model for the future. https://www.linkedin.com/pulse/integrated-finance-sustainable-working-model-future-faheem-aslam-gremf/

Aspinall, N. G., Jones, S. R., McNeill, E. H., Werner, R. A., & Zalk, T. (2018). Sustainability and the financial system Review of literature 2015. *British Actuarial Journal*, *23*, e10. DOI: 10.1017/S1357321718000028

Auer, R. (2022). Embedded supervision: How to build regulation into Decentralised Finance CESifo Working Paper No. 9771. DOI: 10.2139/ssrn.4127658

Auer, R. (2022b). *Embedded Supervision: How to Build Regulation Into Decentralized Finance*. Cryptoeconomic Systems., DOI: 10.21428/58320208.14a4105d

Ayhan Kose, M., Prasad, E. S., & Taylor, A. D. (2011). Thresholds in the process of international financial integration. *Journal of International Money and Finance*, *30*(1), 147–179. DOI: 10.1016/j.jimonfin.2010.08.005

Banerjee, N. (2025, January 14). *IndianRetailer.com*. Indian Retailer. https://www.indianretailer.com/article/retail-business/retail/how-amazon-indias-home-category-leading-retail-game-40-growth

Bank of Ghana. (2019). Annual Report 2019. https://www.bog.gov.gh/wp-content/uploads/2020/06/Annual-Report-2019.pdf

Barbosa, A. D. S., Crispim, M. C., Silva, L. B., Silva, J. M. N., Barbosa, A. M., & Morioka, S. N. (2024). How can organizations measure the integration of environmental, social, and governance (ESG) criteria? *Business Strategy and the Environment*, *33*(4), 3607–3634. DOI: 10.1002/bse.3675

Barman, P. A., & Goon, P. (2024). EMBEDDED FINANCE: THE INTEGRATION OF FINANCIAL SERVICES INTO NON-FINANCIAL PLATFORMS. *IIP Series*. https://www.academia.edu/117967436/EMBEDDED_FINANCE_THE_INTEGRATION_OF_FINANCIAL_SERVICES_INTO_NON_FINANCIAL_PLATFORMS

Barroso, M., & Laborda, J. (2022). Digital transformation and the emergence of the Fintech sector: Systematic literature review. *Digital Business*, *2*(2), 100028. DOI: 10.1016/j.digbus.2022.100028

Barwise, P., & Watkins, L. (2018). The Evolution of Digital Dominance. In *Digital Dominance: The Power of Google*. Amazon, Facebook, and Apple.

Beck, S. (2024, December 18). *Understanding Embedded Finance And The Growth Of White-Label Neobanking*. Forbes. https://www.forbes.com/councils/forbestechcouncil/2024/12/18/understanding-embedded-finance-and-the-growth-of-white-label-neobanking/

Bhutta, U. S., Tariq, A., Farrukh, M., Raza, A., & Iqbal, M. K. (2022). Green bonds for sustainable development: Review of literature on development and impact of green bonds. *Technological Forecasting and Social Change*, *175*, 121378. DOI: 10.1016/j.techfore.2021.121378

Bianchi, G., Testa, F., Tessitore, S., & Iraldo, F. (2022). How to embed environmental sustainability: The role of dynamic capabilities and managerial approaches in a life cycle management perspective. Business Strategy and the Environment, 31(1), 312-325. DOI: wiley.comDOI: 10.1002/bse.2889

BIS. (2020). Central banks and payments in the digital era. Annual Economic Report, Chapter III, June 2020. https://www.bis.org/publ/arpdf/ar2020e3.pdf

Blake, J. (2012). Sustainable communities and social work practice learning: Reflections on emergent learning partnerships. *The Journal of Practice Teaching and Learning*, *9*(2), 93–114. https://journals.whitingbirch.net/index.php/JPTS/article/view/393. DOI: 10.1921/jpts.v9i2.393

Bowden, J., King, T., Koutmos, D., Loncan, T. & Stentella Lopes, F. S. (2021). A taxonomy of FinTech innovation. *Disruptive Technology in Banking and Finance: An International Perspective on FinTech*, 47-91.

Brassett, J., & Rethel, L. (2015). Sexy money: The hetero-normative politics of global finance. *Review of International Studies*, *41*(3), 429–449. Advance online publication. DOI: 10.1017/S0260210514000461

Breckenridge, K. (2010). The world's first biometric money: Ghana's E-Zwich and the contemporary influence of South African biometrics. *Africa*, *80*(4), 642–662. DOI: 10.3366/afr.2010.0406

Brightmore, D. (2024, August 13). *How Embedded Finance is changing the e-commerce landscape*. FinTech Strategy. https://www.fintechstrategy.com/blog/2024/08/13/how-embedded-finance-is-changing-the-e-commerce-landscape/

Bruce, E., Shurong, Z., Ying, D., Yaqi, M., Amoah, J., & Egala, S. B. (2023). The effect of digital marketing adoption on SMEs sustainable growth. *Sustainability (Basel)*, *15*(6), 4760. DOI: 10.3390/su15064760

Bugvi, J. A., & Endress, T. (2023). Making Finance Invisible: Embedded Finance Adoption and User Experience. In *Proceedings of the AIT SOM Doctoral Colloquium 2023* (pp. 42-53).

Bureau, I. (2024, December 6). *Amazon Pay surpasses 1 billion gift cards delivered in India - India Retailing*. India Retailing. https://www.indiaretailing.com/2024/12/06/amazon-pay-surpasses-1-billion-gift-cards-delivered-in-india/

Bursa Malaysia. (2021). Growing your wealth using Exchange-Traded Funds ("ETFs"). https://my.bursamalaysia.com/learn/knowledge/explorer/growing-your-wealth-using-exchange-traded-funds-etfs

Buteau, S., Rao, P., & Valenti, F. (2021). Emerging insights from digital solutions in financial inclusion. *CSI Transactions on ICT*, *9*(2), 105–114. DOI: 10.1007/s40012-021-00330-x

Caldarelli, G. (2021). Wrapping trust for interoperability: A preliminary study of wrapped tokens. *Information (Basel)*, *13*(1), 6. DOI: 10.3390/info13010006

Caldecott, B. (2022). Defining transition finance and embedding it in the post-Covid-19 recovery. *Journal of Sustainable Finance & Investment*, *12*(3), 934–938. Advance online publication. DOI: 10.1080/20430795.2020.1813478

Callaway, B., & Sant'Anna, P. H. C. (2021). Difference-in-Differences with multiple time periods. *Journal of Econometrics*, *225*(2), 200–230. DOI: 10.1016/j.jeconom.2020.12.001

Cao, L. (2022). AI in finance: Challenges, techniques, and opportunities. *ACM Computing Surveys*, *55*(3), 64. Advance online publication. DOI: 10.1145/3502289

Caussat, P., Prime, N., & Wilken, R. (2019). How Multinational Banks in India Gain Legitimacy: Organisational Practices and Resources Required for Implementation. *MIR. Management International Review*, *59*(4), 561–591. DOI: 10.1007/s11575-019-00387-6

CFA Institute. (2023). How FinTech is driving financial inclusion. https://www.cfainstitute.org/insights/articles/how-fintech-is-driving-financial-inclusion

CGAP. (2018). A digital credit revolution: Insights from borrowers in Kenya and Tanzania. https://www.cgap.org/research/publication/digital-credit-revolution-insights-borrowers-in-kenya-and-tanzania

Chan, R. (2021). Ensuring impactful performance in green bonds and sustainability-linked loans. *The Adelaide Kaw Review*, *42*(1), 221–258.

Chao, T., Yunbao, X., Chengbo, D., Bo, L., & Ullah, S. (2023). Financial integration and renewable energy consumption in China. *Environmental Science and Pollution Research International*, *30*(5), 12944–12952. DOI: 10.1007/s11356-022-22852-w PMID: 36121627

Chhikara, H., Chhikara, S., & Gupta, L. (2025). Predictive Analytics in Finance: Leveraging AI and Machine Learning for Investment Strategies. In Utilizing AI and Machine Learning in Financial Analysis (pp. 325-336). IGI Global Scientific Publishing. DOI: [HTML]DOI: 10.4018/979-8-3693-8507-4.ch017

Chinoda, T., & Kapingura, F. M. (2024). Digital financial inclusion and economic growth in Sub-Saharan Africa: The role of institutions and governance. *African Journal of Economic and Management Studies, 15*(1), 15–30. DOI: 10.1108/AJEMS-09-2022-0372

Chitimira, H., & Warikandwa, T. V. (2023). Financial inclusion as an enabler of United Nations sustainable development goals in the twenty-first century: An introduction. In *Financial inclusion and digital transformation regulatory practices in selected SADC countries: South Africa, Namibia, Botswana and Zimbabwe* (pp. 1–22). Springer International Publishing. DOI: 10.1007/978-3-031-23863-5_1

Chiu, I. H. Y. (2021). Regulating Sustainable Finance In Capital Markets:A Perspective From Socially Embedded Decentered Regulation. *Law and Contemporary Problems, 84*(1).

Chowdhary, K. R., & Chowdhary, K. R. (2020). Natural language processing. In *Fundamentals of Artificial Intelligence* (pp. 603–649). DOI: 10.1007/978-81-322-3972-7_19

Chueca Vergara, C. & Ferruz Agudo, L. (2021). Fintech and sustainability: do they affect each other?. Sustainability. / mdpi.comDOI: 10.3390/su13137012

Chuhan-Pole, P., & Angwafo, M. (Eds.). (2011). *Yes, Africa Can: Success Stories from a Dynamic Continent*. The World Bank., DOI: 10.1596/978-0-8213-8745-0

CIMB. (2025). Banking towards tomorrow. https://www.cimb.com.my/en/personal/day-to-day-banking/sustainability-at-cimb.html

Citterio, A., Marques, B. P., & Tanda, A. (2024). The Early Days of Neobanks in Europe: Identification, Performance, and Riskiness. *Journal of Financial Services Research*. Advance online publication. DOI: 10.1007/s10693-024-00433-x

Colombage, S. (2025). Financial Technology (Fintech) and Sustainable Financing. *Journal of Risk and Financial Management, 18*(10), 553. DOI: 10.3390/jrfm18100553

Copestake, A., Kirti, D., & Martinez Peria, M. S. (2025). Growing retail digital payments: The value of interoperability. *IMF Fintech Notes, 2025*(004), 1. Advance online publication. DOI: 10.5089/9798229014250.063

Corneli, F. (2021). Financial integration without financial development. *Atlantic Economic Journal, 49*(2), 201–220. DOI: 10.1007/s11293-021-09709-2 PMID: 34092835

Creswell, J. W., & Plano Clark, V. L. (2010). Designing and conducting mixed methods research. *Sage (Atlanta, Ga.).*

Crisanto, J. C., Ehrentraud, J., Fabian, M., & Monteil, A. (2022). Big tech interdependencies – a key policy blind spot. FSI Insights on policy implementation No 44. https://www.bis.org/fsi/publ/insights44.pdf

Cromwell, R. S., & Peprah, J. A. (2025). Banking Business Models and Sustainable Development: Challenges and Opportunities. Strategic Approaches to Banking Business and Sustainable Development Goals, 3-22. / [HTML]DOI: 10.1007/978-3-031-80744-2_1

Crona, B., Peterson, G., Meacham, M., Parlato, G., Lade, S. J., Rocha, J. C., & Galaz, V. (2025). A systems approach to sustainable finance: Actors, influence mechanisms, and potentially virtuous cycles of sustainability. *iScience*, *112785*(7), 112785. Advance online publication. DOI: 10.1016/j.isci.2025.112785

Cross, J. & Neumark, T. (2021). Solar power and its discontents: critiquing off-grid infrastructures of inclusion in East Africa. Development and Change. DOI: wiley.comDOI: 10.1111/dech.12668

Cummins, J. D., & Weiss, M. A. (2009). Convergence of insurance and financial markets: Hybrid and securitized risk-transfer solutions. *The Journal of Risk and Insurance*, *76*(3), 493–545. DOI: 10.1111/j.1539-6975.2009.01311.x

Cunha, F. A. F. D. S., Meira, E., & Orsato, R. J. (2021). Sustainable finance and investment: Review and research agenda. Business Strategy and the Environment, 30(8), 3821-3838. DOI: researchgate.netDOI: 10.1002/bse.2842

Danisman, G. O., & Tarazi, A. (2020). Financial inclusion and bank stability: Evidence from Europe. *European Journal of Finance*, *26*(18), 1842–1855. DOI: 10.1080/1351847X.2020.1782958

Das, R. (2025, January 29). *Dunzo: A Quick Commerce Case Study*. Linkedin.com. https://www.linkedin.com/pulse/dunzo-quick-commerce-case-study-rupam-das-ocjqc

Datta, D. (2024, June 25). *Strong growth metrics gives food aggregator Zomato an edge over Swiggy*. @Bsindia; Business Standard. https://www.business-standard.com/markets/news/strong-growth-metrics-gives-food-aggregator-zomato-an-edge-over-swiggy-124062501169_1.html

De Gregorio Rebeco, J. (1999). Financial integration, financial development and economic growth. *Estudos Econômicos*, *26*(2), 137–161.

Delle Foglie, A., & Keshminder, J. S. (2022). Challenges and opportunities of SRI sukuk toward financial system sustainability: A bibliometric and systematic literature review. *International Journal of Emerging Markets, 19*(10), 3202–3225. DOI: 10.1108/IJOEM-04-2022-0601

Deloitte. (2023). *2023 financial services industry outlooks | Deloitte China | Financial Services*. Deloitte China. https://www2.deloitte.com/cn/en/pages/financial-services/articles/financial-services-industry-outlooks-2023.html

Dempere, J., Alamash, E., & Mattos, P. (2024). Unveiling the truth: Greenwashing in sustainable finance. *Frontiers in Sustainability, 5*, 1362051. DOI: 10.3389/frsus.2024.1362051

Dikau, S., & Volz, U. (2023). Out of the window? Green monetary policy in China: Window guidance and the promotion of sustainable lending and investment. *Climate Policy*, *23*(1), 122–137. Advance online publication. DOI: 10.1080/14693062.2021.2012122

Dmuchowski, P., Dmuchowski, W., Baczewska-Dąbrowska, A. H., & Gworek, B. (2023). Environmental, social, and governance (ESG) model; impacts and sustainable investment–Global trends and Poland's perspective. *Journal of Environmental Management, 329*, 117023. Bo, S., & Battisti, E. (2024). Green finance and greenwashing: charting a sustainable path forward. *Qualitative Research in Financial Markets*.

Doerr, S., Frost, J., Gambacorta, L., & Shreeti, V. (2025). Big techs in finance. In Berger, A., Molyneux, P., & Wilson, J. (Eds.), *The Oxford Handbook of Banking* (4th ed., pp. 296–325). Oxford University Press., DOI: 10.1093/oxfordhb/9780198897071.013.14

Donner, J. (2015). *After access: Inclusion, development, and a more mobile Internet*. MIT Press. DOI: 10.7551/mitpress/9740.001.0001

Donner, J., & Tellez, C. A. (2008). Mobile banking and economic development: Linking adoption, impact, and use. *Asian Journal of Communication, 18*(4), 318–332. DOI: 10.1080/01292980802344190

Douglas, D. D. (2024). The transformative impact of AI in finance and banking. *Journal of Investment Banking and Finance, 2*(1), 01–08.

Dresner, A., Murati, A., Pike, B., & Zell, J. (2022). Embedded finance: Who will lead the next payments revolution. McKinsey & Company, 18.

Dresner, A., Murati, A., Pike, B., & Zell, J. (2022, August 13). *Embedded finance trends | McKinsey*. Www.mckinsey.com. https://www.mckinsey.com/industries/financial-services/our-insights/embedded-finance-who-will-lead-the-next-payments-revolution

Dresner, A., Pike, B., & Schiff, H. (2024, April 11). *Embedded finance: The choices and trade-offs for US banks | McKinsey*. Www.mckinsey.com. https://www.mckinsey.com/industries/financial-services/our-insights/embedded-finance-the-choices-and-trade-offs-for-us-banks

Dubey, S. (2025). *LinkedIn*. Linkedin.com. https://www.linkedin.com/pulse/dunzo-case-study-sandeep-dubey-zquuf

Dwivedi, P., Alabdooli, J. I., & Dwivedi, R. (2021). Role of FinTech adoption for competitiveness and performance of the bank: A study of banking industry in UAE. *International Journal of Global Business and Competitiveness*, *16*(2), 130–138. DOI: 10.1007/s42943-021-00033-9

Dwivedi, Y. K., Ismagilova, E., Hughes, D. L., Carlson, J., Filieri, R., Jacobson, J., Jain, V., Karjaluoto, H., Kefi, H., Krishen, A. S., Kumar, V., Rahman, M. M., Raman, R., Rauschnabel, P. A., Rowley, J., Salo, J., Tran, G. A., & Wang, Y. (2021). Setting the future of digital and social media marketing research: Perspectives and research propositions. *International Journal of Information Management*, *59*, 102168. DOI: 10.1016/j.ijinfomgt.2020.102168

Economic Times. (2022, February 10). *Ola eyes NBFC acquisition to expand financial services business*. The Economic Times; Economic Times. https://economictimes.indiatimes.com/tech/technology/ola-eyes-nbfc-acquisition-to-expand-financial-services-business/articleshow/89478354.cms?from=mdr

Economic Times. (2024, July 30). *Flipkart consolidates fintech offerings into single vertical ahead of festive sales*. The Economic Times; Economic Times. https://economictimes.indiatimes.com/tech/technology/flipkart-consolidates-fintech-offerings-under-flipkart-pay-ahead-of-festive-sales/articleshow/112131771.cms?from=mdr

Elidrisy, A. (2024). Comparative review of ESG Reporting Standards: ESRS European Sustainability Reporting Standards" versus ISSB "International Sustainability Standards Board. *International Multilingual Journal of Science and Technology*, *9*(3), 7191–7198.

Elkington, J. (1998). Partnerships from cannibals with forks: The triple bottom line of 21st-century business. *Environmental Quality Management*, *8*(1), 37–51. DOI: 10.1002/tqem.3310080106

Elkington, J. (1999). Triple bottom line revolution: Reporting for the third millennium. *Australian CPA*, *69*(11), 75–76.

Engstrom, S. (2019). Recognising the role eco-grief plays in responding to environmental degradation. *Journal of Transdisciplinary Peace Praxis*, *1*(1), 168–186.

Eremeeva, T., & Akulova, A. (2024). The european digital payment wallet ecosystem: key characteristics and insights.

European Commission. (2023). Regulation (EU) 2019/2088 on sustainability-related disclosures in the financial services sector (Sustainable Finance Disclosure Regulation). *Official Journal of the European Union, L, 317*, 1–16.

Falchetta, G., Michoud, B., Hafner, M., & Rother, M. (2022). Harnessing finance for a new era of decentralised electricity access: A review of private investment patterns and emerging business models. Energy Research & Social Science, 90, 102587. / sciencedirect.comDOI: 10.1016/j.erss.2022.102587

Farayola, O. A. (2024). Revolutionizing banking security: integrating artificial intelligence, blockchain, and business intelligence for enhanced cybersecurity. Finance & Accounting Research Journal. DOI: academia.eduDOI: 10.51594/farj.v6i4.990

Farrell, H., & Newman, A. L. (2019). Weaponized interdependence: How global economic networks shape state coercion. *International Security*, *44*(1), 42–79. DOI: 10.1162/isec_a_00351

Fava, D. (2023). Where Behavioral Finance and Embedded Finance Intersect. *Journal of Financial Planning*, *36*(1), 54–57.

Fernandez-Vallado, M. (2025). Towards a Policy Framework for Microfinance: Innovative Financial Solutions for Sustainable Development. In Microfinance, Financial Innovation, and Sustainable Entrepreneurship in Economics (pp. 139-182). IGI Global Scientific Publishing. DOI: [HTML]DOI: 10.4018/979-8-3693-6622-6.ch006

Fiedler, S., & Gomber, P. (2022). Decentralized finance (DeFi): Ein literature review aus wirtschafts- und rechtswissenschaftlicher perspektive. *Journal of Business and Law*, *15*(2), 123–145. DOI: 10.1007/s10257-022-00592-3

Finextra. (2024, September 17). *Embedded finance adoption: What are the real catalysts?* Finextra Research; Finextra. https://www.finextra.com/the-long-read/1118/embedded-finance-adoption-what-are-the-real-catalysts

Finken, S. (2025). *Embedded Finance*. Springer Books. DOI: 10.1007/978-3-658-46863-7

Finken, S., & Hensen, J. (2025). Embedded finance: An evaluation of current and future use cases. *Journal of Digital Banking*, *9*(4), 294–316. DOI: 10.69554/XMNM5451

Fintech Association of Malaysia. (2025). Financial assistance. https://fintechmalaysia.org/financial-assistance-peer-2-peer-lending/

Fintech News Malaysia. (2023). Digital insurance products in Malaysia that caught our attention. https://fintechnews.my/38194/insurtech-malaysia/digital-insurance-products-in-malaysia-that-caught-our-attention/

Fintech News Malaysia. (2025). 5 top e-wallets in Malaysia and what they're best for (2025). https://fintechnews.my/50928/payments-remittance-malaysia/top-ewallets-in-malaysia/

Fintech News Malaysia. (2025). A list of licensed equity crowdfunding (ECF) platforms in Malaysia. https://fintechnews.my/50781/crowdfunding-malaysia/a-list-of-licensed-ecf-platforms-in-malaysia/#:~:text=Behind%20this%20momentum%20is%20a%20network%20of%2013,and%20value%20propositions%20for%20both%20issuers%20and%20investors

Fintech News Malaysia. (2025). Boost Bank and CGC Digital to offer RM130 million in MSME loans. https://fintechnews.my/48719/digital-banking-news-malaysia/boost-bank-msmes-loan/#:~:text=Boost%20Bank%2C%20Malaysia%E2%80%99s%20first%20homegrown%20digital%20bank%2C%20and,in%20Malaysia%2C%20allocating%20RM130%20million%20for%20business%20loans

Fintech News Malaysia. (2025). How to buy cryptocurrency in Malaysia (2025). https://fintechnews.my/47522/blockchain/how-to-buy-cryptocurrency-in-malaysia-2025/

Folqué, M., Escrig-Olmedo, E., & Corzo Santamaría, T. (2021). Sustainable development and financial system: Integrating ESG risks through sustainable investment strategies in a climate change context. *Sustainable Development (Bradford)*, *29*(5), 876–890. DOI: 10.1002/sd.2181

Fratzscher, M., & Imbs, J. (2009). Risk sharing, finance, and institutions in international portfolios. *Journal of Financial Economics*, *94*(3), 428–447. DOI: 10.1016/j.jfineco.2008.12.007

Frederick, D. P., & Parappagoudar, S. K. (2021). *SWOC Analysis of Zomato - A Case of Online Food Delivery Services*. Papers.*ssrn*.com. https://papers.ssrn.com/sol3/papers.cfm?abstract_id=3805485

Freeman, R. E. (1984). *Strategic management: A stakeholder approach.* Cambridge University Press.

Friede, G., Busch, T., & Bassen, A. (2015). ESG and financial performance: Aggregated evidence from more than 2000 empirical studies. *Journal of Sustainable Finance & Investment, 5*(4), 210–233. DOI: 10.1080/20430795.2015.1118917

Fu, C., Lu, L., & Pirabi, M. (2023). Advancing green finance: a review of sustainable development. Digital Economy and Sustainable Development. / springer.comDOI: 10.1007/s44265-023-00020-3

Galeone, G., Ranaldo, S., & Fusco, A. (2024). ESG and FinTech: Are they connected? *Research in International Business and Finance, 69*, 102225. DOI: 10.1016/j.ribaf.2024.102225

Gardner, I. (2008). Capital Rules: The Construction of Global Finance. *Journal of Economic Issues, 42*(4), 1163–1165. Advance online publication. DOI: 10.1080/00213624.2008.11507208

Gema, S. B. (2023). Financing the energy transition: The new paradigm for renewable energy investors. In *The Palgrave Handbook of Zero Carbon Energy Systems and Energy Transitions* (pp. 1–44). Springer International Publishing. [HTML], DOI: 10.1007/978-3-030-74380-2_4-1

Ghazawneh, A., & Henfridsson, O. (2013). Balancing platform control and external contribution in third-party development: The boundary resources model. *Information Systems Journal, 23*(2), 173–192. DOI: 10.1111/j.1365-2575.2012.00406.x

Ghosh, O., Kumar, B., Sharif, M., & Siwach, J. (2025). Regulatory and Legal Implications on Harnessing Blockchain-Digital Twin Fusion for Sustainable Investments. In The Future of Indigenous Inclusivity: Unlocking Finance for Economic Development (pp. 19-38). IGI Global Scientific Publishing. DOI: researchgate.netDOI: 10.4018/979-8-3693-7924-0.ch002

Giakoumelou, A., Salvi, A., Bekiros, S., & Onorato, G. (2024). ESG and FinTech funding in the EU. *Research in International Business and Finance, 69*, 102233. DOI: 10.1016/j.ribaf.2024.102233

Giannetti, M., & Ongena, S. (2007). Financial integration and firm performance: Evidence from foreign bank entry in emerging markets. https://ssrn.com/abstract_id=669421www.ecgi.global/content/working-papers DOI: 10.2139/ssrn.669421

Global Legal Insights. (2025). Fintech laws and regulations: Nigeria. In Global Legal Insights – Fintech Laws and Regulations 2025. London: Global Legal Group. https://www.globallegalinsights.com/practice-areas/fintech-laws-and-regulations/nigeria/

Goel, A. (2024, September 6). *Embedded Finance: A Comprehensive Guide to Integration and Future Trends*. Nucleus Software. https://www.nucleussoftware.com/blog/how-financial-institutions-can-seamlessly-implement-embedded-finance/

Goggin, G. (2025). Mobile AI: Communication and mobility after the smartphone. *Communication and Change, 1*(5), 5. Advance online publication. DOI: 10.1007/s44382-025-00002-3

Goutte, S., & Sanin, M. E. (2024). Main challenges regarding development and sustainability in economics and finance. [HTML]. *Development and Sustainability in Economics and Finance, 100002*, 100002. Advance online publication. DOI: 10.1016/j.dsef.2024.100002

Grand View Research. (2023). *U.S. Embedded Finance Market Size | Industry Report, 2030*. Grandviewresearch.com. https://www.grandviewresearch.com/industry-analysis/us-embedded-finance-market-report

Grand View Research. (2024). *Embedded Finance Market To Reach $588.49 Billion By 2030*. Grandviewresearch.com. https://www.grandviewresearch.com/press-release/global-embedded-finance-market

GRI. (2023). *GRI standards: The global standards for sustainability reporting*. Global Reporting Initiative. https://www.globalreporting.org/standards/

GrowishPay. (2022, December 21). *The Embedded Finance Journey: the view of Goldman Sachs - GrowishPay*. GrowishPay. https://growishpay.com/2022/12/21/embedded-finance-journey-goldman-sachs/

GSMA. (2023). State of the Industry Report on Mobile Money 2023. https://www.gsma.com/sotir/wp-content/uploads/2025/04/GSMA-SOTIR-2023.pdf

Gunjan, R. K. (2024, July 4). *Fintech-as-a-feature has been disabled. Just ask Zomato*. The Ken. https://the-ken.com/kaching/fintech-as-a-feature-has-been-disabled-just-ask-zomato/

Hajian, M. & Kashani, S. J. (2021). 1 - Evolution of the concept of sustainability. From Brundtland Report to Sustainable Development Goals. *Sustainable Resource Management,* 1-24. https://doi.org/.DOI: 10.1016/B978-0-12-824342-8.00018-3

Harris, M., Adams, B., Davis, A., & Tijssen, J. (2022). *Embedded Finance: What It Takes to Prosper in the New Value Chain*. https://www.bain.com/contentassets/a5ad904e61324de88b62707de879f174/bain_brief_embedded-finance.pdf

Hasan, M. M., Yajuan, L., & Khan, S. (2022). Promoting China's inclusive finance through digital financial services. *Global Business Review*, *23*(4), 984–1006. DOI: 10.1177/0972150919895348

Hatch, M., Schmitz, C., & Kaempfer, J. (2025). *Embedded Finance: why banks are at a crossroads*. Ey.com. https://www.ey.com/en_us/insights/banking-capital-markets/how-banks-are-staking-a-claim-in-the-embedded-finance-ecosystem

Hazen, B. T., Russo, I., Confente, I., & Pellathy, D. (2021). Supply chain management for circular economy: conceptual framework and research agenda. The International Journal of Logistics Management, 32(2), 510-537. / emerald.comDOI: 10.1108/IJLM-12-2019-0332

Heeks, R. (2010). Do information and communication technologies (ICTs) contribute to development? *Journal of International Development*, *22*(5), 625–640. DOI: 10.1002/jid.1716

Henry Ntarmah, A., Kong, Y., & Kobina Gyan, M. (2019). Banking system stability and economic sustainability: A panel data analysis of the effect of banking system stability on sustainability of some selected developing countries. *Quantitative Finance and Economics*, *3*(4), 709–738. DOI: 10.3934/QFE.2019.4.709

Hensen, J., & Kötting, B. (2022). From open banking to embedded finance: The essential factors for a successful digital transformation. *Journal of Digital Banking*, *6*(4), 308–318. DOI: 10.69554/SRCL3482

Hidayat-ur-Rehman, I., & Hossain, M. N. (2024). The impacts of Fintech adoption, green finance and competitiveness on banks' sustainable performance: Digital transformation as moderator. *Asia-Pacific Journal of Business Administration*. Advance online publication. DOI: 10.1108/APJBA-10-2023-0497

Hossain, R., Ghose, P., Chowdhury, T. M., Hossen, M. D., Hasan, M. N., & Mani, L. (2024). Ownership Structures and Firm Performance: A Correlation and Regression Analysis of Financial Institutions in Bangladesh. *Pakistan Journal of Life and Social Sciences*, *22*(2), 6278–6295. DOI: 10.57239/PJLSS-2024-22.2.00473

Hove-Sibanda, P., & Mkumatela, Y. (2025). Green Logistics in SMEs for Sustainable Development. In *Eco-Logistics and Sustainable Supply Chain Innovations* (pp. 85–116). IGI Global Scientific Publishing. [HTML], DOI: 10.4018/979-8-3693-6175-7.ch005

Howson, P., & de Vries, A. (2022). Preying on the poor? Opportunities and challenges for tackling the social and environmental threats of cryptocurrencies for vulnerable and low-income communities. [HTML]. *Energy Research & Social Science, 84*, 102394. Advance online publication. DOI: 10.1016/j.erss.2021.102394

Hu, H., Jia, Z., & Yang, S. (2025). Exploring FinTech, green finance, and ESG performance across corporate life-cycles. *International Review of Financial Analysis, 97*, 103871. DOI: 10.1016/j.irfa.2024.103871

IBM. (2023). *Embedded finance*. IBM. https://www.ibm.com/thought-leadership/institute-business-value/en-us/report/embedded-finance

IBM. (2025). What is environmental, social and governance (ESG)? https://www.ibm.com/think/topics/environmental-social-and-governance

Ifrim, O. (2024). Embedded finance and BaaS: Reflections on 2024 and what lies ahead. https://thepaypers.com/fintech/expert-views/embedded-finance-and-baas-reflections-on-2024-and-what-lies-ahead

Industry Arc. (2023). *Embedded Finance Market Size Worth $379 Billion By 2030: IndustryARC*. Big News Network.com. https://www.bignewsnetwork.com/news/273990537/embedded-finance-market-size-worth-379-billion-by-2030-industryarc

Iona cu, A. E., Gheorghiu, G., Spătariu, E. C., Munteanu, I., Grigorescu, A., & Dănilă, A. (2023). Unraveling Digital Transformation in Banking: Evidence from Romania. *Systems, 11*(11), 534. DOI: 10.3390/systems11110534

Iwuanyanwu, O., Gil-Ozoudeh, I., Okwandu, A. C., & Ike, C. S. (2024). Cultural and social dimensions of green architecture: Designing for sustainability and community well-being. *International Journal of Applied Research in Social Sciences, 6*(8), 1951–1968. https://www.academia.edu/118424441/Cultural_and_social_dimensions_of_green_architecture_Designing_for_sustainability_and_community_well_being. DOI: 10.51594/ijarss.v6i8.1477

Jaiwant, S. V., Haridasan, A., & Kureethara, J. V. (2024). The role of financial institutions in addressing climate change. In Naifar, N. (Ed.), *Climate change and finance. Sustainable Finance*. Springer., DOI: 10.1007/978-3-031-56419-2_5

Jalan, A. (2019, December 11). *Dunzo Case Study – Business Model, Funding, History & Much More*. Aryan Jalan. https://aryanjalan.com/dunzo-business-model/

Jarvis, D. (2013). *Environmental justice and social work: A call to expand the social work profession to include environmental justice* [Master's thesis, Columbia University]. Academic Commons. DOI: 10.7916/D8RN36CZ

Jayadev, M. (2013). Basel III implementation: Issues and challenges for Indian banks. *IIMB Management Review, 25*(2), 115–130. DOI: 10.1016/j.iimb.2013.03.010

Jonsdottir, B., Sigurjonsson, T. O., Johannsdottir, L., & Wendt, S. (2022). Barriers to using ESG data for investment decisions. *Sustainability (Basel), 14*(9), 5157. DOI: 10.3390/su14095157

julies chicktanz, J. M. (2025, January 16). *Amazon to Acquire India-Based BNPL Fintech Axio - Finovate.* Finovate. https://finovate.com/amazon-to-acquire-india-based-bnpl-fintech-axio/

Kadam, M. A., Jangid, A., & Singh, N. (2024). Embedded Finance: Scope, Challenges and Opportunities. BVIMSR Journal of Management Research, 16(2).

Kandpal, P. C. (2024). India's policy response to the COVID-19 pandemic: Lessons for a post-COVID society. *Discover Global Society, 2*(1), 16. DOI: 10.1007/s44282-024-00043-x

Kashyap, S., & Iveroth, E. (2020). Transparency and accountability influences of regulation on risk control: The case of a Swedish bank. *The Journal of Management and Governance, 25*(2), 475–508. DOI: 10.1007/s10997-020-09550-w

Kaur, P., & Singh, M. (2025). Exploring the impact of InsurTech adoption in Indian life insurance industry: A customer satisfaction perspective. *The TQM Journal, 37*(2), 457–483. DOI: 10.1108/TQM-06-2023-0186

Kern, A. (2018). *Gender and the Green Economy* (Doctoral dissertation, University of Kansas). KU ScholarWorks. https://kuscholarworks.ku.edu/server/api/core/bitstreams/c4e51a6c-f71c-4802-86e5-7757cb7db960/content

Key, C. (2023, June 17). *Tracking Repeat Purchase Rates on Amazon: Measuring Loyalty to Boost Long-Term Revenue*. Channel Key. https://channelkey.com/amazon-inventory-and-orders/tracking-repeat-purchase-rates-on-amazon-measuring-loyalty-to-boost-long-term-revenue/

Khalid, F., Su, C. Y., Weiwei, K., Voinea, C. L., & Srivastava, M. (2025). Financial mechanism for sustainability: The case of China's green financial system and corporate green investment. *China Finance Review International, 15*(1), 93–116. DOI: 10.1108/CFRI-11-2023-0291

Khalifa, N., Elmedany, W., & Sharif, S. (2024). Leveraging digital identity and open banking data for fraud prevention in the financial industry. *FiCloud, 286*, 286–291. Advance online publication. DOI: 10.1109/FiCloud62933.2024.00051

Khalil, M. A., Sinliamthong, P., & Khalil, R. (2025). From Paper to Pixels for a World of Purpose: A Systematic Review of Sustainable Finance, Blockchain, and Digital Assets. Sustainable Financing—A Contemporary Guide for Green Finance, Crowdfunding and Digital Currencies: Sustainable Financing, 61-78. / [HTML] DOI: 10.1007/978-3-031-80969-9_5

Khan, S. A. R., Yu, Z., Sarwat, S., Godil, D. I., Amin, S., & Shujaat, S. (2021). The role of block chain technology in circular economy practices to improve organisational performance. *International Journal of Logistics*, *25*(4–5), 605–622. DOI: 10.1080/13675567.2021.1872512

Kim, M., & Duvendack, M. (2024). Digital credit for all? An empirical analysis of mobile loans for financial inclusion in Kenya. *Information Technology for Development*, *31*(3), 559–576. DOI: 10.1080/02681102.2024.2402996

Kim, S., & Li, Z. (2021). Understanding the impact of ESG practices in corporate finance. *Sustainability (Basel)*, *13*(7), 3746. DOI: 10.3390/su13073746

Kinara Capital. (2023, July 27). *Embedded Finance Maximizing Financial Opportunities in India*. Kinara Capital. https://kinaracapital.com/power-of-embedded-finance-in-india/

Kiourtis, A., Mavrogiorgou, A., Makridis, G., Fatouros, G., Soldatos, J., & Kyriazis, D. (2023). Data Marketplaces: Best Practices, Challenges, and Advancements for Embedded Finance. *Proceedings - 19th International Conference on Distributed Computing in Smart Systems and the Internet of Things, DCOSS-IoT 2023*. DOI: 10.1109/DCOSS-IoT58021.2023.00088

Klapper, L. (2023). How digital payments can benefit entrepreneurs. *IZA World of Labor: Evidence-Based Policy Making*, *396*. Advance online publication. DOI: 10.15185/izawol.396.v2

Kotsantonis, S., & Serafeim, G. (2019). Four things no one will tell you about ESG data. *The Bank of America Journal of Applied Corporate Finance*, *31*(2), 50–58. DOI: 10.1111/jacf.12346

KPMG International. (2021). ESG risks in banks: Effective strategies to use opportunities and mitigate risks. https://assets.kpmg.com/content/dam/kpmg/xx/pdf/2021/05/esg-risks-in-banks.pdf

Krings, A., Victor, B. G., Mathias, J., & Perron, B. E. (2020). Environmental social work in the disciplinary literature, 1991–2015. *International Social Work*, *63*(5), 652–664. DOI: 10.1177/0020872818788397

Kruger, M., Lavigne, R., & Mckay, J. (2016). *The role of the International Monetary Fund in the post-crisis world Standard-Nutzungsbedingungen*. https://doi.org/DOI: 10.34989/sdp-2016-6

Kshetri, N. (2022). Blockchain systems and ethical sourcing in the mineral and metal industry: A multiple case study. [HTML]. *International Journal of Logistics Management*, *33*(1), 1–27. Advance online publication. DOI: 10.1108/IJLM-02-2021-0108

Kumar, L., Nadeem, F., Sloan, M., Restle-Steinert, J., Deitch, M. J., Ali Naqvi, S., ... & Sassanelli, C. (2022). Fostering green finance for sustainable development: A focus on textile and leather small medium enterprises in Pakistan. Sustainability, 14(19), 11908. / mdpi.comDOI: 10.3390/su141911908

Kumar, N. M. & Chopra, S. S. (2022). Leveraging blockchain and smart contract technologies to overcome circular economy implementation challenges. Sustainability. / mdpi.comDOI: 10.3390/su14159492

Kumar, S., Sharma, D., Rao, S., Lim, W. M., & Mangla, S. K. (2022). Past, present, and future of sustainable finance: insights from big data analytics through machine learning of scholarly research. Annals of Operations Research, 1-44. / springer.comDOI: 10.1007/s10479-021-04410-8

Kumar, B., Kumar, A., Sassanelli, C., & Kumar, L. (2025). Exploring the role of finance in driving circular economy and sustainable business practices. *Journal of Cleaner Production*, *486*, 144480. DOI: 10.1016/j.jclepro.2024.144480

Kuzmina, J., Maditinos, D., Norena-Chavez, D., Grima, S., & Kadłubek, M. (2023). ESG integration as a risk management tool within the financial decision-making process. In Digital Transformation, Strategic Resilience, Cyber Security and Risk Management (pp. 105-113). Emerald Publishing Limited. / [HTML]DOI: 10.1108/S1569-375920230000111A007

Leal Filho, W., Lange Salvia, A., Ruy Portela Vasconcelos, C., Anholon, R., Simon Rampasso, I., Henrique Paulino Pires Eustachio, J., Liakh, O., Alzira Pimenta Dinis, M., Cementina Olpoc, R., Bandanaa, J., Aina, Y. A., Lolekola Lukina, R., & Sharifi, A. (2022). Barriers to institutional social sustainability. *Sustainability Science*, *17*(6), 2615–2630. https://doi.org/ (Full text also available via PMC: https://www.ncbi.nlm.nih.gov/pmc/articles/PMC9688692/)DOI: 10.1007/s11625-022-01204-0

Leal Filho, W., Tripathi, S. K., Andrade Guerra, J. B. S. O. D., Giné-Garriga, R., Orlovic Lovren, V., & Willats, J. (2019). Using the sustainable development goals towards a better understanding of sustainability challenges. *International Journal of Sustainable Development and World Ecology*, *26*(2), 179–190. DOI: 10.1080/13504509.2018.1505674

Lee, C.-C., Lou, R., & Wang, F. (2022). Digital financial inclusion and poverty alleviation: Evidence from the sustainable development of China. *Economic Analysis and Policy*, *77*, 418–434. Advance online publication. DOI: 10.1016/j.eap.2022.12.004

Li, Z. & Chen, P. (2024). Sustainable Finance Meets FinTech: Amplifying Green Credit's Benefits for Banks. Sustainability. / mdpi.comDOI: 10.3390/su16187901

Li, B. (2023). The role of financial markets in the energy transition: An analysis of investment trends and opportunities in renewable energy and clean technology. [HTML]. *Environmental Science and Pollution Research International*, *30*(43), 97948–97964. Advance online publication. DOI: 10.1007/s11356-023-29014-6 PMID: 37599346

Li, L., Fei, C., & Fei, W. (2023). Research on investment incorporating both environmental performance and long (short) term financial performance of firms. *International Journal of Systems Science*, *55*(2), 273–299. DOI: 10.1080/00207721.2023.2270402

Li, N., & Huang, F. (2024). Evaluating the financial returns on investment in sustainable enterprise digitalization initiatives using AI information system. *Journal of Internet Services and Information Security*, *14*(4), 21–44. DOI: 10.58346/JISIS.2024.I4.002

Liu, X., Liang, W., Fu, Y., & Huang, G. Q. (2024). Dual Environmental, Social, and Governance (ESG) Index for corporate sustainability assessment using blockchain technology. *Sustainability (Basel)*, *16*(10), 4272. DOI: 10.3390/su16104272

Louman, B., Girolami, E. D., Shames, S., Primo, L. G., Gitz, V., Scherr, S. J., Meybeck, A., & Brady, M. (2022). Access to landscape finance for small-scale producers and local communities: A literature review. *Land (Basel)*, *11*(9), 1444. DOI: 10.3390/land11091444

Luo, Q., Xue, M., Xiong, Y. & Ge, X. (2024). The backfire of mutual funds balancing financial objectives in ESG investments: Evidence from China. *International Review of Financial Analysis, 96*(Part B), 103686. https://doi.org/.DOI: 10.1016/j.irfa.2024.103686

Luo, D., Luo, M., & Lv, J. (2022). Can digital finance contribute to the promotion of financial sustainability? A financial efficiency perspective. *Sustainability (Basel)*, *14*(7), 3979. DOI: 10.3390/su14073979

Macchiavello, E., & Siri, M. (2022). Sustainable finance and fintech: Can technology contribute to achieving environmental goals? A preliminary assessment of 'green fintech'and 'sustainable digital finance'. *European Company and Financial Law Review*, *19*(1), 128–174. DOI: 10.1515/ecfr-2022-0005

MarketsAndMarkets. (2025). *Embedded Finance Market Size, Growth Analysis & Forecast, [Latest]*. MarketsandMarkets. https://www.marketsandmarkets.com/Market-Reports/embedded-finance-market-126584658.html

Mastercard. (2024, February 16). *Embedded finance: transforming financing for SMEs*. Mastercard Data & Services. https://www.mastercardservices.com/en/industries/financial-institutions/insights/embedded-finance-transforming-financing-smes

Matarneh, S., Piprani, A. Z., Ellahi, R. M., Nguyen, D. N., Le, T. M., & Nazir, S. (2024). Industry 4.0 technologies and circular economy synergies: Enhancing corporate sustainability through sustainable supply chain integration and flexibility. Environmental Technology & Innovation, 35, 103723. / sciencedirect.comDOI: 10.1016/j.eti.2024.103723

Mavrogiorgou, A., Kiourtis, A., Makridis, G., Kotios, D., Koukos, V., Kyriazis, D., Soldatos, J., Fatouros, G., Drakoulis, D., Malo, P., Serrano, M., Isaja, M., Lazcano, R., Vera, J. M., Fournier, F., Limonad, L., Perakis, K., Miltiadou, D., Kranas, P., & Troiano, E. (2023). FAME: Federated Decentralized Trusted Data Marketplace for Embedded Finance. *2023 International Conference on Smart Applications, Communications and Networking, SmartNets 2023*. DOI: 10.1109/SmartNets58706.2023.10215814

Maybank (2022). Maybank launches Sustainable Product Framework to drive sustainable finance. https://www.maybank.com/en/news/2022/09/01.page

Md, R., & Tanvir Rahman, A. (2019). The Effects of Financial Inclusion Initiatives on Economic Development in Underserved Communities. *American Journal of Economics and Business Management*, 2(4), 191–198.

Mehta, J. (2014, August 25). *The LimeRoad Growth Story: 600+ vendors, 5X orders this year and $20 million in funding*. Yourstory.com; YourStory. https://yourstory.com/2014/08/limeroad-growth-story

Meng Sam, K., & Han Chan, W. (2020). FACTORS AFFECTING THE ADOPTION OF EMBEDDED MOBILE FINANCE FUNCTIONS. *FACTORS AFFECTING THE ADOPTION OF EMBEDDED MOBILE FINANCE FUNCTIONS Journal of Information Technology Management, XXXI*(2).

Meng, S., He, X., & Tian, X. (2021). Research on Fintech development issues based on embedded cloud computing and big data analysis. *Microprocessors and Microsystems, 83*, 103977. Advance online publication. DOI: 10.1016/j.micpro.2021.103977

Mensah, B. A. (2024). Predictive Model on Digital Financial Inclusion and Sustainable Development in Sub-Saharan Africa (Doctoral dissertation, University of Cape Coast).

Mhlanga, D. (2022). Introduction to digital financial inclusion: Revisiting poverty theories in the context of the fourth industrial revolution. In *Digital financial inclusion: revisiting poverty theories in the context of the fourth industrial revolution* (pp. 3–15). Springer International Publishing. DOI: 10.1007/978-3-031-16687-7_1

Mishra, D., Kandpal, V., Agarwal, N., & Srivastava, B. (2024). Financial inclusion and its ripple effects on socio-economic development: A comprehensive review. *Journal of Risk and Financial Management, 17*(3), 105. DOI: 10.3390/jrfm17030105

Mocsary, G. A. (2014). The embedded firm: Corporate governance, labor, and finance capitalism - Commentary. *Accounting, Economics, and Law : A Convivium, 4*(2). Advance online publication. DOI: 10.1515/ael-2013-0035

Mogaji, E., & Nguyen, N. P. (2024). High street banking on the app: Branding strategies of traditionally-driven neobanks. *International Journal of Bank Marketing, 42*(2), 301–330. DOI: 10.1108/IJBM-12-2022-0529

Mohammed, M. M., Khan, N., & Ahmad, T. (2022). Opportunity for Islamic Finance in Blockchain Solutions for Climate Change: A Case Study of DCarbonX Model. *, 18*. DOI: 10.33001/M0110202218/105

Monis, E., & Pai, R. (2023). Neo Banks: A Paradigm Shift in Banking. *International Journal of Case Studies in Business, IT, and Education*, 318–332. DOI: 10.47992/IJCSBE.2581.6942.0275

Mordor Intelligence. (2025). *Embedded Finance Market Size & Share Analysis - Industry Research Report - Growth Trends*. Mordorintelligence.com. https://www.mordorintelligence.com/industry-reports/embedded-finance-market

Morgan Stanley. (2025). *Can Food Delivery Apps Deliver Profits for Investors?* Morgan Stanley. https://www.morganstanley.com/ideas/food-delivery-app-profits

Morseletto, P. (2020). Restorative and regenerative-Exploring the concepts in the circular economy. *Journal of Industrial Ecology, 24*(4), 763–773. DOI: 10.1111/jiec.12987

Mukherjee, S. (2015, September 10). *LimeRoad founder Suchi Mukherjee talks about building brand stickiness*. @Bsindia; Business Standard. https://www.business-standard.com/article/companies/limeroad-founder-suchi-mukherjee-talks-about-building-brand-stickiness-115091000791_1.html

Mulye, D. (2021). *What is Embedded Finance and how it will change FinTech*. Finbox.in. https://finbox.in/blog/what-is-embedded-finance-and-how-it-will-change-fintech-in-india/

Murati, A., Skau, O., & Geer, A. D. (2024, July 15). *Embedded finance: How banks and customer platforms are converging | McKinsey*. Www.mckinsey.com. https://www.mckinsey.com/industries/financial-services/our-insights/embedded-finance-how-banks-and-customer-platforms-are-converging

Murinde, V., Rizopoulos, E., & Zachariadis, M. (2022). The impact of the FinTech revolution on the future of banking: Opportunities and risks. *International Review of Financial Analysis*, *81*, 102103. DOI: 10.1016/j.irfa.2022.102103

Musleh Al-Sartawi, A. M., Hussainey, K., & Razzaque, A. (2022). The role of artificial intelligence in sustainable finance. Journal of Sustainable Finance & Investment, 1-6. / tandfonline.comDOI: 10.1080/20430795.2022.2057405

Nagy, S., Molnár, L., & Papp, A. (2024). Customer adoption of neobank services from a technology acceptance perspective–evidence from Hungary. *Decision Making: Applications in Management and Engineering*, *7*(1), 187–208.

Naidoo, C. P. (2020). Relating financial systems to sustainability transitions: Challenges, demands and design features. *Environmental Innovation and Societal Transitions*, *36*, 270–290. DOI: 10.1016/j.eist.2019.10.004

Nair, S., & Kibble, R. (2022, October 6). *Embedded finance: regulation and strategic choices | Deloitte UK*. Deloitte United Kingdom; Deloitte. https://www.deloitte.com/uk/en/Industries/financial-services/blogs/embedded-finance-regulation-and-strategic-choices.html

Negi, S. (2025, February 3). *Order now, pay later! How to unlock Swiggy's best feature*. NewsBytes. https://www.newsbytesapp.com/news/science/order-now-pay-later-how-to-unlock-swiggy-s-best-feature/story

Ng, S. H., Yang, Y., Lee, C. C., & Ong, C. Z. (2023). Nexus of financing constraints and supply chain finance: Evidence from listed SMEs in China. *International Journal of Financial Studies*, *11*(3), 102. DOI: 10.3390/ijfs11030102

Ng, T. H., Lye, C. T., Chan, K. H., Lim, Y. Z., & Lim, Y. S. (2020). Sustainability in Asia: The roles of financial development in environmental, social and governance (ESG) performance. *Social Indicators Research, 150*(1), 17–44. DOI: 10.1007/s11205-020-02288-w

Niemand, T., Rigtering, J. P. C., Kallmünzer, A., Kraus, S., & Maalaoui, A. (2021). Digitalization in the financial industry: A contingency approach of entrepreneurial orientation and strategic vision on digitalization. *European Management Journal, 39*(3), 317–326. DOI: 10.1016/j.emj.2020.04.008

Nyarko, K., Urmee, T., Whale, J., Simsek, Y., & Haigh, Y. (2025). Assessing the effectiveness of energy policies in accelerating renewable energy-based mini-grid deployment: A case study. Energy for Sustainable Development, 85, 101631. / sciencedirect.comDOI: 10.1016/j.esd.2024.101631

Obiora, S. C., Bamisile, O., Opoku-Mensah, E., & Kofi Frimpong, A. N. (2020). Impact of banking and financial systems on environmental sustainability: An overarching study of developing, emerging, and developed economies. *Sustainability (Basel), 12*(19), 8074. DOI: 10.3390/su12198074

Ohnishi, M. (2021). *NEW DIGITAL FINANCIAL SERVICES OFFER THE PROSPECT OF HIGH CUSTOMER RETENTION-EXPECTATIONS FOR THE GROWING TREND OF "EMBEDDED FINANCE."* https://www.mitsui.com/mgssi/en/report/detail/__icsFiles/afieldfile/2021/05/25/2103i_ohnishi_e.pdf

Ohnishi, M. (2021). New Digital Financial Services Offer the Prospect of High Customer Retention-Expectations for the Growing Trend of "Embedded Finance." *Mitsui&Co., March.*

Okekenwa, I. (2025). Legal challenges and opportunities in Nigeria's fintech sector. DOI: 10.2139/ssrn.5228794

Olins, J. (2022, April 19). *How are small businesses using embedded finance? - BusinessCloud.* BusinessCloud. https://businesscloud.co.uk/opinion/how-are-small-businesses-using-embedded-finance/

Omarini, A. (2023). From digital technologies to new economics in banking: how to drive the future of digital money and data information knowledge. In *Digital Transformation and the Economics of Banking* (pp. 31–49). Routledge. DOI: 10.4324/9781003340454-3

Omokhoa, H. E., Odionu, C. S., Azubuike, C., & Sule, A. K. (2022). AI-powered fintech innovations for credit scoring, debt recovery, and financial access in microfinance and SMEs. *Journal of Finance and Technology*, *18*(3), 45–67. DOI: 10.1016/j.fintech.2022.03.004

Omokhoa, H. E., Odionu, C. S., Azubuike, C., & Sule, A. K. (2024). Digital transformation in financial services: Integrating AI, FinTech, and innovative solutions for SME growth and financial inclusion. *Gulf Journal of Advance Business Research*, *2*(6), 423–434. DOI: 10.51594/gjabr.v2i6.56

Onunka, T., Raji, A., Nkemchor Osafiele, A., Daraojimba, C., Afeyokalo Egbokhaebho, B., & Chinazo Okoye, C. (2023). BANKING: A COMPREHENSIVE REVIEW OF THE EVOLUTION AND IMPACT OF INNOVATIVE BANKING SERVICES ON ENTREPRENEURIAL GROWTH. *Economic Growth and Environment Sustainability*, *2*(2), 66–78. DOI: 10.26480/egnes.02.2023.66.78

OpenPayd. (2021, September 17). *Most appealing impacts of embedded finance for European firms in 2021* [Graph]. In Statista. Retrieved April 12, 2025, from https://www-statista-com-culp.knimbus.com/statistics/1286162/benefits-of-embedded-finance-europe/

Ozili, P. K. (2022). Embedded finance: Assessing the benefits, use case, challenges and interest over time. *Journal of Internet and Digital Economics*, *2*(2), 108–123. Advance online publication. DOI: 10.1108/JIDE-05-2022-0014

Ozili, P. K. (2023). Assessing global interest in decentralized finance, embedded finance, open finance, ocean finance and sustainable finance. *Asian Journal of Economics and Banking*, *7*(2), 197–216. DOI: 10.1108/AJEB-03-2022-0029

Ozili, P. K. (2023). Digital finance research and developments around the World: A literature review. *International Journal of Business Forecasting and Marketing Intelligence*, *8*(1), 35. Advance online publication. DOI: 10.1504/IJBFMI.2023.127698

Ozili, P. K. (2023). Role of Embedded Finance in Increasing Financial Inclusion. *Social Science Research Network*. DOI: 10.2139/ssrn.4629444

Ozili, P. K. (2023c). Role of embedded finance in increasing financial inclusion. In *Adoption and Use of Technology Tools and Services by Economically Disadvantaged Communities*. Implications for Growth and Sustainability., DOI: 10.4018/978-1-6684-5347-6.ch011

Pandey, A. (2024, December 13). *How to add a new payment mode on Swiggy*. NewsBytes. https://www.newsbytesapp.com/news/science/process-to-add-new-bank-card-wallet-upi-on-swiggy/story

Parfitt, C. (2024). A foundation for 'ethical capital': The sustainability accounting standards board and integrated reporting. *Critical Perspectives on Accounting*, *98*, 102477. DOI: 10.1016/j.cpa.2022.102477

Paypers (2024). Embedded Finance and Banking-as-a-Service Report 2024. https://thepaypers.com/register?return=/fintech/reports/embedded-finance-and-banking-as-a-service-report-2024

Pedersen, L. H., Fitzgibbons, S., & Pomorski, L. (2023). Responsible investing: The ESG-efficient frontier. *Journal of Financial Economics*, *142*(2), 572–597. DOI: 10.1016/j.jfineco.2020.11.001

Pizzi, S., Corbo, L., & Caputo, A. (2021). Fintech and SMEs sustainable business models: Reflections and considerations for a circular economy. Journal of Cleaner Production. / ucp.ptDOI: 10.1016/j.jclepro.2020.125217

Poiriazi, E., Zournatzidou, G., Konteos, G., & Sariannidis, N. (2025). Analyzing the interconnection between environmental, social, and governance (ESG) criteria and corporate corruption: Revealing the significant impact of greenwashing. *Administrative Sciences*, *15*(3), 100. DOI: 10.3390/admsci15030100

Pradhan, T. K. (2023). A framework for measuring financial inclusion in India: Bridging gaps between theory and practice. Journal of Financial Counseling and Planning Randa, I. O. (2024). Financial infrastructure development for inclusive growth. In *Infrastructure development strategies for empowerment and inclusion* (pp. 209–233). IGI Global.

Precedence Research. (2025). *Embedded Finance Market Size to Hit USD 1,732.53 Bn by 2034*. Precedenceresearch.com; Precedence Research. https://www.precedenceresearch.com/embedded-finance-market

PricewaterhouseCoopers. (2023, April). *Embedded finance: Challenging common assumptions*. PwC. https://www.pwc.com/gx/en/industries/financial-services/publications/embedded-finance-challenging-common-assumptions.html

PricewaterhouseCoopers. (2024, June 18). *What does embedded finance mean for business?* PwC. https://www.pwc.com/gx/en/issues/technology/tech-translated-embedded-finance.html

Prussia, L. (2019). *Natural connections: Social work's role in mending human and environmental relationships* (Doctoral dissertation, University of St. Thomas, Minnesota). SOPHIA. https://ir.stthomas.edu/caps_graddiss/85/

Pu, G., Qamruzzaman, M. D., Mehta, A. M., Naqvi, F. N., & Karim, S. (2021). Innovative finance, technological adaptation and SMEs sustainability: the mediating role of government support during COVID-19 pandemic. Sustainability, 13(16), 9218. / mdpi.comDOI: 10.3390/su13169218

Puaschunder, J. M. (2023). The Future of Resilient Green Finance. In *The Future of Resilient Finance: Finance Politics in the Age of Sustainable Development* (pp. 185–210). Springer International Publishing. [HTML], DOI: 10.1007/978-3-031-30138-4_6

Purwandani, J. A. & Michaud, G. (2021). What are the drivers and barriers for green business practice adoption for SMEs?. Environment systems and decisions. / springer.comDOI: 10.1007/s10669-021-09821-3

PwC Malaysia. (2023). ESG deals creation and impact investing in Malaysia. https://www.pwc.com/my/en/assets/publications/2023/esg-deals-creation-and-impact-investing-in-malaysia.pdf

PwC. (2023). *Embedded finance: A strategic outlook*. https://www.pwc.in/assets/pdfs/consulting/financial-services/fintech/publications/embedded-finance-a-strategic-outlook-final.pdf

Qualtrics. (2023, December 8). *Sample Size Calculator*. Qualtrics. https://www.qualtrics.com/blog/calculating-sample-size/

Rahman, M. H., Tanchangya, T., Rahman, J., Aktar, M. A., & Majumder, S. C. (2024). Corporate social responsibility and green financing behavior in Bangladesh: Towards sustainable tourism. *Innovation and Green Development, 3*(3), Article 100133. https://www.sciencedirect.com/science/article/pii/S2949753124000109DOI: 10.1016/j.igd.2024.100133

Rakočević, S. B., & Rakić, N. (2023). The Future of Banking in FinTech Era: Decentralized and Embedded Finance. In *Contributions to Finance and Accounting: Vol. Part F233*. DOI: 10.1007/978-3-031-23269-5_6

Relja, R., Ward, P., & Zhao, A. L. (2024). Understanding the psychological determinants of buy-now-pay-later. *International Journal of Bank Marketing*, *42*(1), 7–37. DOI: 10.1108/IJBM-07-2022-0324

Research and Markets. (2022). *Embedded Finance Market Size, Competitors & Forecast to 2029*. Researchandmarkets.com. https://www.researchandmarkets.com/report/embedded-finance?srsltid=AfmBOooi6KL7i9WGKcwVtoHs41-gN4RySA2obnNZGiIbPtMV4EEerzz8

Reserve Bank of India (RBI). (2025). Digital lending directions. New Delhi. https://www.argus-p.com/updates/updates/rbi-digital-lending-directions-2025-an-overview/

Saher, L., Tabák, L., Lyeonov, S., & Vasa, L. (2024). Inclusive growth: Literature review. *Journal of International Students*, *17*(1).

Sahu, A. (2025). *M-RCBG Associate Working Paper Series | No. 247 Fintech Reimagined: Exploring the value of embedded finance for small and medium businesses.* https://www.hks.harvard.edu/sites/default/files/centers/mrcbg/Final_AWP_247.pdf

Samans, R., & Nelson, J. (2022). Corporate reporting and accountability. In *Sustainable Enterprise Value Creation: Implementing Stakeholder Capitalism through Full ESG Integration* (pp. 187–218). Springer International Publishing. DOI: 10.1007/978-3-030-93560-3_6

SASB. (2023). *SASB standards: Industry-based standards for disclosure topics & accounting metrics*. Sustainability Accounting Standards Board. https://www.sasb.org/standards/

Scholtens, B. (2006). Finance as a Driver of Corporate Social Responsibility. *Journal of Business Ethics*, *68*(1), 19–33. DOI: 10.1007/s10551-006-9037-1

Schulz, K. & Feist, M. (2021). Leveraging blockchain technology for innovative climate finance under the Green Climate Fund. Earth System Governance. / sciencedirect.comDOI: 10.1016/j.esg.2020.100084

Sciarelli, M., Cosimato, S., Landi, G., & Iandolo, F. (2021). Socially responsible investment strategies for the transition towards sustainable development: The importance of integrating and communicating ESG. The TQM Journal. / emerald.comDOI: 10.1108/TQM-08-2020-0180

SEC. (2024). Enhancement and standardization of climate-related disclosures for investors: Final rule. U.S. Securities and Exchange Commission, Release Nos. 33-11275; 34-99678.

Selvakumar, P., & Manjunath, T. C. (2025). Green Finance and Investment Explore the Role of Sustainable Finance. In Driving Business Success Through Eco-Friendly Strategies (pp. 149-168). IGI Global Scientific Publishing. DOI: [HTML]DOI: 10.4018/979-8-3693-9750-3.ch008

Sethu Pradeep. (2022, May 25). *Flipkart redesigns its app interface with a focus on groceries*. The Indian Express. https://indianexpress.com/article/technology/tech-news-technology/flipkart-redesigns-app-interface-focus-groceries-7936157/

Shafik, W. (2024a). Artificial intelligence and Blockchain technology enabling cybersecurity in telehealth systems. In *Artificial Intelligence and Blockchain Technology in Modern Telehealth Systems*. DOI: 10.1049/PBHE061E_ch11

Shafik, W. (2024e). Factors Affecting Green Purchase Behaviors for Small and Medium Enterprises (SMEs) in Uganda. In *Entrepreneurial Strategies for the Internationalization and Digitalization of SMEs* (pp. 198–224). IGI Global. DOI: 10.4018/979-8-3693-3518-5.ch009

Shafik, W. (2024f). Generative AI for Social Good and Sustainable Development. In *Generative AI: Current Trends and Applications* (pp. 185–217). Springer. DOI: 10.1007/978-981-97-8460-8_10

Shafik, W. (2024b). The Role of Artificial Intelligence in the Emerging Digital Economy Era. In *Artificial Intelligence Enabled Management* (pp. 33–50). De Gruyter., DOI: 10.1515/9783111172408-003

Shafik, W. (2024c). Data Privacy and Security Safeguarding Customer Information in ChatGPT Systems. In *Revolutionizing the Service Industry Wth OpenAI Models* (pp. 52–86). IGI Global., DOI: 10.4018/979-8-3693-1239-1.ch003

Shafik, W. (2024d). Deep Learning Impacts in the Field of Artificial Intelligence. In *Deep Learning Concepts in Operations Research* (pp. 9–26). Auerbach Publications., DOI: 10.1201/9781003433309-2

Shafik, W. (2024g). Navigating Emerging Challenges in Robotics and Artificial Intelligence in Africa. In *Examining the rapid advance of digital technology in Africa* (pp. 126–146). IGI Global., DOI: 10.4018/978-1-6684-9962-7.ch007

Shafik, W. (2024h). Science of Emotional Intelligence. In *Enhancing and Predicting Digital Consumer Behavior with AI* (pp. 284–310). IGI Global., DOI: 10.4018/979-8-3693-4453-8.ch015

Shafik, W. (2024i). Sustainable Development. In Viana Hassan, A. S. S. B. (Ed.), *Building Community Resiliency and Sustainability With Tourism Development* (1st ed., Vol. 1, pp. 1–30). IGI Global., DOI: 10.4018/979-8-3693-5405-6.ch001

Shafik, W. (2024j). Toward a More Ethical Future of Artificial Intelligence and Data Science. In *The Ethical Frontier of AI and Data Analysis* (pp. 362–388). IGI Global., DOI: 10.4018/979-8-3693-2964-1.ch022

Sharma, S. (2024). Digital Disruption in Banking: A Comparative Analysis of Neo Banks and Traditional Institutions. *International Journal of Management and Development Studies, 13*(3), 01–12. DOI: 10.53983/ijmds.v13n3.001

Siddik, A. B., Rahman, M. N., & Yong, L. (2023, October 1). Do fintech adoption and financial literacy improve corporate sustainability performance? The mediating role of access to finance. *Journal of Cleaner Production, 421*, 137658. DOI: 10.1016/j.jclepro.2023.137658

Sieber, S., & Guibaud, S. (2022). *Embedded finance: When payments become an experience*. John Wiley & Sons.

Silver, N. (2017). *Finance, society and sustainability: How to make the financial system work for the economy, people and planet*. Springer. DOI: 10.1057/978-1-137-56061-2

Simanjuntak, R. (2024). Navigating the Dynamics of Corporate Financial Management for Sustainable Growth. *Advances in Economics & Financial Studies, 2*(2), 53–66. DOI: 10.60079/aefs.v2i2.172

Simatele, M. C., Dube, Z., Khumalo, S., Ssonko, G. W., Kawooya, D. R., Bwalya, M., & Mutyavaviri, T. (2021). *Financial inclusion: Basic theories and empirical evidence from African countries*. AOSIS. DOI: 10.4102/aosis.2021.BK255

Sirakova-Yordanova, G. (2024). Banks Go Beyond Banking: The Expansion Towards Non-Banking Services. *Proceedings of the International Conference on Business Excellence, 18*(1), 391–404. DOI: 10.2478/picbe-2024-0034

Skaleet. (2023). *Embedded Finance – an opportunity for growth for SMEs...* Skaleet. https://skaleet.com/en/blog/embedded-finance-growth-opportunity-for-pme-and-financial-institutions

Smith, S. M. (2024). *Determining Sample Size How to Ensure You Get the Correct Sample Size*. https://www.k-state.edu/it/resources/teaching-learning/survey/pdfs/determine-sample-size.pdf

Sneideriene, A., & Legenzova, R. (2025). Greenwashing prevention in environmental, social, and governance (ESG) disclosures: A bibliometric analysis. *Research in International Business and Finance, 74*, 102720. DOI: 10.1016/j.ribaf.2024.102720

Sokolov, M. (2022, February). *Embedded finance use cases from 30 embedded finance companies. - PSP Lab*. PSP Lab. https://psplab.com/embedded-finance-use-cases-embedded-finance-companies/

Soni, S. (2021, March 30). *India's gig economy comprising Zomato, Swiggy, Ola, Dunzo, others may serve 90m jobs, add 1.25% to GDP*. Financialexpress. https://www.financialexpress.com/business/sme-indias-gig-economy-comprising-zomato-swiggy-ola-dunzo-others-may-serve-90m-jobs-add-1-25-to-gdp-2223519/

Soriano, M. A. (2017). Factors driving financial inclusion and financial performance in Fintech new ventures: An empirical study.

Sowndarya, L., & Yashaswini, M. (2024). A Study on Usage of UPI Payment on Food Delivery Industry - A Case Study of Zomato. *International Journal of Research Publication and Reviews*, *5*(4), 8635–8643. DOI: 10.55248/gengpi.5.0424.1101

Sparks, J. L. D., Massey Combs, K., & Yu, J. (2019). Social work students' perspective on environmental justice: Gaps and challenges for preparing students. *Journal of Community Practice*, *27*(3–4), 476–486. DOI: 10.1080/10705422.2019.1655124

Stasytytė, V. (2015). Conceptualization of financial system sustainability.

Statista. (2023). *ECommerce Report 2023 | Statista*. Statista; Statista. https://www.statista.com/study/42335/ecommerce-report/

Stern, N., & Valero, A. (2021). Innovation, growth and the transition to net-zero emissions. *Research Policy*, *50*(9), 104293. DOI: 10.1016/j.respol.2021.104293

Supersourcing. (2025). *Dunzo | Supersourcing*. Supersourcing.com. https://supersourcing.com/case-studies/dunzo.html

Suri, M. (2024, August 9). *Swiggy Business Model & Growth Strategy*. Growthx.club. https://growthx.club/blog/swiggy-business-model

Svoboda, A. (2023). ESG imperative: The role of financial institutions in a sustainable future. *International Journal of Engineering Technology Research & Management*, *7*(11), 34–41.

Swift, T. (2002). Trust, reputation and corporate accountability to stakeholders. *Business Ethics (Oxford, England)*, *10*(1), 16–26. DOI: 10.1111/1467-8608.00208

Talan, G., Sharma, G. D., Pereira, V., & Muschert, G. W. (2024). From ESG to holistic value addition: Rethinking sustainable investment from the lens of stakeholder theory. International Review of Economics & Finance, 96, 103530. /DOI: 10.1016/j.iref.2024.103530

Taneja, B. (2024). Financial Innovations in FinTech: Unleashing the Power of Embedded Finance and AI in Firm Financing and Investment Strategies. In Contemporary Research and Practices for Promoting Financial Literacy and Sustainability (pp. 208-232). IGI Global. DOI: [HTML]DOI: 10.4018/979-8-3693-0863-9.ch008

Tay, L. Y., Tai, H. T., & Tan, G. S. (2022). Digital financial inclusion: A gateway to sustainable development. *Heliyon*, *8*(6), e09766. DOI: 10.1016/j.heliyon.2022.e09766 PMID: 35785228

TCFD. (2022). *Recommendations of the Task Force on Climate-related Financial Disclosures: Final report*. Financial Stability Board. https://www.fsb-tcfd.org/recommendations/

Technuter. (2025). *Page Restricted*. Technuter.com. https://technuter.com/breaking-news/snapdeal-changes-its-website-and-app-look-to-refresh-the-user-experience.html

Teichmann, F. M. J., Wittmann, C., & Sergi, B. S. S. (2023). What are the consequences of corporate greenwashing? A look into the consequences of greenwashing in consumer and financial markets. Journal of Information [HTML]. *Communication and Ethics in Society*, *21*(3), 290–301. DOI: 10.1108/JICES-10-2022-0090

Telukdarie, K. K., & A, T. (2023). Digital Ecosystems in Financial Services driven by Embedded Finance Platforms in South Africa. *SSRN Electronic Journal*. DOI: 10.2139/ssrn.4331766

The Edge Malaysia. (2022). Green financing and incentives in Malaysia. https://theedgemalaysia.com/article/green-financing-and-incentives-malaysia

The United Nations Principles for Responsible Investment. What Is ESG integration? https://www.unpri.org/investor-tools/what-is-esg-integration/3052.article.

TheBigMarketing.com. (2024, April 21). *Snapdeal Marketing Strategy 2025: A Case Study - TheBigMarketing.com*. TheBigMarketing.com. https://thebigmarketing.com/snapdeal-marketing-strategy/

Thommandru, A., & Chakka, D. B. (2023). Recalibrating the Banking Sector with Blockchain Technology for Effective Anti-Money Laundering Compliances by Banks. *Sustainable Futures : An Applied Journal of Technology, Environment and Society*, *5*, 100107. DOI: 10.1016/j.sftr.2023.100107

Torrance, S. (2021). *a $7 Trillion gamechanging opportunity for incumbents*. https://discover.rainmaking.io/hubfs/Embedded%20Finance/Embedded%20Finance%20Report.pdf

Townsend, Z. (2021). *What the embedded-finance and banking-as-a-service trends mean for financial services*. Mckinsey & Company.

Triantafyllidou, E. & Zabaniotou, A. (2021). Digital technology and social innovation promoting a green citizenship: development of the "go sustainable living" digital application. Circular Economy and Sustainability. / academia.eduDOI: 10.1007/s43615-021-00111-3

Tripathy, A. (2022). Careers and climates Becoming and being a climate finance practitioner. *Focaal, 2022*(93). DOI: 10.3167/fcl.2022.930103

Tullio, D. (2020, November 12). *Embedded finance: The future of fintech. | Airbase*. Airbase | Spend Management Done Right | Airbase. https://www.airbase.com/blog/embedded-finance-the-future-of-fintech

UN PRI. (2023). *Annual report 2023: Principles for Responsible Investment*. United Nations-supported Principles for Responsible Investment Initiative. https://www.unpri.org/annual-report-2023

UNCTAD. (2024). World Investment Report 2024: Chapter III Sustainable finance. https://unctad.org/system/files/official-document/wir2024_ch03_en.pdf

United Nations Environment Programme Finance Initiative (UNEP FI). (2021). A systemic approach to finance sustainability. https://www.unepfi.org/

United Nations Environment Programme Finance Initiative (UNEP FI). (2025). Principles for Responsible Banking. https://www.unepfi.org/banking/bankingprinciples/

United Nations Environment Programme. (2022). Why financial institutions are banking on sustainability. https://www.unep.org/news-and-stories/story/why-financial-institutions-are-banking-sustainability

United Nations. (2025). Greenwashing – The deceptive tactics behind environmental claims. https://www.un.org/en/climatechange/science/climate-issues/greenwashing

Unsal, O., & Ozkan, B. (2024). *Technologies and Emerging Trends Shaping Fintech*. The Emerald Handbook of Fintech. [HTML], DOI: 10.1108/978-1-83753-608-520241046

Valavan, T. A. (2024). Sustainable finance and environmental, social, and governance (ESG) investing. *Journal of Critical Reviews*, *11*(3), 10–18.

van Klyton, A., & Rutabayiro-Ngoga, S. (2018). SME finance and the construction of value in Rwanda. *Journal of Small Business and Enterprise Development*, *25*(4), 628–643. Advance online publication. DOI: 10.1108/JSBED-02-2017-0046

van Rijnsoever, F. J. (2022). Intermediaries for the greater good: How entrepreneurial support organizations can embed constrained sustainable development startups in entrepreneurial .... Research Policy. / sciencedirect.comDOI: 10.1016/j.respol.2021.104438

Vijai, & Wisetsri, W. (2024). Circular economy for sustainable development in India. In *Global Sustainability: Trends, Challenges & Case Studies* (pp. 61-87). Cham: Springer Nature Switzerland.

Wagner, M. (2010). The role of corporate sustainability performance for economic performance: A firm-level analysis of moderation effects. *Ecological Economics, 69*(7), 1553–1560. DOI: 10.1016/j.ecolecon.2010.02.017

Waliszewski, K. (2023). Banking-as-a-Service and Embedded Banking as Innovative Methods of Providing Banking Services. In Digital Transformation and the Economics of Banking (pp. 50-66). Routledge. DOI: 10.4324/9781003340454-4

Waliszewski, K. (2023). Socio-economic determinants of financial inclusion in Central and Eastern Europe during the COVID-19 pandemic. *Przegląd Wschodnioeuropejski, 14*(1), 25–41. DOI: 10.31648/pw.9019

Walls, J. L., Berrone, P., & Phan, P. H. (2012). Corporate governance and environmental performance: Is there really a link? *Strategic Management Journal, 33*(8), 885–913. DOI: 10.1002/smj.1952

Wang, L. (2024). Challenges and Opportunities of ESG Integration in Financial Operations. In *International Conference on Finance and Economics* (Vol. 6, No. 1). DOI: 10.22158/mmse.v6n1p162

Wangsong, X. (2022). The Default Risk of Bank Customers Based on Embedded Microprocessor Wireless Communication under the Internet Finance Background. *Mobile Information Systems, 2022*, 1–15. Advance online publication. DOI: 10.1155/2022/8019033

Wang, W., & Qu, Z. (2024). Capital market opening and commercial bank risk: Evidence from "Shanghai–Hong Kong Stock Connect". *Finance Research Letters, 59*, 104827. DOI: 10.1016/j.frl.2023.104827

Widodo, A. (2019). The role of integrated Islamic commercial and social finance in reducing income inequality in Indonesia. *Journal of Islamic Monetary Economics and Finance, 5*(2), 263–286. DOI: 10.21098/jimf.v5i2.1063

Wiek, A., & Weber, O. (2014). Sustainability challenges and the ambivalent role of the financial sector. *Journal of Sustainable Finance & Investment, 4*(1), 9–20. DOI: 10.1080/20430795.2014.887349

World Bank Group. (2022). Unleashing sustainable finance in Southeast Asia. Institute of Finance and Sustainability. https://documents1.worldbank.org/curated/en/099310011232220307/pdf/P177802011f7760130bc49083a7beb1ef43.pdf

World Bank. (2020). *Embedding Digital Finance in e-Commerce Platforms during the COVID-19 Pandemic*. https://documents1.worldbank.org/curated/en/819411608643348469/pdf/Embedding-Digital-Finance-in-e-Commerce-Platforms-during-the-COVID-19-Pandemic

World Bank. (2021). The Global Findex Database 2021. https://openknowledge.worldbank.org/bitstream/handle/10986/37578/9781464818974.pdf

World Bank. (2025). Financial inclusion. https://www.worldbank.org/en/topic/financialinclusion/overview

World Bank. (2025). Sustainable finance. https://www.worldbank.org/en/country/malaysia/publication/malaysia-sustainable-finance

World Commission on Environment and Development (WCED). (1987). *Our common future*. Oxford University Press.

World Economic Forum. (2021). Here's why comparable ESG reporting is crucial for investors. https://www.weforum.org/stories/2021/07/comparable-esg-investors/

Wu, Y., Wu, Y., Cimen, H., Vasquez, J. C., & Guerrero, J. M. (2022). Towards collective energy Community: Potential roles of microgrid and blockchain to go beyond P2P energy trading. Applied Energy. / sciencedirect.comDOI: 10.1016/j.apenergy.2022.119003

Wullweber, J. (2019). Embedded Finance: The Shadow Banking System, Monetary Politics and Sovereign Power. SSRN *Electronic Journal*. DOI: 10.2139/ssrn.3431909

Wullweber, J. (2020). Embedded finance: The shadow banking system, sovereign power, and a new state–market hybridity. *Journal of Cultural Economics*, *13*(5), 592–609. DOI: 10.1080/17530350.2020.1741015

Xie, X., Gong, C., Su, Z., Nie, Y., & Kim, W. (2024). Consumers' Behavioral Willingness to Use Green Financial Products: An Empirical Study within a Theoretical Framework. Behavioral Sciences. / mdpi.comDOI: 10.3390/bs14080634

Yildirim, Z. & Şendeniz-Yüncü, I. (2025). Financial development, international financial integration, and income inequality: An emerging markets perspective. *Research in International Business and Finance, 77*(Part A), 102917. https://doi.org/.DOI: 10.1016/j.ribaf.2025.102917

Young, J., Wong, W., & Taiyabi, S. (2022). *FinTech in ASEAN 2022: Finance, Reimagined. United Overseas Bank Limited ('UOB"), PricewaterhouseCoopers Risk Services Pte. Ltd. ("PwC Singapore") and Singapore FinTech Association*. SFA.

Zervoudi, E. K., Moschos, N., & Christopoulos, A. G. (2025). From the corporate social responsibility (CSR) and the environmental, social and governance (ESG) criteria to the greenwashing phenomenon: A comprehensive literature review about the causes, consequences and solutions of the phenomenon with specific case studies. *Sustainability (Basel)*, *17*(5), 2222. DOI: 10.3390/su17052222

Zetzsche, D. A., & Anker-Sørensen, L. (2022). Regulating sustainable finance in the dark. European Business Organization Law Review, 23(1), 47-85. springer. comDOI: 10.1007/s40804-021-00237-9

Zheng, K., Zheng, L. J., Gauthier, J., Zhou, L., Xu, Y., Behl, A., & Zhang, J. Z. (2022). Blockchain technology for enterprise credit information sharing in supply chain finance. *Journal of Innovation and Knowledge*, *7*(4), 100256. Advance online publication. DOI: 10.1016/j.jik.2022.100256

Zhichao, Y., Farooq, U., Alam, M. M., & Dai, J. (2024). How does environmental, social, and governance (ESG) performance determine investment mix? New empirical evidence from BRICS. *Borsa Istanbul Review*, *24*(3), 520–529. DOI: 10.1016/j.bir.2024.02.007

Ziolo, M., Bak, I., & Cheba, K. (2021). The role of sustainable finance in achieving sustainable development goals: Does it work?. Technological and Economic Development of Economy, 27(1), 45-70. / vgtu.lt Driessen, N. (2021). Methane Emissions and Financial Structures-The role of Finance in mitigating Environmental Degradation.DOI: 10.3846/tede.2020.13863

Zioło, M., Bąk, I., Cheba, K., Spoz, A., & Niedzielski, P. (2021). Sustainable financial systems toward sustainability in finance. Institutional and managerial approach. *Procedia Computer Science*, *192*, 4237–4248. DOI: 10.1016/j.procs.2021.09.200

Ziolo, M., Filipiak, B. Z., Bąk, I., & Cheba, K. (2019). How to design more sustainable financial systems: The roles of environmental, social, and governance factors in the decision-making process. *Sustainability (Basel)*, *11*(20), 5604. DOI: 10.3390/su11205604

Ziouache, A., & Bouteraa, M. (2023). Descriptive approach of neo-banking system: Conception, challenges and global practices. *International Journal of Business and Technology Management*, *5*(2), 194–204.

# About the Contributors

**Lee Chin Yee** is a distinguished Senior Lecturer at Taylor's University, Malaysia, specialising in wealth management, housing finance, transportation, and urban planning. Dr. Lee Chin Yee is deeply committed to research, focusing on data-driven solutions to enhance the sustainability of wealth management, housing finance, sustainable transportation systems, and urban planning strategies. Her extensive expertise and innovative approach enable students to navigate complex data landscapes and address critical issues in financial stability, housing, transportation, and urban planning. She is highly motivated and passionate about conducting significant research that extends beyond academic boundaries. Besides her academic contributions, she was the Division Director for Toastmasters International District 102 during 2023-2024 and serves as Rakan Nasihat Komuniti under KKM. She was awarded a community grant to share her knowledge and experience with the community, aiming to improve their quality of life. In 2024, she was selected as the representative for the Women's Selangor State Assembly.

**Thilageswary Arumugam** is an accomplished academic with over 15 years of diverse experience in lecturing, research, and program management. She specializes in Human Resource Management, Business Management, and Research Methodology, with a strong focus on quantitative research methods and people analytics. Dr. Thilageswary currently serves as a Senior Lecturer and Program Manager (DBA) at the University of Malaya Wales, where she has successfully developed accredited DBA programs and spearheaded initiatives to enhance student retention and satisfaction. She holds a Ph.D. and a Master's degree in Human Resource Development from Universiti Putra Malaysia, along with certifications in People Analytics and Environmental, Social, and Governance (ESG) practices. Throughout her career, Dr. Thilageswary has demonstrated exceptional leadership, including roles as Program Leader for postgraduate programs at Asia Pacific University of Technology & Innovation and Editor-in-Chief of the Electronic

Journal of Business Management. A dedicated researcher, Dr. Thilageswary has supervised numerous postgraduate projects and contributed to an extensive array of publications indexed in SCOPUS and Web of Science. Her research delves into high-impact topics such as workplace engagement, leadership dynamics, and sustainable organizational practices. Dr. Thilageswary is also a recognized trainer, having conducted workshops on SPSS, research methodologies, and academic writing. Her awards include the Best Presenter accolades at various international conferences, highlighting her contributions to the academic and research community. Driven by a passion for continuous learning and innovation, Dr. Thilageswary remains committed to advancing human resource practices and developing future leaders in academia and industry.

***

**Gargee Banerjee**, an Assistant Professor in Commerce teaches in Raja Madhusudan Dev Degree College, Bhubaneswar and holds a Master's Degree in both Commerce (Financial Accounting & Auditing) and Business Management (HR & Finance), also is a research scholar pursuing research in HR. Her experience is enriched in both corporate and academic fields. She delved into academics early on from 2003 and although she had a good career in corporate, her fondness for education has kept her teaching side alive all along, thus being a teacher for more than twenty years. She is a accomplished lecturer who is also into research. Till now she has attended many national and international seminars, workshops and conventions, wherein she has also presented her papers. Some of her chapters have also been published in international books and journals. She is a student friendly teacher and a social worker too. She loves to be kept to herself and her students abreast of latest happenings all around the world, at the same time keeping her moral and social compass alive. She is very sincere and strives for betterment in her field of teaching and learning. She has successfully mentored many students in their career path and life.

**Abhijeet Chandrakant Birari** is an accomplished academic and finance professional, currently serving as an Assistant Professor in the Department of Commerce, Finance, and Accountancy at CHRIST (Deemed to be University), Pune Lavasa Campus. He holds a Ph.D. in Derivatives Market from Swami Ramanand Teerth Marathwada University and an MBA in Finance from D.Y. Patil Institute of Management. With over a decade of experience in stock market trading and training, Dr. Birari specializes in algorithmic trading, technical analysis, financial modeling, and analytics. Dr. Birari has authored three books and mentored more than 5,000 students globally, reflecting his commitment to education and financial literacy. He has contributed to several peer-reviewed journals, including a recent publication on speculative investment decisions in cryptocurrency in the Journal of Decision Systems. His academic involvement extends to presenting at international conferences and delivering invited talks on predictive analysis and financial analytics. Notably, he co-founded the student-led initiative #CenFiL, a YouTube channel aimed at enhancing financial literacy, which contributed to CHRIST University Lavasa's recognition in the WURI 2024 rankings. Dr. Birari's dedication to integrating practical financial skills with academic rigor makes him a valuable asset to the field of commerce and finance education.

**Ela Elliyana** is Senior Lecturer (Lektor) at Universitas Indonesia Timur (UIT). She is an expert in Financial Management, Behavioral Finance, and Entrepreneurship. Dr. Ela completed her undergraduate studies in Financial and Banking Management before pursuing master's and doctoral degrees in Financial Management. Currently serving as a Senior Lecturer, she has demonstrated consistent dedication to advancing education and research in financial management and entrepreneurship. Her research focuses include: Financial literacy and inclusion; Debt management literacy and loan self-control; Behavioral finance among SMEs; and Digital entrepreneurship education. All research projects are institutionally supported and have contributed to strengthening financial empowerment and sustainable business development in Indonesia.

**Garapati Gouri Sathvika** is currently pursuing her final year of Bachelor of Commerce in Financial Analytics at Christ University, Lavasa. Her academic interests lie at the intersection of finance, data analytics, and emerging financial technologies. Throughout her undergraduate program, she has undertaken various research-oriented assignments and simulations, with a focus on portfolio management, financial risk analysis, working capital management, and ESG-based financial performance. She has actively contributed to academic forums, case studies, and institutional events, demonstrating analytical and research capabilities. Sathvika has also gained practical exposure through internships and collaborative projects that emphasize financial modelling, strategic decision-making, and receivables management in real-world business contexts. Her research aims to contribute to contemporary discussions in financial strategy and analytics, with a long-term goal of fostering data-driven and sustainable financial practices.

**Manika Garg** is a visionary Research Analyst, Author, Career Coach, and Mentor with a proven track record of publishing numerous research papers in reputable international journals including Springer, ABDC and Scopus. With expertise in multidisciplinary research, academic writing, and career development,

Dr. Manika has made significant contributions to various fields, including Financial Engineering, Banking Digitalisation, Artificial Intelligence in Banking Sector, Financial Inclusion, Financial Modelling and FinTech. As an author, Dr. Manika has written and published several books and book chapters on topics related to Working Capital Management, Portfolio Management and Financial Engineering etc, showcasing their ability to communicate complex ideas to diverse audiences. As a career coach and mentor, She has provided guidance and support to students and professionals, helping them navigate their academic and professional pursuits. With a strong background in research design, data analysis, and interpretation, She is well-equipped to conduct high-quality research and provide expert mentorship. Through their work, she aims to inspire and empower individuals to achieve their full potential and make a positive impact in their respective fields. She has touched the lives of countless individuals, empowering them to achieve remarkable success and make a lasting impact in their respective fields. What sets Dr. Manika apart is their unique ability to transcend geographical boundaries, providing research coaching to working professionals across the world. From corporate executives to industry leaders, She has worked with diverse professionals, helping them to develop research skills, craft compelling narratives, and drive innovation in their organizations. Their expertise in bridging the gap between academia and industry has made them a sought-after expert in the global research community. Her exceptional expertise, coupled with their passion for knowledge sharing and mentorship, has earned them numerous prestigious awards and recognition from esteemed institutions. As a true trailblazer, Dr. Manika continues to push the frontiers of knowledge, inspiring others to join them on this extraordinary journey of discovery and growth. With a legacy that spans continents and industries, She remains committed to empowering individuals to achieve excellence and make a meaningful difference in the world.

**Shuchi Gupta** has 20 years of teaching experience in the field of Accounting and finance. Currently, she is working as Associate Professor of Accounting & Finance, College of Business and Management, University of Hail, Kingdom of Saudi Arabia. Previously She worked as Associate Professor of Accounting and Finance for 2 years in College of Business Administration at Debre Markos University, Ethiopia. In order to gain international exposure, so far she visited 5 Countries. Before moving abroad, she served in different well-reputed institutes and colleges in India. Actually, her teaching career started 20 years back. She started her teaching career as Faculty in 1999 at Maharaja Agrasen College, Jagadhri where she completed her graduation and post-graduation. During her student life, she achieved 6th University position in M.COM and 4th District Position in B.com. She completed her Ph.D. In commerce from CCS, University, Meerut in 2008. Iin 2011 she did MBA in Finance from MD University, Rohtak. She Published more than 30 research papers in various reputed National and International journals and presented 20 papers in National and International conferences.

**Monika Handayani** is a distinguished academic and consultant with a strong focus on sustainability reporting. She currently serves as a lecturer and senate member at Politeknik Negeri Banjarmasin, as well as an Internal Quality Assurance System Auditor. In addition, she is an Assurer for Sustainability Reporting at the National Center for Sustainability Reporting in Jakarta, specializing in the evaluation of sustainability reports for mining, oil, and gas companies across Indonesia. Her academic qualifications are extensive, including a Bachelor's degree in Economics and Accounting, a Master's degree in Governmental Management Accounting, and a Doctorate in Accounting from Universitas Brawijaya, Malang. Monika Handayani is also a certified specialist in sustainability reporting, quality management auditing, chartered accountancy, and export management, holding several prestigious certifications such as Certified Sustainability Reporting Specialist (CSRS), Certified Sustainability Reporting Assurance (CSRA), Certified Accountant (CA), and Certified International Internal Quality

**Arindam Nag** is a finance enthusiast with a keen interest in AI-driven investment strategies, sustainable finance, and the role of technology in reshaping financial systems. Currently pursuing a BBA in Financial Technology Honors at CHRIST (Deemed to be University), Delhi NCR, he explores how embedded finance can drive sustainable growth.

**Indra Pahala** is Senior Lecturer (Lektor Kepala) at State University of Jakarta (UNJ). He is Expertise in Accounting, Taxation, Corporate Governance. Dr. Indra Pahala completed his undergraduate studies in Accounting before pursuing master's and doctoral degrees. Currently serving as a Senior Lecturer at UNJ with the rank of Penata (Grade III D), demonstrating his significant dedication and contributions to academia. Research focuses include: Corporate governance and accountability; Taxpayer behavior and taxation systems; Financial reporting and accounting standards; All research projects funded by BLU UNJ. Actively contributes to the development of accounting and taxation knowledge in Indonesia. His research has been applied in policy-making and business practices.

**Rismawati** +6281334488341 Universitas Muhammadiyah Palopo Jl. Jenderal Sudirman No. 03 Kota Palopo, Sulawesi Selatan 91922 risma11@umpalopo.ac .id Rismawati is a distinguished academic and consultant with a robust focus on sustainability reporting. She currently holds the position of lecturer and Head of the Quality Assurance Institute at Universitas Muhammadiyah Palopo, where she has been pivotal in ensuring the quality of university processes and outputs since

February 2020. Additionally, she serves as an Assurer for Sustainability Reporting at the National Center for Sustainability Reporting in Jakarta, specializing in the evaluation of sustainability reports for mining companies across Indonesia. Her academic qualifications are extensive, comprising a Bachelor's degree in Economics and Accounting, a Master's degree in Accounting Science, and a Doctorate in Accounting from Universitas Brawijaya, Malang. Rismawati is also a certified specialist in sustainability reporting, risk management, and tax planning, holding several prestigious certifications including Certified Sustainability Reporting Specialist (CSRS), Certified Risk Management Practitioner (CRMP), Certified Management Accountant (CMA) and Certified Enterprise Risk Analysis (CERA). In her professional capacity, she has provided consultancy services in financial management and tax compliance for companies such as PT. Reski Barito Timur and PT. Helay Raya. Furthermore, she has authored multiple publications on Social Accounting, Sustainability Accounting, Management Accounting and CSR, contributing significantly to the academic community. Her interests in reading, writing, and travel reflect her commitment to lifelong learning and professional growth in her field.

**Wasswa Shafik** (Member, IEEE) received a Bachelor of Science degree in information technology from Ndejje University, Uganda, a Master of Engineering degree in Information Technology (Computer and Communication Networks) from Yazd University, Iran, and a PhD in Computer Science with the School of Digital Science, Universiti Brunei Darussalam, Brunei Darussalam. He is also the Founder and Research Director of the Dig Connectivity Research Laboratory (DCRLab) after serving as a Research Associate at the Network Interconnectivity Research Laboratory at Yazd University. Prior to this, he worked as a Community Data Analyst at Population Services International (PSI-Uganda), a Community Data Officer at the Programme for Accessible Health Communication (PACE-Uganda), a Research Assistant at the Socio-Economic Data Centre (SEDC-Uganda), Uganda, an Assistant Data Officer at TechnoServe, Kampala, Uganda, and Asmaah Charity Organization as Cheif Executive Officer. He has hundreds of publications with renowned publishers. His research interests include Artificial Intelligence, Neural Networks, Computer Vision, Smart Agriculture, Digital Health, and Green Computing.

# Index


## A

Aadhaar 1, 2, 32, 40
Advocate 81, 242, 258, 260, 261, 266, 268, 274
AI 14, 16, 28, 50, 55, 57, 58, 67, 77, 78, 81, 85, 91, 93, 96, 97, 101, 103, 107, 120, 121, 129, 130, 131, 132, 133, 134, 135, 136, 137, 138, 139, 140, 141, 142, 143, 145, 146, 147, 148, 150, 152, 153, 154, 155, 156, 160, 161, 163, 165, 166, 169, 173, 174, 177, 178, 179, 180, 181, 183, 188, 189, 190, 194, 197, 199, 202, 203, 204, 205, 206, 207, 216, 217, 223, 224, 225, 226, 233, 235, 242, 245, 251, 252
API 24, 25, 26, 27, 28, 29, 32, 37, 38, 40, 41, 44, 46, 47, 48, 49, 50, 51, 54, 55, 56, 59, 60, 62, 66, 70, 82, 83, 96, 98, 100, 103, 148, 278

## B

Behavioral Finance 65, 86, 200
Business Model Innovation 91, 93, 103, 104, 106, 114

## C

CAPM 197
Carbon Credits 169, 179, 182, 184, 185, 208, 244
Consumer Satisfaction 116, 117, 118
Core Banking Systems 1, 2

## D

DeFi 65, 85, 169, 170, 175, 176, 179, 180, 197, 207, 208, 209, 210, 225, 235
Digital Banking 1, 2, 4, 5, 8, 13, 15, 16, 17, 87, 124, 149, 158, 166, 174, 201, 217
Digital India 1, 2
Digital Payments 2, 21, 36, 45, 53, 58, 99, 104, 108, 111, 166, 172, 173, 182, 183, 185, 188, 225

## E

E-Commerce 22, 31, 36, 38, 48, 60, 61, 62, 74, 75, 76, 80, 91, 92, 95, 96, 97, 98, 100, 102, 104, 105, 106, 107, 108, 109, 114, 115, 119, 122, 128, 156, 167, 169, 201, 216
Economic Growth 19, 62, 63, 66, 68, 69, 76, 81, 82, 86, 96, 130, 157, 164, 189, 233, 237, 238, 248, 258, 260, 261, 262, 263, 268, 273, 275, 276
Economy 16, 22, 24, 29, 36, 40, 42, 45, 46, 48, 54, 69, 75, 88, 91, 95, 97, 107, 114, 121, 127, 131, 133, 135, 140, 143, 144, 146, 148, 149, 153, 160, 165, 166, 169, 170, 171, 178, 183, 184, 185, 186, 187, 189, 191, 192, 193, 194, 195, 235, 236, 237, 239, 242, 245, 250, 251, 252, 257, 258, 259, 262, 263, 264, 265, 266, 267, 268, 270, 271, 272, 273, 274, 275, 276, 277, 278
Embedded Finance 21, 22, 23, 24, 25, 26, 28, 29, 30, 31, 32, 33, 35, 39, 44, 46, 47, 48, 49, 52, 53, 54, 55, 56, 59, 60, 61, 62, 63, 64, 65, 66, 70, 71, 72, 73, 74, 75, 76, 77, 78, 79, 80, 81, 82, 83, 84, 85, 86, 87, 88, 89, 91, 92, 93, 94, 95, 96, 97, 98, 99, 100, 101, 102, 103, 104, 105, 106, 107, 108, 109, 110, 111, 112, 113, 114, 115, 116, 117, 118, 119, 120, 121, 122, 123, 124, 125, 126, 127, 129, 130, 131, 132, 133, 134, 135, 139, 140, 141, 142, 143, 149, 150, 153, 154, 155, 156, 157, 158, 159, 160, 161, 163, 164, 165, 166, 167, 168, 169, 170, 171, 172, 173, 174, 176, 177, 178, 179, 180, 181, 182, 183, 184, 185, 186, 187, 188, 193, 194, 197, 198, 199, 200, 201, 202, 203, 204, 206, 207, 211, 212, 213, 214, 215, 217, 218, 219, 220, 221, 222, 223, 224
Environmental 62, 64, 68, 69, 70, 71, 75,

76, 80, 82, 83, 87, 89, 129, 130, 139, 142, 143, 144, 146, 147, 152, 154, 155, 156, 164, 165, 166, 168, 169, 171, 172, 173, 174, 175, 177, 178, 179, 181, 183, 184, 185, 186, 188, 189, 190, 192, 193, 195, 197, 198, 199, 200, 202, 203, 204, 205, 206, 208, 209, 211, 213, 215, 216, 217, 218, 219, 221, 222, 223, 224, 225, 228, 229, 230, 235, 236, 237, 238, 240, 241, 242, 243, 244, 245, 246, 248, 250, 251, 252, 253, 254, 255, 257, 258, 259, 260, 261, 262, 263, 265, 266, 267, 268, 269, 270, 271, 272, 273, 274, 275, 276, 278, 279
ESG 62, 63, 64, 68, 69, 70, 71, 72, 73, 75, 76, 77, 78, 80, 81, 82, 83, 84, 85, 142, 143, 144, 145, 155, 163, 164, 165, 166, 167, 168, 169, 170, 172, 173, 175, 176, 177, 178, 179, 180, 181, 182, 183, 184, 185, 186, 187, 188, 189, 190, 191, 192, 194, 197, 198, 199, 200, 201, 202, 203, 204, 205, 206, 207, 208, 210, 211, 212, 213, 214, 215, 216, 217, 218, 219, 220, 221, 222, 223, 224, 225, 226, 227, 228, 229, 230, 232, 236, 239, 240, 241, 242, 243, 244, 245, 246, 247, 248, 249, 250, 251, 252, 253, 254, 255
ESG Data Quality 206
ESG Integration 63, 68, 70, 71, 144, 192, 201, 205, 212, 217, 240, 241, 243, 252, 253, 254
ESG Investments 180, 244, 246, 251

# F

Financial Inclusion 1, 2, 10, 13, 15, 16, 17, 18, 21, 22, 23, 25, 27, 32, 39, 44, 45, 46, 49, 53, 54, 56, 57, 59, 61, 62, 63, 65, 66, 67, 68, 70, 71, 72, 73, 74, 75, 77, 78, 79, 80, 82, 83, 84, 85, 86, 87, 88, 92, 96, 97, 100, 102, 103, 107, 108, 111, 124, 126, 129, 130, 131, 135, 147, 154, 160, 168, 170, 182, 183, 189, 195, 224, 231, 232, 233, 237, 238, 248, 251, 252, 254
Financial Inclusion in Emerging Markets 21, 39
Financial Services 2, 3, 8, 9, 11, 13, 14, 15, 16, 18, 21, 22, 23, 25, 26, 27, 28, 31, 42, 48, 49, 53, 60, 61, 62, 63, 64, 65, 66, 67, 71, 74, 75, 78, 80, 82, 83, 86, 87, 92, 93, 94, 97, 98, 99, 100, 101, 104, 105, 106, 107, 110, 111, 112, 115, 118, 119, 121, 122, 125, 129, 130, 131, 132, 133, 134, 135, 148, 149, 150, 151, 152, 155, 159, 161, 166, 167, 168, 169, 175, 182, 198, 200, 201, 202, 206, 207, 209, 210, 211, 221, 222, 225, 227, 229, 230, 231, 232, 233, 236, 237, 239, 245, 252, 262
Fintech 2, 3, 10, 15, 18, 19, 24, 30, 35, 37, 47, 48, 51, 58, 59, 67, 68, 71, 72, 74, 76, 78, 81, 83, 84, 85, 86, 88, 92, 94, 98, 99, 105, 107, 109, 110, 111, 112, 116, 120, 122, 123, 124, 125, 126, 127, 133, 137, 141, 145, 150, 153, 154, 159, 160, 161, 163, 165, 166, 168, 169, 170, 171, 173, 189, 190, 191, 192, 193, 194, 195, 224, 226, 231, 232, 233, 234, 235, 236, 237, 238, 242, 243, 245, 247, 248, 249, 250, 251, 252, 253
Fintech and Green Finance 189
Fintech Innovation 94, 98, 99, 235, 247
Food Delivery 30, 91, 104, 105, 106, 110, 111, 112, 113, 115, 119, 123, 125, 127

# G

Governance 21, 24, 25, 28, 29, 33, 34, 39, 40, 41, 44, 45, 49, 50, 51, 52, 54, 55, 56, 60, 62, 67, 68, 75, 76, 77, 78, 80, 81, 83, 84, 85, 86, 89, 93, 103, 130, 142, 143, 144, 146, 147, 148, 154, 155, 159, 164, 165, 171, 177, 178, 179, 180, 188, 190, 194, 197, 198, 203, 206, 207, 208, 211, 218, 222, 223, 224, 228, 229, 230, 231, 236, 239, 240, 241, 242, 243, 245, 250, 251, 252, 253, 254, 255
Green Finance 69, 72, 75, 78, 144, 154,

169, 170, 171, 172, 175, 176, 180, 189, 190, 191, 192, 194, 218, 224, 230, 243, 250
Green Fintech 193
Greenwashing 77, 81, 142, 145, 167, 171, 172, 175, 176, 178, 179, 180, 185, 186, 187, 188, 190, 194, 197, 199, 202, 204, 206, 213, 217, 223, 243, 244, 245, 248, 252, 253, 255

## I

India 1, 2, 3, 4, 5, 6, 7, 8, 9, 10, 11, 13, 14, 15, 16, 17, 18, 19, 21, 23, 24, 26, 28, 31, 32, 33, 36, 37, 40, 44, 49, 50, 51, 52, 53, 54, 55, 59, 61, 67, 85, 88, 91, 93, 97, 99, 103, 104, 106, 107, 108, 110, 112, 113, 114, 119, 121, 122, 124, 125, 127, 195, 197
Integrated Finance 139, 145, 165, 168, 181, 183, 185, 227, 228, 229, 230, 231, 232, 239, 243, 245, 246, 247
Internet Banking 2
Investors 69, 83, 92, 125, 132, 136, 137, 144, 147, 148, 151, 153, 164, 165, 167, 168, 169, 170, 172, 177, 179, 181, 182, 183, 191, 198, 199, 200, 201, 202, 205, 226, 228, 229, 231, 233, 234, 236, 238, 239, 240, 241, 242, 243, 244, 246, 254, 258

## L

Loss Aversion 197, 198, 200, 201

## M

Machine Learning 12, 30, 57, 67, 96, 136, 137, 145, 150, 154, 169, 181, 190, 192, 197, 198, 199, 201, 202, 203, 204, 205, 206, 214, 217, 235, 239
Mobile Banking 1, 2, 58

## N

Neobanks 1, 2, 3, 4, 5, 6, 7, 8, 9, 10, 11, 12, 13, 14, 15, 16, 17, 18, 44, 226
Non-Financial Platforms 47, 49, 60, 61, 62, 64, 74, 91, 93, 94, 97, 100, 101, 103, 120, 121, 129, 134, 167, 198, 231

## P

Policy 19, 25, 37, 41, 49, 56, 58, 64, 66, 68, 69, 70, 71, 72, 73, 76, 78, 79, 83, 84, 85, 124, 154, 155, 158, 164, 180, 181, 189, 190, 195, 205, 215, 217, 222, 225, 253, 259, 260, 261, 263, 264, 266, 267, 268, 274, 275
Projects 52, 55, 69, 131, 153, 164, 166, 167, 170, 171, 175, 179, 181, 183, 189, 202, 206, 208, 209, 212, 216, 234, 236, 240, 244, 245, 258, 269, 271, 272

## R

Regulatory Challenges in Embedded Finance 204
Robo-Advisors 167, 169, 199, 204

## S

SFDR 213, 217, 223
Smart Contracts 55, 77, 154, 169, 179, 181, 182, 207, 208, 209
Social 18, 22, 25, 27, 32, 33, 34, 35, 42, 45, 46, 54, 57, 61, 62, 63, 64, 66, 67, 68, 75, 76, 80, 81, 83, 84, 86, 89, 120, 126, 130, 139, 142, 143, 144, 145, 146, 147, 148, 152, 154, 155, 157, 160, 164, 165, 166, 177, 178, 182, 183, 188, 189, 190, 191, 192, 194, 197, 198, 199, 203, 204, 205, 206, 211, 213, 217, 218, 219, 221, 223, 224, 228, 229, 230, 235, 236, 237, 238, 239, 240, 241, 243, 245, 247, 250, 251, 252, 253, 254, 255, 257, 258, 259, 260, 261, 262, 263, 264, 265, 266, 267, 268, 269, 270, 271, 272, 273, 274, 275, 276, 277, 278, 279
Social Justice 130, 144, 257, 258, 259, 261, 265, 270, 275, 276
Sustainability 19, 41, 49, 54, 61, 62, 63, 64, 68, 69, 70, 71, 72, 73, 75, 76, 77,

78, 79, 80, 81, 82, 83, 84, 85, 86, 87, 88, 89, 93, 129, 132, 139, 142, 144, 145, 146, 155, 156, 157, 160, 161, 163, 164, 165, 166, 167, 168, 169, 170, 171, 172, 173, 174, 175, 176, 177, 178, 179, 180, 181, 183, 184, 185, 186, 187, 188, 189, 190, 191, 192, 193, 194, 195, 197, 198, 199, 201, 202, 203, 204, 205, 206, 207, 208, 210, 211, 212, 213, 214, 215, 216, 217, 218, 219, 220, 221, 222, 223, 224, 225, 226, 227, 228, 229, 230, 232, 235, 236, 237, 238, 239, 240, 241, 242, 243, 244, 245, 246, 247, 248, 250, 251, 252, 253, 254, 255, 258, 259, 262, 263, 264, 265, 266, 267, 269, 270, 271, 272, 274, 275, 276, 278
Sustainable Development Goals 62, 67, 69, 75, 81, 86, 131, 155, 156, 164, 167, 188, 190, 195, 227, 250, 257, 258, 259, 261, 265, 271, 273, 276, 278
Sustainable Finance 61, 64, 65, 69, 70, 71, 72, 75, 78, 79, 83, 88, 132, 133, 142, 143, 144, 146, 155, 158, 159, 163, 164, 165, 166, 167, 168, 169, 171, 172, 173, 176, 177, 179, 181, 188, 189, 190, 192, 193, 194, 195, 200, 202, 207, 208, 209, 210, 213, 217, 218, 219, 221, 225, 236, 237, 238, 239, 243, 248, 249, 250, 251, 253, 254
Sustainable Investment 144, 165, 166, 177, 190, 191, 194, 197, 198, 199, 200, 201, 202, 203, 204, 205, 206, 207, 213, 215, 217, 218, 219, 220, 221, 222, 237

# T

Technological Enablers 78, 93, 117, 118
Transportation 30, 62, 91, 104, 105, 106, 110, 115, 119, 173, 237

# U

UPI 1, 2, 4, 5, 7, 8, 26, 27, 31, 32, 37, 40, 41, 44, 47, 48, 50, 51, 54, 55, 67, 108, 110, 111, 112, 126, 127

www.ingramcontent.com/pod-product-compliance
Lightning Source LLC
LaVergne TN
LVHW080900300926
849162LV00003B/500